MOROCCO

BUSINESS AND INVESTMENT OPPORTUNITIES YEARBOOK

VOLUME 1

PRACTICAL INFORMATION AND OPPORTUNITIES

International Business Publications, USA
Washington DC, USA - Morocco

MOROCCO

BUSINESS AND INVESTMENT OPPORTUNITIES YEARBOOK

VOLUME 1 PRACTICAL INFORMATION AND OPPORTUNITIES

UPDATED ANNUALLY

We express our sincere appreciation to all government agencies and international organizations which provided information and other materials for this yearbook

Cover Design: International Business Publications, USA

2015 Edition Updated Reprint International Business Publications, USA
ISBN 0-7397-0885-6

For customer service and information, please contact:

in the USA: **International Business Publications, USA**
P.O.Box 15343, Washington, DC 20043
Phone: (202) 546-2103, Fax: (202) 546-3275.
E-mail: rusric@erols.com

Printed in the USA

MOROCCO

BUSINESS AND INVESTMENT OPPORTUNITIES YEARBOOK

VOLUME 1

PRACTICAL INFORMATION AND OPPORTUNITIES

TABLE OF CONTENTS

STRATEGIC AND BUSINESS PROFILES 10
STRATEGIC PROFILE 11
Geography 11
People 13
Government 14
Economy 15
Communications 18
Transportation 19
Military 19
Transnational Issues 20
NARCOTICS CONTROL STRATEGY 20
Status of Country 20
Country Actions Against Drugs 21
U.S. Policy Initiatives Programs 22
IMPORTANT INFORMATION FOR UNDERSTANDING MOROCCO 22
PROFILE 22
PEOPLE 23
HISTORY 24
GOVERNMENT AND POLITICAL CONDITIONS 25
ECONOMY 26
FOREIGN RELATIONS 27
U.S.-MOROCCAN RELATIONS 29
TRAVEL AND BUSINESS INFORMATION 30
INVESTING AND STARTING BUSINESS IN MOROCCO BASICS 32
INVESTING IN MOROCCO 32
BUSINESS FORMS AND STRUCTURES 34
COMPANIES LAW 34
Limited Liability Company 34
Private Limited Company 34
PARTNERSHIPS 35
Limited Partnerships 35
Limited Partnership with Shares 35
Joint Ventures 35

Branch Offices 35
Sole Proprietorships 35
SETTING UP & OPERATING BUSINESS IN MOROCCO 36
TYPE OF BUSINESS 36
TAXATION 36
INCENTIVES 37
EXCHANGE CONTROL 37
VISA REQUIREMENTS 37
INCORPORATING IN MOROCCO 37
COMPANY LAW 38
PRIVATE LIMITED COMPANY - SARL 38
BRANCH 38

INCORPORATING PROCEDURE IN MOROCCO 39

COMPANY REGISTRATION 39
Registration Requirements 39
Registration Requirements Details 39
Registering Property 41
Registration Requirement Details 41
TAXES 44
MOROCCAN CODE OF GOOD CORPORATE GOVERNANCE PRACTICES 44
HOW SHOULD THIS CODE BE USED? 47
GENERAL PRINCIPLES OF GOOD CORPORATE GOVERNANCE PRACTICES 48
II- RIGHTS OF SHAREHOLDERS AND PARTNERS AND THEIR EQUITABLE TREATMENT 56
III- TRANSPARENCY AND THE DISSEMINATION OF FINANCIAL INFORMATION 59
IV- THE ROLE OF STAKEHOLDERS AND THEIR EQUITABLE TREATMENT 62
CHARTER FOR GOVERNING BODY MEMBERS 68

STRATEGIC INFORMATION FOR CONDUCTING BUSINESS 71

POLITICAL ENVIRONMENT 71
Nature of the Political Relationship with the United States: 71
Political System 71
U.S. ASSISTANCE TO MOROCCO 72
USAID Morocco 72
DEVELOPMENT BACKGROUND 72
USAID PROGRAM 73
RESULTS 73
USAID Assistance FUNDS 74
USAID Morocco Projects 74
Training for Development (No. 608-0208) 75
PEACE CORP PROGRAMS IN MOROCCO 81
Contacting the Peace Corps in Morocco 81
Peace Corps Country Overview for Morocco 81
ECONOMY AND ECONOMIC DEVELOPMENT 83
Economic Trends 84
Principal Growth Sectors 84
Government Role in the Economy 85
Balance of Payments Situation 87
Infrastructure Situation 87
TRADE POLICY 89
General Policy Framework 89
2. Exchange Rate Policies 89
3. Structural Policies 90

4. Debt Management Policies *90*
5. Aid *90*
6. Significant Barriers to U.S. Exports and Investment *90*
7. Export Subsidies Policies *91*
8. Protection of U.S. Intellectual Property *91*
9. Workers Rights *92*
INVESTMENT AND BUSINESS CLIMATE 94
1. Openness To, and Restrictions Upon, Foreign Investment *94*
2. Conversion and Transfer Policies *100*
3. Expropriation and Compensation *100*
4. Dispute Settlement *100*
5. Performance Requirements and Investment Incentives *102*
6. Right to Private Ownership and Establishment *103*
7. Protection of Property Rights *103*
8. Transparency of the Regulatory System *105*
9. Efficient Capital Markets and Portfolio Investment *106*
10. Competition from State-Owned Enterprises *107*
11. Corporate Social Responsibility (CSR) *108*
12. Political Violence *109*
13. Corruption *109*
14. Bilateral Investment Agreements (BITs) *111*
15. OPIC and Other Investment Insurance Programs *112*
16. Labor *112*
17. Foreign Trade Zones/Free Ports *114*
18. Foreign Direct Investment and Foreign Portfolio Investment Statistics *114*
PRIVATIZATION *115*
THE CASABLANCA STOCK MARKET *115*
MOROCCO ECONOMY STRUCTURE 116

MAJOR ECONOMIC SECTORS AND BUSINESS OPPORTUNITIES 118

KEY ECONOMIC SECTORS AND BUSINESS OPPORTUNITIES 118
AGRICULTURE *118*
PRODUCTION *118*
FORESTS *119*
FISHERIES *120*
ENERGY *122*
Future projects: *123*
PPER *124*
MINING *125*
MANUFACTURING INDUSTRIES *127*
HANDICRAFTS *127*
MANUFACTURING INDUSTRIES *128*
FOOD PROCESSING INDUSTRIES *128*
TEXTILE AND LEATHER PRODUCTS *129*
CHEMICALS & PARACHEMICALS *130*
METALLURGICAL, MECHANICAL, ELECTRICAL & ELECTRONIC INDUSTRIES *130*
BANKING SYSTEM 130
DYNAMIC MARKET *131*
POST AND TELECOMMUNICATIONS 132
Relations with the World *132*
TOURISM *133*
ENERGY SECTOR 135
Energy Overview *135*

Oil and Gas Industries 135
Environmental Overview 135
Oil and Gas 136
Coal and Electricity 137

PRACTICAL INFORMATION FOR STARTING AND CONDUCTING BUSINESS 138

BASIC REGULATIONS FOR INVESTMENTS 138
INVESTMENT FREEDOM FOR FOREIGNERS 138
DEFINITION 138
FORM OF INVESTMENTS 138
FUNDING MODES 138
TRANSFER OF INVESTMENT REVENUE 139
TRANSFER OF CESSION OR LIQUIDATION PROCEEDS OF FOREIGN INVESTMENTS 139
DOCUMENTS TO SUBMIT TO THE EXCHANGE OFFICE FOR A FOREIGN INVESTMENT PROJECT 139
DOCUMENTS TO SUBMIT TO THE BANK FOR THE TRANSFER OF A FOREIGN INVESTMENT REVENUES 140
DOCUMENTS TO SUBMIT TO THE BANK FOR THE TRANSFER OF THE PRODUCT OF CESSION OR OF LIQUIDATION OF A FOREIGN INVESTMENT 141
CUSTOMS REGULATIONS 141
BONDED WAREHOUSES 141
TEMPORARY IMPORT 142
TEMPORARY IMPORT 142
GOODS EXPORTED FOR FURTHER PROCESSING 143
TEMPORARY EXPORTATION 143
GOODS IN TRANSIT 143
SPECIAL SYSTEMS 144
MOVEMENT AND HOLDING OF GOODS IN BOND 144
DOMESTIC CONSUMER TAXES 144
LITIGATION 144
EXCHANGE REGULATIONS 145
PAYMENTS BY TRANSFER TO FOREIGN COUNTRIES 145
PAYMENTS BY TRANSFER FROM FOREIGN COUNTRIES 145
TYPES OF BANK ACCOUNTS THAT MAY BE OPENED BY FOREIGNERS 145
FOREIGN CURRENCY ACCOUNT AND CONVERTIBLE DIRHAM ACCOUNTS 145
SYSTEM GOVERNING LIQUID ASSETS IN DIRHAM HELD IN MOROCCO BY NONRESIDENT FOREIGNERS 146
OTHER BENEFITS GRANTED TO FOREIGN RESIDENTS IN MOROCCO 147
THE CONVERTIBILITY OF THE DIRHAM 148
OFFSHORE SECTOR 149
EXCHANGE MECHANISMS 149
FISCAL AND CUSTOMS MECHANISMS 149
REGULATIONS FOR FOREIGN STAFF 149
FREE ZONES 150
FOREIGN TRADE, EXCHANGE, CUSTOMS AND FISCAL CONTROLS FOR COMPANIES ESTABLISHED IN FREE ZONES FOR EXPORT 150
LEADING SECTORS FOR BUSINESS AND INVESTMENTS 151
LEADING SECTORS AND OPPORTUNITIES FOR TRADE AND INVESTMENTS 151
Renewable Energy 151
Infrastructure Projects 152
Aviation (Civil and Defense) 157
Environmental Technologies 160
Franchising 165

Healthcare ... 167
Safety and Security ... 168
Agricultural Sectors ... 169
IMPORTANT INVESTMENT OPPORTUNITIES ... 172
INDUSTRY ... 178
SOLAR ENERGY ... 179
WIND ENERGY ... 181
TOURISM ... 182
AGRICULTURE ... 184
FISHING ... 185
LOGISTICS ... 186
INFORMATION AND COMMUNICATION TECHNOLOGY ... 186
RETAIL TRADE ... 194
ISLAMIC BANK ... 195
INVESTMENT INCENTIVES ... 195
INVESTMENT ZONES ... 197
Industrial Zones ... 199
Free Zones ... 199
MARKETING PRODUCTS AND SERVICES ... 199
Finding a Partner ... 200
Direct Marketing ... 200
Joint Ventures/Licensing ... 200
Establishing an Office ... 200
Selling Factors/Techniques ... 200
Advertising and Trade Promotion ... 201
Pricing Product ... 201
Customer Support ... 201
Selling to the Government ... 202
Protecting ProductS from IPR Infringement ... 202
Need for a Local Attorney ... 202
due diligence/checking bona fides of banks/agents/customers ... 203
TRADE AND PROJECT FINANCING ... 204
Banking System ... 204
Foreign Exchange Controls Affecting Trading ... 204
General Financing Availability ... 204
How to Finance Exports/Methods of Payment ... 204
Types of Available Export Financing and Insurance ... 204
Project Financing Available ... 206
Projects Scheduled for Financing by the World Bank ... 206
TRADE REGULATIONS, CUSTOMS AND STANDARDS ... 208
Trade Barriers ... 208
Customs Regulations ... 208
Tariff Rates and Import taxes ... 208
Customs Valuation ... 208
Export Controls ... 208
Import/Export Documentation ... 208
Temporary Goods Entry Requirements ... 209
Labeling Requirements ... 209
Prohibited Imports ... 209
Export Controls ... 209
Standards ... 210
Free Trade Zones/Warehouses ... 210
Membership in Free Trade Agreements ... 210

Customs Contact Information ... *210*
BASIC COSTS FOR CONDUCTING BUSINESS ... 211
INDUSTRIAL WAGE RATES ... *211*
PRICE OF INDUSTRIAL WATER ... *211*
ELECTRIC POWER ... *212*
COAL ... *213*
TAX SYSTEM ... 213
CAPITAL REGISTRATION FEES ... *213*
STAMP DUTY ... *213*
NOTARIAL TAX ... *213*
TAXATION ON IMPORTED PRODUCTION MATERIALS AND OTHER PRODUCTS ... *213*
VALUE ADDED TAX-VAT ... *214*
DOMESTIC CONSUMER TAXES ... *215*
PARAFISCAL TAX AT IMPORTATION ... *215*
INTERNATIONAL ADOPTION - MOROCCO ... 215
General Adoption Information ... *215*
Legal "Adoption" in Morocco ... *215*

BUSINESS TRAVELING ... 218

US STATE DEPARTMENT SUGGESTIONS ... 218
SAFETY/SECURITY ... *218*
GETTING THERE ... 222
GETTING AROUND ... 223
ACCOMMODATION ... 225
Hotels ... *225*
MONEY ... 225
Costs ... *225*
Currency exchange ... *226*
PUBLIC HOLIDAYS ... 226

SUPPLEMENTS ... 228

STRATEGIC STATISTICTS & DATA ... 228
Economy Statistics ... *228*
Trade Statistics ... *229*
INVESTMENT STATISTICS ... 229
Foreign Investment Inflows by Sector ... *230*
Market Research ... *231*
List of USDA/FAS/Commodity Reports & Briefs ... *231*
U.S. AND COUNTRY CONTACTS ... 231
COUNTRY GOVERNMENT AGENCIES ... *232*
COUNTRY TRADE ASSOCIATIONS/CHAMBERS OF COMMERCE ... *232*
COUNTRY MARKET RESEARCH FIRMS: ... *233*
MAJOR COUNTRY COMMERCIAL BANKS ... *233*
U.S. MISSION TRADE PERSONNEL ... *234*
WASHINGTON-BASED USG COUNTRY CONTACTS ... *234*
U.S.-BASED MULTIPLIERS RELEVANT FOR COUNTRY ... *235*
Banks with Correspondent U.S. Banking Arrangements ... *235*
SELECTED GOVERNMENT AGENCIES ... 236
ECONOMIC DEVELOPMENT OFFICES ... 237
CHAMBERS OF COMMERCE ... 239
PROFESIONAL ASSOCIATIONS ... 244
MAROCCO EMBASSIES ... 245
LEADING RESTAURANTS ... 248

LEADING HOTELS 249
AGADIR *249*
CASABLANCA *249*
LAAYOUNE *250*
MARRAKESH *250*
MEKNES *250*
RABAT *250*
TANGIER *250*
PRESIDENTIAL INITIATIVE ON INTERNET FOR ECONOMIC DEVELOPMENT: 251
Part I—Government Policy Considerations in the IT Sector *251*
C. The Financial System *253*
D. The Tax System *257*
Part II—Telecommunications Infrastructure *259*
Part III—Legal and Regulatory Reform Introduction *262*
Part IV—E-Commerce and Business Development *269*
BASIC TITLES FOR MOROCCO 274

STRATEGIC AND BUSINESS PROFILES

Capital	Rabat 34°02′N 6°51′W34.033°N 6.85°W
Largest city	Casablanca
Official language(s)	Arabic[1] Amazigh[2][a]
Native languages	Moroccan Arabic, Tachelhit, Central Atlas Tamazight Tarifit, Hassaniya. [b]
Ethnic groups	99.1% Arab-Berber 0.7% Other 0.2% Jews [3]
Demonym	Moroccan
Government	Unitary parliamentary democracy and Constitutional Monarchy
- King	Mohammed VI
- Prime Minister	Abdelillah Benkirane
Legislature	Parliament
- Upper House	Assembly of Councillors
- Lower House	Assembly of Representatives
	Independence
- from France	March 2, 1956
- from Spain	April 7, 1956
	Area
- Total	446,550 km^2 [c] or 710,850 km^2[c](58th/40th) 172,487 sq mi
- Water (%)	250 km² (0,056%)
	Population
- 2011 estimate	35,000,000[4] (38th)
- 2011 census	35,657,056[5]
- Density	71.6/km^2 (122nd) 185.5/sq mi
GDP (PPP)	2011 estimate
- Total	$151.4 billion[6] (58)
- Per capita	$4,800[6]
GDP (nominal)	2011 estimate
- Total	$103.5 billion[6]
- Per capita	$4,800[6]
HDI (2011)	0.582 (medium) (130th)
Currency	Moroccan dirham (MAD)
Time zone	WET (UTC+0)
- Summer (DST)	WEST (UTC+1)
Drives on the	right
ISO 3166 code	MA
Internet TLD	.ma
Calling code	+212

STRATEGIC PROFILE

Morocco's long struggle for independence from France ended in 1956. The internationalized city of Tangier was turned over to the new country that same year. Morocco virtually annexed Western Sahara during the late 1970s, but final resolution on the status of the territory remains unresolved. Gradual political reforms in the 1990s resulted in the establishment of a bicameral legislature in 1997.

GEOGRAPHY

Location: Northern Africa, bordering the North Atlantic Ocean and the Mediterranean Sea, between Algeria and Western Sahara
Geographic coordinates: 32 00 N, 5 00 W
Map references: Africa

Area:
total: 446,550 sq km
land: 446,300 sq km *water:* 250 sq km

Area - comparative: slightly larger than California
Land boundaries:
total: 2,017.9 km
border countries: Algeria 1,559 km, Western Sahara 443 km, Spain (Ceuta) 6.3 km, Spain (Melilla) 9.6 km
Coastline: 1,835 km

Maritime claims:
contiguous zone: 24 nm
continental shelf: 200-m depth or to the depth of exploitation
exclusive economic zone: 200 nm
territorial sea: 12 nm

Climate: Mediterranean, becoming more extreme in the interior

Terrain: northern coast and interior are mountainous with large areas of bordering plateaus, intermontane valleys, and rich coastal plains
Elevation extremes:
lowest point: Sebkha Tah -55 m
highest point: Jebel Toubkal 4,165 m
Natural resources: phosphates, iron ore, manganese, lead, zinc, fish, salt

arable land: 21%
permanent crops: 1%
permanent pastures: 47% *forests and woodland:* 20% *other:* 11%

Irrigated land: 12,580 sq km
Natural hazards: northern mountains geologically unstable and subject to earthquakes; periodic droughts

Morocco
International boundary
Province or préfecture boundary
National capital
Province or préfecture capital
Railroad
Road or track
Province or préfecture names are the same as their capitals
0 50 100 Kilometers
0 50 100 Miles
SPAIN
Cádiz
Málaga
Mediterranean Sea
Algeciras
Gibraltar (U.K.)
Tangier
Ceuta (Sp.)
Tétouan
Oran
Chechaouene
Al Hoceima
Melilla (Sp.)
Nador
Ghazaouet
Tlemcen
Oujda
Ouezzane
Taounate
Kenitra
Salé
Rabat
Fès
Taza
Meknès
Khemisset
Casablanca
Ben Slimane
Azrou
Boulemane
Al Jadida
Settat
Oued Zem
Khouribga
Khenifra
Bou Arfa
Safi
Beni Mellal
el Kelaa des Srarhna
Figuig
Azilal
Ksar es Souk
Béchar
Marrakech
Essaouira
ATLANTIC
OCEAN
Ouarzazate
Agadir
Tata
Tiznit
Sidi Ifni
Tan-Tan
Tarfaya
Tindouf
ALGERIA
El Aaiún
WESTERN
SAHARA
MAURITANIA
Base 504118 7-79

Environment - current issues: land degradation/desertification (soil erosion resulting from farming of marginal areas, overgrazing, destruction of vegetation); water supplies contaminated by raw sewage; siltation of reservoirs; oil pollution of coastal waters

Land use:

Environment - international agreements:
party to: Biodiversity, Climate Change, Desertification, Endangered Species, Hazardous Wastes, Marine Dumping, Nuclear Test Ban, Ozone Layer Protection, Ship Pollution, Wetlands
signed, but not ratified: Environmental Modification, Law of the Sea
Geography - note: strategic location along Strait of Gibraltar.

PEOPLE

Population: 30,122,350

Age structure:
0-14 years: 35% (male 5,372,393; female 5,175,114)
15-64 years: 60% (male 9,021,259; female 9,163,548)
65 years and over: 5% (male 632,698; female 757,338)

Population growth rate: 1.74%
Birth rate: 24.6 births/1,000 population
Death rate: 6.02 deaths/1,000 population
Net migration rate: -1.21 migrant(s)/1,000 population

Sex ratio:
at birth: 1.05 male(s)/female
under 15 years: 1.04 male(s)/female
15-64 years: 0.98 male(s)/female
65 years and over: 0.84 male(s)/female
total population: 1 male(s)/female

Infant mortality rate: 49.72 deaths/1,000 live births
Life expectancy at birth:
total population: 69.13 years
male: 66.92 years
female: 71.44 years
Total fertility rate: 3.13 children born/woman
Nationality:
noun: Moroccan(s)
adjective: Moroccan
Ethnic groups: Arab-Berber 99.1%, other 0.7%, Jewish 0.2%
Religions: Muslim 98.7%, Christian 1.1%, Jewish 0.2%
Languages: Arabic (official), Berber dialects, French often the language of business, government, and diplomacy

Literacy:
definition: age 15 and over can read and write
total population: 43.7% *male:* 56.6% *female:* 31%

GOVERNMENT

Country name:
conventional long form: Kingdom of Morocco
conventional short form: Morocco
local long form: Al Mamlakah al Maghribiyah
local short form: Al Maghrib

Data code: MO
Government type: constitutional monarchy
Capital: Rabat

Administrative divisions: 37 provinces and 2 wilayas*; Agadir, Al Hoceima, Azilal, Beni Mellal, Ben Slimane, Boulemane, Casablanca*, Chaouen, El Jadida, El Kelaa des Srarhna, Er Rachidia, Essaouira, Fes, Figuig, Guelmim, Ifrane, Kenitra, Khemisset, Khenifra, Khouribga, Laayoune, Larache, Marrakech, Meknes, Nador, Ouarzazate, Oujda, Rabat-Sale*, Safi, Settat, Sidi Kacem, Tanger, Tan-Tan, Taounate, Taroudannt, Tata, Taza, Tetouan, Tiznit
note: three additional provinces of Ad Dakhla (Oued Eddahab), Boujdour, and Es Smara as well as parts of Tan-Tan and Laayoune fall within Moroccan-claimed Western Sahara; decentralization/regionalization law passed by the legislature in March 1997 creating many new provinces/regions; specific details and scope of the reorganization not yet available

Independence: 2 March 1956 (from France)
National holiday: Throne Day or Sete de Throne 30 July (anniversary of King MOHAMED VI's accession to the throne)
Constitution: 10 March 1972, revised 4 September 1992, amended (to create bicameral legislature) September 1996
Legal system: based on Islamic law and French and Spanish civil law system; judicial review of legislative acts in Constitutional Chamber of Supreme Court

Suffrage: 21 years of age; universal

Executive branch:
chief of state: King MOHAMMED VI (since 30 July 1999)
head of government: Prime Minister Abdelilah BENKIRANE (since 29 November 2011)
cabinet: Council of Ministers appointed by the prime minister
elections: the monarchy is hereditary; prime minister appointed by the monarch following legislative elections

Legislative branch:

bicameral Parliament consists of the Chamber of Counselors (or upper house) (270 seats - to be reduced to a maximum of 120; members elected indirectly by local councils, professional organizations, and labor syndicates to serve nine-year terms; one-third of the members are elected every three years) and Chamber of Representatives (or lower house) (395 seats; members elected by popular vote to serve five-year terms)

elections: Chamber of Counselors - last held on 3 October 2009 (next to be held in 2012); Chamber of Representatives - last held on 25 November 2011 (next to be held in 2016) election results: Chamber of Counselors - percent of vote by party - NA; seats by party - NA; Chamber of Representatives - percent of vote by party - NA; seats by party - (partial results as of 6 December 2011) PJD 107, PI 60, RNI 52, PAM 47, USFP 39, MP 32, UC 23, PPS 18Judicial branch: Supreme Court, judges are appointed on the recommendation of the Supreme Council of the Judiciary, presided over by the monarch

Political parties and leaders: Action Party or PA [Ahmed ABAKIL]; Constitutional Union or UC [Abdellatif SEMLALI]; Democratic Forces Front or FFD [Thami KHIARI]; Democratic Socialist Party or PSD [Issa al-OUARDIGHI]; Democratic Party for Independence or PDI [Thami el-OUAZZANI, Said BOUACHRINE]; Istiqlal Party or IP [Abbas EL-FASSI]; Labor Party or UT [leader NA]; National Democratic Party or PND [Mohamed Arsalane EL-JADIDI]; National Popular Movement or MNP [Mahjoubi AHARDANE]; National Rally of Independents or RNI [Ahmed OSMAN]; Organization of Democratic and Popular Action or OADP [Mohamed BENSAID]; Party of Progress and Socialism or PPS [Moulay Ismail al ALAOUI]; Popular Constitutional and Democratic Movement or MPCD [Dr. Abdelkarim al-KHATIB]; Popular Movement or MP [Mohamed LAENSER]; Social Democratic Movement or MDS [Mahmoud ARCHANE]; Socialist Union of Popular Forces or USFP [Abderrahmane YOUSSOUFI]

Political pressure groups and leaders: Association of Popular Trade Unions or ADP [leader NA]; Democratic Confederation of Labor or CDT [Noubir AMAOUI]; Democratic National Trade Union or USND [leader NA]; Democratic Trade Union or SD [leader NA]; General Union of Moroccan Workers or UGTM [Abderrazzak AFILAL]; Labor Union Commissions or CS [leader NA]; Moroccan National Workers Union or UNMT [leader NA]; Moroccan Union of Workers or UTM [Mahjoub BENSEDIQ]; Party of Shura and Istiqla [Abdelwaheb MAASH];

International organization participation: ABEDA, ACCT (associate), AfDB, AFESD, AL, AMF, AMU, CCC, EBRD, ECA, FAO, G-77, IAEA, IBRD, ICAO, ICC, ICFTU, ICRM, IDA, IDB, IFAD, IFC, IFRCS, IHO (pending member), ILO, IMF, IMO, Intelsat, Interpol, IOC, IOM, ISO, ITU, NAM, OAS (observer), OAU, OIC, OPCW, OSCE (partner), UN, UNCTAD, UNESCO, UNHCR, UNIDO, UPU, WHO, WIPO, WMO, WToO, WTrO

Diplomatic representation in the US:
chief of mission: Ambassador (vacant)
chancery: 1601 21st Street NW, Washington, DC 20049
telephone: (202) 462-7979 through 7982
FAX: (202) 265-0161
consulate(s) general: New York

Diplomatic representation from the US:
chief of mission: Ambassador Edward M. GABRIEL
embassy: 2 Avenue de Marrakech, Rabat
mailing address: PSC 74, Box 3, APO AE 09718
telephone: [212] (7) 76 22 65
FAX: [212] (7) 76 56 61
consulate(s) general: Casablanca

Flag description: red with a green pentacle (five-pointed, linear star) known as Solomon's seal in the center of the flag; green is the traditional color of Islam.

ECONOMY

Economy - overview:	Moroccan economic policies brought macroeconomic stability to the country in the early 1990s but have not spurred growth sufficient to reduce unemployment - nearing 20% in urban areas - despite the Moroccan Government's ongoing efforts to diversify the economy. Morocco's GDP growth rose to 5.9% in 2008, with the economy recovering from a drought in 2007 that severely reduced agricultural output and necessitated wheat imports at rising world prices. Moroccan authorities understand that reducing poverty and providing jobs are key to domestic security and development. In 2005, Morocco launched the National Initiative for Human Development (INDH), a $2 billion social development plan to address poverty and unemployment and to improve the living conditions of the country's urban slums. Moroccan authorities are implementing reform efforts to open the economy to international investors. Despite structural adjustment programs supported by the IMF, the World Bank, and the Paris Club, the dirham is only fully convertible for current account transactions. In 2000, Morocco entered an Association Agreement with the EU and, in 2006, entered a Free Trade Agreement (FTA) with the US. Long-term challenges include improving education and job prospects for Morocco's youth, and closing the income gap between the rich and the poor, which the government hopes to achieve by increasing tourist arrivals and boosting competitiveness in textiles.
GDP (purchasing power parity):	$137.9 billion (est.) country comparison to the world: 59 $129.9 billion (2007 est.) $125.9 billion (2006 est.) *note:* data are in 2008 US dollars
GDP (official exchange rate):	$88.88 billion
GDP - real growth rate:	6.2% (est.) country comparison to the world: 53 3.2% (2007 est.) 7.8% (2006 est.)
GDP - per capita (PPP):	$4,500 (est.) country comparison to the world: 148 $4,200 (2007 est.) $4,200 (2006 est.) *note:* data are in 2008 US dollars
GDP - composition by sector:	*agriculture:* 13.3% *industry:* 31.2% *services:* 55.5%
Labor force:	11.25 million

Labor force - by occupation:	*agriculture:* 40% *industry:* 15% *services:* 45%
Unemployment rate:	7.7%
Population below poverty line:	19%
Household income or consumption by percentage share:	*lowest 10%:* 2.6% *highest 10%:* 30.9%
Distribution of family income - Gini index:	40
Inflation rate (consumer prices):	2.8%
Investment (gross fixed):	21.7% of GDP
Budget:	*revenues:* $15.85 billion *expenditures:* $20.39 billion; including capital expenditures of $2.19 billion
Public debt:	70.9% of GDP
Agriculture - products:	barley, wheat, citrus, wine, vegetables, olives; livestock
Industries:	phosphate rock mining and processing, food processing, leather goods, textiles, construction, tourism
Industrial production growth rate:	4%
Electricity - production:	18.48 billion kWh
Electricity - consumption:	18.89 billion kWh
Electricity - exports:	0 kWh
Electricity - imports:	1.7 billion kWh
Oil - production:	300 bbl/day
Oil - consumption:	170,000 bbl/day
Oil - exports:	21,890 bbl/day
Oil - imports:	186,100 bbl/day
Oil - proved reserves:	100 million bbl

Natural gas - production:	50 million cu m
Natural gas - consumption:	50 million cu m
Natural gas - exports:	0 cu m
Natural gas - imports:	0 cu m
Natural gas - proved reserves:	1.218 billion cu m
Current account balance:	$389 million
Exports:	$11.72 billion f.o.b.
Exports - commodities:	clothing, fish, inorganic chemicals, transistors, crude minerals, fertilizers (including phosphates), petroleum products, fruits, vegetables
Exports - partners:	France 21.4%, Spain 20.5%, UK 4.9%, Italy 4.7%, India 4.1%
Imports:	$21.22 billion f.o.b.
Imports - commodities:	crude petroleum, textile fabric, telecommunications equipment, wheat, gas and electricity, transistors, plastics
Imports - partners:	France 17.4%, Spain 13.4%, Saudi Arabia 6.9%, China 6.8%, Italy 6.3%, Germany 5.9% (2006)
Reserves of foreign exchange and gold:	$18.21 billion
Debt - external:	$17.9 billion
Economic aid - recipient:	ODA, $706 million
Currency (code):	Moroccan dirham (MAD)
Exchange rates:	Moroccan dirhams per US dollar - 8.7722 (2006), 8.865 (2005), 8.868 (2004), 9.574 (2003), 11.021 (2002)
Fiscal year:	calendar year

COMMUNICATIONS

Telephones - main lines in use:	1.266 million
Telephones - mobile cellular:	16.005 million
Telephone system:	*general assessment:* modern system with all important capabilities; however, density is low with only 4 main lines available for each 100 persons *domestic:* good system composed of open-wire lines, cables, and microwave radio relay links; Internet available but expensive; principal

	switching centers are Casablanca and Rabat; national network nearly 100% digital using fiber-optic links; improved rural service employs microwave radio relay *international:* country code - 212; 7 submarine cables; satellite earth stations - 2 Intelsat (Atlantic Ocean) and 1 Arabsat; microwave radio relay to Gibraltar, Spain, and Western Sahara; coaxial cable and microwave radio relay to Algeria; participant in Medarabtel; fiber-optic cable link from Agadir to Algeria and Tunisia (1998)
Radio broadcast stations:	AM 27, FM 25, shortwave 6
Television broadcast stations:	35 (plus 66 repeaters)
Internet country code:	.ma
Internet hosts:	3,218
Internet users:	6.1 million

TRANSPORTATION

Railways:
total: 1,907 km
standard gauge: 1,907 km 1.435-m gauge (1,003 km electrified; 540 km double track)
Highways:
total: 57,847 km
paved: 30,254 km (including 327 km of expressways)
unpaved: 27,593 km
Pipelines: crude oil 362 km; petroleum products 491 km (abandoned); natural gas 241 km
Ports and harbors: Agadir, El Jadida, Casablanca, El Jorf Lasfar, Kenitra, Mohammedia, Nador, Rabat, Safi, Tangier; also Spanish-controlled Ceuta and Melilla
Merchant marine:
total: 40 ships (1,000 GRT or over) totaling 218,987 GRT/263,191 DWT
ships by type: cargo 9, chemical tanker 6, container 3, passenger 1, petroleum tanker 3, refrigerated cargo 9, roll-on/roll-off 8, short-sea passenger 1
Airports: 70
Airports - with paved runways:
total: 26
over 3,047 m: 10
2,438 to 3,047 m: 5
1,524 to 2,437 m: 9
914 to 1,523 m: 1
under 914 m: 1
Airports - with unpaved runways:
total: 44
2,438 to 3,047 m: 1
1,524 to 2,437 m: 10
914 to 1,523 m: 22
under 914 m: 11
Heliports: 1

MILITARY

Military branches: Royal Armed Forces (includes Army, Navy, Air Force), Gendarmerie, Auxiliary Forces

Military manpower - military age: 18 years of age
Military manpower - availability:
males age 15-49: 7,961,552
Military manpower - fit for military service:
males age 15-49: 5,026,210
Military manpower - reaching military age annually:
males: 335,264
Military expenditures - dollar figure: $1.361 billion
Military expenditures - percent of GDP: 3.8%

TRANSNATIONAL ISSUES

Disputes - international: claims and administers Western Sahara, but sovereignty is unresolved and the UN is attempting to hold a referendum on the issue; the UN-administered cease-fire has been in effect since September 1991; Spain controls five places of sovereignty (plazas de soberania) on and off the coast of Morocco - the coastal enclaves of Ceuta and Melilla which Morocco contests, as well as the islands of Penon de Alhucemas, Penon de Velez de la Gomera, and Islas Chafarinas

Illicit drugs: illicit producer of hashish; trafficking on the increase for both domestic and international drug markets; shipments of hashish mostly directed to Western Europe; transit point for cocaine from South America destined for Western Europe.

NARCOTICS CONTROL STRATEGY[1]

Despite the Government of Morocco's (GOM's) law enforcement efforts, Morocco remains a major producer and exporter of cannabis. While there continues to be no evidence that Moroccan cannabis reaches the United States in significant amounts, an estimated 2004 tons is believed to reach Europe annually. Estimates vary, however, regarding the extent of cannabis cultivation in Morocco. The Ministry of Interior estimates that an average of 50,000 hectares of cannabis are cultivated illicitly in the Kingdom of Morocco annually.

Since 1995, the GOM's Royal Center for remote sensing, a scientific research facility, independent of UCLAD and the Interior Ministry, estimates primary cannabis growing areas in Morocco in the range of 15,000 to 40,000 hectares. In contrast to these lower Moroccan figures, the European Union (EU) estimates the area of illicit cannabis cultivation at between 80-85,000 hectares. There are reports that Morocco is used as a transshipment point for hard drugs such as heroin and cocaine entering Europe. Clearly, the threat from Moroccan enforcement efforts, as they are, has not been enough to deter drug traffickers. This reality coupled with GOM counternarcotics budgetary constraints does not bode well for near-term or even long-term progress against hashish cultivation, production, and trafficking in Morocco. Morocco is a party to the 1988 UN Drug Convention.

STATUS OF COUNTRY

[1] Bureau for International Narcotics and Law Enforcement Affairs, U.S. Department of State Washington, DC

Morocco consistently ranks among the world's largest producers of cannabis and its cultivation and sale provide the economic base for much of northern Morocco. According to EU law enforcement officials, Moroccan cannabis is typically processed into hashish, resin, or oil and exported to Algeria, Tunisia, and Europe. To date, money laundering and precursor chemicals have virtually been non-factors within the Moroccan drug market.

While cannabis is the traditional drug of choice for Moroccans, there is also a small but growing domestic market for harder drugs, such as heroin and cocaine. Newspaper reports on Morocco's role as a major producer and exporter of drugs allege a connection between local drug traffickers and international cartels such as Latin American cocaine rings. However, these allegations have never been substantiated.

COUNTRY ACTIONS AGAINST DRUGS

Policy Initiatives. In 1996, the GOM established a coordination unit for the fight against narcotics (Unite de Coordination de Lutte Anti-Drogue or UCLAD) in an effort to improve coordination between the various law enforcement services involved in the counter narcotics effort. UCLAD is subordinate to the Ministry of Interior. UCLAD officials report that they have been instrumental in reworking legislation to increase the maximum allowable prison sentence to 30 years and also increase fines for narcotics violations to a range of $20-$80,000. Ten years imprisonment remains the typical sentence for major drug traffickers arrested in Morocco. Coordination among law enforcement agencies remains weak. In short, UCLAD's centralized control of all drug-related matters is not yet completely realized. However, European diplomats believe UNCLAD's problems result partly from a lack of resources to fulfill its mandate.

Law Enforcement Efforts. Approximately every six months, as part of an anti-drug initiative launched by the late King Hassan in 1992, 10,000 police are rotated into the Rif Mountain region to maintain drug control checkpoints. Moroccan forces also man observation posts along the Mediterranean coast, and the navy carries out routine sea patrols and responds to sightings by the observation posts. **Corruption.** The GOM does not promote drug production or trafficking as a matter of policy, and it disputes allegations that government officials in the northern territories are involved in the drug trade. However, most international observers believe that some drug-related corruption exists in that region.

Agreements and Treaties. Morocco is a party to the 1988 UN Drug Convention, the 1961 UN Single Convention on Narcotic Drugs, and the 1971 UN Convention on Psychotropic Substances. With respect to agreements between the U.S. and Morocco, a bilateral narcotics cooperation agreement has been in force since 1989, and a convention on mutual assistance in criminal matters has been in force since 1993. Morocco also has anti-narcotics and or/mutual legal assistance treaties with the EU, France, Spain, Germany, Italy, Portugal, and the UK. Morocco is a party to the World Customs Organization's International Convention on Mutual Administrative Assistance for the Prevention, Investigation, and Repression of Customs Offenses (Nairobi Convention), Annex X on Assistance in Narcotics Cases.

Cultivation/Production. Small scale farmers cultivate most Moroccan cannabis in the northern or Rif region, although some is also grown in the Souss Valley of the south. The average hectare of cannabis produces 2 to 8 metric tons (MT) of raw plant, and although the GOM has stated that it is committed to the total eradication of cannabis production, given the economic dependence of the northern part of the country on cannabis-cannabis crops are estimated to yield two billion U.S. Dollars in revenues annually-eradication is only feasible if accompanied by a highly subsidized crop substitution program. **Drug Flow/Transit.** There are reports that Morocco is used as a transshipment point for hard drugs such as heroin and cocaine entering Europe. However, with the exception of the six tons of cocaine which inadvertently washed up on the Moroccan Coast in July 1997, there have been no substantial seizures of hard drugs in Morocco.

Domestic Programs (Demand Reduction). The GOM does not acknowledge a significant hard drug addiction problem and does not actively promote reduction in domestic demand for cannabis, or other narcotic drugs. It has established a program to train the staffs of psychiatric hospitals in the treatment of drug addiction.

U.S. POLICY INITIATIVES PROGRAMS

Policy Initiatives. U.S. policy goals in Morocco are to: encourage GOM anti-narcotics efforts; cooperate with Moroccan law enforcement officials in curtailing production and transshipment of drugs; provide training in law enforcement techniques; promote GOM adherence to bilateral and international agreement requirements; provide support, as appropriate, for existing Moroccan-European cooperation; and encourage greater international cooperation to control Moroccan production and export of drugs. **Bilateral Cooperation.** The U.S. has trained some Moroccan law enforcement officers in basic narcotics enforcement techniques, and provided anti-narcotics intelligence. The GOM is expected to participate in additional training in FY2004.

The Road Ahead. The U.S. will continue to monitor the narcotics situation in Morocco, cooperate with the GOM in its anti-narcotics efforts, and, together with the more directly affected EU, provide law enforcement training, intelligence, and other support where possible.

IMPORTANT INFORMATION FOR UNDERSTANDING MOROCCO

PROFILE

OFFICIAL NAME: Kingdom of Morocco

Geography
Area: 446,550 sq. km. (172,413 sq. mi.) slightly larger than California. (The disputed territory of Western Sahara comprises another 267,028 sq. km or 102,703 sq. mi.)
Major cities: Rabat (Capital), Casablanca, Marrakech, Fes, Meknes, Tangier.
Terrain: Coastal plains, mountains, desert.
Climate: Mediterranean to more extreme in the interior and south.

People
Nationality: *Noun and adjective*--Moroccan(s).
Population: 31,478,000
Annual growth rate (2004): 1.4%.
Ethnic groups: Arab-Berber 99%.
Religions: Muslim 99.99%, Jewish population estimated at 4,000 people, Christian population estimated at less than 1,000.
Languages: Arabic (official), several Berber dialects; French functions as the language of business, government, and diplomacy.
Education: *Years compulsory*--9. *Literacy*--52.6%.
Health: *Infant mortality rate*--49.72/1,000. *Life expectancy*--66.92 yrs. male, 71.44 yrs. female.
Work force (10.7 million, 2003): *Agriculture*--50%; *services*--35%; *industry*--15%.

Government
Type: Constitutional monarchy.
Constitution: March 1972, revised September 1992 and September 1996 (creating a bicameral legislature).
Independence: March 2, 1956.
Branches: *Executive*--King (head of state), Prime Minister (head of government). *Legislative*--Bicameral Parliament. *Judicial*--Supreme Court.
Major political parties: Socialist Union of Popular Forces (USFP), Istiqlal (Independence) Party (PI), Party of Justice and Development (PJD), National Rally of Independents (RNI), Popular Movement (MP), National Popular Movement (MNP), Constitutional Union Party (UC), Democratic Forces Front, (FFD), National Democratic Party (PND), Party of Progress and Socialism (PPS), Democratic Union (UD), Democratic and Social Movement (MDS), Social Democratic Party (PSD), The Pact (AHD), Liberty Alliance (ADL), United Socialist Leftists (GSU), Moroccan Liberal Party (PML), Party of Reform and Development (PRD), Citizen Forces (FC), National Itihadi (Unity) Congress (CNI), Party of Action (PA), Social Center Party (PCS), Party of Environment and Development (PED), Citizens Initiative for Development (ICD), Party of Renewal and Equity (PRE), Consultation and Independence Party (PCI), Advancing Democratic and Social Party (PAGDS).
Suffrage: Universal starting at 18 years of age.

Economy
GDP: $51.990 billion.
Per capita GDP (2005): $1.725 billion.
Natural resources: Phosphates, fish, manganese, lead, silver, and copper.
Agriculture (13% of GDP): *Products*--barley, citrus fruits, vegetables, olives, livestock, and fishing.
Industry (31% of GDP): *Types*--phosphate mining, manufacturing and handicrafts, construction and public works, energy.
Trade: *Exports*--$14.037 billion (27% GDP). *Major markets*--EU 71.5%, India 4.1%, U.S. 2.6%, and Brazil 2.4%. *Imports*-- $17.68 billion (34% GDP, 2005). *Major suppliers*--EU 52.1%, Saudi Arabia 4.8%, Russia 6.7%, China 5.2%, U.S. 3.4%.

PEOPLE

Moroccans are predominantly Sunni Muslims of Arab, Berber, or mixed Arab-Berber ancestry. The Arabs brought Islam, along with Arabic language and culture, to the region from the Arabian Peninsula during the Muslim conquests of the 7th century. Today, there remains a Jewish community of approximately 5,000, and a largely expatriate Christian population of 5,000, who enjoy religious freedom and full civil rights. Morocco is also home to a 300-500-person Baha'i community which, in recent years, has been able to worship free from government interference.

Arabic is Morocco's official language, but French is widely taught and serves as the primary language of commerce and government. Moroccan colloquial Arabic is composed of a unique combination of Arabic, Berber and French dialects. Along with Arabic, about 10 million Moroccans, predominantly in rural areas, also speak one of the three Moroccan Berber dialects (Tarifit, Tashelhit, and Tamazight). Spanish is also used in the northern part of the country. English is rapidly becoming the foreign language of choice among educated youth and is offered in all public schools from the fourth year on.

Most people live west of the Atlas Mountains, a range that insulates the country from the Sahara Desert. Casablanca is the center of commerce and industry and the leading port; Rabat is the seat of government; Tangier is the gateway to Spain and also a major port; "Arab" Fes is the cultural and religious center; and "Berber" Marrakech is a major tourist center.

Education in Morocco is free and compulsory through primary school (age 15). Nevertheless, many children--particularly girls in rural areas--do not attend school. The country's literacy rates reveals sharp gaps in education, both in terms of gender and location; while country-wide literacy rates are estimated at 39% among women and 64% among men, the female literacy rate in rural areas is only 10%.

Morocco is home to 14 public universities. Mohammed V University in Rabat is one of the country's most famous schools, with faculties of law, sciences, liberal arts, and medicine. Karaouine University, in Fes, is a longstanding center for Islamic studies and is the oldest university in the Maghreb. Morocco has one private, English language university, Al-Akhawayn, in Ifrane, founded in 1993 by King Hassan II and King Fahd of Saudi Arabia. The curriculum is based on an American model.

HISTORY

Morocco's strategic location has shaped its history. Beginning with the Phoenicians, many foreigners were drawn to this area. Romans, Visigoths, Vandals and Byzantine Greeks ruled successively. Arab forces began occupying Morocco in the seventh century A.D., bringing their civilization and Islam. The Alaouite dynasty, which has ruled Morocco since 1649, claims descent from the Prophet Muhammad.

Morocco's location and resources led to early competition among European powers in Africa, beginning with successful Portuguese efforts to control the Atlantic coast in the 15th century. France showed a strong interest in Morocco as early as 1830. Following recognition by the United Kingdom in 1904 of France's "sphere of influence" in Morocco, the Algeciras Conference (1906) formalized France's "special position" and entrusted policing of Morocco to France and Spain jointly. The Treaty of Fes (1912) made Morocco a protectorate of France. By the same treaty, Spain assumed the role of protecting power over the northern and southern (Saharan) zones.

Nationalist political parties, which took shape under the French protectorate, began a strong campaign for independence after World War II. Declarations such as the Atlantic Charter (a joint U.S.-British statement set forth, among other things, the right of all people to choose the form of government under which they live), served as a base for the independence movement. A manifesto of the Istiqlal (Independence) Party in 1944 was one of the earliest public demands for independence. That party subsequently provided most of the leadership for the nationalist movement and remains a dominant political force.

In 1953, France exiled the highly respected Sultan Mohammed V and replaced him with the unpopular Mohammed Ben Aarafa. Ben Aarafa's reign was widely perceived as illegitimate, and sparked active opposition to French rule. France allowed Mohammed V to return in 1955, and by 1956, Morocco had regained its independence.

In the year 2006, Moroccans celebrated their 50th year of independence from France. After gaining independence on March 2, 1956, Morocco regained control over certain Spanish-ruled areas through agreements with Spain in 1956 and 1958. The internationalized city of Tangier was reintegrated with the signing of the Tangier Protocol on October 29, 1956. The Spanish enclave of Ifni in the south became part of Morocco in 1969. Spain, however, retains control over the small coastal enclaves of Ceuta and Melilla in the north.

During the 1990s, King Hassan made great strides toward economic and political liberalization. King Hassan died on July 23, 1999, and was succeeded by his son, Mohammed VI, who pledged to continue these reforms. Under Mohammed VI, the Moroccan Government has undertaken a number of economic, political, and social reforms, including the 2003 Moudawana, a reform of the family status code, and the 2006 Equity and Reconciliation Commission, which investigated allegations of human rights abuse from 1956 to 1999.

GOVERNMENT AND POLITICAL CONDITIONS

Morocco is divided into 16 administrative regions (further broken into provinces and prefectures); the regions are administered by Walis (governors) appointed by the King.

The Moroccan Constitution provides for a monarchy with a Parliament and an independent judiciary. Ultimate authority rests with the King. He presides over the Council of Ministers; appoints the prime minister following legislative elections; appoints all members of the government taking into account the prime minister's recommendations; and may, at his discretion, terminate the tenure of any minister, dissolve the Parliament, call for new elections, or rule by decree. The King is the head of the military and the country's religious leader.

Since the constitutional reform of 1996, the bicameral legislature consists of a lower chamber called the Chamber of Representatives, which is directly elected, and an upper chamber, the Chamber of Counselors, whose members are indirectly elected through various regional, local, and professional councils. The councils' members themselves are elected directly. Parliament's powers, though limited, were expanded under the 1992 and 1996 constitutional revisions to include budgetary matters, approval authority, and establishing commissions of inquiry to investigate the government's actions. The lower chamber of Parliament may dissolve the government through a vote of no confidence.

The last parliamentary elections were held in November 2002 and were considered largely free, fair, and transparent. At that time, King Mohammed VI formed a government appointing then Interior Minister Driss Jettou as Prime Minister. Cabinet level positions were drawn from most major parties in the coalition.

Following the 2002 elections, King Mohammed VI highlighted several goals toward which the new government should work: gainful employment, economic development, meaningful education, and increased housing availability. To meet the King's objectives, the Jettou government embarked on a series of initiatives and reforms, which he laid out in his early days as Prime Minister.

Jettou emphasized that first and foremost, modernization and revitalization of the country's infrastructure (roads, trains, communications, water, etc.) and national economy (support for Moroccan businesses, preparations for competition, modernization of modes of production, etc.), were necessary towards development progress in Morocco.

In order to create employment opportunities, the government is promoting investment in the tourism, industrial, fishing, and service industries, and is ameliorating, restructuring, and modernizing the education system.

Preparations are currently underway for the next parliamentary elections in September 2007.

Principal Government Officials

Office	Name	Party	Since
King	Mohammed VI		23 July 1999
Prime Minister	Abdelillah Benkirane	Justice and Development Party	29 November 2011

Morocco maintains an embassy in the United States at 1601 - 21st Street NW, Washington, DC 20009 (tel. 202-462-7979).

ECONOMY

Macroeconomic stability, coupled with low inflation and relatively slow economic growth, has characterized the Moroccan economy over the past several years. The Jettou government continues to pursue reform, liberalization, and modernization aimed at stimulating growth and creating jobs. Employment, however, remains overly dependent on the agriculture sector, which is extremely vulnerable to inconsistent rainfall. Morocco's primary economic challenge is to accelerate growth in order to reduce high levels of unemployment and underemployment. While overall unemployment stands at 11%, this figure masks significantly higher urban unemployment, as high as 33% among urban youths.

Through a foreign exchange rate anchor and well-managed monetary policy, Morocco has held inflation rates to industrial country levels over the past decade; inflation between 1999 and 2004 remained at 1.5% and fell to 1% in 2005. Despite criticism among exporters that the dirham has become badly overvalued, the country maintains a current account surplus. Foreign exchange reserves are strong, with over $16 billion in reserves, the equivalent of 11 months of imports at the end of 2005. The combination of strong foreign exchange reserves and active external debt management gives Morocco ample capacity to service its debt. Current external debt stands at about $15.6 billion, or 27.8% of GDP.

Economic growth has been hampered by an over-reliance on the agriculture sector. Agriculture production is extremely susceptible to rainfall levels and ranges from 15% to 20% of GDP. Given that almost 50% of Morocco's population depends directly on agriculture, droughts have a severe negative effect on the economy.

The current government is continuing a series of structural reforms begun in recent years. The most promising reforms have been in labor market and financial sectors, and privatization has accelerated the sale of Global System for Mobile Communications (GSM) licenses in the last few years. Morocco also has liberalized rules for oil and gas exploration and has granted concessions for many public services in major cities. The tender process in Morocco is becoming increasingly transparent. Many believe, however, that the process of economic reform must be accelerated in order to reduce urban unemployment.

In January 2006, the bilateral Free Trade Agreement (FTA) between the United States and Morocco went into effect. The FTA represents an important step towards the President Bush's vision of a Middle East Free Trade Area and is the first in Africa. The U.S.-Morocco FTA eliminated tariffs on 95% of bilateral trade in consumer and industrial products with all remaining tariffs to be eliminated within nine years. The negotiations produced a comprehensive agreement covering not only market access but also intellectual property rights protection, transparency in government procurement, investments, services, and e-commerce. The FTA provides new trade and investment opportunities for both countries and will encourage economic reforms and liberalization already underway.

FOREIGN RELATIONS

Morocco is a moderate Arab state which maintains close relations with Europe and the United States. It is a member of the UN and belongs to the Arab League, Arab Maghreb Union (UMA), Organization of the Islamic Conference (OIC), and the Non-Aligned Movement. King Mohammed VI is the chairman of the OIC's Al-Quds Jerusalem Committee. Although not a member of the African Union (formerly the Organization of African Unity--OAU), Morocco remains involved in African diplomacy. It contributes consistently to UN peacekeeping efforts on the continent.

Morocco is active in Maghreb, Arab, and African affairs. It supports the search for peace and moderation in the Middle East. In 1986, then-King Hassan II took the daring step of inviting then-Israeli Prime Minister Peres for talks, becoming only the second Arab leader to host an Israeli leader. Following the September 1993 signing of the Israeli-Palestinian Declaration of Principles, Morocco accelerated its economic ties and political contacts with Israel. In September 1994, Morocco and Israel announced the opening of bilateral liaison offices. These offices were closed in 2000 following sustained Israeli-Palestinian violence, but Moroccan-Israeli diplomatic contacts continue.

Morocco was the first Arab state to condemn Iraq's invasion of Kuwait in 1990, and sent troops to help defend Saudi Arabia. Morocco maintains close relations with Saudi Arabia and the Persian Gulf states, which have provided Morocco with substantial amounts of financial assistance. Morocco has supported efforts to stabilize Iraq following the downfall of Saddam Hussein.

Morocco was among the first Arab and Islamic states to denounce the September 11, 2001 terrorist attacks in the United States and declare solidarity with the American people in the war against terror. Morocco has seen its own terrorism at home as well. On May 16, 2003, Moroccan suicide bombers simultaneously attacked five sites in Casablanca, killing more than 40 people and wounding over 100. More than a million people subsequently demonstrated to condemn the attacks.

The major issue in Morocco's foreign relations is its claim to Western Sahara. As a result of Algeria's continued support for the Polisario Front in the dispute over Western Sahara, relations between Morocco and Algeria have remained strained over the past several decades, although they have full diplomatic relations and there is periodic high-level contact between the two countries.

Western Sahara

For more than 30 years, Morocco and the independence-seeking Popular Front of the Liberation of Saqiat al Hamra and Rio de Oro (Polisario Front) have vied for control of the Western Sahara, a former Spanish territory. Morocco's claim to sovereignty over the Western Sahara is based largely on a historical argument of traditional loyalty of the Sahrawi tribal leaders to the Moroccan sultan as spiritual leader and ruler. The Polisario claims to represent the aspirations of the Western Saharan inhabitants for independence. Algeria claims none of the territory for itself but maintains that Sahrawis should determine the territory's future status.

From 1904 until 1975, Spain occupied the entire territory, which is divided into a northern portion, the Saguia el Hamra, and a southern two-thirds, known as Rio de Oro. In 1969, the Polisario Front was formed to combat the occupation of the territory. In November 1975, King Hassan mobilized 350,000 unarmed Moroccan citizens in what came to be known as the "Green March" into Western Sahara. The march was designed to both demonstrate and strengthen Moroccan claims to the territory. On November 14, Spain, Morocco, and Mauritania announced a tripartite agreement for an interim administration under which Spain agreed to share administrative authority with Morocco and Mauritania, leaving aside the question of sovereignty. With the establishment of a Moroccan and Mauritanian presence throughout the territory, however, Spain's role in the administration of the Western Sahara ceased.

After a period of hostilities, Mauritania withdrew from the territory in 1979 and signed a peace treaty with the Polisario, relinquishing all claims to the territory. Moroccan troops occupied the region vacated by Mauritania and later proclaimed the territory reintegrated into Morocco. Morocco subsequently built a fortified berm around three-fourths of Western Sahara and has de facto administrative control over 80% of the territory.

At the OAU (now African Union) summit in June 1981, King Hassan announced his willingness to hold a referendum in the Western Sahara. Subsequent meetings of an OAU Implementation Committee proposed a cease-fire, a UN peacekeeping force, and an interim administration to assist with an OAU-UN-supervised referendum on the issue of independence or annexation. In 1984, the OAU seated a delegation of the Sahara Democratic Arab Republic (SDAR), the shadow government of the Polisario. Morocco subsequently withdrew from the OAU.

In 1988, Moroccan and Polisario representatives agreed on a joint UN/OAU settlement proposal for a referendum, but due to disagreements it never took place. In 1991, the UN brokered a cease-fire and settlement plan, and established the United Nations Mission for Referendum in Western Sahara (known by its French acronym, MINURSO), which deployed a roughly 200-person monitoring force to the territory.

The UN continues to explore with the parties ways of arriving at a mutually agreed political settlement and to promote confidence-building measures between the parties in the interim. In 2003, former Secretary of State James Baker, working as UN Secretary General Kofi Annan's Personal Envoy, put forward a peace plan calling for a referendum on issues of autonomy or integration with Morocco. While the Polisario Front and the Algerian Government accepted the plan, Morocco rejected it. After a seven-year effort to assist the parties in coming to an agreement, James Baker resigned as Personal Envoy in June 2004. In August of the same year, Kofi Annan appointed Alvaro de Soto Special Representative for the Western Sahara, to continue Baker's work. Special Representative de Soto left MINURSO in May 2005, and was replaced in July 2005 by Peter van Walsum of the Netherlands.

The Western Sahara dispute remains the primary impediment to regional integration and development goals. The parties were able to set aside some of their differences when, in August 2004, U.S. Senator Richard Lugar led a mission to the region that resulted in the release of 404 Moroccan prisoners of war who had long been held by the Polisario. Today, approximately 90,000 Sahrawi refugees live in camps around Tindouf, Algeria. The exact number of refugees living in these camps is not known since there has never been a reliable census of the population. Several thousand Sahrawis also live in the Moroccan-controlled area of Western Sahara among a large number of Moroccan settlers. Morocco considers the Western Sahara part of its national territory, while Polisario insists on the right of the people of the Western Sahara to self-determination. Algeria supports self-determination of the Sahrawis. The issue remains a major stumbling block to Moroccan-Algerian relations and regional integration.

The United States has consistently encouraged the parties to work with the United Nations, and with each other, in a spirit of flexibility and compromise, to find a mutually acceptable settlement. Morocco has recently expressed willingness to lay out its plan for autonomy for the Western Sahara, and the U.S. has encouraged the kingdom to put forward a proposal for all parties to examine and directly discuss.

U.S.-MOROCCAN RELATIONS

Morocco was the first country to seek diplomatic relations with the Government of the United States in 1777, and remains one of our oldest and closest allies in the region. Formal U.S. relations with Morocco date from 1787, when the two nations negotiated a Treaty of Peace and Friendship. Renegotiated in 1836, the treaty is still in force, constituting the longest unbroken treaty relationship in U.S. history. As testament to the special nature of the U.S.-Moroccan relationship, Tangier is home to the oldest U.S. diplomatic property in the world, and the only building on foreign soil that is listed in the U.S. National Register of Historic Places, the American Legation in Tangier (now a museum).

U.S.-Moroccan relations, characterized by mutual respect and friendship, have remained strong through cooperation and sustained high-level dialogue. King Hassan II visited the United States several times during his reign as King, meeting with Presidents Kennedy, Johnson, Carter, Reagan, Bush, and Clinton. King Mohammed VI has continued his father's tradition; he made his first trip to the U.S. as King on June 20, 2000. Prime Minister Jettou visited Washington in January 2004, and King Mohammed came to the United States in July 2004. Secretary of State Colin Powell traveled to Morocco in December 2004 to co-chair with Foreign Minister Benaissa the first meeting of the G8-BMENA "Forum for the Future." In June 2006, Under Secretary for Public Diplomacy and Public Affairs Karen Hughes visited Morocco to meet with Moroccan officials, Moroccan non-governmental organizations, and students.

As a stable, democratizing, and liberalizing Arab Muslim nation, Morocco is important for U.S. interests in the Middle East. Accordingly, U.S. policy toward Morocco seeks sustained and strong engagement, and identifies priorities for reform, conflict resolution, counterterrorism cooperation, and public outreach.

The U.S. Agency for International Development (USAID) and its predecessor agencies have managed an active and effective assistance program in Morocco since 1953, for a cumulative amount exceeding $2 billion. The amount of USAID assistance to Morocco in FY 2005 was $28.2 million. USAID's current multi-sectoral strategy (2004-2008) consists of three strategic objectives in creating more opportunities for trade and investment, basic education and workforce training, and government responsiveness to citizen needs.

The Peace Corps has been active in Morocco for more than 40 years, with the first group of 53 volunteers arriving in the country in 1963. Since that time, nearly 4,000 volunteers have served in Morocco, and have served in a variety of capacities including lab technology, urban development, commercial development, education, rural water supply, small business development, beekeeping, and English training. In 2005, 190 volunteers served in Morocco, working in four sectors: health, youth development, small business, and the environment.

Principal U.S. Embassy Officials
Chargé d'Affaires--Robert Jackson
Director, USAID Mission--Monica Stein-Olson
Political Counselor--Craig Karp
Economic Counselor--Stuart Smith
Agricultural Affairs Officer--Hassan Ahmed
Foreign Commercial Officer--Rick Ortiz
Public Affairs Officer--Mary Jeffers
Consul General, Casablanca--Elisabeth Millard

The U.S. Embassy in Morocco is located at 2 Avenue de Marrakech, Rabat tel. 212 (37) 76-22-65.

TRAVEL AND BUSINESS INFORMATION

The U.S. Department of State's Consular Information Program advises Americans traveling and residing abroad through Consular Information Sheets, Public Announcements, and Travel Warnings.

Consular Information Sheets exist for all countries and include information on entry and exit requirements, currency regulations, health conditions, safety and security, crime, political disturbances, and the addresses of the U.S. embassies and consulates abroad.

Public Announcements are issued to disseminate information quickly about terrorist threats and other relatively short-term conditions overseas that pose significant risks to the security of American travelers.

Travel Warnings are issued when the State Department recommends that Americans avoid travel to a certain country because the situation is dangerous or unstable.

For the latest security information, Americans living and traveling abroad should regularly monitor the Department's Bureau of Consular Affairs Internet web site at http://www.travel.state.gov, where the current Worldwide Caution, Public Announcements, and Travel Warnings can be found. Consular Affairs Publications, which contain information on obtaining passports and planning a safe trip abroad, are also available at http://www.travel.state.gov. For additional information on international travel, see http://www.usa.gov/Citizen/Topics/Travel/International.shtml.

The Department of State encourages all U.S citizens traveling or residing abroad to register via the State Department's travel registration website or at the nearest U.S. embassy or consulate abroad. Registration will make your presence and whereabouts known in case it is necessary to contact you in an emergency and will enable you to receive up-to-date information on security conditions.

Emergency information concerning Americans traveling abroad may be obtained by calling 1-888-407-4747 toll free in the U.S. and Canada or the regular toll line 1-202-501-4444 for callers outside the U.S. and Canada.

The National Passport Information Center (NPIC) is the U.S. Department of State's single, centralized public contact center for U.S. passport information. Telephone: 1-877-4USA-PPT (1-877-487-2778). Customer service representatives and operators for TDD/TTY are available Monday-Friday, 7:00 a.m. to 12:00 midnight, Eastern Time, excluding federal holidays.

Travelers can check the latest health information with the U.S. Centers for Disease Control and Prevention in Atlanta, Georgia. A hotline at 877-FYI-TRIP (877-394-8747) and a web site at http://www.cdc.gov/travel/index.htm give the most recent health advisories, immunization recommendations or requirements, and advice on food and drinking water safety for regions and countries. A booklet entitled "Health Information for International Travel" (HHS publication number CDC-95-8280) is available from the U.S. Government Printing Office, Washington, DC 20402, tel. (202) 512-1800.

INVESTING AND STARTING BUSINESS IN MOROCCO BASICS

INVESTING IN MOROCCO

The Kingdom has drawn up a comprehensive strategy for foreign investment promotion based on three main elements: a more conducive institutional and legal framework for international investors, a regional strategy for FDI promotion, and a sectoral strategy based on outsourcing and delocalisation.

This strategy is based on the following fundamental factors: the right to invest, the right to transfer income from investment (profits, dividends, capital) and earnings from sale or liquidation, without any limits on amounts or duration and the freedom to invest without prior authorisation. All industrial sectors are open to foreign investment, except for agriculture, which is regulated by the Dahir law n°1-69-25, modified by Dahir laws n°1-97-171 and 1-01-55, forming the agricultural investments code. Investment in the money market, offshore export zones, or hydrocarbons are also ruled by specific regulations. Acquisition of arable lands by foreign investors is prohibited, but foreign investors can obtain long-term leases.

The Investment Charter adopted in 1995 provides for additional instruments to encourage investment in the form of contributions and benefits granted by the State to investors. The main incentives are as follows.

Export enterprises are exempt from corporate tax (IS) and the general income tax (IGR) for a five-year period, after which there is a 50 percent reduction in these taxes.

VAT and licence exemptions are good for five years.

Capital goods, equipment, and tools acquired locally are exempt from VAT.

VAT is suspended for products and services slated for export.

For investment in the province of Tangiers, there is a 50 percent reduction in corporate tax (IS), professional tax and licences.

For investment in the Tangiers free trade zone, there is total exemption of corporate tax for five years and taxation at 8.75 percent for the following 10 years.

Stock option capital gains are taxed at 10 percent, under certain conditions.

Acquisition of land intended for an investment initiative is exempt from registration fees. This exemption also applies to companies investing in areas earmarked for priority development.

Full convertibility in foreign currency is available for foreign investment.

Investment is protected and there is free transfer of capital, tax-free profits, and revenue from the sale or total or partial disposal of these investments, including capital gains.

Non-discrimination between foreigners and nationals is guaranteed.

In addition to tax incentives, large-scale investments (exceeding DH 200 million) are also exempt from import duty and VAT on imported capital goods, equipment, and tools for activities that benefit regional development. In order to boost regional development, the State also assumes part of the cost for developing industrial zones. In addition to these tax and customs incentives, foreign investors are also eligible for other advantages in targeted geographic and sector-defined free trade zones. Two types of infrastructure are being developed:

Industrial parks such as Bouskoura, Jorf Lasfar (class A production facilities and controlled pollution) and Meknes.

The Tangiers free trade zone, which relates only to export companies. Investors can also take advantage of a number of benefits pertaining to customs regimes, such as temporary entry for processing, bonded warehousing and storage, as well as advantages provided under the free export zone regime and the offshore financial centre regime.

In 1996, a Foreign Investment Department was set up under the Ministry of the Economy, Finance, Privatisation and Tourism to promote foreign investment in Morocco. In 1998, an Interministerial Investment Commission (CII), chaired by the Prime Minister, was established for purposes of appeal and arbitration. It is responsible for making rulings on obstacles to investment projects and for implementing measures to enhance the investment climate.

16 regional investment centres have been established since 2002, seeking to decentralise, simplify procedures, and decrease the burden of procedures at the regional level. The two main tasks of these regional investment centres are to assist in setting up new businesses and help investors, each with its own-targeted services. For example, the facility that assists in setting up businesses is the sole intermediary for new companies. It provides applicants with the information required by law and undertakes the relevant procedures to obtain required documentation. The government has also created the Hassan II Fund for Economic and Social Development, which grants direct assistance for investment in industrial sectors with strong growth potential. In addition, the Moroccan Corporate Upgrading Fund "FOMAN" has been launched to help companies with their modernisation efforts.

Moroccan legislation governing companies is covered commercial law (law n° 17-95) on limited companies and law n° 5-96 relating to other corporate structures. Foreign investors can acquire holdings in a Moroccan company or set up a new company. Joint stock companies are the most widespread form of corporate structure in Morocco, along with other forms: limited companies, limited-partnership companies, stockholding companies) and partnerships (partnerships, joint-stock limited partnerships).

To assist foreign operators in their investment undertakings, the authorities have adopted a sectoral approach to FDI promotion, based on three target categories: activities related to subcontracting and delocalisation, tourism, and agriculture. 2500 companies in Morocco work in outsourcing, with sales amounting to more than MAD 29 billion (2.6 billion euros), mainly in the textile-clothing sector, electrical and electronic engineering, assembly of commercial vehicles and railway equipment, and manufacture of mopeds and private cars. In the tertiary sector, the strategy to promote FDI for the development of call centres has met with great success.

In the tourism sector, the "2010 Vision" development plan and the "Azure Plan" are the main vectors for attracting foreign investment and four seaside resorts have been sold off to foreign investors. In the agricultural sector, the authorities attacked reprofiling of two public companies (SODEA and SOGETA) in May 2003.

The restructuring process is at an advanced stage, with an international tender launched at the end of October 2004 for these two companies to sell 205 lots involving 56,497 ha of real estate to the private sector. The 2006 finance law introduced a new taxation code. The corporate tax rate has been 35 percent for profits since 1996, down from the previous 39.6 percent rate, which still applies to insurance companies and financial establishments. Non-resident construction and civil engineering companies can opt for an alternative tax amounting to 8 percent of the amount of the contract, under certain conditions. Dividends are taxed at the source at 10 percent maximum and this gives rise to an equivalent tax credit.

Company branches and other companies are also taxed. The standard rate for VAT is 20 percent and reduced rates vary according to product and service, for example 7 percent on water, electricity, pharmaceutical products; 10 percent on restaurants; and 14 percent on real estate, coffee, tea…).

The 1996 association agreement with the European Union went into effective 2000, leading to a free trade area by 2012. A free trade agreement was also signed in June 2004 with the United States, in force since 1 January 2006. The Kingdom is also negotiating several trade agreements targeting regional integration, the so-called "South-South" agreements. Morocco is part of the Agadir agreement signed by Jordan, Egypt, and Tunisia in February 2004, but it has not yet been ratified by Morocco. A free trade agreement was also signed with Turkey in April 2004.

BUSINESS FORMS AND STRUCTURES

COMPANIES LAW

Under Moroccan law, the primary types of corporate structures available are: limited liability companies; private limited companies; limited partnerships with shares; general and limited partnerships; and joint-ventures, all of which generally conform to Western company forms of the same nomenclature. The two most widely used are the SA and the SARL, as described below.

LIMITED LIABILITY COMPANY

Limited liability companies (SA) must have a minimum of five shareholders who can be either legal entities or individuals. As with traditional limited liability companies, the shareholders' liability is limited to the amount of share equity the shareholder hold. Upon incorporation of the limited liability company, a quarter of the equity capital must be paid in advance if paid in cash contributions. If it is paid in contributions in kind, it must be fully paid upon incorporation. Both bearer and registered shares may be issued by the limited liability company. The minimum share value is 50 MDh. The company has no corporate name but a trade name, and there are generally no restrictions on the sale and transfer of shares to third parties.

PRIVATE LIMITED COMPANY

The private limited company (SARL) is an intermediate type between associations of persons and of capital, bearing resemblance to both partnerships and share companies. It is always a trading company, regardless of its corporate name and its minimum equity capital is 10,000 MDh. It may be formed by two or more members who are only liable to the amount of their share of the equity capital in the company. Unlike a general partnership, members of a private limited company do not need to be registered merchants. The private limited company must file a memorandum of association as part of its incorporation process. The capital stock has to be fully described and paid up as the company is formed. Stocks shall have the same face value and are not negotiable; they may be transferred only through contracts. "*Parts Sociales*" may be transferred to third parties outside the company only with the co-associates' consent.

PARTNERSHIPS

GENERAL PARTNERSHIPS

In a general partnership, the partners are jointly and severally liable, without limitation, for the debts of the partnership. Partners may be individuals or corporations, however, they do have to be registered as merchants. There is no restriction on participation by foreign individuals or corporations in general partnerships.

LIMITED PARTNERSHIPS

In a limited partnership at least one partner must have unlimited liability while the others have limited liability. A partner whose liability is limited may not take part in the management of the partnership. Limited partnerships are relatively rare in Morocco.

LIMITED PARTNERSHIP WITH SHARES

This corporate form is essentially a joint stock company wherein the capital is divided into shares to be held by active and inactive partners. There must be at least one active partner who has unlimited liability with regard to the debts of the entity, and three inactive partners who are liable only to the extent of their shares in the equity capital. The limited partnership with shares is operated by the active partners or by external managers. The governing body is a board of trustees composed of at least three of the inactive partners.

JOINT VENTURES

A joint venture does not have a separate legal personality, and its existence is not normally disclosed to third parties, except to the tax authorities. Joint ventures are used for financial syndicates or to undertake specific construction contracts.

BRANCH OFFICES

The branch affiliate or subsidiary of a foreign corporation is regarded as a separate legal entity. The Moroccan branch, however, has to disclose certain details regarding its parent-company, its representatives and its delegated powers. When registering a branch in Morocco, the foreign parent-company must submit its articles of incorporation along with the incorporation documents of the branch.

SOLE PROPRIETORSHIPS

Foreigners may establish in Morocco sole proprietorships. In a sole proprietorship, the business is conducted under the responsibility of an individual personally liable for the debts of the business to the extent of all business and personal assets. The business must be registered with the Commerce Registry and with the tax authority.

SETTING UP & OPERATING BUSINESS IN MOROCCO

TYPE OF BUSINESS

The various forms of business enterprises in Morocco are:

· Share companies : the stock company (SA), the limited liability company (SARL) and the limited company with shares · Partnerships · Entities with specific regulations : investment companies, co-operative societies, consumer cooperative and friendly societies

Besides the sole partnership, the SA and the SARL are the two most widely used types of commercial companies in Morocco.

The Stock Company (SA) The corporation is a commercial company in which the partners are called shareholders due to a right represented by negotiable stocks or shares, and are only liable up to the extent of their contribution. In return, a new law of 17 October 1996 regulates stock companies. This law applies to all stock companies established on or after 17 October 1996.

Companies established prior to that date have until 1 January 2000 to comply with the provisions of the new law. Under the new law, an SA must have paid-in capital of at least DH 300,000 (Dh 3 million for "publicly traded companies") and at least five shareholders which can be either legal entities or individuals. The maximum number of shareholders is unlimited. It can be incorporated only after the capital is entirely subscribed. The minimum nominal value of the shares is DH 100.

All stock companies must appoint at least one statutory auditor. The new law on stock companies, published in October 1996, requires the auditor to express an opinion on the annual accounts.

The Limited Liability Company (SARL) The limited liability company is halfway between partnerships and share companies. Small entities generally adopt this form, in part because the rules governing the formation and operations of limited liability companies are less stringent than those that regulate stock companies. The shareholders are only liable up to the amount of their contribution.

A new law of 1 May 1997 regulates the SARL established on or after 1 May 1997. Companies established before this date are granted a transitional period until January 2000 to comply with the new regulations. Under the new law, a SARL must have paid-in capital of at least DH 100,000 and may have between 1 and 50 shareholders. If the number of partners of a SARL grows to exceed 50, the company must be converted to a stock company. The articles of limited liability companies specify the rules governing transfers of shares. A majority of shareholders, generally 75%, is required to approve the transfer of shares to a third party. The limited liability company must appoint at least one statutory auditor.

TAXATION

Corporate Taxes Moroccan income tax is payable at the corporate rate by resident companies, non-resident companies deriving taxable income from activities carried out in Morocco and branches of foreign companies carrying on business activities independent of those performed by their head office. In general, only Moroccan-source income is subject to tax.

Taxes on Individuals Individuals are liable to Moroccan income tax only on income arising in Morocco. However, in the case of income from employment received by a resident individual, the whole of that income is deemed to arise in Morocco whether the duties of employment are performed in Morocco or abroad and wherever the income is paid. In effect therefore, a resident individual is liable for Moroccan income tax on his worldwide employment income.

Other Taxes · Value Added Tax · Business License Tax · National Solidarity Tax · Professional Training Tax · Urban Tax · Withholding Tax · Registration Duties

INCENTIVES

Prior to 1996, Morocco used to have various investment codes for exports, tourism, industrial , mining, maritime, handicraft and real estate investments. These codes have been cancelled starting from 1 January 1996. Morocco has however adopted and investment charter which sets up the main objectives regarding the promotion and development of investments in Morocco within the next ten years.

The charter's main objectives are to improve the tax environment, review the tax incentives and set up new incentives for investments. More specifically, these objectives consist of the following : · reducing the tax burden relating to the acquisition of equipment, · reducing the income tax rates, · offering tax incentives to promote regional development, · promoting offshore and free-trade zones, · apportioning more equitably the tax charges among taxpayers ...

Moreover, the income tax incentives regarding exports, industrial and handicraft investments have been maintained through their inclusion in the corporate tax law in 1996.

EXCHANGE CONTROL

Remittances of capital and related income to non-residents are guaranteed. No limitations are imposed on the time or amount of profit remitted. Loans must be authorised by the Office of Exchange Control.

VISA REQUIREMENTS

To be employed in a company, a foreigner must be a resident in Morocco and obtain an authorisation from the Ministry of Labour. A non-resident cannot stay more than three months in the country. Nationals of certain countries require visas to enter Morocco.

INCORPORATING IN MOROCCO

Obtain a certificat negatif which registers the company name at the Centre Regional d'Investissement (CRI)

Deposit paid up capital in a bank and obtain an attestation de depot

Legalise statutes at Mayor's office (Commune)

File documents with CRI to register with the Ministry of Finance for patente tax with the Tribunal of Commerce, and for social security and taxation

Prepare declaration for the labor inspector (Ministry of Labor)

COMPANY LAW

Under Moroccan law the primary types of corporate structures available are:

Limited liability companies
Private limited companies
Branch

All of which are similar to European companies. The two most widely used are the SA and the SARL, as described below.

LIMITED LIABILITY COMPANY - SA

Limited liability companies must have a minimum of five shareholders who can be either legal entities or individuals. As with traditional limited liability companies, the shareholders' liability is limited to the amount of share equity the shareholder holds. Upon incorporation of the limited liability company, a quarter of the equity capital must be paid in advance if paid in cash contributions. If it is paid in contributions in kind, it must be fully paid upon incorporation. Both bearer and registered shares may be issued by the limited liability company. The company has no corporate name but a trade name, and **there are generally no restrictions on the sale and transfer of shares to third parties.**

PRIVATE LIMITED COMPANY - SARL

The private limited company is an intermediate type between associations of persons and of capital, bearing resemblance to both partnerships and share companies. It is always a trading company, regardless of its corporate name and its minimum equity capital is 10,000 MDh. It may be incorporated by two or more members. The private limited company must file a memorandum of association as part of its incorporation process. The capital stock has to be fully described and paid up as the company is incorporated. Stocks shall have the same face value and are not negotiable. They may be transferred only through contracts. "Parts Sociales" may be transferred to third parties outside the company only with the co-associates' consent.

BRANCH

The branch affiliate or subsidiary of a foreign corporation is regarded as a separate legal entity. The Moroccan branch, however, has to disclose certain details regarding its parent-company, its representatives and its delegated powers. When registering a branch in Morocco, the foreign parent-company must submit its articles of incorporation along with the incorporation documents of the branch.

INCORPORATING PROCEDURE IN MOROCCO

COMPANY REGISTRATION

Legal Form: Société à Responsabilité Limitée (SARL)
City: Casablanca

REGISTRATION REQUIREMENTS

	Procedure	Time to complete:	Cost to complete:
1	Obtain a certificat negatif, which registers the company name at the Centre Regional d'Investissement (CRI)	1 day	MAD 190 (MAD 170 + MAD 20 droits de timbres)
2	Deposit paid-in capital in a bank and obtain an attestation de depot	1 day	no charge
3	Legalize statutes at Mayor's office (Commune)	1 day	DH 20/page + DH10
4	File documents with CRI to register with the Ministry of Finance for patente tax, with the Tribunal of Commerce, and for social security and taxation	7 days for registration, 30 days for publication	DH 1,350 =DH1,000 (1% of capital, at least DH1,000) + DH200 (registration fee) + DH 350 (registration at commercial registry) + DH 150 publication fee (DH 8-9/ line in business paper, DH4/ line bulletin officiel).
5	File a declaration with the economic office of the Prefecture (Service Economique de la Commune)	1 day	no charge
6	Make company stamp	1 day	MAD 200

REGISTRATION REQUIREMENTS DETAILS

Procedure 1.
Obtain a certificat negatif, which registers the company name at the Centre Regional d'Investissement (CRI)
Time to complete:
1 day
Cost to complete:
MAD 190 (MAD 170 + MAD 20 droits de timbres)
Name of Agency:
Comment:
Procedure 2.
Deposit paid-in capital in a bank and obtain an attestation de depot
Time to complete:
1 day
Cost to complete:
no charge
Name of Agency:
Comment:
Paid-in capital remains frozen until the company formation is completed. Deposits must by accompanied by a copy of the bylaws and a "certificat négatif" from the bank.
Procedure 3.
Legalize statutes at Mayor's office (Commune)
Time to complete:

1 day
Cost to complete:
DH 20/page + DH10
Name of Agency:
Comment:
The mayor's office verifies the identity of the person signing the document.
Procedure 4.
File documents with CRI to register with the Ministry of Finance for patente tax, with the Tribunal of Commerce, and for social security and taxation
Time to complete:
7 days for registration, 30 days for publication
Cost to complete:
DH 1,350 =DH1,000 (1% of capital, at least DH1,000) + DH200 (registration fee) + DH 350 (registration at commercial registry) + DH 150 publication fee (DH 8-9/ line in business paper, DH4/ line bulletin officiel).
Name of Agency:
Comment:
The applicant downloads a single registration form (formulaire unique declaration de creation d'entreprise) from the Internet. With the completed form, the applicant files the following:
- "Certificat négatif" (original + 3 copies).
- Certificate of deposit (attestation de depot) (original + 1copy).
- Signed company statutes (at least five copies).
- Lease contract for company premises (contrat de bail) (two copies).
- Identity cards for managers (three copies).
- Notice to be published in the legal newspaper and in the Official Gazette (two copies).

The Centre Regional d'Investissement (CRI) centralizes the following procedures:
- Deposit of bylaws and registration at the Tribunal of Commerce and the Company Registrar.
- "Patente" tax number.
- Two announcements: in a legal journal and in the Official Bulletin.
- Declaration of fiscal existence.
- Social security affiliation.
- Legalization of legal books.

When submitting the form and all documents, the promoter includes the text for publication in both publications (that is, the legal newspaper and the Official Gazette). The text must be in Arabic and typed. The CRI coordinates the publication process. Although the announcement is published in the Official Gazette in 30 days, a receipt from submitting the publication is enough for filing the registration documents with the Tribunal of Commerce.

In about a week, the promoter receives the "patente," the fiscal identification, the commercial registration certificate, legal books, and the social security registration (CNSS registration). As a new service, the entrepreneur can request to be notified by text message when the file is ready.
Procedure 5.
File a declaration with the economic office of the Prefecture (Service Economique de la Commune)
Time to complete:
1 day
Cost to complete:

no charge
Name of Agency:
Comment:
The company must file a letter of solicitation, a copy of the "patente," a copy of the bylaws, and another application letter (for the second type of authorization), and a map of the establishment, installations, fire controls, waste treatment, and so forth. The Economic Office of the Prefecture assesses the company's security and health conditions and its potential environment effects. The procedure can also be done at the CRI.
Procedure 6.
Make company stamp
Time to complete:
1 day
Cost to complete:
MAD 200
Name of Agency:
Comment:

REGISTERING PROPERTY

	Procedure	Time to complete:	Cost to complete:
1	Complete due diligence	1 day	MAD 75
2	Obtain tax attestation form	1 day	no official cost
3	Obtain Tax clearance certificate from Regional General Tax Authority	15 days	no official cost
4	Obtain Tax clearance certificate from Municipal Tax Authority	15 days	no official cost
5	Give completed tax attestation form to Tax Collection Authority for approval	7 days	no official cost
6	The sale contract is signed by both parties and authenticated by the notary	1 day	0.5% to 1% of the transaction value (notary fees) + 600 dirham in stamps (20 dirham per page, 5 pages, 6 copies)
7	Registration of the deed	2 - 5 days	3% of property price (registration duty)
8	The buyer applies for the inscription of the registered deed on the land registers (Conservation Fonciere)	3 days	MAD 75 + 1% of property value (stamp duty), with a minimum of MAD 450

REGISTRATION REQUIREMENT DETAILS

Procedure 1.
Complete due diligence
Time to complete:
1 day
Cost to complete:
MAD 75
Name of Agency:
Land Registry ("Conservation Fonciere")
Comment:
It is mandatory to complete due diligence by checking the property certificate file from the Conservation Fonciere.
At the same time, the notary will check that the selling company is properly registered in the Company Registry, and its representative is authorized to sell this property.
Procedure 2.
Obtain tax attestation form

Time to complete:
1 day
Cost to complete:
no official cost
Name of Agency:
Tax Collection Authority
Comment:
One obtains a blank form from the tax collection authority (la Perception) in order to obtain approvals from other tax authorities that all relevant obligations have been paid.
Procedure 3.
Obtain Tax clearance certificate from Regional General Tax Authority
Time to complete:
15 days
Cost to complete:
no official cost
Name of Agency:
Regional General Tax Authority
Comment:
As of 2007, taxes from several authorities must be cleared before the transfer takes place and it is the responsibility of the notary to assure that the money for the transaction is sufficient to cover any unpaid taxes.
Procedure 4.
Obtain Tax clearance certificate from Municipal Tax Authority
Time to complete:
15 days
Cost to complete:
no official cost
Name of Agency:
Municipal Tax Authority
Comment:
As of 2007, taxes from several authorities must be cleared before the transfer takes place and it is the responsibility of the notary to assure that the money for the transaction is sufficient to cover any unpaid taxes.
Procedure 5.
Give completed tax attestation form to Tax Collection Authority for approval
Time to complete:
7 days
Cost to complete:
no official cost
Name of Agency:
Tax Collection Authority
Comment:
Once signatures are obtained from local authorities, one reverts to the Tax Collection Authority to complete the attestation that all taxes related to the property have been paid.
Procedure 6.
The sale contract is signed by both parties and authenticated by the notary
Time to complete:
1 day
Cost to complete:
0.5% to 1% of the transaction value (notary fees) + 600 dirham in stamps (20 dirham per page, 5 pages, 6 copies)
Name of Agency:
Comment:

The signatures of the parties in the sales deed are only certified by the public notary if a notarial deed is established. Copies of the document are stamped in each page. The deed can be prepared by the parties, in some cases assisted by their lawyers. At this point the parties will usually pay all fees and taxes to the notary, who will then pay all taxes and fees to the authorities on behalf of the parties.
The documentation shall include:
- the sales agreement signed by the parties
- ID cards of each party; if the parties' signatures are filed with the local authorities, only a certified copy of their ID cards and the date and number under which the deed was filed will be required.
10% TVA on notary fees.

Procedure 7.
Registration of the deed
Time to complete:
2 - 5 days
Cost to complete:
3% of property price (registration duty)
Name of Agency:
Comment:
The deed reflecting the transfer of ownership is registered within 30 days from the date of the deed. According to Article 4 of the Registration and Stamp Code, as amended by Finance Act n°48-03 for budget year 2004, a sales deed must be registered with the registration office in charge of the area where the property being sold is located. Registration can be applied for either by the notary or by the parties--the Registration Code does not include any specific provision stating who is entitled to apply for registration.

The registration duty has been cut to 2.5% in the Loi de Finances pour 2006, 'Livre d'Assiette et de Recouvrement': articles 136.1.B.3 and 136.1.A.1. The duly signed and certified sales deed is the only document that must be provided upon registration. In 2008, the notary tax of 0.5% has been combined with the registration fees, causing no change to the cost to complete this procedure because registration fees have been raised from 2.5 to 3% of property value..

Procedure 8.
The buyer applies for the inscription of the registered deed on the land registers (Conservation Fonciere)
Time to complete:
3 days
Cost to complete:
MAD 75 + 1% of property value (stamp duty), with a minimum of MAD 450
Name of Agency:
Land Registry ("Conservation Fonciere")
Comment:
Listing of the registered sales deed in the land registry is an additional formality, which is separate from registration. The buyer applies for the listing of the registered deed on the land registers. According to Article 65 bis of Royal decree of 5 August 1968 completing the dahir of 1913, such listing must be completed within 18 months from the date the deed was drafted for authentic deeds and as from the date the last signature was certified for private deeds.
Parties submit a statement that must include the following: 1. designation with land title number, of building to be listed; 2. nature of right due to be listed; 3. acquisition method and nature and date of deed testifying to it; 4. if applicable, cause of resolution, restriction or right to dispose of or special notice that needs to be listed at the same time as main

right, together with details of beneficiary.
This statement must be signed by both parties. An original copy of the private deed or a copy of the authentic deed concerned is attached to such application.

One receives an official copy of the property registration certificate at the end of this process for MAD 75, which one can sell immediately.

TAXES

Tax or mandatory contribution	Payments (number)	Notes on Payments	Time (hours)	Statutory tax rate	Tax base	Total tax rate (% profit)	Notes on TTR
Social security contributions	12		48	19.1%	gross salaries	22.2	
Corporate income tax	1		70	30.0%	taxable profits	18.2	
Vehicle tax	1		-	MAD 6100	fixed fee	1.4	
Property tax	1		-	10.0%	rental value of property	0	
Stamp duty	1		-	MAD 20/ page	number of pages in contract		small amount
Value added tax (VAT)	12		240	20.0%	value added		not included
Totals:	28		358			41.7	

Notes:
Name of taxes have been standardized. For instance income tax, profit tax, tax on company's income are all named corporate income tax in this table.
The hours for VAT include all the VAT and sales taxes applicable.
The hours for Social Security include all the hours for labor taxes and mandatory contributions in general.

MOROCCAN CODE OF GOOD CORPORATE GOVERNANCE PRACTICES

Foreword Now that, under the enlightened supervision of His Majesty The King Mohammed VI, our country begins the massive task of modernizing its political, economic and administrative structures, it becomes crucial for us to buttress the competitiveness of our economy and of its enterprises. More than ever, the present environment of globalization and heightened competition requires a convergence between the concept of governance in the private sector and that of the public sector for the emergence of governance practices that protect the interests of those who invest their talents and their capital for the profit of all. This crucial awareness led to the setting up, in February 2007, of a National Commission on Corporate Governance in charge of drafting, following the example of numerous developed and emerging countries, a Moroccan Code of Good Corporate Governance Practices. The National Commission, fruit of a broad consensus between the public and the private Moroccan sectors, brings together all key actors in corporate governance in Morocco who, through their significant commitment and involvement in this matter, are best suited to support this project and to contribute to its success. The Moroccan Code of Good Corporate Governance Practices is, without doubt, a strong signal to the various actors of the business world and helps promote good governance practices within enterprises, both from the private and public sectors, thereby strengthening the necessary trust between all partners and playing a large part in creating more wealth and value for the enterprise and all its stakeholders. Good corporate governance buttresses national and foreign investment, promotes market stability and secures economic growth, an essential lever for national development. These crucial issues require both governmental authorities, through economic and political reforms, and private sector actors, to combine their efforts through continuous improvement of their governance methods and practices so as to build an efficient and united economy. In line with international benchmarks, and widely inspired by the OECD corporate governance principles, the Moroccan Code of Good Corporate Governance Practices has been the subject of broad public consultation, both at the national and international level, so as to adapt it to the local environment and to the specificities of the Moroccan economic fabric. This Code shall be supplemented by provisions and specific regulations to take into account the specificities of small and medium-sized enterprises and family-owned businesses, financial institutions and public enterprises. Corporate governance is an ever-changing process which must be elevated to a culture. Therefore, we shall see to the permanence of the National Commission in order to continuously assess and enhance the provisions of our code and to optimize its impact on the improvement of the business climate and on the performance of our economy and its enterprises. At the same time, consciousness raising and training regarding the new responsibilities and standards set forth in terms of corporate governance shall take place.

We seize this opportunity to sincerely thank again all the members of the National Commission for their considerable effort in drafting this code, and in particular the members of the Anticorruption Commission of the CGEM and the Economic Promotion Unit of the Ministry of Economic and General Affairs who worked on this project with dynamism and conviction and who contributed to create a remarkable synergy between private and public actors. Our warmest thanks also go to the international experts group (GCGF Code Peer Review Group) which accepted to review the initial drafting of this code and to benevolently offer its comments, as well as to all private and public Moroccan institutions and individuals who participated in the consultation process at the national level, for their efficient contribution to enhance the provisions of this code. Finally, we wish to express our special thanks to the Global Corporate Governance Forum (GCGF) for the technical assistance they provided us along this project as well as to the IFC and the OECD for their great support.

Preamble The globalization of markets and competition, the acceleration of information and communications technologies, the advent of individual, institutional, and partner shareholding, and the emergence of new economic, social, societal, and environmental responsibilities are among the factors characterizing the new competitive environment for our companies. Our country's system of institutional and economic reforms has been particularly steadfast in recent years in adapting its legislative and regulatory framework to this new competitive environment, and thereby buttressing the efforts of our firms to achieve greater efficiency and competitiveness. Speaking of corporate governance in particular, an inventory has been conducted through the ROSC study (or *RRNC*) of the World Bank (2001 – Updated in 2003) and the survey on corporate governance in Morocco (2005) carried out by the CGEM. At the same time, it is important to follow the lead of many developed and emerging countries and promote a Moroccan Code of Good Corporate Governance Practices, based on particular principles of sound management and transparency and on ethical standards likely to enhance the performance, competitiveness, and growth of our firms and to improve their image in the eyes of investors and other stakeholders (employees, customers, creditors, the Administration, etc.). Indeed, it is more and more widely acknowledged that good governance practices solidify the trust that is essential among all of a company's partners and contribute to creating greater value for the firm and its stakeholders.

The Moroccan Code of Good Corporate Governance Practices is the outgrowth of an extremely broad consensus reached between the private and public sectors. It was drafted by a National

Commission chaired by the CGEM, with secretariat services and coordination provided by the Ministry of Economic and General Affairs. The Commission brought together all the key stakeholders in corporate governance in Morocco (BAM, CDVM, the Casablanca Exchange, GPBM, CJD, the Association of Auditors, ANPME, FCMCIS, the Ministry of Justice, the Ministry of Economy and Finance, the Ministry of Public Sector Modernization), and benefited from the assistance of the Global Corporate Governance Forum (IFC - OECD). The aim of the Commission was to draw up a code consistent with international benchmarks and the OECD Principles of Corporate Governance, while adapting to local conditions and to the special characteristics of the Moroccan economic fabric.

What is Corporate Governance? Corporate governance involves all the relationships between a company's management and governing bodies and the shareholders, on the one hand, and the other stakeholders, on the other hand, and does so with a view to creating value for the corporation. Corporate governance is thus concerned with the manner in which firms are directed and controlled, and examines the capacities of management bodies to:

- Pursue objectives consistent with the interests of shareholders and other stakeholders, and
- Implement effective control systems for managing potential conflicts of interest and possible risks, and for preventing abuses of power which might cause private interests to hold sway over the "corporate interest."

What is the aim of this Code? Stimulating growth and promoting employment in an ever-more competitive environment is a major concern for all countries. Numerous empirical studies have now demonstrated the interconnections between good corporate governance practices on the one hand and corporate performance and growth on the other. Indeed, it is more and more widely acknowledged that an effective corporate governance mechanism makes it possible to:

- Improve the performance and competitiveness of companies and thereby increase their value over the long term thanks to the quality of their governing bodies (Board of Directors, Supervisory Board, Management Board, Family Council, Managing Board, etc.);
- Optimize access to financing and the cost of capital;
- Build confidence on the part of national and international investors and donors thanks to the improved transparency and quality of financial information on the one hand, and, on the other, the respect for the rights of resident or nonresident majority and/or minority shareholders; and
- Solidify relations with the stakeholders (employees, customers, creditors, the Administration, etc.) thanks to compliance with the prevailing legislative and regulatory provisions (securities law, labor law, company law, commercial law, etc.) and/or the contractual provisions in force.

For the general economy, good practices of corporate governance make it possible in particular to:

-

- Enhance the competitiveness of Moroccan enterprises on the domestic and international markets;
- Contribute to improved growth and employment;
- Contribute to the development of an efficient capital market necessary for the sound and competitive financing of our corporations; and
- Better protect the interests of investors and creditors.

To whom is this Code addressed? This Code is addressed to all firms seeking to increase their performance and value in a sustainable manner thanks to the adoption of best practices for corporate governance. Targeted corporate governance codes will supplement this general code in order to address in particular the special characteristics of the following categories of enterprises:

- SMEs and family-owned businesses
- Credit institutions
- Publicly owned subsidiaries and mixed-capital companies.

HOW SHOULD THIS CODE BE USED?

The principles of good governance are based first and foremost on all the legal and regulatory provisions that must be strictly observed in spirit and to the letter. The Moroccan Code of Good Corporate Governance Practices constitutes a collection of lines of conduct and recommendations that supplement the law and regulations, and any provisions of this Code that are contrary thereto are to be disregarded.

This Code may later be supplemented and enriched by means of circulars and other regulatory texts issued primarily by the Office of the Prime Minister and/or other departments and agencies concerned. At the level of the governing bodies, the Moroccan Code of Good Corporate Governance Practices is built upon the unitary structure (Board of Directors for corporations and management for other forms of companies). This said, the Code's recommendations may also apply, mutatis mutandis, to enterprises that have adopted the dual structure (Supervisory Board and Management Board for corporations). In this case, the provisions of the chapter on "responsibilities of the governing body" apply to the Supervisory Board or to the Management Board depending on the responsibilities of each of these two bodies.

The recommendations and lines of conduct with respect to corporate governance are not to be regarded as hampering corporate dynamism, and enterprises thus have room for maneuver in implementing them flexibly in keeping with their legal structure, size, shareholder composition, activities, risk exposure, and management method. For this reason, each firm will have to take its own position with respect to the Moroccan Code of Good Corporate Governance Practices and explain the extent to which it is applying its recommendations. This system, known as "comply or explain," is recommended by the OECD. It is thus a matter of applying the recommendation (comply) or of explaining (explain) the reasons for any departure from it in the Corporate Governance chapter of the management report and, if need be, in its annual report,.

This Code includes four chapters inspired by the OECD Principles of Corporate Governance (2004), and which constitute the pillars of a sound corporate governance mechanism:

- Responsibilities of the governing body
- Rights of shareholders and partners, and their equitable treatment
- Transparency and the dissemination of financial information
- The role of stakeholders and their equitable treatment.

What is the process for revising this Code? Corporate governance is, by definition, a process that undergoes constant change. For this reason, this Code is intended to evolve and will be revised periodically by the National Corporate Governance Commission in light both of national or international changes in the business environment and of the practices followed by firms.

GENERAL PRINCIPLES OF GOOD CORPORATE GOVERNANCE PRACTICES

I. RESPONSIBILITIES OF THE GOVERNING BODY

1) Functions of the governing body The key functions of the governing body consist in particular in: – Reviewing and guiding the strategy of the company, its action plans, its risk policy, and its annual budgets and activity programs; defining its performance objectives, ensuring monitoring of the implementation of the objectives and enterprise performance, and controlling its principal investments and disinvestments; – Recruiting the principal executives, determining their compensation and ensuring that it is appropriate and transparent, monitoring their activities and performance, and, as necessary, replacing them and preparing succession plans; – Overseeing and managing the conflicts of interest that may arise between management, the members of the governing body, and the shareholders or partners, including abuses of social goods or abuses committed in the context of regulated agreements; – Ensuring the integrity of the accounting and financial and non financial reporting systems of the enterprise, in particular ensuring compliance with accounting principles and the existence of adequate internal control and risk management systems, and organizing independent audits and relations with the external auditors; – Overseeing the information dissemination and communication process of the enterprise, in particular as regards:

The governing body is in charge of the strategic orientation and effective surveillance of the management of the enterprise. It is accountable to majority and minority shareholders and partners, and must be motivated by a genuine "affectio societatis" in its respect for the other enterprise stakeholders (its employees, its customers, its creditors, the Administration, etc.).

The legal and regulatory obligations concerning information
Strategic directions
Social policy
The policy on borrowing and dividends
Regulated agreements, in particular with the principal executives and holding companies
Compensation of executives.

– Ensuring the proper conduct of General Meetings, the implementation of the decisions taken by shareholders, and monitoring corporate governance in all its forms;

– Ensuring the scrupulous observance of laws and regulations (securities law, labor law, company law, commercial law, provisions relating to environmental protection, health and safety legislation, etc.) and professional good practices (high ethical standards and rules, etc.). – Continuously improving corporate governance.

2) Responsibilities and duties of the members of the governing body The members of the governing body must fully exercise their role and contribute genuine added value to the enterprise and its executive management. To this end, it is their duty to act in an informed manner, in good faith, and with diligence in the interest of the firm, its shareholders, and its partners. Their fiduciary responsibility vis-à-vis all shareholders and partners is built upon the duties of diligence and loyalty. The duty of diligence is applicable in particular to their personal involvement and their conviction that the principal management mechanisms facilitate the governing body's exercise of its monitoring and control mission. The duty of loyalty colors the observance of the other principles, relating in particular to independence of judgment, conflicts of interest, ethics, good faith, and professionalism. In general, there are four dimensions to responsibility:

Having the capacity to take decisions in the interest of all shareholders or partners.

To this end, the composition of the governing body must ensure that decisions are taken efficiently and strictly in the company interest. In particular, the diversity of the profiles of the members, with complementary experiences and skills, the assistance provided to members in terms of information and training, and the periodic assessment of members, constitute a guarantee of proper functioning of the governing body.

Having independence of judgment, decision-making, and action.

Decisions must be reached with full independence of judgment on the part of the members of the governing body, whether they are executive or outside members. Similarly, such conflicts as may exist between the moral and material interests of the governing body and those of the firm must be avoided. The governing body must be informed of any possible conflict of interest with the enterprise. All members finding themselves in a direct or indirect conflict of interest situation must abstain from participating in discussions and decision-making on the subjects concerned. Finally, the separation of powers in the corporation by separating the functions of Chairman and Chief Executive (companies with Boards of Directors) or by the adoption of a dual structure (Supervisory Board and Management Board) promotes the independence of decision-making and actions.

Fulfilling the duty of control.

The accounts are one of the main sources of information on corporate performance. The first priority of the governing body is to guarantee the quality of financial information, which must be reliable, comparable, intelligible, and relevant. Similarly, monitoring the implementation of the agreed strategy, examining the internal control procedures applied by the enterprise, risk management, assessing the performance of executives, and monitoring the work of specialized committees are all areas under the responsibility of the governing body. Finally, the adoption of internal by-laws and a charter for the members of the governing body is likely to improve the formalization and control of corporate governance practices.

Fulfilling the reporting obligation.

The obligation to be accountable or render the accounts ("Accountability") constitutes the exercise and justification of responsibilities. This is, in particular, the legal or moral obligation to report to all shareholders, partners, and stakeholders on the manner in which responsibilities have been assumed, corrective measures taken, and, depending on circumstances, agreement to assume the consequences of one's own decisions and acts. The reporting obligation is carried out on the occasion of the General Meeting, the ideal location for shareholders to exercise their rights, but also in connection with the financial and non financial communication process of the enterprise.

3) Structures for the efficient functioning of the governing body 3.1) Independence of the governing body and its members Assessment of the performance of executives and the prevention of conflicts of interest are among the important missions of the governing body. This requires that the governing body be independent both of enterprise management and of its shareholders and partners, and in particular of the shareholders or partners of reference. The independence of the governing body is determined principally by its composition and structure, that is:

The role of non executive or outside senior directors;
The existence of specialized committees, their composition, and the role played in them by the non executive or outside members of the governing body;
The separation of powers between the key executives (Chairman, Chief Executive, manager, co-manager, etc.).

Independence of judgment is a requirement for all members of the governing body, whether executives or not, who must in all circumstances act in the interest of the firm. In particular, the non executive or outside members are full members who must take an objective view of the enterprise and contribute to enriching reflection and decision-making, in particular thanks to their assiduousness, professionalism, and independence. To this end, the enterprise must provide them with the training, information, and resources needed for them to carry out their mission efficiently.

Moreover, for limited liability companies with Boards of Directors, the choice between maintaining combined functions for the Chairman and Chief Executive or separating them should be made by each enterprise, reaching a decision in light of its considerations on good governance. In the interest of ensuring transparency between the key executives and the governing body and transparency vis-à-vis the market and the shareholders and partners, it is necessary that the latter and third parties be properly informed about the option taken, and that the reasons and justifications for the choices made be set forth in the management report. It is recommended that firms opt for the dual structure, or separate the functions of Chairman and Chief Executive. This recommendation is aimed basically at:

Increasing the capacity of the governing body to take decisions completely independently of the key executives;
Avoiding excessive concentration of powers in the hands of a single person;
Strengthening the collegial nature of decision-making.

Such formulas also make it possible to better distribute responsibilities for long-term enterprise strategy and its operational management. 3.2) Ethics of governing body members The following obligations are incumbent on each member of the governing body:

Defend the interests of the enterprise and carry out its responsibilities while dealing impartially with all shareholders or partners.
Take cognizance of the relevant legislative and regulatory texts, the company charter, and the internal operating rules and ethical rules of the governing body. They must also stay informed of changes in the regulatory and competitive environment of the enterprise.
Inform the governing body of any real and/or potential situation of conflict of interest and/or of any regulated agreement, and abstain from voting on the corresponding deliberation.
Be present, involved, and generate added value in the reflections and decisions of the governing body, in order to attain legitimacy and gain the trust of shareholders or partners.
Be properly and correctly informed, and ask the Chairman, managing director, and other key executives for additional information whenever necessary.
Maintain the confidentiality of any privileged information that may come to its attention in the exercise of its duties.
Participate actively in General Meetings.
It is highly recommended that reciprocal mandates be avoided, except when cross-participations are the result of a de facto strategic alliance that has been brought to the attention of shareholders and partners or when the enterprises have significant ties in terms of capital.
It is also recommended to avoid holding several mandates concurrently likely to impair the carrying out of the duties of the member of the governing body in the best conditions.

Each governing body may supplement the above list by special provisions imposed by its own circumstances. 3.3) Specialized committees of the governing body The existence of specialized committees within the governing body is a key component of corporate governance and the efficient functioning thereof. The competence, objectivity, and independence required of members make it essential to entrust certain tasks to committees. This is particularly recommended for enterprises making public offerings. It is up to each governing body to determine the number, structure, and organization of its committees. This said, it is recommended that the:

- Review of the accounts
- Monitoring of internal control
- Selection of the external auditors
- Compensation and nominations policy
- Investment and borrowing policy, and
- Selection of the members of the governing body and corporate agents

be prepared by specialized committees. The establishment of committees does nothing to call into question the responsibility and prerogatives of the governing body, which has the sole legal decision-making power. This is why the committees must report on their work at meetings of the governing body and provide a progress report on their activities, a summary of which must be included in the management report. When and as necessary, the committees may request internal audits of their work or call upon the services of outside consultants paid out of a budget allocated annually for that purpose by the governing body. It is recommended that at least two different committees be created, namely an Audit Committee and a Compensation and

Nominations Committee. The governing body should determine the advisability of adding other committees (risks, investments, etc.). 3.3.1). The Audit Committee The Audit Committee is the governing body's subunit tasked with examining the draft final financial statements and evaluating risks. It therefore plays a central role in respect of the transparency of corporate accounts and the capacity of those accounts to inform shareholders, partners, and stakeholders on all the economic, financial and operational risks to which they are exposed.

Composition of the Audit Committee

The Audit Committee must be made up of governing body members with solid knowledge of the accounting and financial details of the enterprise's activity, and who are capable of assessing the risks to which the enterprise is exposed in view of its line of business and environment. The senior financial and accounting managers of the enterprise, whether corporate agents or otherwise, may be invited to participate in the work of the Audit Committee but may not be members thereof.

– Independence :

It is recommended that the Audit Committee be made up of a majority of non executive or outside members who have the objectivity and freedom of judgment necessary for performing their mission soundly and serenely.

– Resources :

The Audit Committee has the power to meet with the senior financial officers of the firm, the external auditors, and the internal audit managers outside the presence of enterprise management. The Audit Committee may, should it so desire, request external experts to assist in its work. In addition, the committee must receive all reports relating to its area of intervention.

– Duty of care as regards the final accounts :

The Audit Committee ensures the integrity of financial information, and the relevance and consistency of the accounting methods used in closing the accounts. The Committee must request all necessary justifications and documentation for any potential modifications. It must evaluate the consequences thereof and, in particular, those of off-balance-sheet liabilities. It is also responsible for analyzing the scope for accounts consolidation and submitting comments and observations before consolidated accounts are closed by the governing body. The Audit Committee shall meet as necessary and at least twice a year to review its internal by-laws, assess the effectiveness of its operation, assess the accounting choices made by key executives, and make all necessary recommendations to the governing body.

– Control of the independence and objectivity of external auditors :

The Audit Committee makes recommendations to the governing body on the selection, appointment, renewal, and compensation of the external auditors. In accordance with company law, its proposals are submitted to the General Assembly. The Audit Committee regularly interviews candidates for external auditor, whether or not in the presence of key executives and financial, accounting, and treasury officers. It steers the procedure for selecting external auditors and submits the procedure to the governing body. The Committee must examine the fees paid to external auditors by the enterprise or its group in order to verify that the amount is not such as to affect their independence and the quality of their work. For enterprises making public offerings, the double statutory audit enhances the independence and effective control of the external auditors, and the Audit Committee must ensure that the arrangement is effectively implemented, in particular as regards important issues arising when the accounts are closed. It is recommended that the governing body propose the rotation of the external auditor after two successive terms of three years each.

The Audit Committee shall ensure that the external auditor performs no other function that is likely to impair their independence.

– Role of the Audit Committee vis-à-vis internal audit :

The Audit Committee must monitor the efficient functioning and internal control systems of the enterprise. It makes sure that the individual in charge of internal audit is independent and it must be able to meet with him, in the absence of their supervisors, whenever it wishes to have a presentation on the annual program for internal audit, the results of investigations, recommendations, etc. The Audit Committee examines and gives its opinion on the annual program for internal audit prior to its validation and implementation. The Audit Committee must receive internal audit reports, which must touch upon financial and non financial aspects and also include the identification and monitoring of risks. It is informed of the implementation of the recommendations of the internal audit by the company's executives. The composition of Audit Committee members, and the Committee's activities over the previous year, are addressed in the "Corporate Governance" chapter of the management report. 3.3.2. The Compensation and Nominations Committee This Committee helps the governing body to:

Put in place a clear compensation policy that is both equitable and provides incentives for the members of the governing body and other key executives;
Clarify the compensation of the members of the governing body;
Ensure that the quality of the management teams and the governing body matches the strategy of the enterprise.

The compensation policy for corporate agents in particular serves as an example, and the Committee will ensure that the following principles are observed:

Balance between compensation and performance, and between the interests of key executives and those of shareholders, partners, and the enterprise;
Exhaustiveness, consistency, and simplicity;
Coherence with the enterprise compensation policy and with market practices;
Justification and equity with regard to shareholders, partners, and the enterprise.

With regard to the nominations policy, the responsibilities of the Committee will be to:

–

Adopt procedures for the selection and replacement of the members of the governing body;

–

Periodically evaluate the size and composition of the governing body and make all necessary recommendations for improvement;

–

Identify potential candidates with the necessary knowledge, skills, and qualifications, and propose them for approval by the governing body;

–

Express a view on appointment proposals made by shareholders;

–

Devise a succession plan for the members of the governing body and other key executives.

Because independence and transparency must be the principal pillars of the Committee, it is recommended that it include at least one external, unsalaried member of the governing body. The Compensation and Nominations Committee shall meet at least twice a year and whenever it deems it necessary in order to fulfill its obligations, whether or not in the presence of senior management. The "Corporate Governance" chapter of the management report should include a presentation on the members of the Compensation and Nominations Committee and their activities over the preceding year.

3.4 Organization of the governing body 3.4.1. Composition of the governing body The composition of the governing body is critical in enabling it to fulfill its role in the best possible way. It must be made up of members with integrity and competence who are well informed and involved, and who impart a diversity (in terms of training, professional experience, male-female balance, age, nationality, etc.) that will help lead to genuine debate and steer clear of a systematic search for consensus. Each governing body should critically examine its composition, membership, the real balance between the powers of the Chairman as compared to the governing body, and the composition of its committees. In particular, it must seek to reassure the shareholders, partners, and third parties that its missions will be accomplished with the necessary independence and objectivity. 3.4.2. Special characteristics and complementarities of the roles of executive members and non executive or outside members in the governing body

The executive members have the duty of passing on all meaningful financial and extra financial information about the life of the enterprise in order to inform all the non executive or outside members.

The non executive members critically and constructively debate the suggested strategies and policies with the executive members, and enrich them if necessary. The non executive members also rigorously evaluate the performance of the executive members and other key executives in terms of the agreed strategies and objectives. 3.4.3. Training The Committee on Compensation and Nominations ensures that the new members of the governing body have received adequate training to facilitate their integration and participation in its work. This training must cover the general characteristics of the enterprise, its markets, its business lines, its strategy, and its policies, as well as the major challenges and risks to which it is exposed. The members involved in the specialized committees (Audit, Compensation and Nominations) shall receive specialized training so as to enable them to carry out their mission in the best possible manner. For example, new members of the Audit Committee will be informed of the specific operating modalities of that Committee, the accounting, financial, and organizational characteristics of the enterprise, and its internal control and risk management systems. Contact with the external auditor and with those responsible for finance and internal control within the company constitute part and parcel of this training process. Finally, the members of the governing body must always update their knowledge in terms of regulations.

They must also regularly update their skills in terms of best practices in corporate governance and their knowledge of the firm, in order to efficiently carry out their mission within the governing body or its committees, and will dispose of the resources necessary to this end.

3.4.4. Evaluation and transparency It is recommended that the governing body evaluate its size, composition, organization, tasks, and performance, as well as the contribution made by each of its members, the Chairman, and the manager and their interaction with enterprise management This same approach should be applied to the Committees. The aim of this evaluation is to:

Assess the effectiveness of the governing body and ensure, in particular, that important issues are prepared for and debated properly;
Identify the effective contribution of each member in terms of attendance at meetings of the governing body and the Committees, and their involvement in the discussions and decision-making;
Ensure that the size and composition of the governing body are adequate;
Verify the adequacy of the resources allocated to the operation of the governing body and to its missions.

The evaluation should be conducted in accordance with the following modalities:

At least once a year, the governing body should devote an agenda item to exchanges of views on its operation. By way of example, the governing body verifies its independence and the balance of powers exercised within it, ensures that the succession plans for its members are adequate, and ascertains that the selection or reappointment of executive and non executive members guarantee a balance of skills and experience. In effect, each governing body will rank the aspects to be evaluated in terms of the body's strengths and weaknesses with regard to corporate governance.

It is recommended that a formalized evaluation be conducted at least once every three years, perhaps under the direction of a non executive or outside member of the governing body, with assistance from an outside expert.

It is recommended that the non executive members of the governing body evaluate their interaction with the management of the firm, and, to this end, meet at least once a year without the presence of the corporate agents and executive members. It is further recommended that the governing body report on its work and its evaluation in the "Corporate Governance" chapter of the management report.

3.5 Operating tools of the governing body: The internal by-laws and the charter for governing body members : To assist the governing body in fulfilling its transparency mission, it is recommended that firms adopt internal by-laws and a charter for governing body members, which are two key factors in formalizing and implementing corporate governance.

3.5.1. Internal by-laws : The internal by-laws set forth in particular: — The organization of the governing body's meetings; — Its missions; — The distribution of powers among key executives (the Chairman, the Chairman of the

Management Board, the Chief Executive, managers, etc.); — The powers delegated to the Chairman and Chief Executive or to the Chief Executive (in the event of a split structure) with respect to investment, disinvestment, and financing; — Definition of the specialized committees, and, for each of them, its composition, minimum number of meetings annually, mission, resources, and reporting requirements; — The mode and frequency of evaluation of the governing body.

3.5.2. Charter for governing body members (*) : This may optionally be a part of the internal by-laws, but need not be. It sets forth the rights and duties of the members of the governing body and covers the following aspects:

– The knowledge and skills, training, and information of the said member; – The defense of corporate interest and loyalty; – Ethics: confidentiality, conflicts of interest, and transparency of transactions with the

securities held; – The duty to speak up, and independence of spirit; – Availability for and regular attendance at meetings of the governing body; – Presence at the General Meeting; – The criteria for the award of attendance fees.

(*) : See example of Charter in Exhibit p.31

II- RIGHTS OF SHAREHOLDERS AND PARTNERS AND THEIR EQUITABLE TREATMENT

PARTICIPATION AT THE GENERAL MEETING

The General Meeting is the optimal venue for shareholders and partners to exercise their rights in the enterprise, and constitutes a central component of corporate governance.

1.1) The enterprise encourages the effective participation and voting of shareholders or partners at General Meetings.

1.2) The enterprise shall determine the location, date, and timing for holding the General Meeting with the foregoing in mind, and shall make available to shareholders and partners on its website, among other things, all relevant and practical information concerning their participation at the General Meeting, and, in particular, the applicable regulations and voting procedures.

1.3) All the documentation and information relating to the General Meeting must be made available to shareholders and partners as rapidly as possible so as to give them the opportunity to become familiar with same before the Meeting is held.

1.4) The notice calling the General Meeting must clearly include reference to the opportunity offered to shareholders and partners to have items placed on the agenda for the day of the General Meeting and to propose related resolutions.

1.5) The resolutions put forward for voting at the General Meeting must be accompanied by information specifying, among other things, the stakes involved, so as to inform the voting decisions of shareholders and partners.

1.6) Inasmuch as the quality and depth of debate is tied to the presence of the maximum possible number of shareholders and partners, the firm shall encourage the participation of shareholders and partners at the General Meetings and shall seek to identify, with the financial intermediaries or services responsible for holding securities, all means aiming to increase their participation.

1.7) The firm shall encourage methods for distance voting and recommend the use of systems which are simultaneously reliable and rapid, but also secure for the shareholder in terms of confidentiality. Similarly, the enterprise shall authorize the exercise of proxy voting without restriction.

1.8) It is recommended to provide for the right to postal vote in the charter. 1.9) For nonresidents, the enterprise takes into consideration the specifics of exercising voting rights, notably by reducing the period during which shares or partnership shares are blocked.

The enterprise must protect the rights of shareholders and partners, and facilitate the exercise thereof. It must also ensure the equitable treatment of all shareholders and partners, including minority and nonresident shareholders and partners.

1.10) It is recommended that the enterprise provide in its charter for the right to participate in General Meetings without regard to any minimum number of shares.

2) EQUITABLE TREATMENT OF SHAREHOLDERS AND PARTNERS

The rights of shareholders and partners and the equitable treatment thereof must be respected in accordance with the legislation and regulations in force, and at no cost to the shareholder. The equality of majority and minority shareholders and partners, whether resident or nonresident, as regards treatment and the exercise of voting rights, constitutes an essential principle of corporate governance. a) The enterprise must ensure the equitable treatment of all shareholders and partners, including minority and nonresident shareholders and partners. b) The enterprise must respect the rights of minority and nonresident shareholders and partners and facilitate the exercise of those rights, in particular in the following areas:

— Reliability of the methods for registering their securities;

— Freedom to sell or transfer their shares;

— Timely and regular access to relevant and material information on the company; — Participation in and voting at General Meetings; — Participation in important corporate decisions, such as those on:

 New issues; Changes in the charter; Operations of an exceptional nature; The election and removal of directors; The compensation policy for directors and key executives;

 The approval of external auditors. — Dividend policy.

c) It is recommended that the "one share, one vote" principle be applied. d) The enterprise must make public any capital structures and mechanisms which grant some shareholders higher proportions of control than their effective participation in the capital.

3) INFORMATION ON MANAGEMENT

a) The enterprise shall rapidly and systematically make available to shareholders and partners, in particular on its website, information with regard to:

— Description of the rights of shareholders and partners to participate in and vote at General

Meetings; — The shareholding and control structure; — The identity of the major shareholders and partners, with a description of their voting rights

and special control rights and, if they act in concert with others, a description of the key

aspects of existing shareholder agreements; — The schedule for periodic information, meetings, and press conferences; — Other individual events of importance;

– Legal and financial documentation of a non confidential nature (charter, certain non confidential extracts or minutes of corporate bodies, ethical code, annual report, general and special report of the external auditors, letters to shareholders and/or bond holders, charter describing the aspects of corporate governance, etc.);

– The results of votes and minutes of shareholder meetings.

b) The enterprise undertakes to inform shareholders and partners on the legal receivership process or placement in liquidation in the event of composition proceedings. c) The enterprise will ensure in particular that resources and information enabling shareholders and partners to exercise their rights are available. d) The enterprise will ensure compliance with the principle of equivalent information and equivalent access to information on the part of Moroccan shareholders and partners and foreign (nonresident) shareholders and partners in the event of multiple or dual listing on exchanges.

4) MANAGEMENT OVERSIGHT

a) The enterprise communicates information on the organization of the governing body's work and on internal control procedures.

b) Given that the General Meeting is where the governing body reports to shareholders and partners on the exercise of its responsibilities, the enterprise strongly recommends that the members of the governing body attend the General Meetings to answer questions from shareholders and partners, to the extent that responses do not prejudice shareholders or partners or the personnel of the enterprise.

c) The key executives and the members of the governing body must keep the governing body informed of any material interest or special relations of a commercial, family, or other nature which might influence an operation or a matter directly affecting the enterprise. d) The enterprise shall, with complete transparency, announce the general policy on awarding stock options and on the employee incentive system, as well as the consequences thereof for the enterprise, shareholders, and partners.

5) DIVIDEND POLICY

a) The enterprise reports the precise date of payment of dividends upon approval by the General Assembly, and on the allocation of free shares in the event of an increase in capital through the incorporation of reserves. b) The dividend paid by the enterprise is at the same time an important component of remuneration for the risk taken by the shareholder and a key factor in the valuation of the shareholders' shares. Nevertheless, the share of profits allocated to distribution must be compatible with the policy of building reserves (or retaining earnings) required for the sustainable and sound development of the enterprise.

6) VIGILANCE ON SPECIAL OPERATIONS

The enterprise shall, with complete transparency, announce the impact of operations which might call into question the equitable treatment of shareholders. In particular, this refers to the dilution effect which might reduce certain shareholders' percentage of corporate capital (following a capital increase, merger, partial incorporation of assets, etc.) as well as the potential cost to shareholders of option grants, or share purchases, and debt/equity conversions. 7) Management of securities and securities operations The enterprise shall encourage depositories to take practical steps to inform shareholders and partners of the exercise of their subscription and allocation rights.

III- TRANSPARENCY AND THE DISSEMINATION OF FINANCIAL INFORMATION

1) DISSEMINATION OF MATERIAL INFORMATION ON THE LIFE OF THE ENTERPRISE

1.1) Strategies and objectives Alongside the information on the enterprise's strategic vision and operational objectives, it should communicate whatever it can about its social, societal, and environmental policies and its ethical rules.

1.2) Corporate performance and financial situation In its management report, the enterprise will provide a comprehensive view of its financial situation and its main activity and performance indicators. Groups should disseminate, in particular, complete information on intra-group transactions in accordance with the standards in force.

1.3) Information on the main equity participations and voting rights Shareholders or partners must have timely and free-of-charge access to exact, precise, reliable, and complete information on all material matters concerning the enterprise. Such information must be accessible and easy to interpret so as to assist shareholders and investors in their decision-making process.

The enterprise and its governing body have an obligation of transparency vis-à-vis shareholders and partners so as to enable them to take the best possible decisions and act with knowledge of their rights. Alongside the legal or regulatory obligations with respect to information, good practices for corporate governance recommend the dissemination of information relating, for example, to material or foreseeable risks or to the governance policy of the enterprise.

The information must address important or material data on the enterprise and be disseminated simultaneously to all shareholders so as to guarantee their equitable treatment. In particular, the financial and accounting information must be reliable, comparable, sufficiently detailed, and in strict compliance with national or international accounting standards.

Shareholders and partners have the right to have information on the shareholder structure and on their effective rights as compared to other categories of shareholders or partners who may directly or indirectly control the enterprise, notably by means of special voting rights, shareholder agreements, the holding of blocks of shares, or significant cross-shareholdings. Information on the ultimate shareholders is important for purposes of identifying potential conflicts of interest and/or insider offenses, and better analyzing the justification for regulated agreements.

1.4) Compensation policy for key executives and members of the governing body: The shareholders and partners must be informed of the overall policy on the compensation of the key executives in order to have a clear idea of the global cost, and of the criteria for its determination with reference to enterprise objectives and performance. Compensation includes all direct or indirect remuneration of any kind, including stock option plans, or subscriptions or purchases paid for by the enterprise or group of enterprises, Moroccan and foreign, in the scope of consolidation. Shareholders and partners must also be informed of the policy on the meeting fees authorized by the General Assembly and paid to the executive and non executive members of the governing body, as well as the distribution rules adopted (Chairman, members, fixed portion, variable portion, supplementary fees for participation on specialized committees). Shareholders or partners must also receive information on the key executives and members of the governing body in order to assess their professionalism and evaluate possible sources of conflicts of interest. For the members of the governing body, the information will indicate their qualifications, selection process, membership on the governing bodies of other corporations, and impartiality.

1.5) Regulated agreements Shareholders or partners must have a guarantee that the enterprise is managed in the interest of all shareholders and partners.

For the sake of readability, the most important regulated agreements will be the subject of separate resolutions. The enterprise is required to report transparently on the company's transactions with shareholders and the key executives.

1.6) Off-balance-sheet liabilities and material foreseeable risks Shareholders and investors must be informed of the mechanisms established by the enterprise to identify and control offbalance-sheet liabilities and to evaluate material foreseeable risks.

To this end, the enterprise shall maintain an "internal control" function with the authority and resources needed to properly carry out its mission. In its management report, the firm shall indicate the internal procedures implemented and convey to shareholders or partners the following specific information on material off-balance-sheet items, grouped separately:

- Information on the off-balance-sheet items included in the ETIC;
- Information on market risks (interest rate, exchange rate, securities, credit, raw materials).

Where appropriate, the firm shall publish the scores of internationally recognized financial rating agencies and any changes which may have occurred during the course of the financial year.

1.7) Information on internal control and risk management In its management report, the enterprise shall inform shareholders or partners of its internal control and risk management policy. A report on internal control must be submitted to the governing body.

1.8) Information with respect to stakeholders The enterprise must provide shareholders or partners will all information on stakeholders that is likely to affect its performance. The information shall pertain to the relationship between the management of the enterprise and employees and, in particular, the human resource policy (recruitment, training, rotation, incentive mechanisms) and any other significant relationship with other stakeholders (employees, customers, creditors, Administration, etc.). Where appropriate, the firm will report the scores of social, societal, and environmental rating agencies, and any changes which may have occurred during the financial year.

2) FINANCIAL INFORMATION MUST MEET RECOGNIZED ACCOUNTING STANDARDS

Compliance with international standards enhances the quality and comparability of data and builds confidence on the part of shareholders, partners, and investors. The enterprise will ensure compliance with the accounting standards and practices in force and will adopt international best practices. The enterprise will draw up and publish consolidated accounts whenever it controls other entities. It is recommended that these consolidated accounts be prepared in keeping with IFRS standards. The enterprise shall explain to stakeholders any departures from and changes in its accounting methods.

3) DISSEMINATION OF INFORMATION ON THE STRUCTURES AND GOVERNANCE POLICY OF THE FIRM

It is recommended that the enterprise inform shareholders, partners, and stakeholders of its governance practices and report on the manner in which it applies them, in keeping with the "comply or explain" principle. In particular, the enterprise will convey information on:

- The balance of powers within the enterprise;
- The composition and organization of the governing body;
- The work of the specialized committees;
- The compensation policy applicable to the members of the governing body and the key executives;
- Regulated agreements;
- Shareholder agreements;
- Cross-shareholdings.

To this end, the enterprise will include a "Corporate Governance" chapter in its management report and, if applicable, in its annual report.

4) MECHANISMS FOR GUARANTEEING THE RELIABILITY OF INFORMATION

4.1) Audit Committee It is strongly recommended that an Audit Committee be established to examine the draft final accounts and evaluate accounting risks. The Audit Committee will report to the governing body so as to enable it to carry out its missions of monitoring management and verifying the reliability and clarity of the information intended for shareholders or partners and investors. The management report must include a section on the activity of the Audit Committee during the preceding financial year.

The Audit Committee supervises the procedure for selecting the external auditors, provides advice on the level of the fees requested by the latter for performing legal inspection missions, and submits the results of its selection to the governing body. It devotes particular attention to the respect of rules on the independence of the external auditors.

4.2) External Audit The accounts must be examined annually by an independent and competent external auditor who expresses an external and objective opinion on the true and fair characterization of the assets, financial situation, and results of the enterprise. Having two outside auditors is a key means of strengthening the effective control and independence of the external auditors, and the enterprise must ensure its effectiveness.

The external auditors are accountable to the shareholders and partners, and are obligated to perform their mission in accordance with professional standards and due diligence in keeping with national and international ISA standards. For enterprises making public offerings, the audit of the financial statements must be exclusive of any other mission which might undermine its independence.

The length of the appointment is set by law at three years, and its renewable nature constitutes a fundamental guarantee of the independence of the external auditors. The rotation of auditors every two mandates, as well as the phasing over time of the terms of the two external auditors, must be implemented by the enterprise.

5) INFORMATION DISSEMINATION METHOD AND USER ACCESS TO INFORMATION

5.1) Information dissemination method The enterprise shall designate an individual in charge of financial communications, who is tasked with defining a structured communications policy, centralizing information, and serving as interlocutor vis-à-vis third parties. The enterprise shall use the Internet as a complementary information dissemination mechanism. 5.2) Enterprises making public offerings Enterprises making public offerings shall organize meetings to provide explanations to the financial press and financial analysts.

Enterprises making public offerings shall publicly report their principal indicators and results on a quarterly basis. They shall also provide information on the securities transactions of their principal key executives and directors who directly or indirectly hold more than 5% of the capital.

IV- THE ROLE OF STAKEHOLDERS AND THEIR EQUITABLE TREATMENT

The enterprise must respect the rights of stakeholders and take every possible step to treat them equitably and establish mutually profitable relationships with them. Stakeholders are understood to mean shareholders or partners, employees, customers, creditors, the Administration, and generally any party enjoying relations with the enterprise. Relations with the shareholders and partners are addressed in a separate chapter, "The rights of shareholders and partners, and their equitable treatment." Those with the other stakeholders are governed by contractual provisions (as in the case of a loan granted to the enterprise by a bank, for example) and/or by the laws and regulations in force (labor law in the case of employees, for example).

As a supplement to the laws, regulations, and/or contracts, specific recommendations in terms of corporate governance are necessary in order to improve the quality of relations with stakeholders and thereby contribute to the overall process of job and wealth creation and the process of developing competitive and profitable enterprises, the idea being that the interest and long-term success of the enterprise arises from respecting the interests of stakeholders, thanks in particular to professional relationships based on mutually profitable and lasting practices.

1) OBSERVANCE OF LAWS, REGULATIONS, AND CONTRACTUAL COMMITMENTS

The rights of the various stakeholders that are governed by laws, regulations, and contracts must be respected. The enterprise undertakes to scrupulously observe the laws and regulations (Labor Code, Commercial Code, Company Law, Law on Competition, etc.) and its own contractual commitments and, to this end, will introduce suitable internal mechanisms for guaranteeing the scrupulous compliance with laws, regulations, and contracts.

2) ADOPTION OF PRINCIPLES OF CORPORATE RESPONSIBILITY

It is recommended that the enterprise adopt standards exceeding those of the law, regulations, and best practices in terms of corporate, societal, and environmental responsibility, to build its reputation and image and thereby improve the quality of its relations with stakeholders. To this end, it is recommended that the enterprise adopt the Corporate Responsibility Charter espoused by the CGEM in order to benefit notably from the advantages associated with the CGEM label.

3) IMPLEMENTATION OF EMPLOYEE PARTICIPATION AND INCENTIVE PRACTICES

The implementation of employee participation and incentive practices is strongly recommended in order to improve enterprise performance. The involvement and commitment of the enterprise's human capital are critical factors in its performance and competitiveness. This is why the practices of empowerment, delegation, and participation associated with personnel incentive systems are strongly recommended as a means of boosting staff contribution to enterprise performance and increased involvement in the life of the enterprise.

These mechanisms may be mandated by law (the election of employee representatives, for example) or voluntary (incentives, special retirement systems, various social benefits, etc.).

4) STAKEHOLDER ACCESS TO INFORMATION

Stakeholders concerned by corporate governance must, just as shareholders, have timely and regular access to reliable, relevant, and adequate information. In particular, stakeholders must have access to the report of the business trustee in the event of receivership or court-ordered liquidation. Complete and continuous information must be provided to the stakeholders at the time that cessation of payments has been declared through the final phase of the process. Bond holders must also be informed under the same conditions so as to be able to be registered on the list of creditors and thereby safeguard their creditor rights.

5) PROCEDURES FOR MANAGING EMPLOYEE GRIEVANCES

Violation of the law and engaging in unethical practices may have an impact on the rights of stakeholders and be harmful to the interests of the enterprise and of its shareholders or partners. In the interest of the enterprise and its shareholders or partners, the enterprise must therefore establish procedures and protective measures to manage the grievances lodged by employees or their representatives. The grievances will be addressed by the governing body or by a mediator it designates. The enterprise forswears any discriminatory or disciplinary measure against grievants when the grievances are founded.

6) REVIEW OF RELATIONS WITH STAKEHOLDERS

The governing body will include the review of relations with the major stakeholders of the enterprise on the agenda of its meetings. In the event of conflicts of interest, the enterprise takes care to adopt a fair stance that guarantees equitable treatment of all stakeholders.

7) ADOPTION OF AN ETHICS CHARTER

The enterprise must adopt an ethics charter prepared by the governing body, endorsed by the General Assembly, and disseminated to the public. The governing body will ensure that all its operations are consistent with the provisions of this charter.

GLOSSARY

Abuse of majority power: The abuse of majority power assumes that a decision of the majority of shareholders was taken contrary to the general interest of the company, and solely to favor the members of the majority, and to the detriment of minority shareholders. Affectio societatis: Establishing a company, contributing to its capital, and intending to share the profits from it assume that future partners will have the desire to work together, strive toward a common goal, and do so on an equal footing. This combination of conditions constitutes "affectio societatis."

Conflicts of interest: Conflicts of interest are divergences of an ethical nature or which are sanctioned by the regulations between the stakeholders in the enterprise (shareholders and managers, shareholders and lenders, majority shareholders and minority shareholders, employees of the enterprise in their relations with customers, etc.).

Control block: A control block is a packet of securities the acquisition of which gives the buyer majority control of the capital or voting rights of a company.

Corporate agents: The persons who, by virtue of their position, have the authority to represent the company and act in its name, to represent the interests of a legal entity, serve as its representative, have the power to administer it and to commit it vis-à-vis third parties. The corporate agent is appointed by the charter of the legal entity or, depending on the procedure called for in the charter, by the General Assembly of shareholders or partners to which they report. The status of corporate agent is revocable ad nutum. According to French doctrine, the corporate agents of a limited company are: The Chairman of the Board of Directors The Chief Executive The members of the Supervisory Board, and The members of the Management Board.

Corporate governance: In its broad sense, "corporate governance" represents the organization of company control and management. In a more narrow sense, the term is used to designate the interconnection between the shareholder or partner, and the management of the company, hence principally the functioning of the Board of Directors or of the Management Board and the Supervisory Board.

Cost of capital: The weighted average cost of capital is the lowest rate of return required by those providing funds to the enterprise (shareholders and creditors) to finance its investment projects. It represents the overall cost of financing the enterprise.

Creation of shareholder value: This concept is close to that of the creation of value, distinguished only by the appropriation of the value created solely for the advantage of shareholders and not the benefit of all suppliers of funds to the enterprise (shareholders as well as creditors). Some operations may, indeed, be reflected by a transfer of value between creditors and shareholders: destruction of value to the detriment of creditors and the advantage of shareholders. For example, a radical change in financial structure in favor of debt which grossly devalues the existing debt of the enterprise and results in a transfer of value from the creditors to the benefit of shareholders.

Creation of value: The result of the enterprise's capacity to make one or more investments on which the rate of return exceeds the minimum required rate of return (the weighted average cost of capital) with the investment risk taken into account. The creation of value is the rational objective of any company senior management. However, in a competitive world, it is often extremely difficult to sustainably find investments that return more than the capital cost with their risks taken into account because such opportunities naturally attract many candidates, which has the effect of lowering the rate of return. The work of creating value is thus endless, and perpetually restarting. Dilution: The term "dilution" has two quite distinct meanings.

First, dilution is mentioned whenever a change in the financial structure of the enterprise (recourse to borrowing, reduction in capital, etc.) or a merger or acquisition operation brings about a decline in earnings per share. It is then said that it has a dilutive impact on EPS (and a relutive impact when EPS increase). Second, dilution may also characterize the reduction of a shareholder's percentage of the capital in a company following an increase in capital, merger, etc. Dividend policy: The dividend policy or distribution policy constitutes the first source of compensation for shareholders before capital gains at the time of transferring shares. In general, a dividend policy should be assessed in relation to the marginal profitability of the economic asset. If it exceeds the weighted average cost of the capital, the dividend may be low or zero because the enterprise will create value by reinvesting its earnings. In the opposite case, it is better for it to distribute all its gains to shareholders.

Family shareholding: The term family shareholding is used to designate a shareholding group made up of the members of one and the same family for several generations and who, often grouped together in a common holding company, exert influence on management.

This model is dominant in emerging economies. Financial information: Financial information is quite often the only source available for an outside analyst, hence the importance of having access to detailed information reflecting the economic reality of the enterprise. In Morocco, as in most countries, there is a legal obligation to draw up regular and accurate annual accounts providing a true and fair view of the enterprise's net worth, financial situation, and performance.

The key components of financial information are the revenue and expense accounts, the balance sheet, the ETIC, the ESG, and the cash flow statement. Financial intermediaries: Financial intermediation occurs when the financial world serves as a screen between those seeking and those providing capital, that is, when financial intermediaries purchase the securities issued by enterprises and, in order to finance themselves, issue their own securities placed with savers or gather funds in the form of deposits or passbook savings (indirect financing). Financial intermediation is thus very different from the simple role of financial intermediary referred to for direct financing. Governing body: In a joint stock company the governing body is the Board of Directors (in a monist structure), or the Supervisory Board or Management Board depending on the case (in a dual structure). For the other forms of companies, the governing body is the management. Insider offense:

The use of privileged information by any person who has access to it in the exercise of their profession or duties, in order to carry out, or knowingly permit to be carried out on the market, either directly or through another person, one or more operations. It is also the use of privileged information, by any person knowingly in a position of privileged information on the outlook for or situation of a company whose securities are listed on the stock exchange, or on the prospect of changes in a security, to directly or indirectly carry out an operation or permit an operation to be carried out or convey information to a third party, before the public has knowledge of such information.

Internal control System: Process implemented by the Board of directors, the executives and the employees of an organization aimed at providing reasonable assurance with regards to the implementation of objectives within the following categories:

- Implementation and optimization of operations ;
- Reliability of financial information;
- Compliance with laws and regulations into force.

Key executives: Any persons who, in any capacity, participate in the direction or management of the company. These include, in particular, the chief executive officers, general managers, members of the Management Board, the general secretary, directors, and any persons permanently carrying out duties analogous to those of the above.

Non executive member: Non-management member, but not necessarily independent of the company.

Off-balance sheet liability: The main off-balance sheet liabilities may involve lease-purchase operations, interest rate and exchange rate risk management instruments, and guarantees of assets and liabilities at the time an enterprise is conveyed. Outside member: An independent member who has no direct tie of interest with the company (apart from his post as director or member of the Board of Directors). Privileged information: Any information relating to the technical, commercial, or financial performance of an issuer or prospective issuer of a security, that is still unknown to the public and which might affect investor decisions. Public offering: Making a public offering consists in:

- The admission of a security on the securities exchange or any regulated market in Morocco;
- The issuance or sale of securities to the public by directly or indirectly having recourse to solicitation or advertising, or through brokerage firms, banks, or other establishments whose purpose is to place, manage, or provide advice on financial matters, the list of which is set by order of the minister responsible for finance, on the proposal of the CDVM.

Rating agency: This term refers primarily to the financial rating agencies that evaluate the solvency of a borrower in accordance with standardized methods that result in the assignment of a grade. Solvency is of direct concern to the lenders subscribing to bonds or other negotiable debt instruments. It also, however, has an impact on the assessed value of the enterprise and on the price of its capital instruments. In recent years, social, societal, environmental, or corporate governance rating agencies have emerged, with an aim quite distinct from that of the financial rating agencies.

Three universal financial rating agencies dominate the market: Moody's, Standard & Poor's, and Fitch, but there are others that are more or less specialized by geographic area, type of claim, etc. Each agency has its own analytical methods and rating scales for long-term or short-term debt. The grades are accompanied by indicators of a stable, positive, or negative movement, or placement on watch status, etc., which adds more nuance.

Shareholder or partner of reference: The shareholders or partners of reference have an equity interest in the capital and voting rights of the enterprise such that, even if they do not have absolute control, they are in a position to exert strong influence on the enterprise.

Regulated agreements: The risk of conflicts of interest which might oppose individual preferences to the interest of the company prompted the lawgiver to lay down rules of procedure relating to the adoption of agreements concluded directly or indirectly between the company and its directors (or members of the Supervisory Board in a dual structure or managing partners in a limited company) or for agreements entered into between a company and its key executives (members of the Management Board in a dual structure or managers in a limited company) or one of the shareholders directly or indirectly holding over five percent of the capital or voting rights. Such agreements require special authorizations and a special report from the statutory auditors.

Risk management: Corporate risk management includes risk identification, the determination of the existing controls, residual risk, its valuation, and finally the choice of a cover strategy. Currently, increased attention is being focused on such management by enterprises. This has been reflected both in a strengthened regulatory framework and in increasing market pressure for greater transparency and awareness on the part of managerial teams.

Securities: The following are considered to be securities:

- Shares and other instruments or rights which give or can give access, directly or indirectly, to capital and voting rights, and are transmissible by registration to an account or in the traditional manner;
- Debt instruments representing the right to a general claim on the net worth of the legal entity issuing same, transmissible by registration to an account or in the traditional manner, and excluding commercial paper and cash certificates;

The following are treated as if they were securities:

- Shares in mutual funds;
- Shares in securitized mutual funds;
- Shares in venture capital investment organizations.

Shareholder agreement: Legal document that organizes the relationships between various groups of shareholders in a company through the establishment of mechanisms aimed principally at and providing for the implementation of a strategy and regulating changes in the allocation of capital when shares are transferred or sold.

Shareholder structure: Study of the shareholder structure, that is, the distribution of financial interests and voting rights in an enterprise, is particularly important. Indeed, as the shareholders define company strategy, it is worthwhile to determine where the power is vested within the company and to identify the objectives of the various shareholders.

Stakeholders: In addition to shareholders and partners, all those interacting with the enterprise and known as stakeholders, in particular its employees, customers, creditors, and the Administration.

Stock options: Stock options are options to purchase or subscribe to a share at a fixed price, which are generally distributed to the managers of an enterprise in order to give them a direct interest in increasing the value of the enterprise. Granting such instruments may thus be analyzed as a means of aligning the interests of the shareholders and the managers.

True and fair view: The British concept of “true and fair view” has been universally acknowledged and adopted by a great many countries. Summary statements must provide a “true and fair view” of the enterprise’s net worth, financial situation, and performance. The true and fair view is not an additional fundamental accounting principle. Rather, it is an objective assigned to standardized accounting. The originality of this concept pertains in particular to the fact that it is not defined.

CHARTER FOR GOVERNING BODY MEMBERS

Art.1- Administration and corporate interest Each member of the governing body shall in all circumstances act in the corporate interest of the enterprise.

Art.2- Observance of laws, regulations, and by-laws Each member of the governing body shall fully observe all their duties and obligations. Art.3- Exercise of functions: guiding principles Members of the governing body shall exercise their functions with independence, loyalty, and professionalism.

Art.4- Independence and obligation to come forward Members of the governing body shall endeavor to preserve, in all circumstances, their independence of judgment, decision-making, and action. They are forbidden to be influenced by any matter apart from the corporate interest it is their mission to defend. They shall alert the governing body of any matter coming to their attention which might affect the interests of the enterprise. They have the duty of clearly expressing their questions and opinions. They shall endeavor to convince the governing body of the relevance of their positions. In the event of disagreement, they shall ensure that such disagreement is explicitly recorded in the minutes of the deliberations.

Art.5- Independence and conflicts of interest A member of the governing body shall strive to avoid any conflict which might exist between their moral and material interests and those of the enterprise. They shall inform the governing body of any conflict of interest in which they may be involved. In situations in which a conflict of interest cannot be avoided, they shall refrain from participating in debates or any decisions on the subjects concerned.

Art.6- Loyalty and good faith A member of the governing body shall take no initiative which might be harmful to the interests of the enterprise and shall act in good faith in all circumstances. A member shall personally undertake to respect the complete confidentially of all information they receive, debates in which they participate, and the decisions taken. A member is forbidden to use for personal profit or for the profit of anyone any of the privileged information to which they have access.

Art.7- Professionalism and involvement Members of the governing body undertake to devote the time and attention necessary to their duties. Members shall be informed about the lines of business and special characteristics of the enterprise, its issues, and its values, including by making inquiries of its principal key executives. Members shall participate in the meetings of the governing body with assiduousness and diligence.

They shall endeavor to participate in at least one of the specialized committees of the board should any exist. Members shall attend the general meetings of shareholders. Members shall endeavor to obtain, in a timely manner, all items deemed essential for their information for purposes of deliberating within the governing body in a fully informed manner. Members shall endeavor to update areas of knowledge that are of value, and have the right to request from the enterprise such training as they may need for the proper exercise of their mission.

Art.8- Professionalism and efficiency Each member of the governing body shall contribute to the spirit of collegiality and the efficiency of the work of the board and of any specialized committees which may be established in its midst. They shall make any recommendations considered likely to improve the operating modalities of the governing body, in particular on the occasion of the periodic assessment thereof. They shall agree to the evaluation of their own action within the governing body. With the other members of the governing body, they shall endeavor to ensure that control missions are carried out efficiently and without impediments. In particular, they will ensure that procedures are in place within the enterprise to see to compliance with the spirit and letter of the laws and regulations in force. They shall ensure that the positions adopted by the members of the governing body are without exception recorded in formal decisions that are properly documented and recorded in the minutes of its meetings.

Art.9 – Application of the Charter In that it sets forth principles that are essential to the proper functioning of a governing body, each member shall endeavor to ensure that this Charter is properly applied within the governing bodies in which they participate.

ABBREVIATIONS

-ANPME: National Agency for the Promotion of Small and Medium-Sized Enterprises [*Agence Nationale pour la Promotion de la Petite et Moyenne Entreprise*]

- BAM: Bank Al-Maghrib -CDG: *Caisse de Dépôt et de Gestion* - CDVM: Securities Ethics Council [*Conseil Déontologique des Valeurs Mobilières*]
- CGEM: General Confederation of Moroccan Enterprises [*Confédération Générale des Entreprises du Maroc*]
- CJD: Center for Young Managers [*Centre des Jeunes Dirigeants*]

-GCGF: Global Corporate Governance Forum

-DEPP: Directorate of Public Enterprises and Privatization [*Direction des Entreprises Publiques et de la Privatisation*]

-EPS: Earnings Per Share

-ESG: Statement of Management Balances [*Etat des Soldes de Gestion*]

-ETIC: Statement of Supplementary Information [*Etat des Informations Complémentaires*]

- FCMCIS : Moroccan Federation of Commerce, Industry and Services Chambers [*Fédération des Chambres Marocaines de Commerce, d'Industrie et de Services*]
- GPBM: Professional Bankers' Group of Morocco [*Groupement Professionnel des Banques du Maroc*]

-IAS: International Accounting Standards

-IFC: International Finance Corporation

-[*SFI : Société Financière Internationale*] - IFRS: International Financial Reporting Standards

-ISA: International Standard on Auditing

-MAEG: Ministry of Economic and General Affairs [*Ministère des Affaires Economiques et Générales*]

-OECD: Organization for Economic Cooperation and Development
-ROSC : Report on the Observance of Standards and Codes [*RRNC : Rapport sur le Respect des Normes et Codes*]

-SA: Corporation [*Société Anonyme*]

-SMEs: Small and Medium-Sized Enterprises

STRATEGIC INFORMATION FOR CONDUCTING BUSINESS

POLITICAL ENVIRONMENT

NATURE OF THE POLITICAL RELATIONSHIP WITH THE UNITED STATES:

Morocco's bilateral ties with the United States date back to 1787 when Morocco was one of the first nations to recognize the independence of the United States. More recently Morocco's early activism in the search for peace in the Middle East has made the Kingdom a valuable partner on the international stage. King Hassan II, until his death in 1999, enjoyed a warm relationship with a succession of American presidents. A similarly close relationship has been established with King Mohammed VI, whose successful state visit to the U.S. in June 2004 was a high point in the bilateral relationship. Two years into his reign, Mohamed VI remains committed to reforming Morocco's economy and deepening its democratic structures, and modest but promising progress toward these objectives has been achieved to date.

Major Political Issues Affecting the Business Climate:
Among the major political issues that could affect the business climate is the yet unresolved Western Sahara dispute. An armed national liberation force, the Polisario, based in Algeria, clashed with Moroccan troops in the region prior to an UN-brokered cease-fire in 1989. A UN peacekeeping presence remains in the region preparing for an UN-brokered permanent settlement through a United Nations Security Council-sponsored referendum. Civil unrest and religious violence, which continue to plague Morocco's eastern neighbor Algeria, have not spread to Morocco. Islamic extremism has not gained widespread support in Morocco, although social strains caused by increasing economic disparities are leading to growth in the Islamic movement. While there are no accurate election or opinion poll results upon which to base an estimate, it is likely that followers of non-violent political Islam probably account for nearly one fourth of the population. Islamists are for the most part divided between those who have elected to cooperate with the regime and those who have not. The former, a minority of Morocco's Islamists, have a political party and are represented in Parliament. The latter, pertaining to a tightly disciplined organization with considerably more adherents than the aforementioned political party, remain outside the realm of political legitimacy, and their activities remain closely circumscribed by the authorities. Cannabis production in northern Morocco is a major source of regional income and is a concern to Morocco's European neighbors, but has not destabilized the region.

POLITICAL SYSTEM

Morocco is a constitutional monarchy in which the King remains the final arbiter of power and directly controls the key ministries of Interior, Foreign Affairs, Religious Affairs, and Justice plus the military. In September 1996, a constitutional referendum divided the Parliament into two chambers. The lower house is directly elected and the upper house is made up of representatives elected by professional and trade organizations, labor councils, communal councils, and chambers of commerce. King Hassan II selected Abderrahmane Youssoufi, leader of the Popular Union of Socialist Forces (USFP) as Prime Minister following seriously flawed elections in 1997. The next parliamentary elections are scheduled for November 2002. While expectations are high that they will be held on time and be free and fair, the government has not yet drafted necessary legislation that would reform election procedures and reduce the likelihood of fraud.

Morocco is divided into provinces, prefectures and regions. All are administered by non-elected officials (Governors and Walis) from the Ministry of Interior. Cities and rural communes elect communal councils headed by presidents chosen by the council members. Several of Morocco's larger municipal councils elect a President of the Urban Commune, a sort of mayor. These urban communes were recently granted greater budget authority by the Moroccan Parliament. Additionally, each of Morocco's sixteen regions contains an indirectly elected regional authority; however, real control remains in the hands of the non-elected officials of the Ministry of Interior.

U.S. ASSISTANCE TO MOROCCO

USAID MOROCCO

Address, Phone, and Personnel Information

USAID Morocco's street address is: 10, Mehdi Benbarka, Rabat, Morocco Telephone: (212)(7)-63-20-01 -- Fax: (212)(7)-62-20-12

Offices and Key U.S. Personnel

Office/Division	Name
Director (FO)	James Bednar
Population, Health, and Human Resources (PHHR)	Michele Moloney-Kitts
PHHR - Human Resources Division	Monique Bidaoui
Environmental and Natural Resources (ENR)	John Thomas
Office of Economic Growth (EG)	Brad Wallach
Financial Management (OFM)	James E. Schaeffer
Management Office (MO)	Ray Reddy
Program Office	John Wooten

DEVELOPMENT BACKGROUND

Although Morocco is successful in maintaining its macro-economic stability, its irregular rate of growth is not sufficient to keep pace with the fast expansion of the labor force, and the benefits of this growth are not shared equitably. Lack of jobs and inadequate access to housing, land, credit, and other productive resources remain the chief causes of poverty, and are major contributors to social instability. Low labor demand contributes to the creation of a pool of disaffected educated youth, from which extremist appeals find adherents. Poverty and illiteracy remain extensive, especially among women and female-headed households. Large family sizes strain meager incomes and government services. Natural resource degradation and industrial, urban, and agricultural pollution pose threats to the productive base of the economy, to ecosystems, and to human health and productivity.

Predicted water scarcity clouds the horizon. Morocco's problems are reflected in its social indicators, which generally lag behind those of similar nations: (1) an infant mortality rate at 57 per thousand compares unfavorably to 39 as the average for LMI countries; (2) the annual population growth rate is still 2.1% versus 1.5% in LMI countries, and will double the country's population in approximately 33 years; (3) the illiteracy rate is 48% of the adult population, compared to 19% for LMI countries; (4) an estimated 5.9 million people, or 22% of the population, live at or near the poverty level, with two-thirds of the poor in rural areas; and (5) nearly 20% of the labor force is unemployed, and this percentage is increasing at a rate of 7% annually.

USAID PROGRAM

To assist Morocco address these issues, USAID's program focuses on four development areas: (1) population and health, to reduce fertility and improve the health of children and women of child-bearing age; (2) water resources management in the agricultural, urban and industrial sectors; (3) expanding economic opportunities for poorer Moroccans through small business development and employment generation for the poor; and (4) increased primary educational attainment for girls in rural areas, through responsiveness to their educational needs and community support for their education.

USAID assists the Government of Morocco in both public and private sector health care, by training health workers, improving preventive services, decentralizing health-care services, and providing clinical commodities and contraceptives, equipment and vehicles.

USAID also supports development of private health care, and the commercial marketing of contraceptives. In the environment, USAID targets improved water resources management by strengthening policy, regulatory and institutional frameworks, promoting adoption of improved environmental technologies, and broadening public participation for environmental action, including urban housing and sanitation. In economic growth, USAID assists poorer Moroccans through micro- and small-enterprise development and employment generation. USAID support for a competitive and transparent business climate and for overall business development has promoted U.S. exports and investment in Morocco, as well as business development and employment generation for Moroccans of below-medium income. USAID support for rural girls' education, recently initiated, is expected to increase the percentage of rural girls who complete six years of primary school from about 16% in 1996-97 to 35% by 2002-03.

RESULTS

As the principal donor for family planning, USAID has contributed to a decline in the average fertility rate from 7.0 in 1971 to 3.1 children in 1997. As a result, there are 8.8 m. fewer Moroccan people (in 1995) than there would have been without USAID assistance. Contraceptive prevalence increased from 19% in 1979 to 52% in 1997, and infant mortality declined from 91/1,000 in 1979 to 60/1,000 in 1997. In the environment, USAID has provided urban housing with access to sanitation and other services for over 100,000 below-median income families.

USAID support has reduced industrial pollution by promoting energy-saving practices and technologies (resulting in U.S. exports of $2.5 million), while saving over $12 million of foreign exchange to date from annual energy savings of 60,600 tons of oil equivalent, which also decreased emissions of sulfur dioxide by 425 tons, nitrous oxide by 620 tons, and carbon dioxide by 140,000 tons. USAID support has increased the efficiency of water use in irrigated agriculture by 20% in the Tadla region. In economic growth, USAID has supported small businesses, increased access to credit, strengthened 28 business associations, reduced trade barriers, generated 89,000 person-years of employment in labor-intensive agri-business exports, small enterprises and urban housing, expanded the demand for U.S. technologies which resulted in $40 m. of trade with the U.S., and privatized 55 public enterprises valued at about $1.6 billion. Recent support to rural girls' education has encouraged the Ministry of Education to embark upon a program of testing new teaching techniques designed to improve access, retention and attainment of girls and boys in pilot rural primary schools.

USAID ASSISTANCE FUNDS

(figures are in $1,000)

DA (Grants)		Amount
FY-1997	Actual	$18,522
FY-1998	Projected	$12,500
FY-1999	Requested	$11,781

USAID MOROCCO PROJECTS

Following are Information Sheets on the nine major project areas of USAID in Morocco

New Enterprise Development		Training for Development
Morocco Agribusiness Promotion		Tadla Resources Management
Urban and Environment Services		Water Resources Sustainability
Family Planning and Maternal Child Health		Microenterprise Finance
	Morocco Education for Girls	

NEW ENTERPRISE DEVELOPMENT (NO. 608-0204)

Strategic Objective:

Expanded base of stakeholders in the economy, targeting people of below-median income.

Project purpose:

To reduce barriers to entry for new enterprises (men and women owned) and to facilitate the expansion of existing small and medium sized businesses.

Budget: In ($000's)

a. Technical Assistance: 7,750
b. Training: 1,015
b. Equipment: 300
c. Others: 5,685
TOTAL: 14,750

Period:

a. Starting Date: August 16, 1991 **b. Completion Date**: August 15, 1999

Expected Results:

Expanded base of stakeholders in the economy, targeting people of below-median income.
Improved policy and regulatory environment.
Creation and expansion of small and microenterprises.

Implementing Agency:

Ministry of Economic Incentives

TRAINING FOR DEVELOPMENT (NO. 608-0208)

Strategic Objective:

Increased basic educational attainment among girls in selected rural areas.

Project Purpose:

To strengthen Morocco's in country training capacity and to improve Moroccan managerial and technical skills for economic development and private sector expansion.

Budget: In ($000's)

a. Technical Assistance: 8,581
b. Training: 4,800
b. Equipment: 589
c. Others: 30
TOTAL: 14,000

Period:

a. Starting Date: August, 1991 **b. Completion Date**: September 30, 1999

Expected results:

Strengthened capability for human resource development planning at the DFC,
Strengthened human resource development planning in rural primary education at the MNE that is sensitive to the needs for improving access and retention of rural girls in primary school.
Two Moroccan training institutions in the MNE offer curricula and instructional materials relevant to girls primary education needs.
Institutional linkages.

Sufficient numbers of trained personnel in focus areas.

Implementing Agency:

Ministry of Higher Education (Direction de la Formation des Cadres)

MOROCCO AGRIBUSINESS PROMOTION (NO.608-0210)

Strategic Objective:

Expanded base of stakeholders in the economy, targeting people of below-median income.

Project purpose:

To increase the capacity of the private agribusiness sector in Morocco to produce, package and market a wide variety of demand-driven, value-added agricultural commodities.

Budget: In ($000's)

a. Technical Assistance: 6,615
b. Training: 4,026
c. Equipment: 1,526
d. Others: 5,591
TOTAL: 17,758

Period: **a. Starting Date**: August 31,1991 **b. Completion Date**: June 30, 1998

Expected results:

- Expanded base of stakeholders in the economy, targeting people of below-median income.
- Improved policy and regulatory environment.
- Improved competitiveness of USAID-assisted firms which generate employment for below-median income people.
- Increased product and market diversification.
- Increased adoption of improved technology and management practices.

Implementing Agency:

Ministry of Agriculture

TADLA RESOURCES MANAGEMENT (NO. 608-0213)

Strategic Objective:

Improved water resources management in the agricultural, urban and industrial sectors.

Project purpose:

To increase the efficiency, economic yield and environmental sustainability of water resources management and use in the Tadla irrigation perimeter.

Budget: In ($000's)

a. Technical Assistance: 3,805
b. Training: 575
c. Equipment: 1,700
d. Others: 4,545
TOTAL: 10,625

Period:

a. Starting Date: July 31, 1992 **b. Completion Date**: September 30, 1999

Expected results:

Improved Water Resources Management in the Agricultural, Urban and Industrial Sectors.
Improved Environment Technologies.
Broadened Public Participation for Environmental Action.

Implementing Agency:

Ministry of Agriculture (ORMVA du Tadla)

URBAN AND ENVIRONMENT SERVICES (NO. 608-0221)

Strategic Objective:

Improved water resources management in the agricultural, urban and industrial sectors

Project purpose:

To develop a sustainable capacity for increased access by below median income families to sewerage, potable water, urban services and affordable housing.

Budget: In ($000's)

a. Technical Assistance: 4,015
b. Training: 600
c. Equipment: 720
d. Others: 1,865

TOTAL: 7,200

Period:

a. Starting Date: September 29, 1994 **b. Completion Date**: December 31, 1999

Expected results:

- Improved Water Resources Management.
- Improved policy, regulatory and institutional framework.
- Improved environment technologies.
- Broadened public participation for environmental action.
- Expanded Base of Stakeholders in the Economy.
- Increased access to housing for below median income households.

Implementing Agency:

ANHI (Ministry of Housing) - FEC (Ministry of Interior)

WATER RESOURCES SUSTAINABILITY (NO. 608-0222)

Strategic Objective:

Improved water resources management in the agricultural, urban and industrial sectors.

Project purpose:

Improve water resources management and address pollution problems by identifying and implementing demonstration projects which focus on the policy/regulatory and institutional framework, technology, and community participation.

Budget: In ($000's)

a. Technical Assistance: 4,463
b. Training: 418
c. Equipment: 210
d. Others: 10,909

TOTAL: 16,000

Period:

a. Starting Date: August 31, 1995 **b. Completion Date**: September 30, 2002

Expected Results:

Improved water resources management in the agricultural, urban and industrial sectors.
Improved policy, regulatory, and institutional framework.
Improved environmental technologies.
Broadened public participation for environmental action.

Implementing Agency:

Ministry of Environment

FAMILY PLANNING AND MATERNAL CHILD HEALTH (NO. 608-0223)

Strategic Objective:

Reduced fertility and improved health of children under five and women of child-bearing age.

Project purpose:

To increase the effective use of FP/MCH services by improving access, quality and information, and to increase program sustainability by ensuring a favorable policy environment, reinforced decentralized institutional capacity, and diverse resource base.

Budget: In ($000's)

a. Technical Assistance :	6,982	
b. Training:		940
c. Equipment:	11,250	
d. Others:		32,828
TOTAL:		**52,000**

Period:

a. Starting Date: July 2, 1993 **b. Completion Date**: December 31, 1999

Expected results:

Intermediate Results:

Increased use of quality FP/MCH services.
Increased sustainability of FP/MCH services.

Lower Level Results:

Greater access to quality FP/MCH services responsive to client demand.
Improved policy environment supporting expansion of FP/MCH services.

Reinforced capacity to manage FP/MCH programs with particular emphasis on decentralized approaches responsive to client need.
Increased diversification of resource base financing the delivery FP/MCH services.

Implementing Agency:

Ministry of Public Health

MICROENTERPRISE FINANCE (NO. 608-0218)

Strategic Objective:

Expanded base of stakeholders in the economy, targeting people of below-median income.

Project purpose:

To facilitate microenterprise growth through broad access to formal, institutionalized and self-sustainable microfinance.

Budget: In ($,000's)

a. Technical Assistance:	5,745
b. Subcontract:	3,011
c. Collateral Fund	4,500
d. Others:	2,234
TOTAL:	**15,500**

Period:

a. Starting Date: September 19, 1995 **b. Completion Date**: September 30, 2003

Expected results:

Expanded base of stakeholders in the economy, targeting people of below-median income.
Increase in annual operating costs recovered by microfinance institutions' loan and fee revenues.
Increase number of microenterpreneurs receiving loans through the formal credit system.
Increase in the percent of women receiving loans through the project.

Implementing Agency: **Ministry of Commerce, Industry and Handicrafts**

MOROCCO EDUCATION FOR GIRLS (NO. 608-0226)

Strategic Objective:

Increased basic educational attainment among girls in selected rural areas.

Project purpose:

To increase the participation (access and retention) of rural girls in primary schooling through a series of innovative pilot activities at the local, regional and national levels.

a. Starting Date: August 1996 **b. Completion Date**: March 30, 2003

Expected results:

Increased basic educational attainment among girls in selected rural areas.
Increased responsiveness of the primary school system to girls' educational needs.
Increased community involvement in girls' education.
Reduced operational constraints to girls' participation primary education.

Implementing Agency: Ministry of National Education

PEACE CORP PROGRAMS IN MOROCCO

CONTACTING THE PEACE CORPS IN MOROCCO

International Airmail Address:

Peace Corps
1 Rue Benzerte
Rabat, Morocco
Telephone Number: 212-7-706-020

Fax Number: 212-7-708-701

PEACE CORPS COUNTRY OVERVIEW FOR MOROCCO

Peace Corps Volunteers have supported many significant contributions in the quality of life in Morocco over the last 36 years, but the country continues to face a number of pressing development challenges. The maternal mortality rate is exceptionally high in rural areas. Drought, over-grazing, and a lack of veterinary services continue to hamper livestock production and management. There is a high rate of unemployment, particularly among youth. Population growth has contributed to the drainage of wetlands, de-forestation of public areas, and erosion in national park reserves. To help address these problems, Volunteers are assigned to projects in agriculture, education, the environment and health.

AGRICULTURE

Volunteers in the agriculture sector work with rural communities and agriculture extension agents in a variety of projects, including: fruit tree planting, beekeeping, rabbitry, irrigation, potable water, rural women's development, poultry, large animal husbandry, composting and others. Volunteers disseminate much needed technical information for the establishment of innovative agricultural projects. They are also very effective at drawing out the priority needs that local communities feel they have.

ENVIRONMENT

Volunteers work with Morocco's national park management to help implement nature conservation activities and local community outreach programs. They often serve as much needed links between local people that rely on the natural resources of park areas and the park management. They have implemented community projects in environmental education, fruit and forestry tree planting, fuel efficient cook stoves, garbage disposal and irrigation. Volunteers also study and survey the vegetation and wildlife of the nature protected zones and have compiled substantial works on the indigenous natural life in the areas.

EDUCATION

Volunteers and their Moroccan colleagues are working together to improve teaching techniques, expand educational resources, and design targeted technical English curricula. Volunteers are also working in the informal sector, providing English classes at youth centers in small towns and working in a variety of community and youth development activities, such as tree plantings and litter clean up campaigns. Other volunteers are helping to expand the resource centers are Center at Moroccan universities by refining, and in some cases developing library and information management systems.

SMALL BUSINESS DEVELOPMENT

The main goal of volunteers and their Moroccans counterparts of the Ministry of Industry, Commerce and Artisan is to increase the capacity of the artisan sector to generate income and provide jobs. Volunteers will work as Small Business Advisors to support structured small business activity in the artisan sector. Volunteers will provide training in areas such as: marketing, exports, basic finance, information systems and Internets. They will also carry out feasibility studies, business plans and marketing plans.

HEALTH

Volunteers work in rural Moroccan communities (1) to improve maternal and child health care, (2) increase safe water supplies and, (3)promote hygiene and sanitation practices. Hygiene education is a major component of their activities. Volunteers have participated in the implementation of the national campaigns (vaccination, family planning, diarrhea, trachoma), designed and produced safe birth kits, trained first level nurses and traditional birth attendants in communication and patient counseling, developed hygiene awareness campaigns, constructed water supply systems and sanitation facilities for primary schools. Efforts in pit latrine construction, water sources improvement and other community based projects have produced considered results, including skill transfer to local leaders in project design, management and funding.

ECONOMY AND ECONOMIC DEVELOPMENT

One year into his reign, King Mohammed VI has demonstrated the energy and determination to reform Morocco's economy and to deepen its democratic structures. King Mohammed's extensive travel throughout the country has earned him tremendous respect among his people. The King has taken a number of bold steps in his first year on the throne, including replacing the powerful Minister of Interior Driss Basri in November 1999 with Ahmed Midaoui, a Ministry of Interior veteran with a reputation as a reformer. The King has also established a Royal Commission on Investment to improve Morocco's competitiveness in attracting foreign investment.

Relatively strong macroeconomic indicators coupled with stubborn structural problems characterize the Moroccan economy. Morocco's inflation levels are on par with industrialized countries, and foreign currency reserves provide approximately six months of import coverage. Despite these strong macroeconomic figures, however, economic growth has been anemic in Morocco over the last decade, partially as a result of dependence on agricultural and the recurrence of drought. Two consecutive years of worsening drought have led the economy to shrink by 0.7 percent in 1999, with growth predictions in 2004 of only 0.7 percent. Unemployment in Morocco is high, with urban unemployment in excess of 22 percent.

The government headed by Abderrahmane Youssoufi has made progress in reforming Morocco's economy. Under Youssoufi's government, important steps have been taken to make the public tender process more transparent, update Morocco's intellectual property rights legislation, develop a specialized commercial court system, and aggressively liberalize the telecommunications market. The government has embraced a USAID-funded Investor Roadmap process to identify and resolve common barriers to foreign and domestic investment.

Despite the broad progress made by the government on economic reform, there is frequent criticism that the government is not moving quickly enough on reform. The government bureaucracy is extensive and considered top heavy with 43 ministers, many of whom have conflicting or overlapping portfolios.

In order to increase the attractiveness of Morocco and the rest of the Maghreb as a destination for U.S. business, the United States, Morocco, Algeria, and Tunisia have formed the U.S.-North Africa Economic Partnership. The goal of the partnership is to encourage structural reforms and regional economic integration in the hope of unlocking a market of global importance. The Morocco-EU Association Agreement, which went into effect in March 2004, will accelerate Morocco's integration into Europe.

The Foreign Commercial Service in Morocco has identified the following sectors as best prospects for U.S. firms:
(1) Telecommunications/Information Technology, (2) Electric Power Systems, (3) Environmental Technologies, (4) Water and Waste Water Treatment and (5) Tourism (hotel/resort construction, infrastructure, management and services). At the top of the Foreign Agricultural Service's best prospects list are (1) wheat, including durum, (2) feed grains and (3) crude vegetable oil.

An international call for bids in the partial privatization of the telephone company, Maroc Telecom, is expected in fall 2004. Other privatization projects lined up are a strategic stake in the flag carrier, Royal Air Maroc and the sale of the largest bank, Banque Populaire. U.S. Companies are involved in tenders for aircraft (a $1 billion + Royal Air Maroc fleet renewal); the National Office of Electricity's (ONE) tender for a 450 MW combined cycle power plant at Tahaddart; ONE's tender for a 200 MW Wind Park; Electricity, Water and Wastewater Distribution in Tangier and Tetouan;

Controlled Landfill in Fes (these last two through the Ministry of Interior) and a Driver's License and Vehicle Registration tender through the Ministry of Transport.

The second GSM mobile phone license was inaugurated in April, 2004. Meditel, the Spanish Telefonica-led consortium with Portuguese and Moroccan partners, gained 220,000 subscribers in their first quarter. The new license has received unexpectedly stiff competition from the existing license held by the Moroccan state-owned telephone company, Maroc Telecom, all a good sign of opportunities for growth in this sector as well as a very receptive market. Internet cafes abound in Casablanca, and the telecom infrastructure is reliable and dependable compared to other countries in the region.

FY 2001 should see the launch, after many years of waiting, of a tender for solid waste management in Casablanca, covering collection, transfer and treatment of waste from Morocco's largest city. Improvement in waste treatment, pollution control (air and water) as well as alternative energy projects will illustrate the benefits that technology can bring to improve quality of life.

Morocco offers significant investment opportunities, particularly as a packaging and assembly base because of its strategic location for exporting into North and Francophone Africa, Europe and the Middle East. Significant incentives exist for import of capital equipment and raw materials for re-export. The tourism sector is underdeveloped in contrast to the potential offered by Morocco's coastline, deserts, mountains and historic cities. Opportunities exist in this sector for architectural and engineering services, infrastructure development (water, wastewater, telecommunications), franchising, hotel and restaurant management and services. The severity of the drought in 2004 has highlighted the need for more efficient and innovative ways in which water can be used and distributed both in rural areas and agribusiness.

King Mohammed VI's successful state visit to the U.S. in June, 2004 was a high point in the bilateral relationship and demonstrated that the U.S.' relationship with its first friendship treaty partner is strong and durable. Hopefully more U.S. companies will pursue active leads and prospects in Morocco and the Maghreb region to put more American products, services and equipment into the hands of consumers, clients and users – further strengthening the solid bonds between the two countries.

ECONOMIC TRENDS

Morocco boasts the world's largest phosphate reserves, a diverse agricultural sector, rich fisheries, a sizeable and growing tourist industry, a growing manufacturing sector (especially clothing), and a dynamic, deregulated telecommunications sector. There is a considerable inflow of funds from Moroccans working abroad. The illegal production and export of cannabis also plays a role in the Moroccan economy, particularly in the north. Most of Morocco's trade is with Europe, with France alone accounting for about a quarter of Morocco's imports and a third of its exports.

PRINCIPAL GROWTH SECTORS

Agriculture: Agriculture accounts for between 15 and 20 percent of GDP (depending on the harvest) and employs about 40 percent of the workforce. Morocco is a net exporter of fruits and vegetables, and a net importer of cereals. Over 90 percent of agriculture is rain-fed.

Agricultural output has been dampened significantly by insufficient rainfall over the past two years. Fall cereal (wheat and barley) production dropped by over 70 percent compared to the five-year average. This is expected to impact heavily on the growth of the economy because agriculture continues to account for over 15 percent of the total GDP. Also, the insufficient rainfall has resulted in poor pasture conditions that are forcing the government to take several drought relief measures including larger imports of feed.

Fishing: The fishing industry is a key sector of the Moroccan economy, employing about 300,000 people directly and indirectly, and accounting for over $600 million in export earnings. Morocco did renew its fisheries agreement with the European Union (EU), which expired on November 30,1999. The relatively undercapitalized Moroccan fishing fleet has difficulty competing with the highly industrialized European fleet. Working to better manage its fish resources, the GOM has been imposing periodic fishing bans on various types of fish and regions.

Industry: Industrial output rose 2.8 percent in 1999, and is expected to continue to expand by over three percent per year in 2004. Electricity generation is rising as new thermal generating capacity comes on line and hydroelectric production continues at high levels.

World market conditions will determine developments for Morocco's export industries, notably phosphate derivatives, processed agricultural products and clothing. Much of the clothing production is done under contract with European companies that provide the inputs and receive the finished garments.

Mining: Morocco has the world's largest phosphate reserves. The export of phosphates and its derivatives (phosphoric acid and fertilizer) account for about 18.5 percent of Moroccan exports. The export earnings of phosphate and phosphate derivatives reached $1.4 billion in 1999, the same level recorded in 1997.

Morocco's other mineral resources include copper, fluorine, lead, barite, iron, and anthracite. Globally, Morocco is a significant producer and exporter of industrial minerals. It is also a significant regional producer of base metals, primarily for Europe.

Telecommunications: The Moroccan government has decided to open up the entire telecommunications sector to competition by 2002. This year state-owned Maroc Telecom saw its monopoly on voice transmission end with the introduction of competing mobile service by the Spanish-Portuguese consortium Meditel (Meditel paid $1.1 billion in 1999 for the license to provide this service). Morocco has recently awarded four VSAT licenses to provide data transmission. Over the next two years, Morocco will award licenses for closed-loop networks, international service, as well as additional mobile phone licenses. State-owned Maroc Telecom is slated for partial privatization over the course of 2004.

GOVERNMENT ROLE IN THE ECONOMY

The Moroccan government has gradually reduced its role in the economy over the last decade. In particular, it ceased direct credit and foreign exchange allocation, reduced trade barriers, restrained government spending, and embarked on an extensive privatization program, including the telecom sector and concessions in energy and utilities.

Monetary policy: With the inflation rate averaging less than three percent in the 1990's, monetary growth has remained steady in recent years. Foreign exchange reserves have been rebuilt since dipping during the drought of the middle part of the decade. They now stand at about $6 billion, covering almost six months of imports. Broad money grew by about 10.2 percent in 1999.

Fiscal policy: The Moroccan government has made a concerted effort to reduce its budget deficit in recent years, averaging under three percent. The deficit fell to 2.3% of GDP in FY 1998-99 and is slated to remain below 3% of GDP in FY 1999-2004.

Foreign Exchange Regulations: The Moroccan Dirham is convertible for all current transactions (as defined by the IMF's Article VIII) as well as for some capital transactions, notably capital repatriation by foreign investors. Foreign exchange is available through the commercial banks on presentation of appropriate documents. Foreign firms have complained about the complexity of remaining restrictions on foreign exchange. Private Moroccan resident individuals face several foreign exchange restrictions, notably against internationally accepted credit cards.

The Central Bank maintains an exchange rate peg for the Dirham against a basket of currencies of its principal trading partners. The rate against the basket has been fixed since a nine- percent devaluation in May 1990, with changes in the rates of individual currencies reflecting changes in cross rates. Some economists feel the Dirham is overvalued against European currencies, but the government argues consistently against devaluation.

Foreign Trade: Morocco has gradually reduced barriers to trade over the last decade, although the level of protection remains high. The maximum tariff rate is 35 percent, except for a few agricultural products for which quantitative restrictions were replaced by tariffs of up to 290 percent, in line with Morocco's World Trade Organization commitments. In addition to tariffs, there is an import surtax of up to 15 percent on most goods.

Privatization: Morocco launched a privatization program in 1992 and since then 58 out of 114 state enterprises have been sold, raising $1.7 billion. On March 31, 1999 parliament approved an amendment to the privatization law which pared to 28 the remaining enterprises to be sold off, mainly reflecting legal and financial problems in the others. The law also provides a legal framework for other state-owned enterprises to be privatized in the future. Among the entities to be privatized are six sugar plants, nine hotels, three banks (Banque Centrale Populaire, Banque Nationale pour le Development Economique, Credit Immobilier et Hotelier) and the state fertilizer company Fertima. The Ministry of Privatization is preparing for the sale of a strategic stake in the telephone operator Maroc Telecom. The competition is slated to take place during 2004. There are also plans to privatize a share of the national carrier, Royal Air Maroc, through a combination of international tender and placement on the stock market, as well as the privatization of the state-run tobacco marketing company.

European Union Trade Preference: Morocco's Association Agreement with the European Union went into effect on March 1, 2004. The agreement calls for the gradual elimination of tariffs on Morocco-EU trade in industrial goods over the next 12 years. Agricultural products (including Morocco's most important agricultural exports like citrus and tomatoes) are not covered by the agreement. Morocco already enjoys free access to the EU for virtually all non-agricultural products under a 1976 agreement. Thus the major effect of the agreement will be to phase out Moroccan tariffs for EU manufactured goods. The free trade provisions of this agreement do not apply to the exchange of agricultural products between Morocco and the EU.

Trade and Investment Framework Agreement (TIFA): The 1995 TIFA between the United States and Morocco provides that both parties will take appropriate measures to encourage and facilitate trade in goods and services, and to establish favorable conditions for the long-term development of bilateral trade and investment. Working groups of U.S. and Moroccan officials and private sector representatives have been established to address, on a regular basis, specific measures to achieve these objectives. For example, talks to date have covered reduction of tariffs on certain U.S. products, streamlining of customs and bureaucratic procedures, and specific problems faced by U.S. firms in Morocco. An OPIC agreement, signed in 1961, and updated in 1995, was ratified by the Moroccan parliament in June 1999.

BALANCE OF PAYMENTS SITUATION

Morocco runs a chronic merchandise trade deficit, which is generally offset by receipts from tourism, workers remittances and foreign investment. In 1999 imports increased by 7.4 percent while exports increased by 5.4 percent. Exports are only 68.2 percent as large as imports. Foreign investment increased by 240 percent in 1999 as result of the successful sale of a second mobile phone license. In 1999 tourism receipts increased by 14.7 percent while worker remittances fell 1.6 percent.

Merchandise Trade: The trade deficit remained steady in 1999 at 36.5 billion Dirhams. Citrus fruit and phosphates and its derivatives led export growth. Imports of crude oil increased by 65.4 percent in dirham terms, reflecting the increases in world oil prices. Food imports are expected to increase in 2004 due a second successive year of drought.

Tourism: The number of tourists in Morocco increased by 18 percent in 1999, to 2.35 million visitors, and tourism receipts increased by 14.7 percent. The tourism sector has shown strong growth over the past few years, especially in Marrakech and Agadir. The land border with Algeria – formerly the largest single source of foreign tourists – remains closed.

Workers' remittances: Remittances fell in 1999 by 1.6 percent to $1.94 billion. Remittances have fallen four of the last five years. Moroccan economists expect remittances to trend downward in the future if the European economies (where over 1 million Moroccans live) remain slack, and as ties between the overseas Moroccans and their homeland weaken.

Foreign investment: Foreign investment inflows tripled in 1999, almost 50 percent higher than the previous record set in 1997. The level was reached thanks to the sale of a second mobile phone license for $1.1 billion to the Spanish/Portuguese firm Meditel.

Foreign debt: Morocco's foreign debt burden has declined steadily in recent years. Morocco last rescheduled its Paris Club debt in 1992. The French and Spanish governments, and since early 1999 the Italian government, have engaged in debt-equity swaps with Morocco, and Morocco is seeking the cooperation of other lenders. Morocco's current debt service ratio of approximately 20.0 percent of exports of goods and non-factor services appears sustainable. External public debt fell to $17.5 billion in 1999.

INFRASTRUCTURE SITUATION

Morocco is making the development of its communications and transportation networks a top priority. With many improvements already achieved and several projects underway in these two sectors, Morocco's infrastructure for the distribution of goods and services is good.

Roads and Highways: Morocco's 60,000 km road network is among the best in Africa. Most parts of the country are readily accessible by well-surfaced roads. Most agricultural and manufactured goods move by road. With the completion of a toll-highway linking Fez and Rabat, Morocco now boasts 466 kilometers of highways linking the coastal cities of Casablanca, Rabat and Assilah, and the inland cities of Fez and Meknes. However, the slow progress of the highway between Casablanca and Marrakech is a frustration to residents, tourists and distributors, and the road between Casablanca and Jorf Lasfar, passing through the resort town of El Jadida has been the scene of frequent traffic accidents involving fatalities. Traffic in Casablanca continues to be clogged due to insufficient signaling, absence of pedestrian overpasses and lack of parking and traffic enforcement.

Airports: There are eleven major airports in the country. The largest international airport "Mohammed V", located 35 km south of Casablanca, offers about fifty regular flights per day to Europe, the United States, Canada, the Middle East and several African cities. Merchandise can be transported to and from the airport by truck or by train. The Moroccan Airport Authority "Office National Des Aeroports" (ONDA) launched in 1993 an ambitious program to modernize the infrastructure of all national airports. All airports have modern equipment to increase traffic security and safety, and to improve the airspace radio coverage. Runways are being extended to receive large planes and training is provided to airport technical agents.

Air transportation: Royal Air Maroc, Morocco's national airline, has a well-developed route structure, particularly to Europe and the Middle East/Gulf as noted above. The carrier has modernized its middle and short-haul fleet with the purchase of new generation Boeing 737s, and has augmented service to France and Egypt by leasing two additional 737-800s. RAM launched a tender for a fleet renewal to replace its middle/short haul and long haul aircraft. RAM has announced plans to enter a code share agreement with Delta Airlines to go into effect in October 2004. Regional Airlines competes with RAM on certain domestic routes as well as to Lisbon and Malaga. Regional recently ordered five Brazilian-manufactured Embraer Regional Jets 135 & 145 for the expansion of its fleet. The jets are equipped with U.S. state of the art avionics from Honeywell. The engines are from Allison Rolls Royce out of Cincinnati and the cabin design is manufactured by C&D, a California firm.

The Rail Network: The rail company, the "Office National des Chemins de Fer"(ONCF), plays an important role in the Moroccan economy. It employs 13,820 people and operates on some 2,000 km of track. ONCF handles the transportation of phosphates, fertilizers, chemical products and other minerals. Ambitious plans are scheduled to modernize and extend the network.

Shipping Network: The National Port Authority, "Office d'Exploitation des Ports" (ODEP) is the managing body. The port infrastructure handles 98% of the country's foreign trade. Morocco's twenty-four ports posted a record of 52.9 million tons in 1999, an increase of 9% compared to 1998. The port of Casablanca, the second largest in Africa handled 37% of goods imported and/or exported. Morocco's shipping costs are high in comparison to its Mediterranean competitors. There is frequent ferry service to and from Spain and France for tourists.

Telecommunications: The telephone system has greatly improved in the last five years. The national telecommunications network offers a range of services including cellular, paging, video conferencing, voice mail and Internet. Total telephone lines reached close to 1,455,853 at the end of 1999, still low on a per capita basis. In July 1999, a second GSM license was awarded. The competition with the existing license (held by state-owned Maroc Telecom) brought about intense marketing and promotion. As a result, the existing Maroc Telecom increased its subscribers from 173,000 in 1998 to over 1,000,000 by summer, 2004; the second license holder, Meditel, gained close to a quarter million subscribers in it's first three months. Licenses were also awarded during 1999-2004 for GMPCS and VSAT.

TRADE POLICY[2]

GENERAL POLICY FRAMEWORK

Morocco boasts the largest phosphate reserves in the world, a diverse agricultural (including fishing) sector, a large tourist industry, a growing manufacturing sector (especially clothing), and considerable inflows of funds from Moroccans working abroad. Most of Morocco's trade is with Europe, France alone accounts for about a quarter of Morocco's imports and a third of its exports. Morocco is a member of the WTO.

The Moroccan government has pursued an economic reform program since the early 1980s. It has restrained government spending, revised the tax system, reformed the banking system, pursued appropriate monetary policies, eased import restrictions, lowered tariffs, launched a privatization program and liberalized the foreign exchange regime. These reforms have helped restore macroeconomic equilibria: the current account deficit, fiscal deficit and inflation rates are well below their early 1980s levels. Economic growth has been modest, with wide year-to-year fluctuations due largely to variations in rainfall.
The reform program continues to move forward although slowly and unevenly. An anti-corruption campaign in early 1996 considerably slowed customs clearances, and put a damper on some economic activity. The privatization program has progressed slower than expected, but trading privatized companies has given a huge boost to the Casablanca stock exchange. The Moroccan government has embraced private financing, construction and operation of some highways, a new Atlantic Ocean port for Tangier and other large infrastructure projects, including a $1.5 billion electric power project awarded to a joint venture between an American and a European firm.

GDP growth topped twelve percent in 1996 following heavy rains that nourished a record harvest. Erratic rains in 1997 led to a 25 percent drop in agriculture GDP. The economy as a whole is expected to contract by 2.5 percent in 1997. Foreign exchange reserves have bounced back after falling during the 1994-1995 drought. The government has recently announced an easing of exchange controls for Moroccan tourists. Morocco's chronic merchandise trade deficit narrowed slightly in 1996. This trend has continued into 1997. Receipts from remittances, tourism and foreign investment recovered in 1996, and have increased sharply in 1997, led by a significant increase in foreign investment.

2. EXCHANGE RATE POLICIES

The Moroccan dirham is convertible for all current transactions (as defined by the International Monetary Fund's Article VIII) as well as for some capital transactions, notably capital repatriation by foreign investors. Foreign exchange is routinely available through commercial banks for such transactions on presentation of documents. Moroccan companies may borrow abroad without prior government approval. Investment abroad by Moroccan individuals or corporations is subject to approval by the Foreign Exchange Board. Approval is routinely denied for projects that do not directly benefit Morocco.

The Central Bank sets the exchange rate for the dirham against a basket of currencies of its principal trading partners, particularly the French franc and other European currencies. The rate

[2] Department of State report submitted to the Senate Committees on Foreign Relations and on Finance and to the House Committees on Foreign Affairs and on Ways and Means

against the basket has remained steady since a nine percent devaluation in May 1990, with changes in the rates of individual currencies reflecting changes in cross rates.

The large weight given to European currencies in the basket results in a greater volatility of the dollar than the European currencies against the dirham. This increases the foreign exchange risk of importing from the United States as compared to importing from Europe.

3. STRUCTURAL POLICIES

The 1992 Foreign Trade Law committed Morocco to the principles of free trade, reversing the legal presumption of import protection. It replaced quantitative restrictions with tariffs (both ad valorem and variable) on the importation of politically sensitive items.

Interest rate policy has also changed in recent years. In 1994 the Government revised the interest rate ceilings on bank loans. The new ceiling is set as a three to four percent markup over the rate received on deposits, including the below-market-rates on required deposits. The effect of the change is to lower the interest rate ceilings, although real rates remain high

Morocco has a three-part tax structure consisting of a value added tax, a corporate income tax, and an individual income tax. The new investment code passed by the Parliament in October 1995 calls for reductions in corporate and individual income taxes, and the reduction of import duties and elimination of the value added tax on certain capital goods and equipment. A plethora of minor taxes can significantly raise the cost of certain imported goods.

4. DEBT MANAGEMENT POLICIES

Morocco's foreign debt burden has declined steadily in recent years. Foreign debt fell from 128 percent of GDP in 1985 to about 58 percent of GDP in 1996. Similarly, debt service payments before rescheduling, as a share of goods and services exports, fell from over 58 percent in 1985 to about 32 percent in 1996. The Moroccan government does not foresee the need for further Paris Club rescheduling, although it is pursuing other forms of debt relief with major official creditors.

5. AID

Less than two percent of the aid listed in the economic indicators section of the report is military assistance.

6. SIGNIFICANT BARRIERS TO U.S. EXPORTS AND INVESTMENT

Import Licenses: Morocco has eliminated import licensing requirements on a number of items in recent years. Licensing requirements remain for motor vehicles, used clothing and explosives.

Tariffs: Tariffs have been gradually reduced in recent years. By 1993 the maximum tariff was 35 percent and the (trade-weighted) average tariff was about 13 percent. Despite the downward trend, tariffs on some products have increased as quantitative restrictions were replaced with higher tariffs. For example, following the elimination of licensing requirements, tariffs on dairy products, cereals, vegetable oils and sugar have increased. There is also a 10 to 15 percent surtax on imports of most goods.

Services Barriers: In November 1989 Parliament abrogated a 1973 law requiring majority Moroccan ownership of firms in a wide range of industries, thus eliminating what had been a barrier to U.S. investment in Morocco. In 1993 the Moroccan government repealed a 1974 decree limiting foreign ownership in the petroleum refining and distribution sector, which allowed Mobil Oil to buy back the Moroccan government's 50 percent share of Mobil's Moroccan subsidiary in 1994.

Standards, Testing, Labeling and Certification: Morocco applies approximately 500 industrial standards based on international norms. These apply primarily to packaging, metallurgy and construction. Sanitary regulations apply to virtually all food imports. Meat should be slaughtered according to Islamic law.

Investment Barriers: The Moroccan government actively encourages foreign investment. The Parliament passed a new investment code in 1995 which applies equally to foreign and Moroccan investors, except for the foreign exchange provisions which favor foreign investors. Unlike the previous sectoral investment codes, the advantages offered under the new code are to be granted automatically. There are no foreign investor performance requirements, although the new code provides income tax breaks for investments in certain regions, and in crafts and export industries.

Government Procurement Practices: While Moroccan government procurement regulations allow for preferences for Moroccan bidders, the effect of the preference on U.S. companies is limited. Virtually all of the government procurement contracts that interest U.S. companies are large projects for which the competition is non-Moroccan (mainly European) companies. Many of these projects are financed by multilateral development banks which impose their own nondiscriminatory procurement regulations. U.S. companies sometimes have difficulty with the requirement that bids for government procurement be in French.

Customs Procedures: In principle, customs procedures are simple and straightforward, but in practice they are sometimes marked by delays. A commercial invoice is required, but no special invoice form is necessary. Certification as to country of origin of the goods is required.

7. EXPORT SUBSIDIES POLICIES

There are no direct export subsidies, although the 1995 investment code provides a five-year corporate income tax holiday for export industries. Morocco has a temporary admission scheme which allows for suspension of duties and licensing requirements on imported inputs for export production. This scheme includes indirect exporters (local suppliers to exporters). In addition, a "prior export" program exists, whereby exporters can claim a refund on duties paid on imports which were subsequently transformed and exported. Morocco is not a signatory of the GATT Subsidies Code.

8. PROTECTION OF U.S. INTELLECTUAL PROPERTY

Morocco is a member of the World Intellectual Property Organization and is a party to the Bern Copyright, Paris Industrial Property, and Universal Copyright Conventions, the Brussels Satellite Convention, and the Madrid, Nice, and the Hague agreements for the protection of intellectual property.

Copyright: Computer software is not specifically covered by Morocco's copyright law and violations of software copyrights are widespread. Moroccan officials have announced the imminent introduction of legislation to offer protection for computer software.

Patents: Morocco has a relatively complete regulatory and legislative system for the protection of intellectual property. A quirk dating from the era of the French and Spanish protectorates requires patent applications for industrial property to be filed in both Casablanca and Tangier for complete protection. The proposed 1996 industrial property code will amend this provision and require that applications be filed only in Casablanca.
Trademarks: Counterfeiting of clothing, luggage, and other consumer goods is not uncommon; however, anti-counterfeiting has been increasingly enforced. Counterfeiting is primarily for local sales rather than for export. Trademarks must be filed in both Casablanca and Tangier, though this too will be amended in the new law.

9. WORKERS RIGHTS

a. The Right of Association: Workers are free to form and join unions throughout the country. The right is exercised widely but not universally. About ten percent of Morocco's 4.9 million urban workers is unionized, mostly in the public sector. The selection of union officers and the carrying out of their duties are subject to government pressure. More narrowly focused strikes continue to occur, although strikers have encountered police harassment and arrest. Work stoppages are normally intended to advertise grievances and last 24-48 hours.

b. The Right to Organize and Bargain Collectively: While the protection of the right to organize and bargain collectively exists in the Constitution and labor law, the government does not always enforce the protections fully. The laws governing collective bargaining are inadequate. Collective bargaining has been a long standing tradition in some parts of the economy, but the practice is not spreading. A 1996 social dialogue between labor, government and management resulted in an agreement for a 10 percent pay raise, increased money for housing construction and an understanding to continue such tri-partite discussions. Some of the provisions of this agreement have yet to be implemented, and there remains some dissatisfaction among workers.

The multiplicity of trade union federations creates competition to organize workers. As a result, a single factory may contain several independent locals. However, this also tends to weaken the unions' negotiating position with management. Labor laws are observed most often in the corporate and parastatal sectors of the economy. In the informal economy, labor regulations are routinely ignored. As a practical matter, the unions in Morocco have no judicial recourse to oblige the Government to act when it has not met its obligations under the law.

c. Prohibition of Forced or Compulsory Labor: Forced or compulsory labor is prohibited in Morocco.

d. Minimum Age for Employment of Children: The law prohibits the employment or apprenticeship of any child under 12 years of age. Special regulations cover the employment of children between the ages of 12 and 16. In practice, however, children are often apprenticed before age 12, particularly in the handicraft industry.

The use of minors is common in the rug-making, textile, and tanning industries. Children are also employed informally as domestics and usually receive little or no wages. Child labor laws are generally well-observed in the industrialized, unionized sector of the economy.

e. Acceptable Conditions of Work: The minimum wage is about $165 a month and is not considered adequate to provide a decent standard of living for a worker and his or her family. The minimum wage is not enforced effectively in the informal sector of the economy. It is enforced fairly effectively throughout the industrialized, unionized sectors where most workers earn more than the minimum wage. They are generally paid between 13 and 16 months salary, including bonuses, each year.

The law provides for a 48-hour maximum workweek with not more than 10 hours any single day, premium pay for overtime, paid public and annual holidays, and minimum conditions for health and safety, including the prohibition of night work for women and minors. As with other regulations and laws, these are not universally observed in the informal sector.

f. Rights in Sections with U.S. Investment: Worker rights in sectors with U.S. investment do not differ from those described above, all of which is in the formal, industrial sector of the Moroccan economy.

U.S. INVESTMENT IN SELECTED INDUSTRIES

(Millions of U.S. dollars)

Category	Amount	
Petroleum		(1)
Total Manufacturing		92
Food & Kindred Products	37	
Chemicals & Allied Products	22	
Metals, Primary & Fabricated	(1)	
Machinery, except Electrical	0	
Electric & Electronic Equipment	0	
Transportation Equipment	0	
Other Manufacturing	(1)	
Wholesale Trade		0
Banking		(1)
Finance/Insurance/Real Estate		0
Services		0
Other Industries		0
TOTAL ALL INDUSTRIES		122

(1) Suppressed to avoid disclosing data of individual companies.
Source: U.S. Department of Commerce, Bureau of Economic Analysis

INVESTMENT AND BUSINESS CLIMATE

Douglas Wallace
Senior Commercial Officer
U.S. Consulate, Casablanca
+212 522 264 550
Douglas.Wallace@trade.gov

Despite global economic uncertainty and slowed capital inflows into North Africa following the regional upheaval linked to the Arab Spring, the Moroccan government is making great strides in attracting foreign direct investment (FDI) to the country. Morocco's overarching economic development plan is based on leveraging its location, along the Strait of Gibraltar between Spain and Africa, to transform the country into a regional hub for North, West, and Sub-Saharan Africa for shipping, logistics, finance, assembly, and sales.

The Government of Morocco has implemented a series of sector strategies aimed at raising performance and output in key revenue-earning sectors, boosting employment, and attracting foreign investment. Notably, its National Plan for Industrial Development set the groundwork for large-scale global investments, such as those by France's Renault in Tangier and Canada's Bombardier in Casablanca. The strategy focused on developing export-oriented economic sectors (aeronautics, automotive, offshoring, and electronics). The manufacturing sector created 75,000 jobs in the past ten years and the new 2014 industrial strategy aims to accelerate this effort by creating 500,000 new jobs in manufacturing by 2020.

Casablanca Finance City (CFC), Morocco's flagship project launched in 2010 by King Mohammed VI, is aimed at developing a state-of-the-art financial center and business hub in Casablanca. The platform is a comprehensive business ecosystem that gives international financial institutions, professional services firms, and regional headquarters access to African markets and preferential benefits. Due to its political stability and strategic location, Morocco is rapidly becoming a regional manufacturing and export base for international companies.

Morocco actively encourages foreign investment and has sought to facilitate it through macro-economic policies, trade liberalization, and structural reforms. Morocco has ratified 62 bilateral agreements for the promotion and protection of investments and 51 double taxation avoidance agreements. Its Investment Charter has put in place a convertibility system for foreign investors and gives investors the freedom to transfer profits.

Morocco's Free Trade Agreement (FTA) with the United States entered into force in 2006. Since then, overall trade between the two countries has increased by more than 300 percent. The U.S. has a long standing and close bilateral relationship with Morocco. This cooperation has been reinvigorated with the U.S.-Morocco Strategic Dialogue and the Business Development Conferences.

While Morocco has improved its World Bank "Doing Business" rank by ten points from the previous year, many challenges remain. Multinational companies cite Morocco's security and stability as positive factors influencing their interest in Morocco, and stress the country's appeal as a base for regional activities. However, they also express concern over the lack of skilled labor, weak intellectual property rights protection, and the lack of regulatory transparency. These issues could affect a company's willingness to increase investment in Morocco. Nevertheless, foreign companies still find Morocco profitable and envision maintaining their presence.

1. OPENNESS TO, AND RESTRICTIONS UPON, FOREIGN INVESTMENT

Attitude towards FDI
Morocco is positioning itself as a platform for Africa. The U.S. Mission is increasingly seeing multinational companies leverage Morocco's geographical position by setting up their regional headquarters in the country.

Morocco actively encourages foreign investment and has sought to facilitate it through macro-economic policies, trade liberalization, and structural reforms. Under the U.S.-Morocco Free Trade Agreement (FTA) and the Association Agreement with the EU, Morocco has reduced its tariffs on imports from the U.S. and the EU. Morocco has also signed a quadrilateral FTA with Tunisia, Egypt and Jordan (under the Agadir Declaration), an FTA with Turkey, and concluded third round FTA talks with Canada in June, 2012. In 2008, Morocco was the first country in the region to be granted "advanced status" with the EU. In January 2014, Morocco concluded third round talks with the EU on a Deep and Comprehensive FTA. This will be the first such agreement between the EU and a North African country.

Additionally, Morocco is seeking trade and investment accords with other African, Asian and Latin American countries.

The U.S.-Morocco FTA is a comprehensive agreement that supports the economic and political reforms that are underway in Morocco. It provides for improved bilateral commercial opportunities by reducing and eliminating trade barriers. Its entry into force in 2006 has facilitated a significant increase in U.S.-Moroccan trade and investment.

In September 2012, the U.S. and Morocco launched a Strategic Dialogue, a framework to deepen bilateral cooperation on strategic issues and mutual priorities. The U.S.-Morocco Business Development Conference (BDC) provides a platform to strengthen business-to-business ties, further capitalize on the U.S.-Morocco FTA, promote increased investment, and encourage regional economic integration. The second U.S.-Morocco BDC took place in Morocco in March 2014 and attracted the participation of over 50 U.S.-based companies.

The Joint Committee established by the U.S.-Morocco FTA held its third meeting in December 2012. At that meeting, the United States and Morocco announced an agreement on two new initiatives: the Joint Principles for International Investment and the Joint Principles for Information and Communication Technology (ICT) Services. Morocco became the first Middle East and North Africa partner to endorse both principles, sending a strong signal to domestic and international investors that Morocco embraces an open, 21st century approach to investment and growth.

A bilateral trade facilitation agreement was signed during King Mohammed VI's visit to Washington, DC in November 2013.

Morocco's ranking in the World Bank's 2014 Doing Business report out of 189 countries:

Area	Rank
Ease of Doing Business	87
Starting a Business	39
Dealing with Construction Permits	83
Getting Electricity	97
Registering Property	156
Protecting Investors	115
Getting Credit	109

Enforcing Contracts	83

Morocco is ranked 87 out of 189 economies in the 2014 Doing Business report. This rank is a ten-position improvement over last year, due mainly to positive reforms related to starting a business, registering property, and tax administration. The business climate is still weak in areas of investor protection and the credit market. And while improvements have been made in property registration, Morocco still lags behind in the region due to the time and cost of registration.

Other Investment Policy Reviews

UNCTAD's 2008 Investment Policy Review of Morocco can be found here (French): http://unctad.org/en/Docs/iteipc200616_fr.pdf. The Investment Policy Review noted that Morocco had the potential to attract increased FDI inflows and FDI of a high quality in order to meet the development objective of the "Plan Emergence" of moving into high value added activities.

The WTO's 2009 Trade Policy Review (TPR) of Morocco can be found here: http://www.wto.org/english/tratop_e/tpr_e/tp317_e.htm. The review found that the macroeconomic and structural reforms, including trade reforms, pursued by Morocco since the previous TPR (2003) have contributed to the growth diversification and positive overall performance of its economy.

The OECD's 2010 Investment Policy Review of Morocco can be found here: http://www.oecd.org/daf/inv/internationalinvestmentagreements/morocco-investmentpolicyreview-oecd.htm. The review found that Morocco has adopted a series of laws and amendments needed to improve the local investment climate. Progress has been made in improving transparency and business access to information, and in reducing the time and cost of administrative procedures.

Laws/Regulations of FDI

Law 18-95 of October 1995, constituting the Investment Charter, (http://www.usa-morocco.org/Charte.htm) is the principal Moroccan text concerning investment and applies to both domestic and foreign investment.

The Foreign Exchange Office's Circular 1589 of September 1992 instituted a convertibility regime that allows foreign investors to conduct their investment operations in Morocco freely. The 1995 Charter guarantees free transfer of funds (Article 16) and gives foreign investors the freedom to transfer profits and capital for persons who make investments in foreign currency (Article 15).

Morocco accepted Article VIII of the Articles of Agreement of the International Monetary Fund in January 1993.

Sector Strategies

On April 2, 2014, the Moroccan Minister of Industry, Trade, Investment, and the Digital Economy, unveiled an ambitious seven-year industrial growth and acceleration plan. It allocates $2.5 billion for programs to increase manufacturing's share from 14 to 23 percent of the economy and to create 500,000 new jobs by 2020. The plan targets manufacturing-sector challenges including underdeveloped small and medium-sized enterprises (SMEs), weak youth employability, unbalanced growth, and integrated industrial platforms (P2Is aka industrial parks). The Minister's industrial plan seeks to promote exports and use increased foreign investment to boost knowledge sharing and technology transfer. At the same time, it aims to protect local industries against 'unfair' competition and reduce import dependency.

Overall, the new plan contains many positive aspects such as a) creating links between large enterprises and SMEs; b) formalizing the informal sector; c) addressing skills mismatch; d) creating new industrial parks and improving existing facilities; e) improving coordination among export promotion agencies; f) encouraging FDI; and g) looking more towards sub-Saharan Africa for growth, in particular by leveraging CFC.

The Moroccan government established the CFC in December 2010 to position Casablanca as a financial hub for Francophone Africa. The CFC exclusively targets financial institutions (investment banks, asset management firms, private equity firms, and insurance companies), multinational regional headquarters, and professional services firms (consulting, law, audit, and credit rating agencies).

Morocco's 2009 National Plan for Industrial Development set the groundwork for large-scale global investments, such as those by France's Renault in Tangier and Canada's Bombardier in Casablanca. The strategy focused on developing export-oriented economic sectors in which Morocco had a comparative advantage, including four that had attracted significant FDI – automobile, aeronautics, electronics, and offshoring – and three that were largely financed by domestic investment – leather, food processing, and textiles. The plan also developed Morocco's P2Is that offered investors land for new or expanding businesses, special tax breaks, transport connections, and services such as security, telecommunications, and recruitment support. In the past ten years, the manufacturing sector created 75,000 jobs.

More information on this strategy can be found here: http://www.emergence.gov.ma/en/Pacte/Pages/LePacte.aspx.

By 2020, Morocco plans to have invested $18.95 billion in its Energy Strategy to decrease energy dependence, preserve the environment, and generate 50,000 jobs. Its goal is to have 42 percent of its total electrical power produced by renewable energy (solar, wind, and hydraulic). With a goal to make solar energy 14 percent of total electric capacity, Morocco aims to increase solar electric production capacity to 2000 MW by 2020 principally using two technologies: concentrated solar power and photovoltaic. It plans to increase installed wind-generated electrical capacity from 280 MW in 2010 to 2000 MW by 2020, reducing CO_2 emissions by 5.6 million tons per year.

Morocco has 15 commercial ports that generated 92.3 million tons in merchandise traffic in 2012. Morocco has two port management agencies, the National Port Agency (ANP) and Tanger-Med Special Agency (TMSA). TMSA manages Tanger Med, the largest port by volume in Morocco. Tanger-Med Port terminals 1 and 2 are operational. It is expected to process 8 million containers, 7 million passengers, 700,000 trucks, 2 million vehicles, and 10 million MT of oil products by 2015. Once fully operational, it will be the largest transshipment port in Africa.

Morocco has implemented other sector strategies including the Green Morocco Plan (to revive Morocco's agriculture sector), Digital Morocco 2013 Plan (to position Morocco as a dynamic emerging country in information technology), Halieutis Plan (to improve the competitiveness of Morocco's fishing industry), Logistics Strategy (to improve logistic services and transportation infrastructure), National Strategy for the Craft Industry (to promote production and sales of handicrafts), and Tourism Vision 2020 strategy (to double the number of foreign tourists and triple the number of national domestic travelers).

To support the tourism strategy, Morocco's Ministry of Equipment and Transport and the National Airports Office, which manages Airports and air traffic control, are implementing a development strategy. It aims to promote the Casablanca airport as an international hub for traffic to Central and West Africa, and develop Marrakech airport as a hub for African traffic toward Europe. It also seeks to improve Morocco's airport infrastructure through airport extension, modernization, and new construction.

Limits on Foreign Control

According to the OECD 2010 Investment Policy Review, Morocco places limits on foreign investment in air and maritime transport companies and maritime fisheries.

Although foreigners are prohibited from owning and cultivating agricultural land, they can purchase it for non-agricultural purposes. Morocco has sought to encourage foreign investment in the agricultural sector by making land available to foreigners through leases of up to 99 years. French, Spanish and Middle Eastern investment in the sector centers mostly on citrus and olives, with smaller investment in grapes and berries.

Morocco adheres to the OECD Declaration on International Investment and Multinational Enterprises. Morocco's OECD FDI Regulatory Restrictiveness Index in 2010 was 0.067 (closed economy = 1; open = 0).
http://www.oecd.org/daf/inv/internationalinvestmentagreements/45563285.pdf.

Privatization Program

In 1993, an ambitious program of privatization was initiated. When it ended in August 2011, total revenue from divestment in state-owned enterprise (SOE) and the granting of telecom licenses totaled about 107 billion dirhams (approximately $13 billion). Privatization has attracted FDI, giving a boost to Morocco's economy.

While the 2010 budget law envisioned 4 billion dirhams ($490 million) in privatization revenues, actual sales totaled only 35 million dirhams ($4 million). Sales of government-owned companies picked up in 2011, with 5.3 billion dirhams raised by selling a twenty-percent stake in *Banque Populaire* to its regional affiliates. (The government still holds 18 percent interest in the bank.) Financial institutions still controlled by the government include Credit Agricole Maroc, investment bank *Caisse de Depot et de Gestion Capital*, and the *Al Barid Bank*, which is a division of Morocco's postal service.

Competition Law

Restrictive agreements and practices are regulated by the Competition Law.

Morocco's Competition Law (French): http://www.wipo.int/wipolex/en/text.jsp?file_id=191407.

Law no. 06-99 on Free Pricing and Competition (June 2000) outlines the authority of the Competition Council (http://conseil-concurrence.ma/) as an independent executive body with investigatory powers. Together with the Central Authority for the Prevention of Corruption, the Competition Council is one of the main actors in charge of improving public governance and advocating for further market liberalization.

Morocco hosted the 13th Annual International Competition Network (ICN) Conference – a conference that promotes implementing more effective enforcement of antitrust law – in April, 2014.

TABLE 1: Morocco's Ranking on Various Indices

Measure	Year	Rank or value	Website Address
TI Corruption Perceptions Index	2013	(91 of 177)	http://cpi.transparency.org/cpi2013/results/
Heritage Foundation's Economic Freedom index	2013	(103 of 177)	http://www.heritage.org/index/ranking
World Bank's Doing Business Report "Ease of Doing Business"	2013	(87 of 189)	http//doingbusiness.org/rankings
Global Innovation Index	2013	(92 of 142)	http://www.globalinnovationindex.org/content.aspx?page=gii-full-report-2013#pdfopener
World Bank GNI per capita	2012	$ 2,960	http://data.worldbank.org/indicator/NY.GNP.PCAP.CD

TABLE 1B: Millennium Challenge Corporation* Scorecard for Morocco:

Year	Index	Ranking	Meets Performance Standards
2014	MCC Gov Effectiveness	77th Percentile	Yes
2014	MCC Rule of Law	69th Percentile	Yes
2014	MCC Control of Corruption	62nd Percentile	Yes
2014	MCC Fiscal Policy	23th Percentile	No
2014	MCC Trade Policy	17th Percentile	No
2014	MCC Regulatory Quality	77th Percentile	Yes
2014	MCC Business Start Up	77nd Percentile	Yes
2014	MCC Land Rights Access	41th Percentile	No
2014	MCC Natural Resource Protection	27st Percentile	No
2014	MCC Access to Credit	31th Percentile	No
2014	MCC Inflation	88th Percentile	Yes
2014	MCC Gender in the Economy	41st Percentile	No

*The Millennium Challenge Corporation, a U.S. Government entity charged with delivering development grants to countries that have demonstrated a commitment to reform, produced scorecards for countries with a 2012 per capita gross national income (GNI) of $4,085 or less. A list of countries/economies with MCC scorecards is available here: http://www.mcc.gov/pages/selection/scorecards. Details on each of the MCC's indicators and a guide to reading the scorecards are available here: http://www.mcc.gov/documents/reports/reference-2013001142401-fy14-guide-to-the-indicators.pdf

2. CONVERSION AND TRANSFER POLICIES

Foreign Exchange

Morocco has achieved relatively stable macroeconomic and financial conditions under an exchange rate peg. The peg (to an 80 percent euro/20 percent U.S. dollar basket) has helped achieve price stability and insulate the economy from nominal shocks. However, according to the International Monetary Fund (IMF), growth has been relatively volatile. The IMF advocates a more flexible exchange rate, which would allow Morocco to respond better to shocks and support competitiveness as the economy opens up and becomes more vulnerable to external shocks.

On November 16, 2011, the legislature enacted the Moroccan Office of Exchange (OC) Circular. The Circular permits local banks to open accounts in dirham and foreign currency for corporate and individual clients. Moroccan or foreign non-residents may import foreign currencies or negotiable instruments in Morocco up to a maximum value of 100,000 dirhams ($12,300), provided it is declared with Customs. The Circular also regulates the importation of goods into Morocco, stipulating that locally established entities may import goods without prior authorization from the OC provided that an import license has been provided by Customs.

The Circular's general rule on foreign investment is that the foreign investor must notify the OC of his/her investment within six months of the transaction. With respect to the cross-border transfer of investment proceeds to foreign investors, the rules vary depending on the type of investment.

Morocco guarantees full currency convertibility for capital transactions, free transfer of profits, and free repatriation of invested capital.

Morocco is a member of the Middle East and North Africa Financial Action Task Force. The 2013 International Narcotics Control Strategy Report (INCSR), Volume II: Money Laundering and Financial Crimes Country Database, classifies Morocco as a "jurisdiction of concern" http://www.state.gov/j/inl/rls/nrcrpt/2013/database/211176.htm.

More information on Morocco's foreign exchange regulation can be found here: http://www.moroccobusinessnews.com/Invest_Morocco/Foreign_Exchange_Regulation.asp.

3. EXPROPRIATION AND COMPENSATION

The Moroccan Constitution (Article 15) stipulates that no expropriation can take place except in the cases and forms provided by law. The right to own property is guaranteed, but its extent and use may be restricted by law if the needs of economic and social planning and development require it.

U.S. Mission Morocco is not aware of any recent, confirmed instances of private property being expropriated for other than public purposes, or being expropriated in a manner that is discriminatory or not in accordance with established principles of international law.

4. DISPUTE SETTLEMENT

Legal System, Specialized Courts, Judicial Independence, Judgments of Foreign Courts

The principal sources of commercial legislation in Morocco are the 1913 Dahir of Obligations and Contracts, as amended, and the 1996 Code of Commerce.

According to the European Bank for Reconstruction and Development's 2012 Morocco Country Assessment Report (http://www.ebrd.com/downloads/sector/legal/morocco.pdf), the establishment of special commercial courts in 1997 led to some improvement in the handling of commercial disputes. Nevertheless, the lack of training for judges on general commercial matters remains one of the key challenges to effective commercial dispute resolution in the country. In general, litigation procedures are time consuming and resource-intensive, and there is no legal requirement with respect to case publishing.

Law No. 53-95 establishes Morocco's Commercial Courts. A Moroccan WTO submission states: "This law gives these courts exclusive jurisdiction to hear trade disputes. These courts also have sole competence to entertain industrial property disputes, as provided for in Law No. 17-97 on the Protection of Industrial Property, irrespective of the nature of the parties."

Arbitration is increasingly used in Morocco. The U.S. Agency for International Development (USAID) and the International Finance Corporation (IFC) assisted Morocco in 2008 and 2009 to establish a national commission on Alternative Dispute Resolution (ADR) with a mandate to regulate mediation training centers and develop mediator certification systems. The goal of this program was to increase the use of mediation in the prevention phase of bankruptcy proceedings and in the resolution of business disputes outside of the courts. Although the program remained limited in its implementation, the business community generally viewed early use of the system in Rabat and Casablanca as favorable.

Bankruptcy

Commercial Courts have jurisdiction over all cases related to insolvency. The Ministry of Justice and Liberties (MOJL) is currently reviewing bankruptcy legislation. Sources indicate that it would like to implement a bankruptcy system similar to U.S. Chapter 11.

The World Bank's 2006 Morocco Report on the Observance of Standards and Codes - Insolvency and Creditor Rights Systems: http://www.worldbank.org/ifa/rosc_icr_mor_eng.pdf. According to the study, the absence of a regulatory body and of competency requirements for insolvency administrators and liquidators are major impediments to the effective functioning of the insolvency system.

The World Bank's 2014 Doing Business report ranked Morocco 69 out of 189 countries in "Resolving Insolvency" (up 15 positions from 2013).

Investment Disputes

In an effort to promote foreign investment, the Moroccan legislature has adopted laws to protect both foreign investors and their Moroccan counterparts. Morocco is a member of the International Center for the Settlement of Investment Disputes (ICSID) and a party to the 1958 Convention on the Recognition and Enforcement of Foreign Arbitral Awards (with reservations) and the 1965 Convention on the Settlement of Investment Disputes between States and Nationals of Other states.

In general, investor rights are backed by an impartial procedure for dispute settlement that is transparent. No U.S. company had investment disputes with the Government of Morocco in 2010 or 2011. Several new cases emerged in 2012, which are the subject of continuing U.S. advocacy with the relevant Moroccan government agencies.

International Arbitration

Foreign companies have cited their ability to choose arbitration outside Morocco (in the case of litigation) as a strong benefit for doing business in the country.

Law No. 08-05 established a system of conventional arbitration and mediation, while allowing parties to apply the Code of Civil Procedure in their dispute resolution. Disputes may be brought before eight Commercial Courts, (located in Rabat, Casablanca, Fez, Tangier, Marrakech, Agadir, Oujda and Meknes) and three Commercial Courts of Appeal (located in Casablanca, Fez and Marrakech). These are comprised of professional judges and will consider all commercial disputes.

ICSID Convention and New York Convention

Morocco is party to the Convention on the Settlement of Investment Disputes between States and Nationals of Other States (entry into force: June 1967) and to the New York Convention of 1958 on the Recognition and Enforcement of Foreign Arbitral Awards.

5. PERFORMANCE REQUIREMENTS AND INVESTMENT INCENTIVES

WTO/TRIMS

The WTO Trade Related Investment Measures' (TRIMs) database does not reveal any reported Moroccan measures to be inconsistent with TRIMs requirements. However, many measures, regarding public procurement for example, reportedly show preferences to companies utilizing local content or establishing local production facilities. The government also maintains several "free zones" in which companies enjoy lower tax rates and relaxed labor laws in exchange for an obligation to export at least 85 percent of their product. In some cases, the government provides generous incentives for companies to locate production facilities in the country but stipulates other requirements in return.

Investment Incentives

Morocco offers incentives designed to encourage foreign and local investment. Morocco's Investment Charter gives the same benefits to all investors regardless of the industry in which they operate (except agriculture which remains outside the scope of the Charter.)

Morocco provides a range of investment incentives including:

> A corporate tax holiday during the first five years of business and a 17.5 percent rate thereafter.
>
> VAT exemptions: Equipment goods, materials, and tools needed to achieve investment projects involving an amount higher than or equal to 200 million dirhams (around $24 million) are exempt from VAT on imports, within the framework of an agreement concluded with the state, during a period of 36 months from the start of business.
>
> Import duty exemptions: Businesses that commit to making an investment of an amount higher than or equal to 200 million dirhams are exempt from import duties (applicable to

goods, materials, and tools needed for their project and imported directly by the companies) within the framework of an agreement concluded with the state.

Morocco created six integrated industrial zones within the region of Tangier, each dedicated to a different sector of the economy, including car manufacturing and aeronautics. Morocco has set up many free zones to offer companies incentives ranging from tax breaks, subsidies, and reduced customs duties. One of this strategy's biggest successes is the opening of a new facility for French car manufacturer Renault in 2012 in Tanger Automotive City.

Financial institutions and professional services firms that have CFC status are exempt from corporate taxes for the first five years after receiving CFC status. Afterwards, companies will be taxed a reduced rate of 8.75 percent instead of the standard 17.5 percent tax on export turnovers. Companies with regional headquarters in the CFC pay a reduced ten percent rate on profits, versus the average 30 percent standard rate. Employees of CFC-status companies also benefit from reduced personal income tax rates.

Other CFC advantages include administrative assistance. CFC-status companies are exempt from having to produce an official certificate from the National Agency of Employment Promotion and Competences, certifying that no other local candidate can fill the position offered to the foreign employee. In addition, CFC-status companies benefit from a simplified procedure for obtaining work permits for their foreign employees, cutting wait times from six months to one week. Additionally, foreign exchange regulations are eased for CFC status companies whereby certain transfers may be carried out freely without needing approval for each transaction, as is generally required.

More details on investment incentives:
http://www.invest.gov.ma/upload/documents/en_Doc_236.pdf

6. RIGHT TO PRIVATE OWNERSHIP AND ESTABLISHMENT

Private ownership is permitted in all but a few sectors reserved for the state, such as phosphate mining. Economic analysts, however, speculate that as Morocco's phosphate processing increasingly becomes open to foreign investment, its mining sector may follow suit. Apart from a few exceptions, private entities may freely establish, acquire and dispose of interests in business enterprises.

7. PROTECTION OF PROPERTY RIGHTS

Real Property

The World Bank's 2014 Doing Business Report ranked Morocco 156 out of 188 countries in 2014 (up 10 positions from 2013) on "Registering Property." Some of the report's findings on registering property in Morocco are below:

Indicator	Morocco	Middle East & North Africa	OECD
Procedures (number)	8	6	5
Time (days)	60	33.0	24.1
Cost (% of property value)	5.9	5.9	4.4

Information on the procedures to register property:
http://www.doingbusiness.org/data/exploreeconomies/morocco/registering-property.

USAID's report on Morocco's Property Rights:
http://usaidlandtenure.net/sites/default/files/country-profiles/full-reports/USAID_Land_Tenure_Morocco_Profile.pdf. According to the report, land and natural resource issues facing Morocco include: (1) lack of comprehensive policies governing land, water, forests and mineral resources; (2) underdeveloped legal frameworks and limited, ambiguous formal laws governing land and other natural resources; (3) a limited rural land market; (4) limited water; (5) undeveloped programs for participatory forest management; and (6) slow progress on women's rights of access to and control over land and natural resources.

Intellectual Property Rights

According to the 2013 International Property Rights (IPR) Index, Morocco ranks 64 out of 130 countries in protecting physical and intellectual property rights. In December 2004, the Moroccan Parliament passed amendments to its intellectual property legislation bringing it into compliance with its commitments under the WTO TRIPS Agreement. Morocco has been a member of the World Intellectual Property Organization (WIPO) since 1971. It is party to the Bern Copyright, Paris Industrial Property, and Universal Copyright Conventions; the Brussels Satellite Convention; and the Madrid, Nice, and Hague Agreements for the Protection of Intellectual Property.

In 2011, Morocco took the significant step of completing its accession to the Budapest treaty on patents and to the WIPO treaties on Copyright and Phonograms. In addition, it signed the Beijing Treaty on Audiovisual Performances in 2012. Morocco is also a signatory to the Anti-Counterfeiting Trade Agreement (ACTA), though it has not yet entered into force. The ACTA establishes an international framework that will assist parties in their efforts to effectively combat the infringement of IPR, in particular the proliferation of counterfeiting and piracy, which undermines legitimate trade and the sustainable development of the world economy.

Morocco is working with the U.S. to fulfill its commitments under the U.S.-Morocco FTA. The FTA contains strong intellectual property protections, which were incorporated in Moroccan intellectual property legislation in 2006. However, like neighboring countries, copyright protection remains problematic and counterfeit goods are widely available.

The Ministry of Industry, Trade, Investment, and the Digital Economy oversees the Moroccan Office of Industrial and Commercial Property (OMPIC). Based in Casablanca, it serves as a registry for intellectual property rights for patents and trademarks in the industrial and commercial sectors. In 2012, Morocco granted 993 patents, including 867 to non-residents, registered 11,323 trademarks, including 5,312 to non-residents, and recorded 422 industrial designs, including 363 to non-residents. The Ministry of Communications oversees the Moroccan Copyright Office (BMDA) in Rabat. It registers copyrights for literary and artistic works, including software.

Morocco has a non-discriminatory legal system that is accessible to foreign business. While criminal and civil courts can hear IPR-related cases, Commercial Courts, particularly those in the Casablanca region, are becoming adept at adjudicating patent, trademark, and copyright cases. Between 2008 and 2011, the largest commercial courts in Tangier, Oujda, Agadir, and Casablanca heard 595 cases related to counterfeiting. Casablanca courts hear approximately 85 percent of counterfeiting cases in Morocco. From filing until judgment, the average case takes 18 months.

Moroccan Customs, BMDA, and OMPIC have initiated campaigns to target Morocco's largest counterfeit manufacturers and importers. To support these ends, OMPIC partnered with the Moroccan General Business Confederation (CGEM) to form the National Committee for Industrial Property and Anti-Counterfeiting (CONPIAC), a bridge between the public and private sectors. CONPIAC has been active in supporting research regarding counterfeiting in Morocco and sponsored public events to raise awareness of the problem.

CONPIAC estimates that counterfeiting in Morocco results in a loss for the economy of between 6 billion dirhams ($734 million) and 12 billion dirhams ($1.47 billion) or 0.7 percent to 1.3 percent of gross domestic product (GDP). Preliminary studies show that counterfeiting is highest in textiles, followed by leather products, electrical goods, automobile parts, and cosmetics. A 2013 CONPIAC study estimated that the government loses 1 billion dirhams ($122 million) in tax revenue annually and that the economy loses 30,000 jobs due to counterfeiting.

Regarding software piracy, the U.S.-Morocco FTA obligates the government of Morocco to "issue appropriate laws, orders, regulations, or administrative or executive decrees mandating that its agencies use computer software only as authorized by the right holder," and specifies that "these measures shall actively regulate the acquisition and management of software for government use." The software industry has tried to work with the Moroccan government to meet this obligation. However, it reports continuing a lack of progress in the private and public sector. Public tenders of hardware contain no provision for the legal acquisition of software. Government IT managers copy software illegally, often claiming they lack the budget to buy legal software. The estimated level of piracy in the public sector in Morocco is 80 percent, well above the estimated 66 percent piracy level for the rest of the country (and still far above the regional or global average piracy rate).

For additional information about treaty obligations and points of contact at local IP offices, please see WIPO's country profiles at http://www.wipo.int/directory/en/.

Embassy point of contact: Douglas Wallace, U.S. Consulate, Casablanca
Douglas.Wallace@trade.gov

Resources for Rights Holders:

The American Chamber of Commerce (AmCham) in Morocco can provide a list of lawyers: http://www.amcham.ma/

8. TRANSPARENCY OF THE REGULATORY SYSTEM

Despite government efforts to increase transparency, Morocco's administration is opaque and difficult to navigate. The lack of transparency in the government's regulatory system is frequently cited by multinational companies as a challenge to doing business in the country. Routine permits, especially those required by local government agencies, can be difficult to obtain and regulations that can alter the market are often changed without proper consultation or notification. Notably, multinational pharmaceutical companies express their concern over the lack of a clear regulatory framework governing the health care industry and policy changes that may inhibit investment in the market.

As noted above, the Competition Council and the Central Authority for the Prevention of Corruption have responsibility for improving public governance and advocating for further market liberalization.

Morocco's World Economic Forum's Global Competitiveness Report 2013-2014: http://www3.weforum.org/docs/GCR2013-14/Morocco.pdf. The surveyed companies cite inefficient government bureaucracy as the most problematic factor for doing business in Morocco, followed by corruption and lack of access to finance.

9. EFFICIENT CAPITAL MARKETS AND PORTFOLIO INVESTMENT

Money and Banking System

The Casablanca Stock Exchange (CSE), founded in 1929 and re-launched as a private institution in 1993, is one of the few regional exchanges with no restrictions on foreign participation.

With a market capitalization of $55 billion and 76 listed companies, it is the third largest exchange in Africa, after South Africa and Egypt. The market is currently dominated by institutional investors which act on long-term trends. Short-selling, which would enable investors to profit from the downward trend, is not allowed on the CSE at present.

The market in Morocco is shallow and illiquid compared to other emerging and frontier markets, with many large firms controlled by privately owned holding groups. The Morgan Stanley Capital International's (MSCI) 2012 Annual Market Classification Review announced in June 2012 Morocco's reclassification to "Frontier Markets" from "Emerging Market" status, mainly due to its illiquidity. The report stated that, "the MSCI Morocco Index is more in line with the size and liquidity requirements of Frontier Markets following a significant decrease in liquidity since 2008, which resulted in a simultaneous decrease in the number of constituents in the MSCI Morocco Index."

The 1993 Law on the CSE has changed little over the years, and efforts are ongoing to further liberalize the management of the CSE and to empower the market regulator.

Morocco's banking system is one of the most liberalized in North Africa. Nonetheless, it is highly concentrated, with the six largest banks accounting for 85 percent of banking sector assets and access to finance, particularly for small and medium sized enterprises, remains challenging.

Credit is allocated on market terms, and foreign investors are able to obtain credit on the local market. There are some cross-shareholding arrangements, but they are not tailored to exclude foreign investment. The U.S. Mission has not received any reports of efforts by the private sector or industry to restrict foreign participation in standard-setting organizations. The government has actively sought out the participation of foreign investors for discussions on improving the business climate in Morocco.

In the 2013-2014 World Economic Forum's Global Competitiveness Report (http://reports.weforum.org/the-global-competitiveness-report-2013-2014/) Morocco dropped from 70th to 77th place out of 148 countries. In the report's eighth pillar, "Financial Market Development" Morocco received a score of 4.6 (down from 4.8 a year before) for "availability of financial services" (where 1 = not at all; 7 = provides a wide variety). Morocco received a 2.8 (down from 3.2 a year before) for "ease of access to loans" (where 1 = difficult; 7 = easy). Morocco improved its score from a year before from 5.3 to 5.7 for "soundness of banks" (where 1 = insolvent and may require bailout; 7 = generally healthy with sound balance sheet). Morocco was ranked 41 out of 148 countries on soundness of banks.

Several international financial institutions (IFIs) and major regional and bilateral organizations continue to be active in Morocco. In August, 2012 the IMF approved a $6.2 billion precautionary and liquidity line (PLL) as a buffer against fluctuations in oil prices and potential fallout from the downturn in Europe. According to the IMF survey, "the liquidity line provides Morocco with a useful insurance policy for meeting immediate financing needs should these risks materialize. It aims to strengthen investors' confidence and facilitate international market access by signaling that Morocco's current policies are sound, and that the authorities have adequate resources to draw upon if needed. The PLL is precautionary, and Morocco has said that it does not intend to draw on it in the absence of exogenous shocks."

According to the IMF's Third Review under the PLL Arrangement, "Morocco's macroeconomic performance improved in 2013, supported by strong policy commitment and implementation, as well as the insurance provided by the PLL. Important measures taken by the authorities helped reduce fiscal and external vulnerabilities and strengthen the economy's resilience." The review can be found here: http://www.imf.org/external/pubs/ft/scr/2014/cr1465.pdf

Among the main legal reform projects for the banking sector is the creation of a new provision that will enable banks to specialize in offering Islamic products. These new banks, called participatory banks, will be supervised by the Sharia Financial Committee to ensure the products are sharia-compliant.

On April 24, 2014 the Ministry of Economy and Finance (MoEF) released a draft law allowing for the creation of Islamic insurance companies, known as solidarity insurance, based on Sharia rules. Minister of Economy and Finance Mohamed Boussaid indicated that interest in Islamic insurance is growing steadily and will occupy a more prominent place within the international financial system. The draft law highlights the need for contracts to precisely stipulate the form of financial compensation of the insurance company, the amount of this compensation, how surpluses are distributed between participants, and the insurance company's financial investment policy. The law also forbids the Islamic insurance company from providing any other conventional insurance services.

A new chapter called "macro-prudential supervision" is also being added to the current banking Law 34-03 to create a new governmental supervisory body (the Supervisory and Coordination Committee of Systemic Risks) to analyze the risks of the financial market.

10. COMPETITION FROM STATE-OWNED ENTERPRISES

Reform of the state-owned enterprise sector in Morocco has undergone three distinct phases: 1) structural reforms in the 1980s; 2) modernization of their environment in the 1990s; and 3) the liberalization of numerous industries in the 2000s.

The public enterprise portfolio consists of 241 state-owned enterprises (SOEs), 42 percent of which operate in productive sectors and 38 percent in the social domain, according to a 2012 report by the OECD (http://www.keepeek.com/Digital-Asset-Management/oecd/governance/towards-new-arrangements-for-state-ownership-in-the-middle-east-and-north-africa/corporate-governance-of-state-owned-enterprises-in-morocco_9789264169111-8-en#page4). The Treasury has direct equity interest in 44 companies, 43 percent of which operate in the infrastructure sector. Act No. 69-00 on State Financial Control of Public Enterprises, adopted in 2003, defined Moroccan SOEs for the first time using three distinct categories: (1) state companies are those in which public bodies hold all the equity, (2) public subsidiaries are companies of which public bodies hold more than half the equity, and (3) semi-public companies are companies of which public bodies hold less than half of the equity.

Forty-nine percent of SOE firms are affiliated with three public holding companies (*Caisse de Depot et de Gestion*, OCP SA, and *Banque Centrale Populaire*); 119 are local or regional in scope; 53 have subsidiaries or affiliates abroad; and 11 are publicly traded.

Several sectors remain under public monopoly, managed either directly by public institutions (phosphate production, rail transport, some postal services, acceptance of savings through the national savings bank, airport services) or by the municipalities (wholesale distribution of fruit and vegetables, fish, slaughterhouses). Several activities that were traditionally run by the government are now open to private domestic or foreign operators, under the delegated management or concession arrangements generally subject to tendering procedures. This is the case, for example, with water and electricity distribution, construction and operation of motorways, and the management of non-hazardous wastes.

OECD Guidelines on Corporate Governance of SOEs

The Moroccan National Commission on Corporate Governance was established in 2007. It prepared the first Moroccan Code of Good Corporate Governance Practices in 2008. Based on the OECD Principles of Corporate Governance, it applies to both the private and public sectors. Recognizing the specific features of the SOE sector, the Commission drafted in 2011 a code dedicated to state-owned enterprises, drawing on the OECD Guidelines on Corporate Governance of SOEs. The code, which came into effect in 2012, is aimed at enhancing SOE's overall performance. It requires greater use of standardized public procurement and accounting rules, outside audits, the inclusion of independent directors, board evaluations, greater transparency, and better disclosure.

Moroccan SOEs are overseen by boards of directors or supervisory boards. These bodies are governed by the Financial Control Act and the Limited Liability Companies Act. The MoEF's Department of Public Enterprises and Privatization monitors SOE governance. Pursuant to Act No. 69-00, SOE annual accounts are published. Under Act No. 62-99, or the Financial Jurisdictions Code, the Court of Accounts and the Regional Courts of Accounts audit the management of a number of public enterprises.

Currently, a number of governance-related initiatives are a priority. These include an initiative that aims to help SOEs contribute to the emergence of regional development clusters. The government is also attempting to improve the use of multi-year contracts with major SOEs as tool to enhance performance and transparency.

11. CORPORATE SOCIAL RESPONSIBILITY (CSR)

OECD Guidelines for Multinational Enterprises

While there is no legislation mandating specific levels of CSR, foreign and some local enterprises follow generally accepted principles such as the OECD CSR guidelines for multinational companies. NGOs are also taking an increasingly active role in monitoring corporations' CSR performance. Morocco's national contact point is the Moroccan Investment Agency (www.invest.gov.ma).

CSR has gained strength in tandem with Morocco's economic expansion and stability. The country's businesses are slowly taking responsibility for the impact of their activities on the environment, communities, employees and consumers. For example, CGEM has awarded "social labels" to companies based on a systematic analysis of the effects of their activities. The

Moroccan Association of Textile and Apparel Industries also award a "*Fibre Citoyenne*" label to worthy companies. Additionally, Morocco launched the UN Global Compact network in 2006 in Casablanca. The project provides support to companies who affirm their commitment to social responsibility. The major trade unions (CDT, UMT, UGMT, and FDT) and CGEM were among its initial members. Maroc Telecom joined in November 2012, demonstrating its commitment to adhere to the Compact's principles in the area of human rights, labor law, environment, and corruption.

AmCham in Morocco has five committees, including one that promotes good corporate citizenship and social responsibility. The Director General of Dell is currently the Chairperson of this committee, which focuses on recognizing excellence in CSR of AmCham members. The committee also develops public-private sector partnerships and implements programs that have an educational, philanthropic, and/or socially responsible nature within the broader context of U.S.-Morocco economic relations.

12. POLITICAL VIOLENCE

Morocco is a monarchy with a constitution, government, Parliament and judiciary, in which ultimate power and authority rest with the King. A process of qualified democratic reform is underway, and the country is broadly regarded as politically stable. The U.S. government maintains excellent relations with Morocco and designated Morocco a Major Non-NATO Ally in 2004. A series of terrorist bombings in Casablanca in March 2003, March and April 2007, as well as the bombing of the Argana Café in Marrakesh in April 2011, underscore that Morocco continues to face a terrorist threat. Counterterrorism cooperation is excellent. The Moroccan Government aggressively investigates terrorist suspects and has dismantled a number of terrorist cells over the past years.

Demonstrations occur frequently in Morocco and usually center on domestic issues. Most demonstrations have been peaceful and orderly. There are infrequent reports of anti-American sentiment and isolated instances of violence. In September 2012, protesters held demonstrations in Casablanca in response to the video, *The Innocence of Muslims,* produced in the U.S. The largest turnout of the two demonstrations consisted of 200 - 300 protesters who gathered near the U.S. Consulate.

During periods of heightened regional tension, large demonstrations may take place in major cities. Additionally, the Arab Spring of 2011 led to the creation of the February 20th Movement in Morocco. This disparate group of protesters took to the street in numbers of between a few hundred to tens of thousands almost every Sunday from its inception through March 2012. It has since attempted to inspire new popular protests, but attendance is often low. Unions and labor groups occasionally organize public demonstrations to protest working conditions, salary levels, or other social benefit issues.

The sparsely settled Western Sahara was the site of armed conflict between the Moroccan government and the POLISARIO Front, which demands independence. A cease-fire has been in effect since 1991, but sovereignty over the territory remains disputed. Negotiations to reach a settlement resumed in 2007 under UN auspices, but the dispute hampers development in the territory, as well as economic and political integration in the North Africa region.

13. CORRUPTION

According to the 2013 State Department's Country Report on Human Rights Practices, Moroccan law provides criminal penalties for official corruption, but the government does not implement the law effectively. Officials often engage in corrupt practices with impunity. Corruption is a serious problem in the executive branch, including police, as well as the legislative and judicial branches of government. There have been reports of government corruption and several notable prosecutions. In July 2013 courts sentenced the director general of the National Airports Office to five years in prison for embezzlement of public funds. Observers generally consider corruption a serious problem, particularly among magistrates. In 2013, courts sentenced magistrates from Kenitra, Taza, Meknes, and Inezgane to prison terms for corruption.

The King, who has made statements calling for judicial system reform since 2009, acknowledged the judiciary's lack of independence and susceptibility to influence. Many members of the well-entrenched and conservative judicial community are loath to adopt new procedures.

The Central Commission for the Prevention of Corruption (ICPC) is the agency responsible for combating corruption but lacks authority to require responses from government institutions. In 2010 ICPC set up an internet portal for civil society and small businesses to identify instances of corruption: www.stopcorruption.ma. ICPC also publishes quarterly reports covering specific cases of corruption and the outcome of any subsequent prosecution. ICPC acknowledges that the anticorruption situation has not improved significantly and that governmental policy continues to lack a strategic dimension and effective commitment.

In addition to ICPC, MOJL and the government accountability court have jurisdiction over corruption issues but have pursued no high-profile cases. The inspector general of MOJL investigated 107 ethics complaints against judges in 2012, which resulted in the referral of three judges to the Supreme Judicial Council for disciplinary measures.

Observers have noted that there is widespread corruption in the police force. The government claims to investigate corruption and other instances of police malfeasance through an internal mechanism. Authorities did not provide official information on the results of the investigations.

In the 2013 Corruption Perception Index published by Transparency International (TI) http://www.libertadciudadana.org/archivos/ipc2013/2013_CPIBrochure_EN.pdf, Morocco dropped 3 spots from its 2012 rank of 88 to 91 out of 177 countries. Government officials have criticized the Index, which reflects public perceptions concerning corruption, for not emphasizing recent anti-corruption efforts. These include enhancing the transparency of public tenders and implementation of a requirement that senior government officials declare their assets at the start and end of their government service.

The latest TI report on Morocco:
http://www.transparency.org/gcb2013/country/?country=morocco.

Transparency International National Chapter:

Mr. Abdessamad Saddouq
transparency@menara.ma
+212-522-542-699
http://www.transparencymaroc.ma/index.php

UN Anticorruption Convention

Morocco signed the UN Convention against Corruption in 2007 and hosted the States Parties to the Convention's Fourth Session in 2011.

Morocco has published its anti-corruption measures here:http://www.invest.gov.ma/upload/documents/en_Doc_223.pdf

14. BILATERAL INVESTMENT AGREEMENTS (BITS)

Morocco has BITs with the following countries:

Argentina
Austria
Bahrain
Belgium
Benin
Cameroon
Central African Republic
Chad
China
Croatia
Czech Republic
Denmark
Dominican Republic
Egypt
El Salvador
Equatorial Guinea
Finland
France
Gabon
Germany
Greece
Hungary
India
Indonesia
Iran
Italy
Jordan
Kuwait
Lebanon
Libyan Arab Jamahiriya
Luxembourg
Malaysia
Mauritania
Netherlands
Oman
Pakistan
Poland
Portugal
Qatar
Republic of Korea
Romania
Senegal
Slovakia
Spain
Sudan
Sweden
Syrian Arab Republic
Tunisia
Turkey
Ukraine
United Arab Emirates
United Kingdom
United States of America
Yemen

The U.S. and Morocco signed a BIT on July 22, 1985, but its provisions were subsumed by the investment chapter of the U.S.-Morocco FTA, which entered into force on January 1, 2006. The BIT's dispute settlement provisions remain in effect for ten years after the effective date of the FTA for certain investments and investment disputes which predate the Agreement.

Investment Chapter of the FTA:
http://www.ustr.gov/sites/default/files/uploads/agreements/fta/morocco/asset_upload_file651_3838.pdf

Bilateral Taxation Treaties

The U.S. signed an income tax treaty with Morocco in 1977: http://www.irs.gov/pub/irs-trty/morocco.pdf.

15. OPIC AND OTHER INVESTMENT INSURANCE PROGRAMS

Morocco signed an agreement with OPIC in 1961. The agreement was updated in 1995 and ratified by the Moroccan parliament in June 2004. The agreement can be found here: http://www.opic.gov/sites/default/files/docs/africa/Morocco-1995.pdf

In August 2013, OPIC provided its consent for a new $40 million, eight-year term loan facility with Attijariwafa Bank to support loans to small and medium-sized enterprises (SMEs) in Morocco under a risk sharing agreement between OPIC and Citi Maghreb. OPIC has a long history of supporting projects in Morocco and has provided finance or insurance support to 22 deals over the past four decades. This recent agreement between Citi Maghreb and OPIC is OPIC's first risk-sharing agreement for the banking sector in Morocco.

16. LABOR

Morocco is in a paradoxical situation: large numbers of graduates are unable to find jobs commensurate with their education and training, while employers complain of skills shortages and mismatches. According to some U.S. companies in Morocco, qualified labor is not only rare, it is also expensive, with wages equivalent to those in France.

In 2012 the World Bank described the problem of youth unemployment in Morocco as "very serious." Youth (aged 15 to 29) make up about 30 percent of Morocco's total population and 44 percent of the working age population (aged 15 to 64). According to a June 2012 World Bank report, Moroccan youth are largely excluded from the sustained economic growth the country has experienced in the last decade.

World Bank report: http://www.youthpolicy.org/national/Morocco_2012_Youth_Report.pdf

The national unemployment rate for the first trimester of 2014 was 10.2 percent (up from 9.4 percent from the same period last year) with urban unemployment reaching 14.6 percent compared to 5.1 percent rural unemployment. Overall, 20.2 percent of youth aged 15-24 were unemployed (36.7 percent urban youth unemployed versus 9.9 percent rural youth unemployed) and 17.5 percent of university graduates were unemployed. Nearly 20 percent of graduates in urban areas were unemployed. Unemployment rates are disproportionately higher for graduates from universities, secondary schools, and vocational training institutions that have open enrollment.

Source : *Haut Commissariat au Plan* http://www.hcp.ma

Lowering youth unemployment is a government priority since high youth unemployment has historically resulted in serious social and political tensions. Moreover, without a trained workforce capable of increasing productivity, Morocco cannot generate sufficient prosperity through private-sector growth.

USAID is launching a $38 million project to address this challenge and enhance the employability of young Moroccans. The project will help university and vocational students' transition from school to work by building stronger links between education institutions and the private sector.

According to the State Department's Country Report on Human Rights Practices (http://www.state.gov/j/drl/rls/hrrpt/humanrightsreport/index.htm#wrapper), the Moroccan constitution grants workers the right to form and join unions, strike, and bargain collectively, with some restrictions (S 396-429 Labor Code Act 1999, No. 65/99). The law prohibits certain categories of government employees, including members of the armed forces, police, and some members of the judiciary, from forming and joining unions and from conducting strikes. The labor code does not cover domestic workers.

The law concerning strikes requires compulsory arbitration of disputes, prohibits sit-ins, calls for a ten-day notice of a strike, and allows for the hiring of replacement workers. The government may intervene in strikes. The government generally respects freedom of association and the right to collective bargaining. Labor disputes (S 549-581 Labor Code Act 1999, No. 65/99) are common and in some cases result in employers failing to implement collective bargaining agreements and withholding wages. Trade unions complain that the government at times uses Article 288 of the penal code to prosecute workers for striking and to suppress strikes.

Once strong and politically influential, the Moroccan trade union movement is now fragmented and no longer possesses the political clout it had 50 years ago when it helped lead the country to independence. Nevertheless, 5 of the more than 25 trade union federations remain strong enough to wield some political influence. Although unions claim high membership rates, Morocco has about 600,000 unionized workers, less than six percent of the 11.26 million person workforce.

Investors continue to view labor regulations as a significant constraint. They complain that procedures regarding lay-offs remain complicated and onerous, imposing a significant financial burden on companies. Rules regarding foreign personnel are also vague and can lead to conflicting interpretations and arbitrary decisions.

Morocco's labor code prohibits all forms of forced or compulsory labor. Penalties for forced labor include a fine for the first offense and jail term of up to three months for subsequent offences. The minimum age for employment in all sectors is 15 (S 143 Labor Code Act 1999, No. 65/99). The law prohibits any employee from working more than 10 hours per day except under specific circumstances.

Morocco's minimum wage for the industrial sector (SMIG) was recently renegotiated and will increase by ten percent to 13.46 dh/hour (or $1.66/hour) by July 2015. While the minimum wage will increase consumer purchasing power, many in the business community fear a loss of competitiveness. According to Morocco's business association CGEM, minimum wage has increased annually between 2001 and 2012 by 9.7 percent while inflation has increased by 1.7 percent. In exchange for the increase in minimum wage, CGEM has asked for the government to update its regulation on strikes and the Labor Code.

Morocco has ratified the following International Labor Organization (ILO) conventions:

Forced Labor Convention (1957); Right to Organize and Collective Bargaining (1957); Equal Remuneration (1979); Abolition of Forced labor (1966); Discrimination-Employment and Occupation (1963); Minimum Age (2000); and the Worst Forms of Child Labor Convention (2001). Morocco has yet to ratify the Freedom of Association and Protection of the Right to Organize Convention.

For a list of the 62 ILO conventions Morocco has ratified, see here: http://www.ilo.org/dyn/normlex/en/f?p=1000:11200:0::NO:11200:P11200_COUNTRY_ID:102993.

17. FOREIGN TRADE ZONES/FREE PORTS

Instituted by Law 19-94 (Dahir No. 1-95-1 dated January 26, 1995), export processing zones are identified areas of the customs territory where industrial and commercial export activities are exempted from customs regulations, foreign trade and exchange control. Each zone is created and defined by a decree which stipulates the nature and activities of the companies that can operate in the zone.

Free zones in Morocco include: Nouaceur Free Zone in Casablanca; Tanger Free Zone; Tanger Automotive City; Tetouan Shore; Oujda Free Zone; and the Atlantic Free Zone.

Detailed information on Morocco's free zones (French): http://www.ilo.org/wcmsp5/groups/public/@ed_dialogue/@actrav/documents/publication/wcms_183548.pdf.

General information on Morocco's free zones (English): http://www.invest.gov.ma

Morocco's National Pact for Industrial Emergence aims to attract investment in aeronautics, automobile, offshoring, electronics, textile and leather, and the food industry.

18. FOREIGN DIRECT INVESTMENT AND FOREIGN PORTFOLIO INVESTMENT STATISTICS

TABLE 2: Key Macroeconomic data, U.S. FDI in host country/economy

	Host Country Statistical source		USG or international statistical source		Source of Data
Economic Data	Year	Amount	Year	Amount	
Host Country Gross Domestic Product (GDP) (billion U.S. Dollars)	(2012)	$96.75	(2012)	$95.98	International Source: http://www.worldbank.org/en/country Local Source: http://www.bkam.ma/
Foreign Direct Investment	Host Country Statistical source		USG or international statistical source		
U.S. FDI in partner country (Millions U.S. Dollars, stock position)	(2012)	$217.72 $1,900 $600	(2012)	$613	USG Source: Bureau of Economic Analysis Morocco's government statistical source provides information on FDI flows* http://www.oc.gov.ma/portal/ Moroccan Ministry of the Economy and Finance reports stock: http://www.finances.gov.ma/fr/SitePages/Home.aspx Unofficial host country press cites

					the total value of U.S. FDI stock to Morocco $600 million: http://financenews.press.ma/Economie/maroc-usa-une-visite-royale-a-forte-connotation-economique.html
Total inbound stock of FDI as % host GDP	(2012)	3.8% 49.2%	(2011)	22%	International Source: The IMF's Coordinated Direct Investment Survey reported that total FDI stock* to Morocco in 2011 were estimated at $21 billion: http://cdis.imf.org/ Morocco's government reported that total FDI flows* to Morocco in 2012 were estimated at $3.7 billion: http://www.oc.gov.ma/portal/ Morocco's Ministry of the Economy and Finance reported that total FDI stock to Morocco in 2012 was $47 billion http://www.finances.gov.ma/fr/SitePages/Home.aspx

*Official statistics from the host country on FDI stock are unavailable.

TABLE 3: Sources and Destination of FDI

Inward Direct Investment		
From Top Five Sources (US Dollars, Millions) End of 2011		
Total Inward investment	21,059	100%
France	15,580	74%
Sweden	1,203	6%
Spain	1,109	5%
Kuwait	607	3%
Switzerland	535	3%

Source: http://cdis.imf.org

PRIVATIZATION

Morocco started in 1993 a new stage of its privatization program. This program completed liberal measures taken in the 1980s to liberalize Morocco's economy and industry.

The law authorizes the transfer to the private sector of 112 enterprises (75 companies and 37 hotels). A law amendment extended the deadline of the privatization program from December 31, 1995 to December 31, 1998 and added to the list two enterprises: SAMIR and SCP. If the two companies' equity shares in other companies is taken into account, privatization involves 40% of the state portfolio.

THE CASABLANCA STOCK MARKET

The Moroccan financial market has witnessed a considerable evolution during the last years, due mainly to the privatization program. The turnover went up from 672 million DH in 1989 to 23.9 billion Dh in 1995.

Meanwhile, the stock market capitalization progressed from 5 billion Dh in 1989 to 39.0 billion Dh in 1995.

During the same period, the average turnover for each session went up 167 folds, from a daily 0.5 million to 82.6 million. The improvement of these indicators was even consolidated since privatization was made through the stock market.

Under the law adopted in 1993, the Casablanca stock market status changed from a public institution to a private one whose capital is equally shared by the stock market firms. In parallel, the creation of the Deontologic Council of Stocks and Bonds (Conseil Déontologique des Valeurs Mobilières) helped in the smooth running of thee market and ensured the protection of savers. In 1995, reforms were carried on with the setting forth of the new implement regulating the Stock Market activity.

MOROCCO ECONOMY STRUCTURE

The structures of the Moroccan economy was built in various stages from the turn of the century.

Originally, the economy was pre-capitalistic based on agriculture and handicrafts.
The modern economy started developing from 1912 around the following:

* A modern agricultural sector, the production of which was geared to export.
* An industrial sector, mainly manufacturing industries linked to French enterprises.

* A mining sector to meet the raw material demands of the French market.
A vigorous equipment policy made it possible for the country to acquire the necessary infrastructures.

This development had nonetheless some negative aspects: the traditional agricultural sector did not benefit from modernization trends; the handicraft sector was disorganized by competition from the industrial sector; and industry only met the needs of the French economy rather than those of the local population.

As from independence, the Moroccan authorities devoted their efforts to ensuring economic development linked to the national economy.

To achieve that, this country had to create an industrial sector that would seek to tap natural resources and exploit all the agricultural production potentiality. This led to important state intervention.

The first signs of such a policy lie in the initiation of development plans, the lion's share going to the public and para-public sectors, especially at the investment level.

However, in the last thirty years, Morocco has undertaken several economic and institutional changes which are positive assets for development strategies. To improve the economic environment and ensure greater openness on the outside world, encouragement of private industrial investments was developed as follows:

- Incentives within the framework of the Investment Codes regulations,
- Creation of the Office for Industrial Development, to design an implement industrial projects.

- Liberalization of the economy,
- Simplification of administrative procedures,
- Privatization of large sectors of the economy.

This policy of reforms has produced remarkable results.
From 1982 to 1991, average annual growth was about 4%, the balance of payments deficit and the budget deficit improved, and hard currency reserves rose to 6 months of imports.

Major changes have affected most productive sectors, in industry, mining or tourism.

The structure of Gross Domestic Product also improved: primary sector: 20%, secondary sector: 27% , tertiary sector: 37%, and the public administration 16%.

MAJOR ECONOMIC SECTORS AND BUSINESS OPPORTUNITIES

KEY ECONOMIC SECTORS AND BUSINESS OPPORTUNITIES

AGRICULTURE

The agricultural sector is among the priority sectors of economic activity in Morocco. Almost 50% of the working population is involved in agriculture related activities.

The policy of dam construction initiated in the early 1960's coupled with the development of irrigation projects made it possible to alleviate the impact of capricious climatic changes on agricultural production.

84 large dams are currently operational in Morocco. The launching of other works such as the Alwahda and the Hachef dams will increase water storage capacity from the current 10 billion cubic meters to 14 billion cubic meters.

The national irrigation plan is to irrigate 250,000 extra hectares which will benefit from the waters of the dams already in operation and to restore making 200,000 hectares of land currently under irrigation.

The total irrigated area is 899,150 hectares, making it possible to alleviate the impact of droughts . Projects for the year 2004 aim at irrigating 1 million hectares.

PRODUCTION

Cereals

Area in 100ha Production in 1000qs Yield (qs/ha)

Soft wheat	1714	31809	18.6	
Hard wheat	1336	23423	17.6	
Barley	2582	37199	14.4	
Maize	324	2026		6.3

Pulses

Area in 100ha Production in 1000 qs Yield (qs/ha)

broad beans		123	1111	9.0 Chickpeas 66 468 7.1
Peas		42	288	7.7
Lentils	42	357	8.5	
other	74	543	7.3	
TOTAL	347	2767	8.1	

Early vegetables and citrus fruit

Production per 1000t Exports per 1000t

Early vegetables 648

including: Tomatoes 375 175 .Potatoes 149 83 .other vegetables 124 33

Citrus fruits 1324

including: Oranges 925 358. Tangerines 343 177 .Other products 56 21

LIVESTOCK

Livestock total 20.2 million head including :
- cattle 2.23 million
- sheep 13.9 million
- goats 4.06 million

Meat production
- red meat 295,000 t
- white meat 160,000 t

FORESTS

The total forest area is 9 million hectares. 5.3 million ha are natural forests, 0.5 million ha afforestation and 3.2 million ha of Alfa grossland. The natural forest is rich in tree species: evergreen oak 24% , argan tree 15%, thuya 11%, juniper 6%, cork oak 6%, cedar 2%, pine and fir 2%, other secondary species 34%. The main forest regions are in the Centre -North 32% and the North-West 22%.

WORKS IN PROGRESS AND PROJECTS

1. Works in progress:

Project « Haut service des Doukkala »
Aim : Development of 16,000 ha irrigated agriculture.
Cost : 4 billion DH.

Entire Right Bank of the Loukkos River.
Aim : development of 7,000 ha of irrigated agriculture.
Cost : 689 million DH.

Project for the Improvement of Large Scale Irrigation: Phase 2.
Aim : rehabilitation of obsolete equipment.
Cost : 367 million DH.

Project Had Cort Ouezzane
Integrated project.
Aim : improvement of agricultural production and livestock.
Cost : 295 million DH.

Eastern Project
Aim : development of livestock and pastures.
Cost : 412 million DH.

Support Project for Agricultural Development
Aim : increase agricultural production and farmer's income by introducing modern techniques.
Cost : 312.7 million DH.

Forestry Project, Phase I
Aim : preservation and rehabilitation of forest soil
Cost : 270 million DH.

Pipeline Project
Central Haouz Project, Phase II
Aim : Development of irrigation agriculture (20,000 ha)
Cost : 556 MDHS
Implementation duration : 1995-2004

FISHERIES

With almost 3,500 km of coastline and a 200 mile exclusive economic zone, Morocco has a big maritime fishing potentialities. Morocco is the first African and Arab producer or exporter of fish products.

Production	741,000 tons
Consumption	190,000 tons
Processing	419,000 tons
Exports	5.8 billion DH
Investments	29 billion DH
Job Opportunities	400,000

Maritime fishing production is made up of benthic species mainly white fish and crustaceans, as well as the pelagic species like sardines, mackerel, anchovies, tuna, etc. The pelagic fish is partly destined for the food processing industry.

Sardines are the most plentiful and represent almost 70% of coastal fishing activity.

PRODUCTION

Activity Sectors: Group Species: Weight (tons) Value(MDHS)

Coastal	547,570 686,271
Pelagic	61,367 792,189
Total	608,937 1,478,460

fishing Cephalopods white fish	89,500	2,810
bentics pelagic	32,700	91
shrimps	5,900	243
other	6,500	108
Total coastal fishing	134,600	3,252
Aquaculture	1,363	96
Algae	5,367	58
coral	5	6
madrague(tuna)	422 21	
Total	**7,147 181**	

EXPORTS

Products weight (tons) value (thousand Dhs)

fresh salted fish	32,031 741,941	
crustaceas		
and shell-fish	112,051	3,520,622
canned fish	59,381	1,439,843

bone meal	2,968	8,810
fish oil	705	1,897
algae	962	11,991
agar-agar	962	143,635
coral	6 5,752	
TOTAL:	209,230	5,874,448

MAIN FISHING PORTS

Agadir, Tan Tan, Essaouira, Safi, El Jadida, Casablanca, Mohammedia, Rabat, Kenitra, Larache, Tangier, Alhoceima, Nador, Layoune, Dakhla

FISHING FLEET:

Number of fishing vessels and boats : 14,991 units, including:
Coastal fleet : 2,564 totaling 72,125 gross tons
boats : 12,000 totaling 14,000 "
high sea fleet : 427 totaling 135,500 "

LEGISLATIVE INCENTIVES:

The maritime investment code grants maritime fishing and merchant shipping enterprises and harbor craft fiscal advantages, equipment bonuses and currency transfer guarantees for non residents. (See chapter on maritime investment code).

Major Guidelines of The Agreement Pertaining to the Relations Between

Morocco and the E.U. on Maritime Fishing

Morocco and the EU have signed the UN Convention on Maritime Law.

In compliance with this Convention, Morocco has sovereignty over a 200 nautical mile exclusive zone.

The 1992 fishing accord signed between Morocco and the EU was established with the aim of setting up a free exchange zone.

In accordance with the agreement :

Morocco grants EU fishing fleet fishing opportunities within its zone in accordance with the limits and conditions stated in the protocol.

In return, the EU grants Morocco financial aid and backing to implement programs, research and specific studies to improve management of fishing resources, the creation and development of joint ventures, the training of ship crews, the development of aqua culture and the search for new fishing techniques.

THE PROTOCOL'S BROAD LINES :

The protocol specifies the conditions for fishing by EU fleets inside the Moroccan fishing zone. Hence, it deals with :

- Provisions for applicaitons, issue and validity of fishing licences;

- The fees to be paid;

- Payment modalities for fishing rights and dues;

- Ship logs and data communication on fish catches;

- Import modalities within EU for fish products and canned sardines

Moroccan origin: Partial suspension of customs duties for these imports

- The amount of the financial equivalent and support of the EU to Morocco;

- Technical files for each fishing category indicating the fishing zones, tonnage,

MAXIMUM NUMBER OF AUTHORIZED FISHING BOATS AND THE TYPE OF EQUIPMENT USED.

OBJECTIVES:

- From 800,000 to 1,000,000 tons
- $1 billion exports
- Consumption doubling
- Job opportunities doubling

ENERGY

Being a non oil-producing country, Morocco imports more than 80% of its energy requirements.

Imports in 1993: 8.9 billion DH , 41% of total imports.

OIL PRODUCTS

Nearly all products are imported as raw materials. Refining is done by the Société Marocaine de l'Industrie et du Raffinage (Samir) and the Société Chérifienne des Pétroles (SCP). Consumption: 5.8 million tons of oil equivalent.

COAL

The Jerada coal deposit was discovered in the northeast Morocco in 1927 and has been run since 1932 by Société des Charbonnages du Maroc.

-Potential reserves : 100 million tons of which more than 20 million have already been extracted.
- Production : 615,000 tons .
- Coke imports : 1 million tons worth 483 million DH

POWER

In 1993 power production in Morocco reached 10 billion Kwh and 1 billion Kwh was imported. This production is provided by :

- 22 hydro-electric plants of 686,750 Kw capacity;
- 5 thermal plants of 1,151,000 Kw capacity;
- 8 gas-powered turbine plants of 498,500 Kw capacity;
- 16 diesel-powered plants of 55,500 Kw capacity.

Other thermal and hydro-electric production units are either under construction or projected for construction by the year 2004.

Consumption, which amounts to 9,800 million Kw, is broken down as follows:

Domestic	37%
Industry	36%
Mining	9%
Agriculture	6%
Transport	3%
Other	9%

FUTURE PROJECTS:

NUCLEAR POWER PROJECT:

This project aims, to diversify energy resources necessary for power production, and on the other hand develop the uranium content of phosphate rock which could supply the projected nuclear power plants.

For this purpose, the Centre National de l'Energie des Science et des Techniques Nucleaires was created and will be fitted with a 2 Megawatt nuclear reactor. This organization will foster nuclear techniques utilization in vital sectors of the national economy. Site and center location studies have identified of a site in the Maamora forest near Rabat. The site is currently being investigated and the necessary reconnaissance works are under way prior to its adoption.

THE TARFAYA OIL SHALE PROJECT

The national power authority « O.N.E. » is about to complete a feasibility study on the use of fluidised bed furnace technology. The aim is to determine oil shale combustion parameters in order to analyze performance on an industrial scale.

RURAL POWER SUPPLY

3 programs are under way :

- PNER: national program for rural power supply;
- PNED: national program for decentralized power supply (renewable energy);
- PNER II: 1990-2004.
- PPER : rural pre-electric program.

The project aims at providing electricity for 600 centers. It will also make it possible to supply 190,000 households with electricity.

The total cost of the second phase is 2,532 million DH.

* The PNED 1993-2004

The PNED project is implemented to supply quick and adapted power networks to villages not connected by the PNER in the short or medium terms. 12 provinces, of which more than half are located in the North, will benefit from the project. Power supply is ensured by renewable energy resources: solar and wind energy. Power will also be supplied via micro hydropower stations.

- 180 villages were electrified.

- power supply to 200 villages

- power supply to 240 villages

PPER

It is a pilot program undertaken in three provinces (Azilal, Safi and Errachidia) and plans to supply power to rural centers via renewable energy resources.

240 villages are planned for power supply connection.

¤ The Spanish - Moroccan interconnection: 150 MW capacity

The aim of this project is to link the Spanish and Moroccan power supply networks.

Capacity: 150 MW for the first 1996 semester extended to 300 MW from the second 1996 semester on to the end of 1998.

¤ Program of equipment and operational schedules for thermal and hydraulic power supply stations

THERMAL PLANTS

Works under construction operational date

TAG Tetouan 99Mw
JORF LASFAR II 330 Mw
Works scheduled to be completed by 2004
* Koudia Blanco windmill park 30-50 Mw
(concessional production of electricity)
JORF LASFAR III 330 Mw mid 1999
JORF LASFAR IV 330 Mw mid 1999
* First cycle 300-600Mw beginning 1998
(Mohammedia)

HYDRAULIC PLANTS:

dams under construction:
Allal El Fassi 240 MW end 2nd quarter 94
Dams scheduled for completion in 2004:
Al Wahda 248MW first semester 97
SIDI DRISS 31 MW end 1997

M'DEZ 52 MW end of 1999
El MENZEL 148MW end of 2004
Dachar El Oued 6.4 MW end of 2004

MAGHREB - EUROPE GAS PIPELINE:

This project will enable Morocco to use natural gas. The aim is to supply the Spanish and Portuguese markets with Algerian gas in the first place, then the French and German markets in a subsequent phase. Progress report on the project:

A factory in Nador completed the preparation of 400 km of pipes. Sea works were started in July 1994 and will be followed by the laying down of gas pipelines between November and December 1995.

- Investment: 383.3 million $
- Investment: 440 million $

The Maghreb - Europe gas pipeline project will be operational at the beginning of 1996.

MINING

The sector represents 30% of export earnings and employs almost 60,000 persons. Moreover, it contributes 3% to GDP. Mining production is north 4.5 billion DH for 19.3 million tons, mainly phosphates.

PHOSPHATES

Moroccan soil contains ¾ of world reserves. Morocco is the first world exporter and the third largest producer after the USA and Russia. Phosphate mining is a state monopoly run by the Cherifian Office of Phosphates « OCP ». Extraction is carried out in Khouribga, Youssoufia, Benguerir and Boukraa. Phosphate production reached 18.3 million tons.

OTHER MINERALS

There are mainly iron ore, zinc, lead, copper, manganese, fluorine, barytine, etc. For the other minerals, the state carries out research through the Bureau des Recherches et d'Exploitation Pétrolière (BRPM). The BRPM field of activity covers the whole of the mining sector - except for phosphates- from research, exploitation, to processing and marketing activities.

THE MAJOR MINING ZONES IN MOROCCO

- 60 to 120 km from the Atlantic coast and central Morocco where phosphates, lead, fluorine and antimony are found.
- The Anti-Atlas contains deposits of copper, manganese, precious and strategic metals (cobalt, tin, titanium and sulfur).
- The High Atlas contains deposits of lead, zinc, copper, manganese, iron ore and barytine.
- The Rif contains iron ore, zinc, antimony, strategic metals and fuller's earth.
- The East contains lead and zinc.

MINERAL PROCESSING

In the field of Mineral Processing, Morocco has been active since 1965 with:

- Maroc-Chimie I and II chemical complexes which process Youssoufia

PHOSPHATES.

- Maroc Phosphore I and II works which process Benguerir phosphates.
- Oued El Heimer foundry in Oujda which processes most of the extracted lead.

Production and Exports of Mining Products per 1000 tons

On 1000 tons	Production	Exports
Phosphate rock	18,307	8,398
Barytine	364.6	323.1
Iron ore	66.3	55.1
Lead	111.9	35.6
Chemical manganese	42.6	39.6
Copper	35.8	37.1
Fluorine	70.0	59.2
Zinc	125.7	115.7

INCENTIVES

There is an investment code for the mining sector wich offers fiscal and financial benefits for mining and miningrelated enterprises (see "Investemnt Codes"section).

PROCESSING AND LOADING OF PHOSPHATES

The project is for a 4 million ton/year are washing plant in Khouribga for enriching through washing and flotation « low content » phosphates from Sidi Chennane, a raw phosphate rock train station with a 4.9 million ton/year capacity at Jorf Lasfar. It will take 24 months to complete. The total cost excluding tax amounts to 95.5 million $.

Maroc Phosphore V and VI

The Maroc Phosphore V and VI project comprise mainly include :

- A sulfur unit with an annual capacity of 4,500,000 tons

- An eight-line phosphoric acid unit of 500 tons, P205/day/line, or an annual capacity of 1,400,000 tons.

- A fertilizer production unit of 90 tons /hour/line, or, an annual capacity of 2,600,000 tons DAP.

This complex will be located in Jorf Lasfar, and work will be spread over a 4- year period. Production is due to start in 1998. The total cost of the project is 1,348.3 million $.

Purchase of three chemical tankers

The building of three ships equipped with stainless steel central tanks to carry phosphoric acid exported by Maroc Phosphore and also fitted with specially-coated lateral tanks for the transport of chemical products on the return leg. The project will be completed in 36 months and the total cost is 97.8 million $.

MANUFACTURING INDUSTRIES

The industrial sector is the mainstay of our economy because of its potential and performance. It offers important opportunities for direct investment, joint ventures and subcontracting opportunities. Industrial production totaled 117 billion DH yielded by 6,200 companies which employ a workforce of 444,000

Companies with foreign participation (1,038 units) contributed 32% of the industrial output. The added value of manufacturing industries amounted to 36 billion DH, or 15% of the GDP. Exports of industrial products rose to 287 billion DH in 2003 : over 81% of total exports against 39% in 1981 and 45% in 1985.

Branches contributing most to exports are textiles (25%), chemicals and para-chemicals (23%), food industries (19%), hosiery (16%) of total industrial exports.

APPROVED INDUSTRIAL INVESTMENTS

The total amounts to 8.3 billion DH, broken down as follows :

INDUSTRIAL SECTORS	VALUE (1000 DH)
Chemicals & para-chemicals	2,368,561
Agribusiness	1,805,410
Industrial enterprises	1,707,073
Textile & leather	1,555,724
Mechanic & metallurgy	467,613
Electric and electronic	332,199
Industry-linked Service Enterprises	43,677
TOTAL	**8,280,257**

¤ Investment distribution

Moroccan private sector	68%
Public sector	15%
Foreign investment	17%

¤ Incentives

The industrial sector is governed by the Code of Industrial Investments which grants fiscal advantages, bonuses, and transfer guarantees for industrial enterprises and also for enterprises of an industrial nature and service enterprises linked to industry (see « Code of Industrial investments » in « Investment Codes»).

HANDICRAFTS

Handicrafts is one of the most important sectors due to its contribution to investment, employment and exports.

- Investment : 42 million DHS
- Total work force 1.5 million workers.
- Number of projects: 119
- Number of cooperatives: nearly 440 production units

EXPORTS :

In addition to the European market, Morocco has a foothold in other markets such as the United States, Canada, Arab and African countries.

Exports have reached 532 million DHS, of which 53% represented by carpet exports. Traditional garments and leather work represent respectively 11.8% and 7.8% of total exports. The remainder, i., e., 27%, consists of blankets, copper, wood, basket weaving and others products.

With 72.18% of total exported goods, the EU represents Morocco's first customer, followed by the USA (11%), Arab and African countries (9%).

INCENTIVES :

The Handicrafts Code of Investments grants fiscal advantages in addition to transfer guarantees to Moroccan handicrafts manufactures (cf. Code of Handicrafts Investments in « Investment Codes»).

MANUFACTURING INDUSTRIES

With the liberalization of its economy, Morocco has strengthened market mechanisms and excluded progressively the distortions, A better distribution of resources a good equilibrium between economic activities, and the improvement of productivity are reached through the application of adjusting measures.

In 2005, processing industries provided about 18.8 percent of Morocco's gross domestic product. They recorded an added value of US$ 5.2 billion. The total production of processing industries maintained their growth rate of recent years. Investments increased by 26 percent in 1995, reaching US$ 1.7 billion which 92 percent were provided by the private sector.

Foreign investment represented 21% of the total investment (US $ 345 million) a 19 percent increase from the previous year. Moroccan processing industries include the following sectors: Agriculture and food, chemicals and pharmaceuticals, textiles and leather, metallurgy and machinery, electrical equipment.

FOOD PROCESSING INDUSTRIES

The food processing sector plays a leading role in the Moroccan economy and includes the transformation of agricultural production, the supply of basic products for the country and the development of exports. Foreign investment in the food processing industry represents 27 percent of the total investment input and 17 percent of the sector's manpower. Leading areas of foreign investment in recent years included vegetable canning, the extraction of essential oils, greenhouse cultivation and industrial cold processing (frozen and deep-freeze). Examples of major foreign investments in this sector include:

NESTLE, which has developed a large range of products for both the local market and for export : dehydrated soups, evaporated and powdered milk, baby food, etc...

LUKUS, which farms several thousand acres for the production of oil resins, powdered tomatoes and powdered red pepper mainly for export.

THE SAUDI EL BARAKA GROUP, which invested in fish canneries and greenhouses.

BEL CHEESE- producing group.

LE SAFRE, specializing in baking yeast.

INVESTMENT OPPORTUNITIES

Agriculture, including gray champs, sea bream and bass as well as fresh water trout

Yeast and in particular baking yeast, with strong development possibilities both for the local market and export.

Vegetable conservation, including frozen goods as well as canned and dehydrated products.

TEXTILE AND LEATHER PRODUCTS

The textile and leather products sector is one of Morocco's leading activities. This sector has been the greatest source of new employment for two decades and has been a major factor in the growth of industrial production. All textile branches, including yarn-making, clothes manufacturing and weaving are expanding with exports driven production.

Exports of leather goods play an important role. Over 60 percent were concentrated in haberdashery and ready made clothes manufacturing. Development possibilities remain high, with advantageous production conditions, the proximity of the European market and the largely unexplored possibilities of the North American market.

Thus, several international groups are present in Morocco, including: NAF NAF, COURTAULDS, TRIUMPH,JORDACHE, ARTLANDER, LEGO,COATS VIYELLA, SARALEE, FRUIT OF THE LOOM, BENETTON, CARRERA, VAN GILS, YVES ST-LAURENT, TAVEX. Several prestigious brands are manufactured in Morocco, including: CATIMINI, CHEVIGNON, DANIEL HECHTER, PETIT BATEAU, NEW MAN, BOYE, GALOPIN, MARINER, C17, EMINENCE, ABSORBA, ESCADA, KUNERT, CORTIEFIEL, K-WAY, FASHION TREND, DELTEX.

INVESTMENT OPPORTUNITIES

Weaving, finishing, yarn-making, knitwear, hosiery and women's lingerie, sports and leisure articles,suits, etc...

Unwoven products for use in agriculture and construction (insulation,waterproofing, etc.), fishing nets, technical fibers.

Luxury leather goods
Chemical fibers

CHEMICALS & PARACHEMICALS

Chemicals and related industries include such activities as wood processing, cardboard manufacturing, chemical products and construction materials using rubble, plastics and cement processing accounts for the highest share of investments. Phosphates lead the market in general and exports in particular. Foreign investments grew by 300 percent during the last 5 years. In five years, Procter and Gamble invested more than US$ 40 million in Morocco. These investments were mainly directed to the construction of a new Household Cleaning Products plant in Mohammedia as well as the expansion to new ranges of products such as shampoo, baby diapers, hygienic towels, ete

INVESTMENT OPPORTUNITIES

Ammonia, uric acid
Polyethylene
Tripolyphosphates

METALLURGICAL, MECHANICAL, ELECTRICAL & ELECTRONIC INDUSTRIES

The Metallurgical, Mechanical, Electrical &, Electronic industries play an important role in the industrial development, by providing goods to industry and consumers and by maintaining technical infrastructures. the most important branches include metal structures, electrical and electronic products. Foreign investors are present in some 30 percent of the companies in the sector, including joint ventures.

Sub-Contracting in electronics offers interesting investment possibilities due to competitive costs. For example, SGS Thomson manufactures semiconductors for the export market in its Casablanca plant, employing 2,000 persons and is developing its investment in Morocco. The Alcatel CIT group recently opened a new plant in Morocco, employing 140 people to manufacture electrical transformers for switching units, smart cards and CNS concentrators.

INVESTMENT OPPORTUNITIES

Basic Metallurgy
Steel- making
Copper Refining
Industrial equipment .
Industrial tools: molds, matrixes .
Agricultural equipment : seeders, Pulverizers, harvesters
Automotive spare parts.
Electronics: .

Telecommunication facilities .

Sub-contracting of electronics for export.

BANKING SYSTEM

The Moroccan banking system is composed of Bank AL Maghrib, 15 commercial banks, several development banks and specialized financial institutions. The three largest banks account for over 63 percent of banking assets and deposits and cover 55 percent of credit.

The 1993 banking law regulates banking and credit activities. All banks must be corporations and must be incorporated in Morocco. Other than the minimum capital requirement, Central Bank regulations consist of certain liquidity,solvency and legal lending limit ratios. Credit ceilings were lifted in 1991 and were replaced by indirect monitoring by means of changes in reserve requirements and controlled access to the Central Bank rediscount window. The legal lending limit is set at 7% of net capital funds. Recent changes, however, increased the level of legal lending limit fivefold for credits guaranteed by OECD (Organization Economic of Cooperation and Development) based banks.

Traditional commercial banking in Morocco has reached an advanced stage of maturity and sophistication. Moroccan banks offer a wide range of standard banking products. Several of them currently offer electronic banking services to their corporate clients and a wide array of consumer banking products including credit cards, automatic teller machines, and telephone banking. Most Moroccan banks are connected to the SWIFT global payment system allowing them quick execution of foreign currency transfers world-wide. Furthermore, banks are permitted to open foreign currency and convertible Dirham accounts to non resident individuals and companies.

They can also automatically repatriate earnings of foreign companies operating in the country. Through the assistance of commercial banks and special financial institutions, local financing is available to foreign investors on the same basis as to Moroccan companies. In force since January 1996, credit rate liberalization should allow companies to benefit from less expansive liquidity costs.
In summary, there are several investor considerations:
- The banking network offers a wide range of services.
- Financing is available from semi- public and private institutions.
- Opportunities exist for long-term foreign investment.

DYNAMIC MARKET

THE CASABLANCA STOCK EXCHANGE (CSE) AN INTERNATIONAL FINANCIAL MARKET

Recently, the CSE witnessed a resurgence of activity driven by the privatization program, and enhanced interest on the part of institutional investors. The lackluster performance of the stock exchange was partly due to the relatively high yield that investors were able to get from treasury bonds, and partly because Moroccan investors have traditionally favored other types of investments such as real estate and bank deposits. Furthermore, large business groups traditionally relied on banks for their financing needs. Nevertheless, the reform is continuing, leading to:

- greater access to a secondary financial market,
- the institution of a control body for trade practices (conseil deontoligique des valeurs mobilieres),and

the implementation of financial market mechanisms such as the Stock exchange society, and mutual funds (SICAV, FCP, OPCVM)
Currently, in 1995, market capitalization stands at about US$ 6 billion with 26.6 percent growth from the previous year, representing 17.7 percent of GDP. It is generally anticipated that this rate will edge upwards as the privatization program continues to be implemented. Market capitalization of the CSE increased 6.5 times from 1990 to 1995. The CSE is highly concentrated. Among the 65 listed companies, 12 of them account for 80 percent of market capitalisation.

The most active stocks include banks (BCM, BMCE, SNI, Wafabank, Credit du Maroc, CIH, BMCI) and large corporations such as ONA and its main subsidiaries, as well as other large companies. it is generally estimated that Morocco's equity market is undervalued relative to other developing economies. This partly explains the important interest shown by institutional investors in the equity market in Morocco. Thus far, foreign institutional investors hold approximately $200 million of Moroccan equities, with ONA accounting for about half of this amount. This is expected to increase in the foreseeable future as new issues are introduced to the CSE. Under the new law, the CSE was privatized. Its new owners are all stockbrokers, including foreign companies, having a seat on the exchange market. Fourteen brokers have been licensed, thirteen are now in operation. Seventeen mutual funds (FCP) are now operating.

POST AND TELECOMMUNICATIONS

In Morocco, telecommunications are considered as a support to other sectors of activity, a development factor and a backing to the reform of structures.

Morocco possesses one of the largest telecommunications network in Africa, with top quality facilities and services. The network was improved and developed, mainly with the adoption of new telecommunication techniques.

Most of operation activity is supervised by the National Posts and Telecommunication Board (O.N.P.T.), a state owned-industrial and economic institution.

New companies marketing telecommunication services are emerging, part of the privatization and openness policy adopted for goods and services.

Increasingly important needs and demand are set to consolidate the role of private operators in the fields of sub-contracting and marketing of telecommunications services and value added goods: radio-cellular mobile services, data transfer, large width networks and RNIS.

RELATIONS WITH THE WORLD

Morocco is represented in various meetings held by regional and international organizations, and particularly :

- the ministers council of posts and telecommunications of the Arab Maghreb Union;

- the arab ministers council of telecommunications ;

- ARABSAT;

- The international telecommunications union;

- The World Trade Organization (W.T.O);

- The Gulf Cooperation Council (G.C.C.);

- The European Telecommunications Organization (EUTELSAT)

At the international level, the development of the telecommunications network takes into account Morocco's geo-strategic location and its role as a linking point between Africa and the Arab world.

Indeed, Morocco possesses state-of-the-art telecommunications means. It is linked to Europe and North America through sub-marine cables and satellites. These means are set to be further consolidated and adapted to match the evolution of technology through Morocco's participation in major international projects planned by Europe and America through sub-marine optic fibers and "Intelsat" and "Arabsat" satellites.

Morocco's participation in the African satellites projects "AFROSAT" will help the country diversify its relations with African countries. Morocco is presently linked to 150 countries.

Secretary of State delegate to the Prime Minister, in charge of Posts and New Information Technology

ONPT Investments since 1984

Years	Turnout (million dh)	Subscribers (thousand)	Investments million dh)
1984	1.320	220	350
1985	1.834	240	560
1986	1.612	252	343
1987	2.010	286	519
1988	2.423	287	941
1989	2.688	335	1.902
1990	3.130	403	2.157
1991	3.579	498	3.238
1992	4.187	657	2.253
1993	5.128	827	1.778
1994	5.656	1.007	2.738
1995	6.380	1.771	2.064
1996	7.178	1.351	3.058
1997	8.300	1.560	1.322

TOURISM

Morocco boasts important natural and historical assets and a rich and diversified cultural legacy.

TOURIST FLOW

National tourism has considerably recovered in 1996, after three consecutive years of an activity slump.

In 1996, the number of foreign tourists who visited Morocco reached 1,801,165 visitors. Out of this figure, visitors who came on cruise reached 163,193, which is an annual increase of 8.7% while visitors who stayed in Morocco were estimated at 1.6 millions, marking an increase of 7.2% in comparison with the previous year.

European tourists exceeded 1.3 million persons, which is an increase of 7.9%. This evolution is the result of more French and German visitors, whose number posted an increase of respectively 17.8% and 31.1%.

Meanwhile, the number of Spanish tourists was lower and the decrease was even sharper among English, Italian and American tourists.

Hotel Occupancy

Like arrivals to hotels, nights spent by tourists in various accommodating categories in 1996 increased by 1.5%, with a total of 28,703,206 against 28,266,744 in 1995.

Out of this total, 35.1% nights were spent in graded hotels, which is 10,073,206 against 9,941,390 in 1995, which is an increase of 1.3 %.

Tourism Remittances

Tourism remittances in 1996 were worth 11,789.9 Million DH, increasing by 18.7% in comparison with 1995 (9,928.6 Million DH).

Infrastructure and Investments

By end of 1996, there was a total number 543 graded hotels.

Morocco's accommodation infrastructure was consolidated in 1996 by the launching of 17 hotel projects with a total of 1,512 beds, bringing the total capacity of graded hotels to 92,023 beds.

The total capacity of authorized hotels which received state advantages in 1996 comprises 39 tourism projects. Investments allocated to their constructions are estimated at 1,697 million DH.

In addition, 31 projects for the extension and refurbishment of tourism facilities received the final agreement of the technical coordination committee of tourism projects, for a total investment amount of 561 million DH.

New measures to support tourism were adopted by the authorities. Some hotels were re-graded in the respect of international standards.

In order to improve the competitiveness of enterprises operating in the tourism sector, the VAT applicable to tourism activities was reduced from 14% to 10% starting July 1st, 1996. In addition, laws regulating some tourism-related activities, mainly those regulating the guide profession and travel agencies, were amended.

Lastly, investments in tourism benefit, since the adoption in November 1995 of the investment charter, automatically from the advantages in force, a move likely to promote investments mainly in areas which are still unexploited.

ENERGY SECTOR

ENERGY OVERVIEW

Minister of Energy and Mines: Youssef Tahiri
Proven Oil Reserves (1/1/00E): 1.9 million barrels
Crude Oil Production (1998E): 1,000 barrels per day (bbl/d)
Oil Consumption (1998E): 145,000 bbl/d
Net Oil Imports (1998E): 144,000 bbl/d
Crude Refining Capacity (1/1/00E): 156,630 bbl/d
Natural Gas Reserves (1/1/00E): 49 billion cubic feet (Bcf)
Natural Gas Production/Consumption (1997E): 1.4 Bcf
Recoverable Coal Reserves (12/31/96): 6 million short tons (Mmst)
Coal Production (1998E): 0.4 Mmst
Coal Consumption (1998E): 3.5 Mmst
Net Coal Imports (1998E): 3.1 Mmst
Electric Generation Capacity (1/1/98E): 4.0 gigawatts (75% thermal, 25% hydroelectric)
Electricity Generation (1998E): 13.2 billion kilowatthours (bkwh)

OIL AND GAS INDUSTRIES

Organization: Office Nationale de Recherches et d'Exploitation Petrolieres (ONAREP) is the national (upstream) oil company.
Major Oil Fields: None
Refineries (capacity-bbl/d): Samir -- Mohammedia (125,230); Ste. Cherifienne des Petroles -- Sidi Kacem (31,400)
Ports: Jorf Lasfar, Casablanca
Pipelines: The Maghreb-Europe Gas (MEG) pipeline passes through Morocco from Algeria en route to Spain.
Major Foreign Energy Company Involvement: Cepsa, Lasmo, Mobil, Repsol, Shell, Total.

ENVIRONMENTAL OVERVIEW

Minister in Charge of Country Planning, Environment, Town Planning and Housing: Mr. Mohamed El-Yazghi
Total Energy Consumption (1998E): 0.41 quadrillion Btu* (0.1% of world total energy consumption)
Energy-Related Carbon Emissions (1998E): 7.5 million metric tons of carbon (0.1% of world carbon emissions)
Per Capita Energy Consumption (1998E): 14.7 million Btu (vs U.S. value of 350.7 million Btu)
Per Capita Carbon Emissions (1998E): 0.27 metric tons of carbon (vs U.S. value of 5.5 metric tons of carbon)
Energy Intensity (1998E): 12,800 Btu/ $1990 (vs U.S. value of 13,400 Btu/ $1990)**
Carbon Intensity (1998E): 0.24 metric tons of carbon/thousand $1990 (vs U.S. value of 0.21 metric tons/thousand $1990)**
Sectoral Share of Energy Consumption (1997E): Transportation (34.4%), Industrial (36.2%), Residential (24.4%), Commercial (5.0%)
Sectoral Share of Carbon Emissions (1997E): Transportation (36.6%), Industrial (36.6%), Residential (21.7%), Commercial (5.1%)
Fuel Share of Energy Consumption (1998E): Oil (71.7%), Coal (22.0%), Natural Gas (0.5%)
Fuel Share of Carbon Emissions (1998E): Oil (69.5%), Coal (30.1%), Natural Gas (0.36%)
Renewable Energy Consumption (1997E): 38.6 trillion Btu* (5% increase from 1996)

Number of People per Motor Vehicle (1997): 20.8 (vs U.S. value of 1.3)
Status in Climate Change Negotiations: Non-Annex I country under the United Nations Framework Convention on Climate Change (ratified December 28th, 1995). Not a signatory to the Kyoto Protocol
Major Environmental Issues: Land degradation/desertification (soil erosion resulting from farming of marginal areas, overgrazing, destruction of vegetation); water supplies contaminated by raw sewage; siltation of reservoirs; oil pollution of coastal waters
Major International Environmental Agreements: A party to Conventions on Biodiversity, Climate Change, Desertification, Endangered Species, Hazardous Wastes, Marine Dumping, Nuclear Test Ban, Ozone Layer Protection, Ship Pollution and Wetlands. Has signed, but not ratified, Environmental Modification and Law of the Sea

Although Morocco has limited energy resources, the country is a major phosphate producer, as well as an important transit center for natural gas exports from Algeria to Europe.

Information contained in this report is the best available as of February 2004 and is subject to change.

OIL AND GAS

Morocco contains no significant proven oil, although most sedimentary basins in the country have not been explored, and relies on imports for all of its oil needs. In 1999, despite efforts by Morocco's energy minister to attract foreign investors to explore for oil and gas, only a few companies signed agreements. These included Saudi Aramco, Australia's ROC, Sweden's Taurus, and U.S.-based Skidmore, which reportedly will invest $50 million in oil exploration onshore in Ounara, on the Atlantic Coast near Essaouira. Lasmo already has a concession at the Ras Tafalney block, located offshore the coastal town of Essaouira.

The block is similar geologically to large hydrocarbon basins off Angola, Congo, and Nigeria. Morocco has oil shale deposits in the Atlas Mountains, but these have not been exploited for economic reasons. Morocco produces small volumes of natural gas from the Gharb Basin in the north, and appears to have a considerable gas field at Meskala just north of Essaouira. In January 2004, an energy ministry spokesman said that Morocco would soon issue new tax ememptions and other incentives to help attract foreign investors to explore for oil in Morocco. In late December 1999, Morocco's Parliament unanimously adopted a new hydrocarbon law, which, among other things, would offer a 10-year tax break to offshore oil production firms and reduce the government's stake in future oil concessions (to a maximum of 25%).

In October 1998, IPIC and Cepsa formed a 50-50 joint venture called Cepsa Maghreb to market and distribute petroleum products and Liquefied Petroleum Gas (LPG) in Morocco. Products are to be supplied from Cepsa's refineries in Spain, and French company Vitogaz is building an LPG import terminal and tank farm near Casablanca. Meanwhile, Spanish oil and gas group Repsol has announced its intentions to invest $20 million in Morocco's energy sector over the next 5 years.

Morocco has two refineries and consumes 145,000 barrels per day (bbl/d) of oil. Two refining companies -- Samir and SCP -- agreed in late 1998 to merge as of the first quarter of 1999. The two companies, which are owned largely by Corral Petroleum Holding of Sweden, have a combined refining capacity of around 156,000 bbl/d. In July 1998, Samir announced that it was planning to invest around $500 million in various oil projects, including increased output at its 125,000-bbl/d refinery at Mohammedia (near Casablanca).

Although it contains only small natural gas reserves of its own, Morocco is a major transit center for Algerian gas exports across the Strait of Gibraltar to Spain, via the 300-billion-cubic-foot-per-year Maghreb-Europe Gas (MEG) pipeline. In November 1999, Spanish company Natural Gaz SDG announced its intention to invest up to $400 million in a natural gas distribution network for Morocco.

COAL AND ELECTRICITY

Morocco produces coal from its one mine at Jerada, and imports coal from the United States, Colombia, and South Africa. Coal is consumed largely by power plants at Mohammedia and Jorf Lasfar. With electricity demand increasing around 7% annually, Morocco plans to expand the Jorf Lasfar plant with the addition of two 330-megawatt (MW) units on a build-operate-transfer (BOT) basis. Mohammedia is supplied through the port of Casablanca, which has been stretched to its limits by increased coal imports.

Morocco's National Office of Electricity (ONE) has an ambitious plan to supply the countryside with electricity by 2010 (currently, only around 15% of the rural population has access to electricity). Morocco plans to spend around $3.7 billion on energy projects through 2003, and part of this money will go towards building power plants and towards rural electrification. As part of this plan, a new, $500-million, 350-400-MW combined-cycle power plant, to be fired by natural gas from the MEG pipeline, is planned. The plant, Morocco's third independent power project (IPP), is to be built at Tahaddart, near Tangier in northern Morocco, with the first stage operational by 2002 and the second stage completed by 2004. As of early 2004, three energy consortia reportedly were competing for the project: Germany's Siemens; General Electric; and a group led by ABB Alsthom.

ONE also is looking at solar power, as well as at building wind power parks throughout the country (including farms at Tangier and Tarfaya). In late 1998, ONE awarded a $56-million construction contract to a French joint venture (CED) for a 50-MW wind farm to be built at Koudia el Beida near the Straight of Gibraltar. If completed, this would be the first wind farm in Africa and the Arab world, according to ONE. In September 1998, Endesa signed a deal with ONE to supply Morocco with 300 gigawatt hours of electricity through November 1998. Meanwhile, a potential project to build a 50-MW solar power plant at Ouarzazate has been postponed. Morocco also is interested in nuclear power for desalination and other purposes, but currently has no nuclear plants.

* The total energy consumption statistic includes petroleum, dry natural gas, coal, net hydro, nuclear, geothermal, solar and wind electric power. The renewable energy consumption statistic is based on International Energy Agency (IEA) data and includes hydropower, solar, wind, tide, geothermal, solid biomass and animal products, biomass gas and liquids, industrial and municipal wastes. Sectoral shares of energy consumption and carbon emissions are also based on IEA data.

PRACTICAL INFORMATION FOR STARTING AND CONDUCTING BUSINESS

BASIC REGULATIONS FOR INVESTMENTS

INVESTMENT FREEDOM FOR FOREIGNERS

To associate Moroccan capital in locally-held foreign investments, Morocco enacted on May 7 1973 a law which enabled Moroccan capital, private as well as public, to take over from foreign capital.

The law required that a minimum of 50% of compang capital be held by Moroccans. Moreover, the presidency and the majority of the board of directors was to be held by nationals.

However, the May 7 1973 Law was abrogated by the January 8, 1990 Law and thus the requirements for Moroccan national shareholding have since been waived. Thus the capital of a commercial enterprise can be held either totally or partially by foreign companies. In addition, the presidency and the majority of the board of directors do not have to be held by nationals any longer.

Foreign investors now have free investment access opportunities to economic activities (cf. Statutory framework, foreign investment code) as well as agricultural land on long term leases.

DEFINITION

Foreign investment means any input in kind or financial input, meant to help realizing a project, in any form,and carried out by aliens, should they reside or not in Morocco and by Moroccan individuals residing abroad.

FORM OF INVESTMENTS

Such investments may take the form of :

Firm setting up ;
Participation in the capital of a company in the making ;
Application to increase the capital of an existing company ;
Setting up of a branch or a liaison office;
Acquisition of Moroccan stocks and shares;
Payment into the current account associates in cash or in trade loans;
Non-remunerated short term financial participation;
Acquisition of real property or the use rights related to the said property;
Financing of construction works by proper funds;
Setting up or acquisition of an individual business;
In kind participation.

These operations can be made in all economic sectors.

FUNDING MODES

Foreign investments can be funded in currencies :

- through cession of currencies to Bank Al Maghrib or - through debiting a currency account or an account in convertible dirham.

Investment operations funded in currencies could be carried out without prior permit of the exchange office.

The following cases are considered similar to investments funded in currencies : - The investment share funded by debiting a convertible account. This partial funding cannot be over 50 p.c. the rest is cover by the cession of currencies to Bank Al-Maghrib. - The consolidation of shareholders current accounts, reserves incorporation, postponement of reserves that became available, in such a way that the corresponding amounts reflect the transferable character. - The consolidation of trade loans materialized by the regular importing of goods or equipment and which were not paid in currencies. - The consolidation of loans under foreign technical assistance, materialized by patents, exploitation licenses, trade marks, know-how... duly conceded by foreign enterprises.

TRANSFER OF INVESTMENT REVENUE

The revenues of foreign investments can be transferred without a prior permit for the concerned investors without limiting the time nor the amount.

The revenues of investment are :

- Dividends or parts in the income distributed by Moroccan companies; - Attendance fees and percentages; - Profits made by Moroccan branches of foreign companies; - Rental income; - Interest accued from loans.

The transfers are made after the payment of duties and taxes in force in Morocco (15 p.c representing Tax on share proceeds, firms shares and assimilated revenues).

TRANSFER OF CESSION OR LIQUIDATION PROCEEDS OF FOREIGN INVESTMENTS

The cession and liquidation operations of foreign investments in Morocco are free. Banks can transfer for the concerned investors the proceeds of the cession or liquidation of their investment as well as the payment in capital principal, of concluded loans.

The transfers deal with the nominal value of the investment and on the potential plue-value.

The cessions between foreign investors can directly result in a payment abroad.

DOCUMENTS TO SUBMIT TO THE EXCHANGE OFFICE FOR A FOREIGN INVESTMENT PROJECT

Foreign investors including Moroccan residents abroad should submit, within six months as of the date of the realization of the investment project, to the exchange office (the investment sub-division) directly or via their bank, fiduciary, notary, lawyer. ... a report including :

- Identity, nationality, place of residence of the investor; - Field of activity; - The investment amount; - The investment form.

The report should be accompanied with the following documents :

- For investments financed in currency :

*A bank certificate * The status of the firm, minutes of the consecutive general assembly and a declaration of subscription or of payment. * Minutes of the extraordinary general assembly ratifying the increase of the firm's capial, accord concluded with the partners. * Purchase contract or other documents.

- For the investments financed by goods or equipment : importation duly imputed by the customs and indirect taxes administration and non-payment bank certificates.

- For investments financed by the consolidation of loans for foreign technical assistance, a contract duly set, showing the nature and facilities.

DOCUMENTS TO SUBMIT TO THE BANK FOR THE TRANSFER OF A FOREIGN INVESTMENT REVENUES

a) For the transfer of dividends, the percentage of profit, profit shares :

- Accounting balance sheets and accounts (exploitation, lesses and profit accounts) the annexed documents related to the payment for which the transfer is requested and the extra-accounting rectifications state made to obtain the fiscal result. These documents should be coupled by a visa by the taxes administration.

- The minute(s) of the ordinary general assemblies of shareholders deciding on the results of the enterprise and dividing the profits, the amount of dividends and the distribution of percentages.

- The list of foreign or Moroccan administrators indicating their name, nationality, address, number of bonds held by each of them, and if need be, the gross amount of percentage obtained by them.

b) For the transfer of director's fees :

The list of foreign or Moroccan nationals residing abroad administrators with the indication of their names, nationality, address, gross and net amount granted to each of them as well as the minute setting the global amount of director's fees allowed to the governing board during the fiscal concerned.

c) For the transfer of exploitation benefits of the branches of foreign firms :

The balance sheets and the accounts of the accounting results, the annexed documents related to the fiscal of which payment is requested as well as the stage of the extra-accounting rectifications to obtain the fiscal results. These documents should be certified by the Taxes Administration.

d) For the transfer of the leasing revenues :

inventory of the manager showing the amounts registered through the rents the related fees, including the taxes. The inventory should be coupled with a leasing contract or any other necessary documents and justificative of the taxes payment.

e) For the transfer of payment and loans interests :

Bank certificates justifying the repatriation of the loan the corresponding book of paying back and, if need be the references of the general or particular consent of the exchange office.

DOCUMENTS TO SUBMIT TO THE BANK FOR THE TRANSFER OF THE PRODUCT OF CESSION OR OF LIQUIDATION OF A FOREIGN INVESTMENT

For the transfer of the product of cession or of liquidation of a foreign investment, the investors concerned should submit to the bank any document justifying the financing of investment in currency.

In addition to these documents, the concerned investors should submit the following documents :

a) For the transfer of the product of the mobile of shares cession :

the accounting documents related to the fiscal year of the firm the bonds of which are ceded, the minute of the ordinary general assembly as well as copies of the certificates of the transfer of bonds ceded showing the price of the cession.

b) For the transfer the real-estate product :

copy of the sale certificate coupled with the documents justifying the payment of taxes related to the fiscal during which the transaction was made.

c) For the transfer of the liquidation product :

the balance sheet of the liquidation duly certified by the fiscal administration, the minute of the general assembly of the shareholders or a copy of the juridical decision pronouncing the dissolution of the partial or total liquidation of the investment, the report of the liquidator showing the net product to divide as well as any document justifying the payment of taxes, if need be.

CUSTOMS REGULATIONS

In addition to the advantages of the Investment Code, investors can get extra benefits granted under special customs conditions.

The special customs conditions apply to the following : bonded warehouses, temporary admission, temporary import, movements for further processing abroad, temporary export, goods in transit and drawback.

BONDED WAREHOUSES

This makes it possible to store goods in establishments controlled by the Customs Administration for a set period of time.

There are two categories of bonded warehouses :

- public bonded warehouses ;
- private bonded warehouse that may be either ordinary or special.

Such warehouses are called :

. Export warehouses when the admitted goods either require special facilities for their conservation or are meant to be presented to the public in fairs, exhibits and other related events, or else to be sold for home consumption under one of the full or partial customs exemption schemes provided by law. . A public bonded warehouse concession is granted when the warehouse meets general requirements; . an ordinary private bonded warehouse is granted to legal/individuals the primary or secondary purpose of stet is to store goods on behalf of third parties; . a special private bonded warehouse concession is granted to industrial or commercial business entities for their exclusive use.

The maximum time allowable to store goods in bonded warehouse is 3 years for public warehouses and 2 years for private warehouses.

TEMPORARY IMPORT

Temporary import is the admission into the regulated area free of applicable customs for goods meant to be processed, undergo extra work or require additional labor.

Such goods having been processed, having benefited from extra work and labor shall be either exported or stored in bond.

Those who may benefit by temporary admission conditions are individuals who hold or may hold the facilities and equipment necessary for the manufacture, extra work or labor envisaged.

All goods to be processed, or require additional work or labor may benefit from such conditions with the exception of agricultural and fishery goods on list B of "le Programme General des Importations" (General Importation Program). The initial duration is 6 months; the maximum duration is 2 years from the registration date of the "Soumission d'Admission Temporaire" (Temporary Admission Submission) statement.

Under temporary admission conditions, it is possible to transfer manufactured products at various levels of completion. The transferee shall, after further extra working, export the products thus obtained.

The products may be :

- either put to consumption - or re-exported - or abandoned to the Customs - or destroyed in the presence of customs officers.

TEMPORARY IMPORT

Temporary Import is the admission into the regulated area, free of all applicable custom import prohibitions and restrictions of :

- objects brought in by individuals usually residing abroad and coming to stay temporarily in Morocco ; - exportable equipment and products in the same condition as when they were imported after having been used as scheduled.

Are admitted to benefit from Temporary Importation conditions all products and capital equipment earmarked either to be integrated into an industrial process, or to be used in manufacturing products meant chiefly for export.

The duration for equipment put in this system is limited to the time the equipment will be used. For other products, the duration does not exceed 2 years.

GOODS EXPORTED FOR FURTHER PROCESSING

This provision makes it possible to export out of the regulated area, products designed to undergo extra work or processing overseas. The said products and goods are liable to customs and other taxes and duties payable depending on the kind of imported products and goods.

TEMPORARY EXPORTATION

This allows the shipping abroad of equipment and products to be used overseas for a period determined according to the nature of the equipment, products and work involved.

The time is limited, and should not be more than one year.

GOODS IN TRANSIT

The Administration limits the time of the transit operation, as well as, if applicable, the route to be followed by the carriers.

The system allows the transportation within the regulated area, of bonded goods, from one warehouse to another office or warehouse.

DRAWBACK

System applies during the export of some products made in Morocco.

It allows for the reimbusement of custom duties, special tax (replaced by the fiscal levy on import) and potential internal consumption taxes.

Average reimbursement rates are set by decree.

PRIOR EXPORT

Prior export allows the export of products obtained from foreign goods whose customs duties and import taxes are paid and the reimporting of the equivalent sum in raw materials and semi-products free of charge.

CLEARING AT HOME

This procedure enables the operator to accomplish all custom payments inside the industrial units by the relevant bureau of the customs services.

The system is granted to imports and exports at the request of the operator concerned :

- To operations to benefit for a privileged treatment such as export, special custom conditions, investments and operations necessary for the proper running of the enterprise such as imports of spare parts destined for machine maintenance. - To repeated operations made by enterprises and which are constantly related to the customs services including the production enterprises for their regular supply of raw materials and semi-products, assembly lines for the import CKD or SKD and trade enterprises specialized in the import of products known to the service.

SPECIAL SYSTEMS

1) In addtion to goods imported free of duty under special legislative provisions are also imported free of all customs duties :

- Goods and products destined for H.M. the King; - Shipments destined for ambassadors, consular and diplomatic services, foreign members of official international organizations established in Morocco; - Shipments destined for charities; - Exceptional, noncommercial shipments.

2) Motor fuel, fuel and lubricants, foods and provisions necessary for outbound sea or air travel to overseas are free of customs dues.

3) Moroccan-made products, products from abroad admitted freely in the regulated area, conveyed by sea from one point to another of the regulated area, are not liable to customs duty.

MOVEMENT AND HOLDING OF GOODS IN BOND

- Some goods are not allowed in the maritime zone of the regulated area except for those on ships the tonnage of which is equal to or higher than 100 net register tons (list of goods as per decree in the Customs Code).

- Cattle, products liable to domestic consumption taxes, products the import/export of which is subject to restrictions are admitted to the land zone in the range of customs, only with a pass delivered by the Administration or local authorities.

DOMESTIC CONSUMER TAXES

The administration is responsible for the collection of domestic consumer taxes applicable to imported goods/pieces of work either imported or produced within the regulated area, i.e. :

- Lemonade, sodawater, plain drinking water, mineral water, other water flavored or unflavored. - Beer. - Wines and spirits. - Sugar, sugar products and dried beet pulp. - Oil products. - Rubber treads, bands, inner tubes and tires. - Platinum, gold or silver artifacts.

LITIGATION

Non compliance with the provisions of the Customs Code are punishable in accordance with the laws governing such breaches of regulations. de are punishable in accordance with the laws governing such breaches of regulations.

EXCHANGE REGULATIONS

The terms and conditions of overseas payment for commercial and financial operations are expressed in either Dirhams or one of the foreign currencies the rates of which are quoted by "Bank Al Maghrib" (Morocco's central bank).

PAYMENTS BY TRANSFER TO FOREIGN COUNTRIES

Such transfers are made in foreign currencies quoted by "Bank Al Maghrib" through :

- a transfer to a foreign transferee, or, - credit either to a foreign currency account or foreign convertible dirham account entered into the books of a bank in favor of the foreign payee, or - international credit card in cases specified by foreign exchange regulations.

PAYMENTS BY TRANSFER FROM FOREIGN COUNTRIES

Such payments are made by :

- repatriating currencies rated by "Bank Al Maghrib", or - debiting either a foreign currency account or foreign convertible dirham account entered into the books of a bank in favor of the foreign payee.

Moreover, payments may be made by international money orders or by crediting/debiting postal transfer accounts.

TYPES OF BANK ACCOUNTS THAT MAY BE OPENED BY FOREIGNERS

These accounts are :

* Foreign currency accounts
* Foreign accounts in convertible Dirhams
* Convertible time deposit accounts
* Special account

FOREIGN CURRENCY ACCOUNT AND CONVERTIBLE DIRHAM ACCOUNTS

Foreign currency accounts and convertible dirham accounts can be opened without prior approval of the "Exchange Office" in the name of foreign resident/non resident individuals or entities.

- Operation of Foreign Currency Accounts :

. Debit

- Transfer overseas;
- Transfer of foreign currencies to "Bank Al Maghrib";

- Payments of checks expressed in foreign currency;
- Amounts destined for the world capital market;
- Transfers to other foreign currency accounts.

. **Credit**

- Transfers from overseas;
- Cashing of checks, traveller checks, or any other means of payment expressed in foreign currency;
- Depositing of foreign bank-notes imported or obtained by arbitrage;
- Drawings of foreign currencies from "Bank Al Maghrib";
- Payments of interests from investments on the world capital market;
- Previously debited sums with a view to investing on the world capital market;
- Transfers from other foreign currency accounts.

- Operation of Convertible Foreign Accounts in Dirhams

. **Debit**

- Purchase from "Bank Al Maghrib" of foreign currencies quoted by the central bank;
- Payments in convertible dirhams to another foreign account;
- Sums earmarked for fixed deposits.

. Credit

- Dirham proceeds transfers of foreign currency to "Bank Al Maghrib";
- Proceeds of the transfer of foreign currencies/banknotes imported or obtained by arbitrage;
- Sums having been approved for transfer;
- Sums from a convertible dirham account;
- Amounts of interest paid.

SYSTEM GOVERNING LIQUID ASSETS IN DIRHAM HELD IN MOROCCO BY NONRESIDENT FOREIGNERS

Convertible Time Account

Convertible time deposit accounts are accounts for funds owned by foreign non-resident individuals or entities who are not entitled to any repatriation guarantee.

Such accounts can be opened without Exchange Office approval.

Available assets of the convertible time deposit accounts are used freely by the original holders.

They can freely cede the assets of their accounts to foreign residents or non-residents or to Moroccan nationals living abroad.

The beneficiaris can use the assets of the said accounts for :

- The partial funding of investments in Morocco at 50 p.c of the participation of the concerned investor. The rest, 50 p.c. , should be paid in foreign currencies. - The payment of all expenses in dirhams in Morocco by foreign movie production firms. - The acquisition of secondary residences, which should be located in a tourist development zone, and should be personally used by the beneficiary. - The subscription by foreign legal entities to the increase in capital of their branch in Morocco at 50 p.c. of their participation. The rest should be paid in foreign currency.

- Operation of Convertible Time Deposit Accounts

- Credit Side :

- Funds that are not transferable.
- The interests from such funds.
- Debit Side : Free use of available assets.

The funds may be used to :

- Finance investment operations in Morocco in all economic sectors and regardless of the form of support.
- Application for Treasury Bills.
- Advances by foreign legal entities in favor of their subsidiary company in Morocco.
- Acquisition of stocks and shares quoted on the Casablanca stock exchange.
- Payment of hotel expenses and any other expense in dirhams incurred by the holder of account, his/her spouse, parents and descendants in direct line or proxies, without limitation of the amount.
- Payment of taxes due in Morocco by the holder of the account.

- Special Accounts

Banks may open special Dirham accounts in their books in favor of non- resident individuals or entities for their temporary activities in Morocco.

Special accounts can be opened without prior approval of the Exchange Office:

- Credit Side :

- encashments in dirhams for work or services performed by the holder of the account;
- advances of funds from overseas made by the holder.

- Debit Side :

- dirham expenses incurred in Morocco;
- reimbursements under advances from overseas.

OTHER BENEFITS GRANTED TO FOREIGN RESIDENTS IN MOROCCO

* Transfer of capital owned by Foreigners about to leave Morocco for good

The amount of the capital that may be transferred is DH 25,000 per year of stay in Morocco, without any ceiling.

* Transfer of savings on profits, salaries and professional fees

Persons who benefit from the transfer at a rate up to 50 p.c. of the savings on profits, salaries, professional fees, and without prior permit of the Exchange Office, foreign resident individuals including foreign spouses of Moroccan nationals and belonging to one of the following socio-economic categories :

- wage-earners of the private sector with a work contract approved by the employment ministry;
- wage-earners of the public sector, offices, public establishments and conceded services;
- members of liberal professions;
- industrialists, tradesmen, farmers and craftsmen;
- pensioners benefiting from a pension payable in Morocco.

For wage-earners and pensioners, transfers can be monthly or at a specific date. The applicant can however accumulate the transfer of many monthly payments.

For other categories, the transfer of savings after paying tax can be made at the end of each year either globally or partially.

* Allowances in currencies for foreign spouses of Moroccan nationals

Foreign spouses of Moroccan nationals can benefit once a year from an allowance in currency valued at 5,000 DHS.

* Social Fees Transfer

Foreign nationals affiliated to foreign pension funds can transfer, in addition to their savings or in the absence of such transfers, contributions due to social security and pension bodies of their countries except contributions due to private bodies of their countries or to insurance companies for the coverage of disease, death or disability risks.

* Transfer of compensation due for foreign technical assistance

In matters of technical assistance, Moroccan enterprises can freely conclude technical assistance contracts with foreign firms and transfer through banks the compensation for such operations.

* Insurance and Re-insurance

Banks can transfer for non-residents the damage compensation without limitating the amount, the yields and the alloted capital under the life insurance contracts.

THE CONVERTIBILITY OF THE DIRHAM

Within the convertibility of the Dirham, economic operators enjoy free access to the purchase of currencies backed by Bank Al Maghrib for the payment of current operations. The transfer of outstanding sums for these operations are also free. They are made without the license of the Exchange Office.

Among the current operations for which Morocco ensures convertibility are :

. Foreign trade operations including fees;
. The transfer of foreign investment;

. The savings on income of foreign individuals residing in Morocco;
. Foreign technical assistance.

OFFSHORE SECTOR

«Offshore Banks » are any legal entities or individuals, regardless of nationality, whose headquarters are based in an offshore financial location, and whose activities consist in dealing in convertible foreign currency deposits, and undertaking with these same currencies any credit, exchange and or financial activity.

An offshore bank can be a subsidiary set up in an offshore financial location to represent and act for its central bank whose headquarters are outside the offshore location.

Is termed « offshore holding corporation » any legal entity or individual whose purpose is capital management and share participation in corporations whose capital is in convertible foreign currencies, on condition that these operations are undertaken in convertible foreign currencies.

Offshore banks and holding corporations benefit from a number of advantages.

EXCHANGE MECHANISMS

Offshore banks and holding corporations are not obliged to repatriate any income or foreign revenues and have total exchange freedom with regard to their transactions with non-resident entities.

All transactions in Morocco are undertaken through foreign currency accounts or convertible Moroccan Dirham foreign accounts opened in Moroccan banks.

In order to meet their operating expenses in Morocco, banks are entitled to run an account in Moroccan Dirhams.

Moreover, offshore banks and holding corporations have free access to investment activities in Morocco and to capital participation operations in local corporations.

FISCAL AND CUSTOMS MECHANISMS

Offshore banks and corporations benefit from the following tax exonerations : Registration fees, VAT, patente tax and urban tax, import duties and taxes, TPA on distributed dividends. Corporate tax is negociable and all other tax for offshore companies is fixed at a nominal $5,000 per year for 15 years. For offshore banks it is either $25,000 U.S a year or 10% of profits.

REGULATIONS FOR FOREIGN STAFF

Freedom to recruit staff required for the activity; staffare is entitled to choose welfare schemes other than the Moroccan one.

Tax exemption for imported personal belongings and application of transit import system for imported vehicles.

The infrastructure required for the setting up the Tangier Offshore market has featured to additional development infrastructure and telecommunication facilities. With this system already in operation, application to open business are deposited at the Crédit Lyonnais in partnership with Crédit du Maroc or through la Banque Nationale de Paris in partnership with "la Banque Marocaine pour le Commerce et l'Industrie".

THE TANGIER OFFSHORE FINANCIAL MARKET

The offshore banks: Since 1993, two offshore financial institutions have been set up in Tangier, namely:

- Banque Nationale de Paris, Offshore subsidiary of Tangier
- Banque Internationale de Tanger, which was set up by Crédit Lyonnais and Crédit du Maroc.

A third bank secured approval in July 1994 : Attijari International Bank to be created by Banque Commerciale du Maroc and Banco Central Espano Americano.

The offshore holding corporations: currently, many offshore holding corporations are established in Tangier, namely :

- La financière Holding Offshore,
- Société Internationale des Participations,
- Investissement Marocain Holding Offshore,
- New Investment Holding Offshore,
- Euro Detroit International Holding Offshore,
- Hyphen Holding Offshore,
- Euromaroc Holding Offshore,
- J & J Holding Offshore,
- Investment Financement Overseas Holding Offshore,
- Energytech Offshore Holding Company,
- Estar Holding International Offshore.

FREE ZONES

Created by the law No 19-94, the "Free Zone for Export" are specific areas of the customs territory where all export activity of an industrial or commercial nature, as well as related services, can be authorized without being subjected to customs or exchange regulations and controls on foreign trade. The agencies responsible for the development and management of the free zones are "L'Office d'Exploitation des Ports" and "L'Office d'Exploitation des Aeroports". Apart from creating, developing and maintaining the said zones, they are also responsible for dealing with investors, helping them in the preparation of their applications for authorizations and assisting them in every way in their projects.

FOREIGN TRADE, EXCHANGE, CUSTOMS AND FISCAL CONTROLS FOR COMPANIES ESTABLISHED IN FREE ZONES FOR EXPORT

A - Foreign Trade and exchange Controls :

- In Free Zones for Export, the entry and exit of merchandise are not subject to foreign trade or exchange control legislation;

- In the same zones, commercial, industrial and services operations with foreign countries enjoy complete

LEADING SECTORS FOR BUSINESS AND INVESTMENTS

LEADING SECTORS AND OPPORTUNITIES FOR TRADE AND INVESTMENTS

RENEWABLE ENERGY

Morocco is the only North African country with no known substantial fossil fuel deposits. The Moroccan government adopted a strategy based on an accelerated development of renewable resources. Morocco's electric power production is insufficient to meet a demand that has been increasing at an average annual rate of 8% for the past five years. The energy plan expects to increase the renewable share of installed capacity in electricity generation to 42% by 2020, up from 26% in 2008. In 2012, Morocco had an installed capacity from renewable energy of 2.853 GW, of which 90% was large-scale hydroelectric plants. Of the remainder, 82% was wind parks, 12% thermo-solar plants, 5% photovoltaic solar installations and the rest micro-hydroelectric plants and biomass treatment plants.

SUB-SECTOR BEST PROSPECTS

Morocco offers excellent opportunities to U.S. firms in the following segments:

- Electrical components
- EPC Contracting
- Connections
- Switches
- Fittings
- High, medium and low-voltage applications.
- Technical training for facilities repair and maintenance

OPPORTUNITIES

All power production projects in Morocco are conducted through international tenders for development on a concession basis. U.S. manufacturers of solar/wind/biomass equipment are encouraged to partner with U.S. developers, in order to participate in tenders as joint consortiums. It is also important to have reliable local partners. More information on upcoming tenders can be found at: https://www.marchespublics.gov.ma/pmmp/?lang=fr

Most government originated tenders have local content requirements. Entering into joint ventures with local partners can be an effective way to win contracts.

In order to increase the renewable share in its power production, Morocco will be undertaking the following projects:

Solar: In addition to the 2GW solar plan managed by the Moroccan Agency for Solar Energy (MASEN) to be completed by 2020, Morocco's Office of Electricity and Water launched 3 PV plants in the east of Morocco with capacities ranging between 10 and 25MW. MASEN's solar plan will require $9 billion in investment and will create a

significant Moroccan solar industry, as well as establish leading R&D infrastructure for Africa.

Wind: While Morocco's wind power potential capacity is estimated at 6,000 MW, the existing installed capacity of Morocco's eight wind farms is limited to 487 MW. Four wind projects under construction are expected to provide an installed capacity of 720 MW by 2015. Six wind farms of a total installed capacity of 1,000MW are in the tendering phase and expected to be implemented by 2020.

Hydro: The current hydroelectric power capacity amounts to 1,770 MW. Among the 580 MW that is under construction, 12 hydroelectric plants will start producing 92 MW in 2016.

Biomass: Biomass has the potential of 950MW based on abundant agricultural resources, including wide areas for livestock breeding (2.6 million cattle, 16.3 million sheep and 5.3 million goats). The Green Morocco Plan to boost agricultural production and new regulations for waste management represents an additional potential of 400MW by the year 2030. In 2002, the U.S. consortium (GESI-Edgeboro-SADAT) won a government tender for the management of the first controlled landfill in Fez. It plans to convert methane gas from the landfill into electricity to power all Fez public lighting.

Web Resources

- Moroccan Ministry of Energy, Mining, Water and Environment: www.mem.gov.ma
- Office National de l'Electricité: www.one.org.ma
- Moroccan Agency for Solar Energy (MASEN): http://www.masen.org.ma/
- Agency for the Development of Renewable Energy and Electrical Efficiency (ADEERE): http://www.aderee.ma/
- Company for Energy Investments (SIE): http://www.siem.ma/

INFRASTRUCTURE PROJECTS

Morocco is solidifying its age-old position as a commercial bridge between Europe and West Africa, and modern infrastructure in the form of world-class ports, airports, and rail links are key to realizing this goal. Strategically located along the Strait of Gibraltar, just a seven-hour flight from New York, NY and three hours from Paris, Morocco is seen more and more as a regional hub in North West Africa for transportation and business. Morocco's moderate Mediterranean climate on 2,750 miles (3,500 kilometers (km)) of coastline and its developing infrastructure make it an attractive location for business and leisure. To meet the domestic demand for infrastructure, the Moroccan government plans to invest, by 2015, more than $15 billion to upgrade its basic infrastructure. In addition, given Morocco's growing population and the economic importance of agriculture, a plethora of projects are underway in water technologies including wastewater treatment, water distribution and irrigation.

SUB-SECTOR BEST PROSPECTS

Morocco offers excellent opportunities to U.S. firms in the following segments:

Building materials:

• Innovative building materials

• Steel

• Prefabricated building

• Glass

• Aluminium doors, windows and frame

• Luxury bath tubs, washbasins, and toilet seats

• Luxury bath and kitchen hardware and accessories

• Luxury door and window knobs and fixtures

• Pigments

• Paints, varnishes

• Vinyl floor covering

• Solar water heaters

• Heating/Air conditioning

Equipment:

• Bulldozers and angle dozers

• Rock drilling and earth boring equipment

• Integral tractor shovel loaders

• Shovels, excavators

- Sorting, screening, separating and washing machines for earth, stone, ores, or other mineral substances in solid form

- Crushing machines for earth, stone, ores, etc.

- Grinding machines for earth, stones, etc.

- Concrete/Mortar mixers

- Machines for mixing mineral substances with bitumen

- Escalators and moving walkways

    - Motorway and rail signalling

    - Motorway and rail monitoring

Services:

- Architecture and design

    - Engineering Consulting

    - Infrastructure Maintenance

    - Road and Rail bed maintenance

    - Signalling

    - Construction Supervision

OPPORTUNITIES

Transport

Roads: Morocco values it high quality network of roads and aims to reach 1,800 km of highways in 2015 (1,416 in 2012), 1,300 km in 2016 of express ways (700 km in 2012) and 2,500 km of country roads by the end of 2014 (11,236 km in 2012). Moreover, improving transportation safety in some areas of Morocco will result in the implementation of tunnels and beltways, especially around the Atlas mountain areas. Currently, les Autoroutes du Maroc, a state owned company, has the monopoly on highway construction and operations. To enhance road expansion, the government is working on the liberalization of highway operations.

Railway: Morocco's railway network comprises 2,110 km of track, with 120 rail stations. Future development plans include the completion of the Tanger-Casablanca (370 Km) high-speed rail, to be implemented by 2015, and the studies for the Casablanca-Marrakech high-speed line (230 km). This will require the creation of maintenance centers dedicated to high-speed rail activity. The Office National Des Chemins de Fer (ONCF) is in charge of railway development and the sole railway operator. It intends to modernize rail lines, rail stations, as well as several regional rail networks around large urban centers. ONCF is committed to developing logistic platforms close to its lines.

Airports: In order to support the tourism's strategy "2020 Vision", Morocco's Ministry of Transports and the Office National des Aeroports (ONDA - in charge of Airport management and air traffic control) is engaged in a development strategy that aims to:

a) Strengthen the status of the Casablanca airport as an international hub to and from Central and West Africa, and develop Marrakech airport as a hub towards Europe

b) Sustain the development of airport infrastructure through airport extensions, modernizations and new construction projects.

Current ONDA projects include:

1. The extension of Nador airport (40 mil USD)

2. The construction of new terminals at Marrakech airport ($132 million) and Fes airport ($58 million)

3. The construction of new airports at Beni-Mellal ($20 million) and Zagora (15 million)

All projects are to be completed between September 2014 and December 2015. Future airport upgrades will include Essaoura, Oujda, and Al Hoceima.

Shipping, Ports and Container Handling

Morocco has 15 commercial ports that generated 92.3 million tons in merchandise traffic in 2012. Major developers of ports are Agence National des Port (ANP) and Tanger-Med Special Agency (TMSA). Tanger-Med Port terminals 1 and 2 are operational. It is expected to reach full capacity by 2015 and to operate 8 million containers, 7 million passengers, 700,000 trucks, 2 million vehicles, and 10 million MT of oil products, becoming the largest transshipment port in Africa. After this successful project that transformed the economic conditions of the Tangier region, the government intends to

develop six new fully integrated ports around Morocco (East / North-east/ Kenitra-Casablanca/ Doukkala-Abda/ Souss-Tensift/ South)

Building Construction

Urban population is growing at 4 percent per year. To meet the demand for property, the government began a New Cities program aimed at creating 15 new cities by 2020. Under the program, the government provides land to the public at competitive prices and tax incentives to developers who commit to build 500 low-cost units within five years. The government established three funds that grant loans at advantageous rates to government employees (Fogaloge-Public Fund), to teachers (Mohammed VI/FOGALEF Fund) and to low-income or temporarily employed people (FOGARIM Fund). Two new cities started in 2004, Tamansourt near Marrakesh, and Tamesna, near Rabat, will provide 88,000 and 54,000 units, respectively, for a total investment of USD 7.2 billion. Morocco needs to build approximately 158,500 units annually.

To meet demand in the education sector, the Ministry of Education, under its 2009-2012 Emergency Plan, began to build 4,774 new schools and extend 187 existing schools. To encourage construction of private schools, Morocco established the "Fonds de Promotion de l'Enseignement Privé" (FOPEP) to co-finance the construction of private schools.

Tourism

Morocco is one of the world's most attractive and well-established tourism destinations. Marrakesh was ranked among the world's top 25 destinations by Trip Advisor in April 2014. The American Association of Travel Agents will hold its annual conference in Marrakesh in 2015. Morocco is the most stable country in North Africa and is already a well-established tourism destination, especially for Europeans. With on-going and probably long-term unrest in competing tourism markets in North Africa, Morocco is expected to experience higher volume in the short and medium term. However, recent reports indicate that the quality of Moroccan hotels and resorts is slipping. Given the importance of the sector to the Moroccan economy, we expect enhanced tourism construction projects and cultural renovations throughout the country will demand U.S. project management expertise, construction equipment, and building services.

Trade Events

The United States Department of Commerce's International Trade Administration is organizing an Executive-led infrastructure Business Development Mission to Morocco, Egypt, and Jordan from December 3-11, 2014.

The purpose of the mission is to introduce U.S. firms and trade associations to Morocco, Egypt, and Jordan's rapidly expanding infrastructure markets and to assist U.S. companies in pursuing export opportunities in these markets. The mission is intended to include representatives from U.S. companies and U.S. trade associations with members that provide infrastructure-related technologies, project managers and implementers, as well as companies with efficient energy equipment and technologies. The mission will visit three countries, Morocco, Egypt and Jordan, where the delegates will receive market briefings and participate in customized meetings with key port officials and prospective partners. Participants may also opt to receive briefings on opportunities and have meetings in the efficient energy infrastructure market in the West Bank for an additional cost. U.S. firms can register at:

http://export.gov/eac/show_detail_trade_events.asp?EventID=34104&InputType=EVENT

Public Tenders

1. From 2010-2015, the Moroccan government plans to invest more than USD 15 billion to upgrade its basic infrastructure of roads, ports and airports.

2. Morocco recently signed a USD 2.4 billion contract with Alstom (France) for the first phase of a high speed train system connecting Casablanca to Tangier by 2015. Additional segments will be opened for bid in the next two to three years. By 2030, ONCF will issue tenders to connect Tangier to Agadir via Rabat, Casablanca, Marrakech and Essaouira, then Casablanca to Oujda via Meknes and Fez.

3. The African Development Bank (AfDB) is providing a EUR 300 million loan to Morocco to support the investment plans of the national rail company Office National des Chemins de Fer (ONCF). ONCF is investing heavily in Morocco's transport infrastructure with a

USD 13 billion planned into 2035. Plans include the construction of almost 2,000km of major rail lines linking the country's largest cities, in addition to urban and high speed rail.

4. Casablanca has plans for 48 miles of rail lines to link Casablanca, its suburbs and a 13-mile metro line. Other large cities, such as Agadir, Fez, Marrakesh and Tangier also plan to build light metro lines and trams.

5. Construction of 50 large dams (3 large dams per year) and 1000 small and mid-sized dams by 2030

6. A North-South transfer pipeline at the Bouregreg, Oum Er Rbia and Tensift basins: 800 million m3 of water per year

7. Rainwater capture pilot projects which could lead to larger-scale deployment similar to what has been done in India and Australia.

Current USTDA Infrastructure Oriented Studies:

1. National Office of Potable Water Industrial Wastewater Treatment projects http://www.devex.com/en/projects/86854/print

2. National Office of Potable Water GIS System: http://www.ustda.gov/RFP/200821025A_MOR.pdf

3. Moroccan Ports VTMS and Surveillance Study http://www.ustda.gov/news/pressreleases/2009/MENA/Morocco/MoroccoVTMS_060809.asp

WEB RESOURCES

• Moroccan Tendering Platform: https://www.marchespublics.gov.ma/pmmp/?lang=fr

• Ministry of Housing: http://www.mhu.gov.ma

• National Railway Authority: http://oncf.ma/

• National Airport Authority: http://www.onda.ma/onda/an

• National Ministry of Equipment and Transport: http://www.mtpnet.gov.ma/MET_New/

• Federation of Builders: http://www.fnbtp.ma , http://www.fnpi.co.ma /

• International Building and Public Works Trade Show (Salon international du Bâtiment et des travaux publics), November 21-25, 2012, Casablanca http://www.sib.ma /

AVIATION (CIVIL AND DEFENSE)

Royal Air Maroc (RAM), the main Moroccan airline, is 96 percent owned by the government. It operates short-haul flights within the country, medium-haul flights to Europe and Africa and long-haul flights across the Atlantic to the U.S. and Canada. It has the largest fleet of 737s in Africa (42) and is scheduled to operate up to four Boeing 787s. Its headquarters is in Casablanca and it has its hub at the Mohammed V International Airport.

Morocco has 24 airports: 15 international, six domestic and three secondary platforms. Half the air traffic goes through Casablanca Mohamed V Airport, followed by Marrakech Menara (24 percent) and Agadir (14 percent). The Mohammed V International Airport is operated by ONDA (National Airports Authority) and it is located in Nouaceur Province, a suburb 30 km south-east of Casablanca. It is the busiest airport in Morocco with almost 7.25 million passengers passing through the airport in 2010.

Established in 1999, ONDA is the operator and administrator of airports in Morocco. Since 2004, they have upgraded the facilities of most airports in the country. In the ONDA 2011-2016 strategy, Morocco will become the North African hub for commercial aviation services. The strategy designates the Casablanca airport to become the service center. The following key measures are to be implemented:

- Training 700 additional engineers by 2016

- Increasing the airport capacity – from 22 million passengers to 42 million and double the airspace use

- Making the airport a major player in regional development by doubling the capacity of freight stations

- Strengthening the role of the airports into regional leaders in Africa by developing the ecosystems of companies that provide aircraft services.

The growth of the aeronautics industry relies on a highly professional and qualified supply chain of local subcontractors who have achieved certifications from international organizations. The newly created Moroccan Aerospace Institute (IMA) offers practical, continuous training and education to the industry of aviation. It is all based on the specific needs of the companies in Morocco.

Morocco plays an important regional role in aircraft sales. The bi-annual Marrakech Air Show is a must for U.S. companies selling into Africa. The last Air show took place in April 2014. The next event will take place in April 2016. For more information: http://marrakechairshow.com/en/ and email Commercial Specialist Thanae Bennani: Thanae.bennani@trade.gov

SUB-SECTOR BEST PROSPECTS

The sub-sectors of the aviation industry are equally important and represent great opportunity for future growth.

These subsectors are:

- Maintenance for all types of aircraft

- Cabling production for aircrafts (or other commercial vehicles)

- Service providers – VIP lounges, catering
- Parts and Equipment Suppliers for aircraft
- Parts and Equipment suppliers to airport facilities
- Pilot and Crew Training
- Air navigation control systems
- Radio communication systems
- Baggage handling
- Scanning equipment
- Passenger security devices,
- Aviation Consulting services
- Security Systems

OPPORTUNITIES

The Casablanca Free Zone in Nouaceur near the Casablanca Airport is a designated Industrial Integrated Platform (P2i) with special support for investors in the aerospace sector. Incentives include a corporate tax break of five years followed by a cap at 8.75 percent during the next 20 years. For example, Bombardier signed an agreement with Midparc Investment S.A., a Moroccan property holding and management company, to purchase land for its new plant in this P2i. Both Bombardier and United Technologies have invested around USD 200 million in new Moroccan factories. U.S. firm Eaton has started the construction of a USD 12 million plant in 2014 to manufacture aeronautics components and systems.

Specific Opportunities at Nouaceur Include:

1. A space "Ready for Output" offers to investors 1200 m2 of well-equipped (electricity, water, compressed air, IT network) modular production space (in units of 200 m2), making it possible to start the production rapidly.

2. A space "Ready for Services" is addressed to service firms related to the aeronautics industry and other innovating sectors. It offers modular offices (of 100, 200 and 300 m2) connected to IT networks and joint-services (conference rooms, copy centers, etc).

Public Tenders

All government contracts must be tendered through the national public tendering portal managed by the Moroccan treasury: https://www.marchespublics.gov.ma/pmmp/?lang=fr

The Office National des Aeroport's (National Office of Airports) website has a list of current Call for aviation related Bids (http://www.onda.ma/ONDA/Fr/Divers/MenuStructure/Appels+doffress/)

Contracting Opportunities:

1. Renovation of Oujda Airport with a new 20,000 m2 terminal to increase capacity to 2 million passengers and a new air traffic control tower for USD 120 million.

2. The construction of a new Terminal III at Marrakech Menara Airport will require USD 108 million and will double the airport's current capacity of 4.5 million passengers.

USTDA Sponsored Opportunities

A feasibility study grant was provided by USTDA to assist RAM in developing an operations optimization program in support of the establishment of a hub for RAM's operations at Casablanca's Mohammed V Airport. For more information, please go to:

https://www.fbo.gov/index?s=opportunity&mode=form&id=b6e27209bb8494f0a987628da2f2f48f&tab=core&tabmode=list& =

WEB RESOURCES

• ONDA's development plan:
http://www.onda.ma/ONDA/An/Espaces/EspaceONDA/Major+Projects/

• USTDA's grant:
http://www.ustda.gov/news/pressreleases/2009/MENA/Morocco/MoroccoRAM_111009.asp

• Direction Generale de l' Aviation Civile

http://www.aviationcivile.gov.ma/def.asp?codelangue=23&po=2

• GIMAS – Groupement des Industries Marocaines Aeronautiques et Spatiales

http://www.gimas.org/fr/Home.aspx

ENVIRONMENTAL TECHNOLOGIES

Waste Management

The Moroccan Government developed a 15 year (2008-2023) National Solid Waste Management Plan, called PNDM (Programme National des Gestion des Dechets Menagers) which was developed in cooperation between the ministries of the Interior, Finance, and the Environment. For a summary of the plan: http://www.environnement.gov.ma/PDFs/PNDM.pdf

The program targets include:

• Total Investment of USD 5 billion

• Collection rates of 82 percent (2005), 90 percent by 2015 and 100 percent by 2020

• Creation of 350 controlled dumps

• Closure and rehabilitation of existing illegal dumps

• Organization and development "sorting-recycling-valorization" in order to reach a recycling rate of 20 percent of all the waste generated in 2014, with pilot actions for source sorting

• Privatization of waste management in urban areas

This program is divided into three subsequent phases:

• 2008 – 2012: Initialization phase which allows for the integration of ongoing projects into priority projects

• 2013 – 2017: Scalability phase

• 2018 – 2020: Phase during which all untreated projects would be validated and implemented

International companies including Segedema, Sita, Veolia, Le Floque (France); Tecmed (Spain) and GESI and Edgeboro (U.S.) have been the main players in this sector.

Water Supply

Water supply in urban areas is almost universal. It reaches over 90% in rural areas. Morocco has developed several models for water management through the construction of dams, large reservoirs and water transfers. Though not yet fully implemented, Law 10-95 of 1995 allows for the establishment of river basin agencies to protect water resources, measures to promote water use efficiency, better allocation of water resources and protection of water quality through the application of user-pays and polluter-pays principles.

Note that L'Office National de l'Electricité (ONE) and the Office National de l'Electricite et de l'Eau Potable (ONEP) were merged and are now known as L'Office National de l'Electricité et de l'Eau Potable (ONEE). This state owned company is the main operator

in Morocco in the area of water and sanitation. ONEE – Water Branch is responsible for the production of drinking water as it produces 860 million m3, which represents 83 percent of the nation's potable water. It is also responsible for quality management and water supply transmission to the local agencies.

Four private operators supply Casablanca, Rabat, Tangier and Tetouan. ONEE – Water Branch's investment plan 2011-2015 includes the reinforcement of existing infrastructure and the upgrade of dams at Fez and Meknes. The investment volume is approximately USD 1.8 billion. A further USD 700 million will aim to increase access to water in rural areas to 95 percent.

For a list of tenders in different regions of the country related to water sanitation and potable water, U.S. companies can consult ONEE – Water Branch's website: http://achats.onep.org.ma/ao_liste.php

Waste Water

Only 70 percent of the urban population is connected to sewage systems. It is estimated that urban wastewater will increase to 900 million m3 in 2020. Wastewater is either discharged into the ocean with only physical treatment or is concentrated in regional basins. Only 20 percent of waste water is currently treated (up from 8 percent in 2005). To meet expected demand growth for waste water management, Morocco launched the National Sanitation Program (NSP) in 2006. The program is called the Programme National d'Assainissement Liquide et d'Epuration des Eaux Usées.

The Program's objective is to:

- Develop and improve wastewater collection and reuse to 60 percent
- Provision of sanitation services to 330 municipalities
- Increase the rate of sanitation access to 80 percent in urban areas
- Cover 10 million people in 260 cities and towns by the year 2020, at an estimated cost of USD 5.5 billion.

Several governmental agencies have roles in the Moroccan water sector:

ONEE – Water Branch is the main player and contributes to wastewater collection and treatment and the management of sanitation services. ONEE – Water Branch, which has been assigned since 2000 a global ambitious objective by the Moroccan Government to manage the sanitation service, now, manages sewerage and wastewater treatment, on behalf of the municipalities to which it supplies drinking water in 72 towns. For a list of tenders in different regions of the country related to water sanitation and potable water, U.S. companies can consult ONEE – Water Branch's website: http://www.onep.ma

Other than ONEE – Water Branch, major entities include:

- The Ministry of Interior ensures the provision of technical assistance and implementation of infrastructure, control, and application of the drainage policy.
- The Ministry of Agriculture and Maritime Fishing is responsible for policy concerning the reuse of wastewater in agriculture.
- The Secretariat of State in Charge of Water and Environment is responsible for environmental policy.
- Basin Agencies ("Régies") are located in different regions of Morocco and are in charge of evaluating, planning, and managing water resources at the hydraulic basin level. These agencies have authorization for defining conditions required for using treated wastewater.

• A Commune Rurale (CR) is responsible for planning, organizing and managing public services, including water supply and sanitation, within its jurisdiction. CRs have the option to provide public services directly, or through a Régie, ONEE – Water Branch, a private operator, or a water user association (WUA).

SUB-SECTOR BEST PROSPECTS

Plans for improving environment services in Morocco offer a growing market to U.S. suppliers of:

• Water and wastewater equipment

• State-of-the-art technology adapted to new water purification

• State of the art wastewater treatment equipment.

• Water and wastewater treatment projects management

• Rural water distribution technology

• Desalination project equipment

• High-pressure water pumps

• Monitoring equipment

• Demineralization systems

• Water treatment

• Distribution equipment

• Chemicals for water treatment

• Remote control equipment.

• Service contracts

• Maintenance contracts

• Technical advisory

• Water efficiency devices

• Solid waste management equipment

• Solid waste management engineers or consultants

OPPORTUNITIES

Internationally Financed Opportunities

The African Development Bank and the World Bank are financing several projects for water supply, sanitation and flood protection. For more information U.S companies can visit the following websites:

- http://www.afdb.org/en/countries/north-africa/morocco/

Upcoming ONEE – Water Branch Tenders

ONEE – Water Branch has ambitious projects to improve urban facilities, improve potable water access in rural areas to 95 percent and waste water treatment:

- Conversion to modern irrigation systems and improvement of existing systems with a potential to save 2.4 billion m3 per year.

- In tourism, developing norms and incentives to use water-efficient devices: pipes, water-closets etc with a potential to save 120 million m3 per year.

- Construction of 50 large (3 large dams per year) and 1000 small and mid-sized dams by 2030

- A North-South transfer at the Bouregreg, Oum Er Rbia and Tensift basins: 800 million m3 per year

- Rainwater capture pilot projects which could lead to larger-scale deployment similar to what has been done in India and Australia.

- Extension of artificial cloud seeding where possible.

- Desalinization of seawater and demineralization of brackish waters: 400 million m3 per year

- Reuse of treated wastewater in golf courses, green spaces and crop irrigation: 300 million m3 per year.

- A National Plan for the Prevention and Fight Against Industrial Pollution.

- Implementation of the National Plan for the Management of Household and Similar Waste.

- A project to de-mineralize brackish waters for reuse in irrigation and drinking water.

- A five-year project to artificially recharge aquifers.

For information on upcoming tenders: https://www.marchespublics.gov.ma/pmmp/?lang=fr

WEB RESOURCES

• L'Office National de l'Electricité et de l'Eau Potable – Branche Eau Potable (ONEE – Water Branch): http://www.onep.org.ma

FRANCHISING

Over 400 franchises operate in the fast food, clothing, office supply, furniture, cosmetics, office cleaning and auto repair sectors. Recent statistics indicate that 55 percent of the franchising activity is dominated by retail franchises and 45 percent is occupied by services. The clothing, food services, home furnishing and shoe retail occupy 45 percent of the market. Franchise holders are attracted to the marketing image and name

recognition of well-known U.S. products and brands such as Hertz, McDonald's, Pizza Hut, Domino's Pizza, KFC, Papa Johns, Haegen Dazs, Burger King, Pinkberry,TGI Friday's, Papa John's, Budget, New Balance, FutureKids, Century21, Starbucks and Midas. The most recent highlight of consumerism in Morocco was the opening of the Morocco Mall in Casablanca. This is Africa's largest shopping center and hosts many familiar brands.

Moroccan macro-economic trends are ideal for developing a franchise network. The country has benefited from a stable GDP growth rate of 3-5 percent over the past decade. Many Moroccans are entering the middle class where convenience and brand awareness become much more important. There is a huge demographic bulge in the 15-25 year old segment, which means a steady future supply of consumers with increasing purchasing power. The distribution of sales points shows a strong concentration in the metropolitan area of Rabat-Casablanca due to its high population density and purchasing power. As other urban centers become wealthier, they too will become attractive for development.

The success of franchising in Morocco stems from an expanding base of young entrepreneurs, many of whom are U.S. educated and have the financial means to develop master franchises. Franchising is also seen as an efficient way to promote small business creation and employment in Morocco. The Moroccan Government specifically promotes franchising in the Plan Rawaj which aims to create12 commercial activity zones (ZAC) by 2020. These zones will offer an attractive, safe and high quality shopping experience adapted to the needs of the local population. They will be familiar to all American franchises as they are highly similar to a mall or shopping center.

While French franchises have a predominant position in the market, American franchises are a close second and have the lion's share in the food business (McDonald's, Pizza Hut, El Rancho, Domino's, KFC, TGI Friday's, etc., car rental (Budget, Avis, Hertz, Dollar), and education (Futurekids, The Fourth R, Dale Carnegie, Wall Street Institute, Berlitz).

The following four points are main challenges that new market entrants must overcome:

• Trademark protection

• Counterfeiting

• Lack of a financing mode adapted to the specifics of franchising. In fact, although banks prefer to finance a franchise than an independent business, financing usually excludes the franchise fees, which are, most of the time, the bulkiest part of the investment.

• Absence of consulting firms specialized in the franchising activity.

• The sector remains non-regulated and there is still no specific franchising legislation.

SUB-SECTOR BEST PROSPECTS

The following sectors are considered to be the most attractive industries that would interest Moroccan franchisees:

• Fast-Food/Beverages

• Education/training (Languages, Executive training and Higher education)

• Supermarket, Hyper-mart chains

• Housewares and Linen retail

• Temporary employment services

• Business building management services

• Entertainment (movie houses, family parks)

OPPORTUNITIES

There is a strong concentration of international franchisees in the urban center of Casablanca, but secondary markets remain underdeveloped. There are a number of locations in Morocco that have a very low penetration rate of U.S. franchises and offer excellent opportunities:

• *Secondary Metropolitan Centers:* The cities of Rabat, Agadir and Tangier remain very open.

• *Plan Rawaj Commercial Zones:* As highlighted in Chapter 1, there are 12 commercial centers planned to be opened in Morocco. These centers will be specifically zoned for stores and suitable for retail franchises.

• *Morocco Mall:* This is Africa's largest mall and there are opportunities for new companies to occupy available retail spaces.

• *Airport Terminals:* The comprehensive renovation plan for Morocco's airports will create very interesting new opportunities for franchises, specifically for those who operate well in airports.

The Mega Franchise & Corporate Exposition is a great opportunity for advantageous meetings between Franchisors, Franchisees and Master Franchisees, investors looking for business opportunities as well as anyone concerned by this new culture. For more information about future Franchising Trade Shows in Morocco contact:

• Office des Foires et Expositions de Casablanca

Mr. Aziz Alami Gouraftei E-mail: aziz.alami@gmail.com

• Federation Marocaine de la Franchise

Mr. Abderrahmane Belghiti E-mail: fmf@menara.ma

WEB RESOURCES

International Franchise Association (IFA) - Assists franchisees and franchisors with the necessary information to properly set up and manage the franchise. The following list compiled by the IFA includes over 1,200 franchises: http://franchise.org/SearchFranchise.aspx

Fédération Marocaine de la Franchise (FMF) :
Président : Mr Abderrahmane BELGHITI.
Address : Angle rue Ain Taoujdate et rue Ain Ifrane Résidence Kacimi
2 éme étage Appt N° 9 Bourgogne - Casablanca
Tel: + (212) 537 77 05 70 03 or +(212) 522 48 58 10 Fax : +(212) 522 48 58 10
E-mail: fmf@menara.ma

Association Marocaine des Commerces en Réseau (AMCR) :
President: Ms Salwa Akhennouch.
3 Rue El Messaoudi Angle Bd Al Massira Khadra Maârif , Casablanca.
Tel : +(212) 522 36 22 88/96/33/41 Fax : +(212) 522 36 22 91
E-mail : amcrmaroc@yahoo.com
www.observatoiredelafranchise.ma

Legal firms specializing in Business Transactions and Joint Ventures
Bennani & Associés LLP 157 Boulevard d'Anfa 20 000 Casablanca, Morocco Tel : +(212) 522 95 96 02 Fax : +(212) 522 95 96 10

HEALTHCARE

The state remains the main health care provider with 70% of Moroccan patients going to state-run hospitals. Private clinics are increasing though, and the MOH is considering opening up private clinics to private investment. Morocco has the second-largest pharmaceutical industry in Africa and its 40 pharmaceutical factories produce 70% of the drugs that are consumed domestically. However, it should be noted that in 2013 the Moroccan Government implemented a pharmaceutical price cutting decree which has dramatically worsened the market for pharmaceuticals manufacturers. There are five university hospitals, six military hospitals, and 147 public hospitals with a total bed capacity of 27,325. These hospitals, plus Morocco's 2,698 basic health centers and 360 private clinics, are insufficient to adequately cover all of Morocco's healthcare needs. The medical device market is estimated at $230 million with $181 million constituting imports. 15% of Morocco's medical device imports come from the United States, which follows France (19%) and Germany (16%).

SUB-SECTOR BEST PROSPECTS

• Magnetic resonance imaging and ultra-sonic scanning equipment

• X-Ray equipment

• Emergency aid (equipment and services)

• Monitoring and electro-diagnostic equipment

• Computerized tomography equipment

• ICT (E-medicine, equipment and related software).

OPPORTUNITIES

Morocco plans to build 30 new hospitals, including two university hospitals in Agadir and Tangier, and expand mobile hospital and emergency units. The UAE will build the Sheikh Khalifa Hospital in Casablanca (200 beds) and Marrakech Health Care City (160

beds) with state-of-the-art medical technology. This expansion will encourage medical tourism as Sub-Saharan countries consider Morocco as a healthcare center and Europe sees Morocco as a low-cost provider. To stem imported second-hand medical equipment, the MOH will require registration within 12 months of all medical devices and equipment. This will improve the quality of medical equipment in Morocco, expand opportunities for U.S. firms, and offer a better quality of medical care to patients treated in Morocco.

WEB RESOURCES

• Association of Biomedical Equipments Professionals (APMB) : http://www.apmb.ma/

• Ministry of Health : www.sante.gov.ma

SAFETY AND SECURITY

Morocco has successfully maintained internal security in a region where Arab Spring revolts have resulted in unprecedented instability, and the government's highest priority is protecting its people, economy and political system from terrorist and criminal elements in the wider neighborhood. Morocco's geographic location as a gateway to Europe also requires the protection of borders and checkpoints against illegal immigration, human trafficking and narcotics. Customs and ports agreements with the United States and other countries require Morocco to implement major upgrades at airports, seaports, border crossings, and government buildings.

SUB-SECTOR BEST PROSPECTS

• All security and safety equipment and related solutions for seaports, airports, border crossings, security and safety agencies such as the police, and buildings,

• Integrated monitoring and surveillance solutions,

• Luggage screening devices,

• Biometrics,

• Fire prevention and control equipment, alarm equipment for building safety, emergency evacuation systems

- Radio communication systems,

- Inspection equipment for containers, and seaport cargo.

OPPORTUNITIES

The Moroccan market for equipment and services is expected to increase by 20% in the next five years. Local production is nonexistent and therefore imported safety and security products supply nearly 95% of the entire market, which until recently, was dominated by European firms. Morocco's implementation of an ambitious infrastructure development plan that includes ports, airports, hospitals, power plants, and new logistics

platforms increases sales opportunities for U.S. safety and security equipment and expertise. In addition, as Morocco depends on international tourism for economic growth, hotels and various tourism facilities provide constant opportunities for U.S. firms in this sector, and the current Open Skies Agreements with European and U.S. air space require continuous upgrades of safety and security equipment and procedures in airports. Moreover, the U.S. – Morocco strategic dialog, initiated in 2012, has a considerable security component that builds on a long history of U.S. – Morocco security and military cooperation.

As a developing economy, Moroccan governmental budgets may be constrained. There is no single Moroccan government agency that sets security policy, and this may complicate market intelligence gathering for U.S. firms. Gravitation towards Europe, though this trends has been weakening over the years.

AGRICULTURAL SECTORS

The agricultural sector's contribution to Morocco's GDP varies between 13 and 21 percent, thus heavily impacting the economy as a whole. Moroccan agricultural production depends a great deal on rainfall as only 16 percent of total arable land is irrigated. As a result, agricultural output fluctuates heavily from year to year. With its significant contribution to the country's GDP, the agriculture sector largely determines the growth of the whole Moroccan economy. The large fluctuations in output are also reflected in fluctuations in agricultural imports of some commodities such as animal feed, wheat and oilseeds.

The agriculture, fishing and forestry sector employs about 40 percent of the total workforce. Over 40 percent of the population lives in rural areas. Morocco's agriculture can be divided into three major sectors: 1) modern, private, irrigated, highly capitalized, and export oriented farms producing mostly fruit and vegetables; 2) agriculture within reorganized large scale dam-irrigated perimeters producing mostly dairy, sugar crops, seeds, fruits and vegetables mostly for the local market; 3) rain-fed agriculture with more favorable land in the northwest (growing mostly grains, olives, pulses, red meat and dairy) and less favorable land in the south and east (growing mostly grains and non-intensive sheep production). Grains account for over 60 percent of agricultural production, and area planted to wheat has expanded dramatically over the last 20 years with increased government support. The prevalence of small farms, complicated inherited land status, and increasing land prices pose serious challenges to agricultural policy makers. Policy makers struggle with the conflicting underlying principles of economies of scale and the capitalization requirements necessary to modernize the agriculture sector and the desire to alleviate poverty and maintain the social structure of the traditional rural society. In April 2008, the Moroccan Government unveiled a new strategy for agricultural development called "Green Plan" that aims at encouraging domestic and foreign investment in agriculture as a means to generate employment, transfer new technologies and achieve a better integration with the world economy.

Main areas for investment included olives, citrus, grapevines, dairy, and fruit trees. The new strategy also aims at providing leverage for small farmers to consolidate outputs and increase value-added production.

Moroccan agriculture remains mostly traditional with limited applications of production inputs such as fertilizers, pesticides and mechanization. However, many of the export-oriented farms, especially fruits and vegetables, have made a great deal of investment in modern irrigation equipment, new production and marketing technologies that help them meet international standards. Morocco agricultural exports consist mostly of fresh citrus, fruits and vegetables mostly targeted at nearby European markets. In 2013, Morocco's exports of agricultural products were estimated at about US$ 3.92 billion, while its imports were estimated at US$ 6.9 billion. In recent years, Morocco's exports to European Union (EU) market accounted for about 60 percent of its total agricultural and food export.

In 2013, U.S. agricultural and food product exports to Morocco totaled US$ 441 million, which represented about 34 percent decline compared to 2012. U.S. agricultural and food product imports from Morocco for 2013, however, were estimated at US$ 128.5 million. Morocco's demand for U.S. products is expected to recover in the coming years, though at a slower pace.

U.S. agricultural and food exports to Morocco are mostly bulk and intermediate commodities. Following the implementation of the U.S.-Morocco Free Trade Agreement (FTA) in January 2006, U.S. exporters increased their market shares of many traditional commodities. In addition, the implementation of the FTA boosted the demand for several U.S. high-value agricultural products, such as dairy products, soybean meal, and cotton. More detailed information on the FTA provisions can be found at: http://www.ustr.gov

Moroccan Agricultural Imports from the United States (USD Thousands)

Product	2009	2010	2011	2012	2013
Bulk Products	213,348	261,674	221,051	115.416	95,089
Coarse Grains (Corn/Sorghum)	123,008	67,578	82,311	7,281	-
Wheat	27,727	101,440	59,901	35	27,716
Cotton	19,335	38,415	58,857	53,119	43,641
Soybeans	42,574	53,103	18,475	43,847	23,732
Intermediate Products	259,946	426,164	642,513	467,880	157,450
Soybean Oil	140,281	197,601	317,708	161,842	21,417
Soybean Meal	76,285	164,921	225,225	217,660	113,924
DDGS/Corn Gluten/Beet Pulp	25,831	38,575	67,633	63,176	17,447
Tallow	7,020	13,024	19,506	12,027	4,662
Consumer Products	31,490	76,644	66,654	83.505	127,996
Dairy Products	21,767	64,394	55,828	70,990	116,675
Tree Nuts	5,603	7,824	8,627	8,585	11,321
Forest Products	958	1,106	2,065	2,664	-

Other products	-	-	-	-	60,439
Grand Total	505,814	765,628	932,500	670,088	440,958

Source: GATS

Best Prospects for Morocco are:

- Dairy product (dry milk, cheese, butter)
- Oilseeds and products (soybean oil and meal)
- Soybeans
- Grain and feed (wheat, barley, corn)
- Crude vegetable oil (Soybean oil)
- Dried fruits and nuts (pistachios, walnuts, non-pitted prunes, raisins, and almonds)
- Confectionary items
- Seafood/frozen
- Canned products.

Several consumer-oriented food products offer good opportunity for U.S. suppliers in spite of the high freight cost. These include processed fruit, fruit and vegetable juices, condiment and sauces, prepared food, confectionary and snack foods.

U.S. Trade Associations:

Mme. Mina EL HACHIMI
Regional Programs Manager - US WHEAT ASSOCIATES
c/o, Institut de Formation en Industrie
Meunière, IFIM, Sidi Bernoussi
Ancienne Route de Rabat km11,5 Ain Sebaa
Casablanca 20600, Maroc
Tel : 05 22 74 14 59
Fax 05 22 74 14 60
melhachi@uswheat.org http://www.uswheat.org

Mr. Khalid BENABDELJELIL
US Soybean Association (Consultant)
Tel : (053) 777 0517 / 777 1745
Cell : (066) 456 8828
kbenabdeljelil@yahoo.fr

Mr. Abdellah AIT BOULAHSEN
US Grain Council (Poultry)
Cell: 06 61 33 37 84
aitboulahsen@gmail.com
Mr. My Mustapha EL YOUSSOUFI
US Grain Council (Livestock)
Tel: 05 35 30 02 39 / 05 35 30 02 40 / 05 35 51 09 12
Cell: 06 61 35 24 47
Fax: 05 35 51 09 12
myoussoufi@menara.ma

In country USDA contacts:
Office of Agricultural Affairs, U.S. Embassy Rabat
Sarah Hanson, *Agricultural Attaché*
Khalid Boukantar, Agricultural Specialist
Phone: +(212) 357 76 59 87 Fax: +(212) 357 76 54 93
Email: AgRabat@fas.usda.gov

IMPORTANT INVESTMENT OPPORTUNITIES

Aiming for a strong and durable economic growth capable of producing wealth, the government has implemented a series of sectorial plans through a public-private partnership.

These plans are twofold:

The modernisation of traditional sectors, following the example of the agricultural, fishing and mining sectors; The development of innovative sectors, such as the following: renewable energy, logistics, automobile, aeronautics and services with a strong added value, where Morocco offers significant competitive advantages.

Priority sectors:

The National Pact for Industrial Emergence is a contract program between the State and the private sector targets 6 priority sectors called “Moroccan World Crafts”, each of which offers competitive advantages:

Offshoring Automobile Aeronautics and Space Electronics Textile and Leather Agribusiness

This strategy has also implemented the following:

The establishment of Integrated Industrial Zones to receive investments Improved competitiveness of Small and Medium Enterprises The adaptation of training to the needs of the sector Improved business climate.

Objectives

The objectives set for 2015 include:

The creation of sustainable employment and reduced urban unemployment; Increased industrial GDP; Decreased trade deficit; Support for national and foreign industrial investment; Contributing to land-planning policies.

Impact

220,000 direct jobs and reduced unemployment 50 Billion Dirham GDP increase 95 Billion Dirham in additional exports 50 Billion Dirham in additional private investments.

New sector strategy

The state has signed new contract programs with the private players in order to give

new impetus to the following sectors: Chemicals and Parachemicals Pharmaceutical Industry Metallurgical and Mechanical Industries (under signature)

Objectives

economic operators and improve the attractiveness. Take advantage of new market opportunities in 2025. Development of the pharmaceutical industry for export.

Impact

Chemicals and Parachemicals : Potential turnover of 150 Billion Dirham in 2020. Contribution of 47 Billion Dirham in GDP of 2020. The creation of 43,000 additional jobs.

Pharmaceutical : Potential export turnover of 1 to 2 Billion USD in 2020. The potential creation of 5,000 direct jobs and 22,500 indirect jobs by 2020.

Metallurgical and Mechanical Industries: Reduce the contribution of these industries on the trade deficit of the Moroccan industry 29%.

The Green Morocco Plan is a political initiative aiming to revive Morocco's agriculture, the main driver of the nation's economic growth.

Objectives

Economically: to develop an intensive and modern agriculture Socially: to modernise small-scale farming and improve the revenues of small fellahs Tools: aggregation, infrastructure development, training, technical assistance To increase GDP To create jobs To further ensure food security To protect the natural resources of the various regions To integrate the Moroccan agriculture into the national and international markets.

Impact

Nearly 150 Billion Dirham to be invested by 2020 An added value to be more than doubled (from 38 Billion to 99 Billion Dirham) 70-100 Billion Dirham in additional agricultural GDP

1.5 million jobs created This plan also aims to encourage a new wave of investments across the country, with a yearly objective of 1000 to 1500 projects translating into 10 Billion Dirham Growth of exports from 8 Billion to 44 Billion Dirham, for fields where Morocco is competitive (citrus, olives, fruits and vegetables)

Two- to three-fold improvement in agricultural revenue for 3 million farmers.

Digital Morocco 2013 is the National Strategy for Information Society and Digital Economy which aims to position Morocco as a dynamic emerging country in information technology.

Objectives

To make high-speed internet available to citizens

E-government programme for the administration to answer to the user's needs

To encourage the digitalisation of SMEs

To develop local IT, favouring the emergence of centres of excellence with high export potential.

Impact

58,000 jobs by 2013, as compared to 32,000 in 2008

- 7 Billion Dirham in direct additional GDP
- 20 Billion Dirham in indirect additional GDP
- 100% of schools fully equipped by 2013, versus only 20% in 2008
- 89 customer-oriented public services by 2013, versus 16 in 2008.

HALIEUTIS PLAN

The Halieutis Plan is an integrated strategy for the development and competitiveness of the fishing industry. It aims to bring up to standard and modernise various segments of the fishing industry, all the while improving its performance.

Objectives

To make aquaculture a powerful engine of economic growth;

To develop landing infrastructures and equipment;

To dedicate port spaces to fishing and to manage them efficiently;

To improve the attractiveness of fish markets and of Industrial Fish Sorting Stations (Comptoirs d'Agréage du Poisson Industriel – CAPI)

Impact

GDP: 21.9 Billion Dirham by 2020

Jobs: to jump from 61,650 to 115,000

Indirect jobs: 510,200

Size of informal sector reduced by half, to 15% of industry turnover

Seafood exports turnover of over 3 Billion Dirham

Over 1.6 million tonnes of fishing production.

LOGISTICS STRATEGY

The national strategy for the development of logistical competitiveness, part of the 2010-2015 programme contract, aims to optimally manage the increasing flow of imported and exported good. It is an essential part of all sectorial strategies, directly serving the interest of businesses and strengthening their competitiveness.

Objectives

Bringing up to standard of logistic services

Reforms and liberalisation of transportation methods (road, maritime, aerial)

Development of transportation infrastructures (ports, roads, highways, railways, airports)

Reduction of logistical costs

Environmental protection

Logistical costs reduced from 20% to 15% of GDP by 2015

70 logistical zones (2,080 ha) by 2015

20 Billion Dirham in direct capital gain

Impact

- 36,000 jobs created
- CO_2 emissions resulting from the transportation of goods reduced by 35%

NATIONAL STRATEGY FOR THE CRAFT INDUSTRY

This strategy aims to revive and develop Morocco's craft industry.

Objectives

The development of Moroccan know-how;

The implementation of a certification and labelling programme for the industry;

The creation of new jobs;

Aid for the emergence and development of a benchmark player-manufacturer base;

Aid to rural and urban single-craftsmen aiming to improve their production, sales, and living conditions.

Impact

Increase craft industry turnover to 24 Billion Dirham;;

Increase formal exports to 7 Billion Dirham;

Generate 4 Billion Dirham in additional GDP;

Create 117,500 jobs.

TOURISM: VISION 2020

This plan aims to perpetuate the progress of Vision 2010 and to again boost the tourism industry. The strategy is centred around tourism regionalisation, quality, and sustainable development.

It was conceived to showcase each of Morocco's regions, while preserving their natural resources, maintaining their socio-cultural authenticity and their population's well-being.

Objectives

To make Morocco one of the Top-20 tourist destinations;

To double the tourist accommodation capacity;

To double the number of foreign tourist arrivals;

To triple the number of national travellers;

Impact

- 8 new destinations;

- 200.000 new hotel beds and assimilated;

- 1 Million tourists from target emerging markets;

470,000 direct jobs created;

140 Billion Dirham in tourism income in 2020;

150 Billion Dirham in tourism GDP;

MOROCCAN ENERGY STRATEGY

The Moroccan energy programme will invest an estimated $18.95 Billion by 2020, or

close to 156 Billion Dirham, and will generate some 50,000 jobs. It predicts that, by 2020, electrical power produced by renewable energy (solar, wind, and hydraulic) will account for 42% of the total power produced.

Objectives

Decreased energy dependence;

Environmental preservation;

Limits on greenhouse gas emissions;

Fighting against climate change.

Impact

Solar Plan

Total electric production capacity of 2000 MW in 2020;

5 locations (Ouarzazate, Ain Bni Mathar, Foum Al Oued, Boujdour et Sebkhat Tah)

2 technologies : Concentrated Solar Power and Photovoltaic;

Increase of solar energy to 14% of total electric capacity;

Fuel savings of 1 Million tonnes of Oil Equivalent (TOE) and 3.7 Million tonnes of avoided CO_2 emissions per year.

Wind Energy Plan

Increased installed electrical capacity from 280 MW in 2010, to 2000 MW by 2020 (38% of current installed capacity);

Annual energy production estimated at 6600 GWh (26% of current national production)

5 new locations: Sendouk (Tanger), Koudia Baida II (Tetouan), Taza (Taza), Tiskrad (Laâyoune), Boujdour

Yearly savings of 1.5 Million TOE and 5.6 Million tonnes of avoided CO_2 emissions per year

RAWAJ 2020

Rawaj 2020 aims to revive and modernise interior trade.

Objectives

Improve procurement conditions for Moroccan citizens;

Improve the quality of life of traders;

Increase the participation of this sector to the national GDP;

Fight against counterfeiting;

Create employment opportunities.

SOURCES

National Pact of Industrial Emergence (www.emergence.gov.ma)

Moroccan Agency For Solar Energy (http://www.masen.org.ma)

Ministry of Energy, Mines ,Water and Environment (http://www.mem.gov.ma)

Agency for Agricultural Development (http://www.ada.gov.ma/)

Ministry of Tourism and Crafts – Administration du Tourisme (http://www.tourisme.gov.ma)

Ministry of Tourism and Crafts – Département de l'Artisanat (http://wwwfr.artisanat.gov.ma)

Rawaj 2020

INDUSTRY

Facing the challenges of an evolving global economy, the National Pact for Industrial Emergence aims to build a strong industrial sector and create a virtuous circle of growth.

The state and the private sector have sealed this covenant by signing a contract program covering the period 2009-2015. By consolidating into one document their mutual commitments, partners bring to all investors the necessary visibility on the changes of the future Moroccan industry. This contractual formula also guarantees the proper execution of measures agreed upon, by ensuring the involvement of all parties concerned, around specific, concrete, concerted and budgeted actions.

Gathering efforts to revive the industrial sectors for which Morocco has clear competitive and exploitable advantages (World Crafts of Morocco), through dedicated development programs.

Improving the competitiveness of companies through 4 major "Cross-cutting Projects":

Strengthening SMEs' Competitiveness

Improving business climate

Training

Creating the next generation industrial parks, called "P2I - Integrated Industrial Platforms".

Establishing an institutional structure to enable the implementation of effective and efficient programs

Targets for 2015:

Creating 220 000 direct jobs and reducing unemployment

Creating wealth through an increase in GDP by MAD 50 billion

Generating an additional volume of exports by MAD 95 billion

Generating additional private investment by up to MAD 50 billion

Program Cost: MAD 12.4 billion over the 2009-2015 period

34% of the total cost dedicated to Training and Human Capital

24% of the total cost dedicated to incentives for investors

Establishing an enforcement tool dedicated to the promotion and development of investments: the Moroccan Agency for Investment Development (AMDI)

SOLAR ENERGY

As part of its strategy towards energy use, Morocco gives priority to developing renewable energy and sustainable development. With abundant solar resources (a potential of 2 600 kWh/m²/year) and a strategic position at the heart of an energy hub (Connexion with Spanish Network through two electric lines 400kV/700 MW), Morocco offers a wide range of investment opportunities in the sector of thermal and photovoltaic solar energy, including the launch of the following structuring programs:

The Moroccan Project of Solar Energy: This integrated development project aims to set up in 2020 a capacity of electricity production driven from solar energy with a total capacity of 2000 MW in five major sites: Ouarzazate, Ain Bni Mathar, Foum Al Oued, Boujdour and Sebkhat Tah. The two technologies - Concentrated Solar Power (CSP) and Photovoltaic-are designated to be used in these stations. This program will increase by 14% the role of solar energy in total electricity capacity by 2020 and prevent the emission of 3.7 million tonnes of CO^2 per year.

Development Program of the Moroccan market for solar water heaters (PROMASOL): This program involves the installation of 440,000 m2 of thermal solar sensors in 2012 and 1.7 million m2 in 2020. In terms of thermal energy produced annually, these figures will correspond to 1190 GWh by 2020. This program will avoid the emission of 920,000 tons of CO_2 per year and create 920 permanent jobs. Both plans were designed to fall under the criteria of a Clean Development Mechanism.

National Solar Plan aims to develop in our country, on the occasion of the completion of power projects, economic and industrial sector in the solar technology sector. Masen invests with all parties stakeholders to create the conditions for the emergence of a competitive local industry. For this purpose, Masen launched with the support of specialized agencies a study on value chains with high potential for domestic industry in the solar sector to adopt appropriate accompanying measures. The FENELEC the AMISOLE the FIMME, and FNBTP among professional associations of the most affected sectors. These organizations are committed to facilitate the identification of key players from industry. The companies within these sectors are invited to register ; The aim is to create a national database of companies involved in the value chain for solar projects. -

Regulatory Framework:

The Renewable Energy Law (No. 13-09) aims to promote energy production from renewable resources, to market and to export by public entities or private. It also introduces the subjugation of facilities producing energy from renewable sources to a system of prior authorization if their power is equal to or greater than 2 MW, or prior notification for operating activities which necessitate power between 20 KW and 2 MW. Finally, it provides the right for an operator to produce electricity from renewable energy sources on behalf of a consumer or a group of consumers connected to the national grid of medium voltage (MV), high voltage (HV) and extra high voltage (EHV), under an agreement whereby they undertake to remove and consume the electricity produced exclusively for their own use.

Financing:

This strategy benefits from the resources mobilized under the pole of the Energy Development Fund with an amount equivalent to $ 1 billion donation from the Kingdom of Saudi Arabia (U.S. $ 500 million), UAE (U.S. $300 million) and the contribution of the Hassan II Fund for Economic and Social Development (200 million U.S.). The year 2010 was highlighted by the establishment of the Energy Investment Corporation (EIS) with a capital of one billion dirhams endorsed by the state (71%) and the Hassan II Fund for Economic and Social Development (29%).

Training

Creation of specialized energy courses within the major Engineering Schools and Universities s

Training of technicians in wind energy by Vocational Training Institutes

Conclusion of Industry partnerships-Large Schools - Universities, Institutes specializing in R & D applies.

Governance:

Moroccan Agency For Solar Energy (MASEN)

MASEN's mission is to ensure the implementation of the Moroccan Solar Plan (see more)

ADEREE

The National Agency for the Development of Renewable Energy and Energy Efficiency, which aims to contribute to the implementation of government policy on renewable energy and energy efficiency (see more).

AMISOLE

The Moroccan Association of Solar Industries and Windmills (Amisola) was created to promote the interests of industrialists and Moroccan professionals working in the renewable energy sector

WIND ENERGY

As part of its strategy towards energy use, Morocco has undertaken a vast wind energy program, to support the development of renewable energy and energy efficiency in the country. The Moroccan Integrated Wind Energy Project, spanning over a period of 10 years with a total investment estimated at 31.5 billion dirhams, will enable the country to bring the installed capacity, from wind energy, from 280 MW in 2010 to 2000 MW in 2020.

The development of 1720 MW of new wind energy farms are planned as follow:

720 MW under development in Tarfaya (300 MW), Akhfenir (200 MW), Bab El Oued-Laayoune (50 MW), Haouma (50 MW) and Jbel Khalladi (120 MW)
1000 MW planned in 5 new sites chosen for their great potential: Tanger2 (150 MW), El BaidaKoudia in Tetouan (300 MW), Taza (150 MW), Tiskrad Laayoune (300 MW) and Boujdour (100 MW).
Objectives of the wind energy program are:

Increase the share of wind power in the national energy balance to 14% by 2020
Achieve a production capacity from wind power of 2 GW and annual production capacity of 6600 GWh, corresponding to 26% of current electricity generation
Save annually 1.5 million tons of fuel, matching the sum of 750 million U.S. dollars, and prevent the emission of 5.6 million tonnes of CO_2 per year.
Value proposition

Real assets:

Huge potential in wind power estimated at 25,000 MW (see wind map)
A strategic location in the heart of an energy hub (connected to the Spanish electrical grid)

Regulatory Framework:

The Renewable Energy Law (No. 13-09) aims to promote energy production from renewable resources, to market and to export by public entities or private. It also introduces the subjugation of facilities producing energy from renewable sources to a system of prior authorization if their power is equal to or greater than 2 MW, or prior notification for operating activities which necessitate power between 20 KW and 2 MW. Finally, it provides the right for an operator to produce electricity from renewable energy sources on behalf of a consumer or a group of consumers connected to the national grid of medium voltage (MV), high voltage (HV) and extra high voltage (EHV), under an agreement whereby they undertake to remove and consume the electricity produced exclusively for their own use.

Financing:

To support the national plan for renewable energy development, an energy investment company for developing renewable energy (SIE) was created specifically for this purpose with a 1 billion dirhams capital.

This strategy benefits from the resources mobilized under the frame of the Energy Development Fund with an amount equivalent to $ 1 billion donation from the Kingdom of Saudi Arabia (U.S. $ 500 million), UAE (U.S. $300 million) and the contribution of the Hassan II Fund for Economic and Social Development (200 million U.S.).

Training

Creation of specialized courses in wind energy in large engineering schools anduniversities
Training of technicians in wind energy by Vocational Training Institutes
Conclusion of Industry partnerships-Large Schools - Universities, Institutes specializing in R & D applies.

Governace:

Energy Investment Company (SIE)

ADEREE
The National Agency for the Development of Renewable Energy and Energy Efficiency, which aims to contribute to the implementation of government policy on renewable energy and energy efficiency.

National Electricity Office (ONE)

TOURISM

Morocco is a tourist destination that has many strengths and clear potential that allowed it to become a highly popular tourist destination. With varied and contrasting landscapes (3500 km of coastline, mountains, deserts ...), a rich cultural heritage (imperial cities, old towns, food and crafts), Morocco is a unique and diverse touristic experience only 2h30 flight from major European cities .

Between 2005 and 2010, the number of tourists visiting Morocco has increased from 5.8 to over 9.3 million, and a mounts of foreign direct investments are around € 30 billion over this period combined. In addition, in 2009, Morocco was the only Mediterranean countries to havev increased more than 6% while the world market decreased by 5%.

Value proposition

Sectoral incentives:

Exemption of import duty preference for all capital equipment needed for the promotion and development of the project
VAT exemption for capital goods, machinery and equipment acquired in Moroccofor a period of twenty four (24) months from the date of commencement of business of the company

Exemption from import VAT for a period of thirty six (36) months for capital goods, machinery and equipment acquired on importation.
Total relief of the SI of turnover in foreign exchange business and hotel for a period of5 years from the year in which the first accommodation was made in foreign currencies and a reduction of 17.5% over this period.
Total exemption from IR to the amount of turnover in foreign currency by the hotel companies and for a period of 5 years and a reduction of 50% over this period.
Conventional Terms
For investments that meet a number of criteria, the investor may conclude with the State, investment agreements granting implementation aid for the project (for details, see the Factsheet Investment Incentives)

Financing offers
To remove the constraints on the access to financial resources, Vision 2020 considers the establishment of an instrument for national and international investment mobilization: the Moroccan Fund for Tourism Development (FMDT). Investment premiums will be implemented taking into account the level of risk perceived by investors for each type of product and for each destination.

To strengthen its commitment in supporting the implementation of Vision 2020, the banking sector is willing to mobilize a budget of 24 billion DH.

Aside from commercial banks responsible for financing the sector, funds for national investments were created to support the dynamic development of tourist projects. Some of them are Actif Invest, Madaef, H Partners, capital T and Saham Hotels.

Investment Opportunities

Azur 2020 Program : Establishment of a considerable Morocco seaside offer internationally competitive.

Program Green / Eco / Sustainability: Valuation of natural resources and rural areas in respect to socio-cultural authenticity of host communities.

Heritage and Legacy Program: Promotion of the Moroccan cultural identity through the structuring and valuation of tangible and intangible heritage of the Kingdom together with the construction of coherent and attractive tourist products.

Animation Program, Sport & Leisure: Creating consistent animation offers, varied and complementary to the basic tourist infrastructure in order to consolidate Moroccan tourism and make it more competitive and attractive to many tourists.

Niche Program with high added value (or business and Welfare): Strengthening the position of Morocco as a tourist destination for Business, welfare and health.

Biladi Program: Strengthening the tourist offer for natives through a suitable product that takes account of their habits and customs.

Governance:

Moroccan Society of Tourism Engineering (SMIT)

AGRICULTURE

The agricultural sector contributes with 19% to the national GDP, divided between agriculture (15%) and agro-industry (4%). This sector employs over 4 million people including about 100,000 in agro-industry.

The new agricultural strategy, Green Morocco Plan, established by the Ministry of Agriculture and Fishing, aims to consolidate the success achieved and to meet new challenges facing Morocco's competitiveness and opening of markets.

Value proposition

Green Morocco Plan designed to promote the development of the entire agricultural and territorial potential. The new Moroccan agricultural sector is meant to be open to all using different strategies depending on the targeted issues.

Green Morocco Plan will contribute to GDP with 174 billion dirhams, creating 1.15 million jobs by 2020 and triple the income of nearly 3 million people in rural areas.

Green Morocco Plan focuses on two pillars.

The accelerated development of a modern and competitive agriculture, vital for the national economy, through the realization of a thousand new projects with high added value in both productions and agro-food
Support to smallholder agriculture through the implementation or professionalization of 545 projects of small farms in difficult rural areas, thereby promoting greater productivity, greater recovery of production and sustainability of farm income . This second pillar also seeks the conversion of cereal crops with higher value added (or less sensitive to precipitation) and processing of local products.

To strengthen the projects of these two pillars, the VMS is based on projects consisting of the so-called cross-sector framework redesign and improvement of water policies, land tenure and the This plan revolves around the concept of aggregation for overcoming constraints to the fragmentation of land ownership patterns, while providing access to aggregated holdings of modern production techniques, finance and markets. It is based on the implementation of a new wave of investment around new players with high managerial ability.

The regional declination of the Green Morocco Plan in farm aims to build a regional vision and a regionalized agricultural production, eco-balance between two pillars and to mobilize regional and national funds, credit agencies, and investors as well as other donors wishing to support Morocco in the implementation of this Plan. □

Measures used

Total Investment: 10 billion dirhams per year in the horizon of 2020
Creation of 6 agropoli (Meknes, Berkane, Souss, Gharb, Tadla and Haouz)

Governance

Creating of the AGENCY FOR AGRICULTURAL DEVELOPMENT (ADA), which oversees the implementation of Green Morocco Plan. □

FISHING

The fishing sector in Morocco has developed an integrated, ambitious and comprehensive development in 2020 called "Halieutis. It aims at upgrading and modernization of various sectors of the fishing industry and improve its competitiveness and performance.

The grand strategy of sector development meansbuild the sector into a genuine development opportunity in the Kingdom, and is basedon three main axes declined as projects: Sustainable use of resources and promotionof responsible fishing involving Fishermen also considered as major players in sector development The development of an efficient and quality fishing StrengtheningCompetitiveness

Value proposition

Promote a sustainable manner the fish wealth Moroccan
Strengthen the sector's contribution to the national economy by nearly tripling thevalue-added fish to pass it by 8.3 billion dirhams in 2007 to 22 billion dirhams in 2020;
Increase the number of work stations on land used by industry and aquaculture of 61 650-115 000 and the indirect employment of 488 500-510 200 for 2020
Reduce by half the weight of the informal sector to reduce it to 15% of turnover in the sector
Raise the value of exports of seafood products to more than 3.1 billion dollarsagainst 1.2 billion dollars in 2007
Raise the volume of fish production of 1.035 million tonnes currently to 1.6 milliontons with a special effort to develop aquaculture
To encourage domestic consumption of fish to carry 10 kg per capita per year on average currently 16/kg/an/habitant

Means

The cost of this program for 2008-2012 is estimated at five billion dirhams of which 1 billion dirhams at the expense of the General Budget of the State.

To ensure the success of this strategy, there will be the establishment of the necessary instruments:

At the institutional level by the upgrading of professional associations and thecreation of new ad hoc organizations dedicated to the new strategy
Legally by the update of the rules governing the sector
At the organizational level by establishing a monitoring system to ensureappropriate traceability of products throughout the production chain and marketing
In terms of financing the establishment of appropriate means and in terms of infrastructure by adopting a broad program of investment in ports, landing equipment,aquaculture sites, chain cold, fish markets, wholesale markets and detail.

Governance:

Halieutis provided for the establishment of a strong public governance and mobilizingto modernize the fisheries sector. With the ultimate goal the establishment of a system of sectoral governance allowing gradual transfer of power to regions and the private sector.

National Committee for Fisheries
Funds for the adjustment and modernization of fishing effort
National Agency for the Development of Aquaculture
National Center for promotion of seafood

Monitoring the use of the fisheries sector

LOGISTICS

The national strategy for the development of logistics competitiveness, which has been the program contract 2010-2015, plans to reduce logistics costs by 20 to 15% of GDP. Wearing including the realization of 70 logistics platforms in several towns (2,080 ha) by 2015, the new logistics strategy of the Kingdom, aims to accelerate economic growth by 0.5 percentage point of GDP per year, or 5 percent of GDP in 10 years.

The new logistics strategy, which aims to optimally manage the increasing flow of goods both import and export, therefore wants an essential part of all sectoral strategies and their keystone to serve the interests directly economic operators and enhance their competitiveness.
Through the organization of transport and the flow of goods around the 70 logistics platforms (logistics Zones Multi-stream) directly connected to ports and highway and rail infrastructure and near the sites of production and consumption, logistics strategy will allow regulating the transport of goods by truck, especially in cities and reduced congestion in town centers limiting urban flows to small tonnage trucks to supply.
The new logistics strategy will also have a very significant impact on the environment, as it will allow for a 35% reduction in CO_2 emissions from freight transport, thus contributing to the improvement of environmental policy objectives.
These improvements are expected to generate direct economic added value of 20 billion dirhams (billion dirhams) and overall (direct and indirect) from 40 billion dirhams in the same period and the creation of 36,000 new jobs by 2015 and about 100,000 to fulfill strategy 15 years later.
Means used

Total investment of 60 billion DH, two-thirds by the private sector,
Development and implementation of an integrated national network of 70 Zones Multi-Flow Logistics (ZLMF)
Upgrade and incentive to the emergence of integrated and efficient logistics players
Skills development through a national training plan in the fields of logistics (61,000 people by 2015)
Establishment of an industry governance framework and measurement appropriate regulation

Governance

Creation of the Moroccan Agency for logistics development and an observatory for monitoring sector performance indicators

INFORMATION AND COMMUNICATION TECHNOLOGY

Information Communication and Technology (ICT) usage is essential for the emergence of the knowledge society and can actively contribute to human development, improvment of social cohesion and national economy growth. The challenge for Morocco in the ICT sector for years to come is not only to sustain the progress already made, but also to allow the insertion of Morocco in the global knowledge economy, through amplified and widely distributed integration of ICT across all actors of society: government, governments, businesses and citizens.

Morocco Numeric Plan 2013 has been built around a clear vision and ambition for Morocco: position Morocco among the top emerging countries in the Information Technology and Communication.

Make IT a vector of human development

Make IT a source of productivity and added value for other economic sectors and Public Administration
Make the IT industry a pillar of the economy
Position Morocco as a regional technology hub

IMPORTANT PROJECTS

Title	Description	Entity	Beneficiary	Status
DAMANCOM Portal: Social declarations for employees	Called e-BDS, the portal is designed to serve the community of companies affiliated to the CNSS or their agents by offering two online services: TV statement: To allow affiliates of the CNSS to submit their statements of an electronic manner. The online payment: To allow CNSS affiliates pay their dues over the Internet thanks to a simple and highly secure system. Currently, 80% of the employed mass is expressed via the portal DAMANCOM	National Social Security Fund	Businesses Citizens	Operational
Collaborative messaging platform	A messaging platform made available to all teachers and Moroccan candidates for IBC	Ministry of Education	Citizens Administrations	Operational, being extended
EParticipation site	New priority area with the implementation of several e-participation initiatives to improve citizen access to information, public services and enhance its participation in public decision making.	Ministry of Industry, Investment and Commerce of the Digital Economy	Administrations Citizens	In progress
Establishment of national data center	New priority project with the aim of pooling national assets in terms of ICT in a centralized and manageable environment that guarantees cost efficiency, transparency, compliance with standards and efficient use of resources	Ministry of Industry, Investment and Commerce of the Digital Economy	Administrations	In progress
Online publication of legal notices	TV for online ordering of the publication in the Official Gazette	Government Secretariat	Businesses	In progress
Multi-platform access to e-Gov Services	System for sending and receiving SMS messages and voice calls to provide an interface for eGov services via the telephone.	Ministry of Industry, Investment and Commerce of the Digital Economy	People	In progress
Mobile application for tracking eGov services	Mobile application for tracking eGov services.	Ministry of Industry, Investment and Commerce of the Digital Economy	Citizens Administrations	Operational
Administration Portal Maroc.ma	In addition to the informational component maroc.ma National Portal facilitates access to online services grouped by theme and user profile. It also can search services and access	Ministry of Communication	Citizens Business Administration	Operational

Title	Description	Entity	Beneficiary	Status
	contact pages of various departments.			
Common charter websites	Set of rules and standards to be implemented for institutional websites, supported by a circular from the Head of Government	Ministry of Industry, Investment and Commerce of the Digital Economy	Administrations	Operational
Site unifying eGov	Corporate website eGov program	Ministry of Industry, Investment and Commerce of the Digital Economy	People	Operational
Platform fikra e-participation	Collection service proposals and votes on the new online services	Ministry of Industry, Investment and Commerce of the Digital Economy	Citizens Businesses	Operational
Unifying portal Opendata of Morocco	National Portal of open public data	Ministry of Industry, Investment and Commerce of the Digital Economy	Citizens Businesses	Operational
Digital platform of Morocco Post	This is a digital platform that includes all the online services offered by Morocco Post.	Morocco Post	Citizens Businesses	Operational
E-government administrative documents control	E-government administrative documents control, with the first documents the extract of birth certificate and a full copy of the birth certificate.	Ministry of the Interior	People	Operational, being extended
Complaint Online	To improve services to citizens, companies, associations, users and elected ... etc, and strengthen communication with them, some ministries have given their websites a system for receiving and processing complaints and claims. This claim online platform is being extended on all the websites of the Kingdom Ministries. The online claim service is available at the: - Ministry of Infrastructure, Transport and Logistics; - Ministry responsible for the relationship with the parliament and civil society - Ministry of Housing and urban policy; - Customs and Excise; - Urban Commune of Tetouan,	Ministry of Industry, Investment and Commerce of the Digital Economy	Citizens Businesses	Operational, being extended
Making appointments online	To better accommodate its patients, the Department of Health has set up this management information system of appointments, which allows patients to make an appointment online or by phone.	Ministry of Industry, Investment and Commerce of the Digital Economy	People	Operational, being extended

Title	Description	Entity	Beneficiary	Status
Unique identifier of the citizen	An interministerial committee is working on the development of a unique identifier of the citizen to facilitate reconciliation of data between administrations and ensure better interoperability.	Ministry of Industry, Investment and Commerce of the Digital Economy	Administrations	In progress
System Information and booking of tourism products in Morocco	Information portal and booking of tourism products in Morocco.	Moroccan National Tourist Office	People	Operational
Industrial property related services	This portal offers TV services that allow online filing of trademarks, industrial designs and patents of invention and online ordering of balance sheets, statutes and company information.	Moroccan Office of Industrial and Commercial Property	Businesses Citizens	Operational
Trade register online	The portal includes several eServices Issuing extracts and certificates, and consultation documents on business	Moroccan Office of Industrial and Commercial Property	Citizens Businesses	Operational

Title	Description	Entity	Beneficiary	Status
Administrative procedures Guide	service-public.ma is a national portal that publishes a guide administrative procedures and a directory of public administrations, the portal also allows governments to update their procedures directly via access to the back office of the portal.	Ministry of Communication	Citizens Business Administration	Operational
Integrated Management of expenditure	The Integrated Management System Expenditures (GID), screw computerize the management of public expenditure, allowing optimal management with better terms of reliability, speed and efficiency.	Ministry of Economy and Finance	Administrations Businesses	Operational
Moroccan Government Procurement Portal	the Portal Moroccan Public Procurement is a common exchange platform between procurers and suppliers. It allows the consultation of markets and online submission	General Treasury of the Kingdom	Businesses Administrations	Operational
Online payment of taxes	Online payment of council tax, the tax on communal services, business tax, and income tax	General Treasury of the Kingdom	Citizens Businesses	Operational
BADR: Base Automated Networked Customs	BADR project aims to modernize the management and control of customs activity and offer users a set of remote services related to customs clearance.	Administration of Customs and Indirect Taxes	Businesses	Operational
Simpl-IR	The Simpl-IR remote service has been set up by the Directorate General of Taxation to allow users ?? s' pay in	Directorate General of Taxes	Citizens Businesses	Operational, being extended

Title	Description	Entity	Beneficiary	Status
	line with their tax obligations related to statements and payments relating to Income Tax.			
Simpl-VAT	The Simpl VAT-TV service was set up by the Directorate General of Taxation to allow users ?? s' pay in line with their tax obligations related to statements and payments connected with the Value Added Tax.	Directorate General of Taxes	Businesses	Operational, being extended
Simpl-IS	The Simpl-IS TV service has been set up by the Directorate General of Taxation to allow users to s ?? pay online with their tax obligations related to statements and payments relating to corporation tax.	Directorate General of Taxes	Businesses	Operational, being extended
Payroll System	Officials payroll system	Ministry of Economy and Finance	Administrations	Operational
Unifying portal e-finance services	Directory of remote services of the Ministry of the Economy, Finance.	Ministry of Economy and Finance	Citizens Businesses	Operational
Web portal of the Ministry of Solidarity, Women, Family and Social Development	This project aims to provide the Ministry of Social Development, Family and Solidarity, its informative web portal.	Ministry of Solidarity of Women, Family and Social Development	Citizens Business Administration	Operational
Visa Secure	Labels for secure visas for foreigners	Ministry of Foreign Affairs and Cooperation	People	Operational
e-Consulate	Publishing Portal administrative procedures and consular services online for the Moroccans Living Abroad	Ministry of Foreign Affairs and Cooperation	People	Operational
Consumer Portal	Following the adoption of the Law on Consumer Protection, the Ministry of Industry, Trade, Investment and the Digital Economy launched the consumer portal. This portal contains mainly informative content as well as a TV service for the online filing of claims.	Ministry of Industry, Investment and Commerce of the Digital Economy	Citizens Businesses	Operational
Biometric passport	This project aims to replace ordinary passports by biometric passports that include security features based on the most advanced technologies to increase reliability and thus, protect incumbents against fraudulent use in the event of loss, theft or identity theft attempt.	Ministry of the Interior	People	Operational
National	NIEC: a new secure identity as aiming	Ministry of the	People	Operational

Title	Description	Entity	Beneficiary	Status
Identity Card Electronics	to protect citizens against possible tampering and theft of identity.	Interior		
Driver's license and vehicle registration	This project is part of a major project to modernize the road transport management system launched by the Ministry of Equipment and Transport. This remote service package for users regarding the dematerialization of procedures for registration of vehicles, the management of driving licenses	Ministry of Infrastructure Transport and Logistics	Citizens Businesses	Operational, being extended
Online Application qualifications and classifications	TV RFQ's dematerialization and service classification that allows the filing of the record and monitor the progress of the online processing of the application.	Ministry of Infrastructure Transport and Logistics	Businesses	In progress
Home Services Portal foreign	Information services in relation to the jobs to migrants in Morocco	Ministry of Employment	Citizens Businesses	Operational
Repository of trades and skills ICT Online	This repository provides information sheets describing SI activities and related skills. These key information enables HR and IT to establish knowingly SI multidisciplinary project teams based on skills held or acquire and develop collective or individual skills development plans.	Department of Vocational Training	Businesses Administrations Citizens	Operational

Title	Description	Entity	Beneficiary	Status
Request criminal record	This service allows TV to the request of the criminal record online and removal in court the plaintiff's choice	Ministry of Justice and Liberties	People	Operational, being extended
Borne consultation rights in courts	Touch screens available in the courts help to learn about the action taken on court cases	Ministry of Justice and Liberties	People	Operational
E-Justice Portal	Legal information portal on several components, for example: Legal texts Circulars Conventions Jurisprudence	Ministry of Justice and Liberties	Citizens Businesses	Operational
Public and academic libraries online	Portal of the National Library which includes catalogs and digitized books with the ability to view online	National Library of the Kingdom of Morocco	Citizens Businesses	Operational
OMTIC: National Observatory of Information and Communication Technologies	The OMTIC is a portal created by the MICIEN to allow monitoring and evaluation of the ICT sector in Morocco strategies as well as anticipation and the day compared to the change in the ICT environment	Ministry of Industry, Investment and Commerce of the Digital Economy	Citizens Businesses	Operational
Government Gateway	The objective of the "Government Gateway" project is to set up:	Ministry of Industry,	Administrations Businesses	In progress

Title	Description	Entity	Beneficiary	Status
	1. an electronic platform for the exchange between administrations (Gov2Gov). 2. tele-service portal for citizens and businesses The expected benefits of the Gateway are: • Simplify administrative procedures by replacing paper documentation with electronic exchange Gov2Gov • Simplify for administrations to create remote services to users through an electronic administration forms generator • Create a one-stop-shop e-government bringing together all the online services in a single portal	Investment and Commerce of the Digital Economy	Citizens	
Creating Online Business	In order to improve the long process and business creation complex, an electronic platform for online business creation will be established. This platform plays firstly a one-stop role for submission of creating folders, and secondly an orchestration role of these files with stakeholders in the process.	Directorate General of Taxes	Businesses Administrations	In progress
General Interoperability Framework	Norms and standards for the interoperability of information systems. A first version was adopted by Circular Head of Government. A second version is planned including semantic interoperability (data structures, nomenclature, common reference)	Ministry of Industry, Investment and Commerce of the Digital Economy	Administrations	Operational
Establishment of an electronic certification operator platform	Barid e-Sign is an electronic certification service provider that has implemented an infrastructure to meet the needs of business, government and the general public in digital trust through the use of digital certificates	Morocco Post	Citizens Business Administration	Operational
Online publication of vacancies in the public service	National portal that brings together all the job opportunities in government and public bodies	Ministry of Civil Service and Modernisation of Administration	Administrations Citizens	Operational
Portal "Invest in Morocco"	Information portal on investment opportunities in Morocco	Moroccan Investment Development Agency	Businesses Citizens	Operational
MASSAR: the schooling of the Management Information System	"Massar" is an integrated information system for the management of education, it is composed of several blocks: School management SI and basic student data Websites of schools	Ministry of Education	Citizens Administrations	Operational, being extended

Title	Description	Entity	Beneficiary	Status
	Online services for parents and students			
SIAS: Information System Administration School	Issuing laptops and 3G connections to the principals	Ministry of Education	Administrations	Operational
MASIRH: HR Portal of Education	HR management at the Ministry of Education has a strategic challenge of modernization and reform of the entire sector. The information system is the cornerstone of this management, several studies have been HR management at the Ministry of Education has a strategic challenge of modernization and reform of the entire sector. The information system is the cornerstone of this management, several studies have been conducted by the DES and that led to the launch of a structured program of HRIS. This program consists of the following projects: - The project MASIRH (Administrative HR Management) - the Harraka project (HR Quantitative Management) - the GPEEC project (HR Qualitative Management) - the Administrative Portal MASIRH The project is the base stand HRIS, covering all the administrative management of human resources and seeks the integration and decentralization of management processes at the regional academies, delegations and schools.	Ministry of Education	Administrations	Operational, being extended
Portal of the integration of ICT in education (Engineering Program)	This portal is an initiative of the GENIE program is the realization of the national strategy of generalization of information and communication technologies for teaching (CTBT) in all Moroccan schools	Ministry of Education	People	Operational
Portal of the High Commission for Planning	Collection and dissemination of statistical data on Morocco in general	High Planning Commission	Citizens Business Administration	Operational
Tracking portal refunds	The CNOPS portal provides online services for employers and allows policyholders the online monitoring of health care claims.	National Fund of Social Welfare Organizations	Citizens Businesses	Operational
Management of public and	RCAR portal is a dynamic space that allows to have remote 24h / 24 and 7/7	Collective Retirement	Administrations Businesses	Operational

Title	Description	Entity	Beneficiary	Status
private pensions	of all RCAR services. Several online services are offered to employers, affiliates, beneficiaries and providers of RCAR all remote services are also available on mobile	Allowance Plan	Citizens	
Maps / access to property titles for notaries	Efoncier is a service offering web consulting service of land and cadastral databases with Agency partners (Notaries, IGT, Public Administration, ...). The available information concerning the properties such as the owner's name, the size, consistency, land charges, etc. ... Efoncier has 3 land services: 1. Land Title information 2. Land archives digitized archive of digitized cadastral 3.Fonds	National Agency of Land Conservation Land Registry and Mapping	People	Operational
E-Mediation in the labor market	Electronic platform matchmaking between job seekers and employers in the private sector.	National Agency for Promotion of Employment and Skills	Citizens Businesses	Operational
Portnet: Port Data Exchange Platform	Portnet seeks to implement Recommendation 33 of the United Nations concerning the single window for formalities related to foreign trade, to provide the port community a centralized database and to share.	Agence Nationale des Ports	Businesses	Operational, being extended

RETAIL TRADE

Retail contributes to 11% of GDP and employs about 1.2 million people or 12.8% of the labor force in Morocco. Retail has experienced over the past decade, the emergence of new patterns of trade and especially franchise networks and retail.

The Department of Trade and Industry has developed the Vision 2020 Rawaj plan for sector development and trade distribution. Rawaj plan revolves around four main axes:

The large and medium distribution
The independent commerce
Trade Network and the franchise
Public spaces merchants under the responsibility of municipalities (wholesale markets, slaughterhouses and fish markets).
Value proposition

Make Morocco a platform par excellence for shopping with an offer that meets the needs of all consumers
Modernize the local shops (labeling, central purchasing, networking traders ...)
Contribute to the emergence of national champions (assistance and support of national operators in the creation and development of commercial networks)
Implementation of 600 supermarkets and hypermarkets in 2020, with more than 50 hypermarkets generating nearly 80,000 jobs
Creation of 15 malls that can accommodate almost 3000 franchise stores and modern trade and generating nearly 21,000 jobs
Creation of 15 outlets, discount stores and factory outlets generating 5,000 jobs

Increase the current GDP of trade to 98 billion MAD
Bring the contribution of trade to GDP at 12.5%
Increase sector growth to 8% annually

In order to encourage merchants to join the modernization plan, program Rawaj VISION 2020 provides for the establishment of a dedicated funding mechanism, including the creation of a development fund for commerce. The fund will finance and support projects initiated by local communities in order to organize the commercial spaces and develop sites for the settlement of itinerant traders. The endowment fund is 200 million MAD per year over the period 2009 to 2012.

ISLAMIC BANK

Opportunity/Project
Establishment of an Islamic Bank in Morocco

INVESTMENT INCENTIVES

In addition to the tax exemptions granted under the common law, Moroccan law provides specific financial, tax and customs advantages to investors, as part of agreements or investment contracts to be concluded with the State, provided that they meet the required criteria. (Download the Factsheet Investment Incentives)

This concerns:

The contribution of the state to certain investment expenses: Investment Promotion Fund;
The contribution of the state to certain expenses for the promotion of investment in specific industrial sectors and the development of modern technologies: the Hassan II Fund for Economic and Social Development;
Exemption from customs duties under Article 7.I of the Finance Act No. 12/98;
Exemption from import VAT under Section 123-22 °-b of the General Tax Code.
These four advantages can be benefited from in a single investment project. And for more information on each of these advantages:

Investment Promotion Fund
The Investment Promotion Fund (IFP) manages operations relating to the state's taking charge of the cost of some advantage granted to the investments that meet the criteria, within the framework of contracts, and in accordance with the investment charter and its implementation decree:

Land support: the IFP takes charge of 20% of the expenses of land acquisition necessary for the realization of the investment;
External infrastructure: the IFP participates in the expenses of external infrastructure with up to 5% of the overall amount of the investment program;
Training: the IFP participates in the expense of vocational training provided as part of the investment program with up to 20% of the cost of this training.
These advantages are cumulative, provided that the state'sparticipation does not exceed 5% of the total investment program. However, if the investment project is expected in a suburban or rural area or in the case of investment in spinning, weaving and textiles finishing, the participation of State may reach 10% of the total investment program.

The investment project must meet at least one of the following criteria:

Invest an amount equal to or greater than MAD 200 million,
Create a number of stable jobs equal to or above 250;

Realize the project within one of these provinces or prefectures: Al Hoceima, Berkane, Boujdour, Chefchaouen, Es-Smara, Guelmim, Laayoune, Larache, Nador, Oued Ed-Dahab, Oujda-Angad, Tangier-Asilah, Fahs-Bni-Makada, Tan-Tan, Taounate, Taourirt, Tata, Taza and Tetouan;
Ensure transfer of technology;

Contribute to the environment protection

HASSAN II FUND

Hassan II Fund for Economic and Social Development (FHII) grants financial assistance for investment projects in some industrial sectors for:

Building or acquiring professional buildings: the Fund can support up to 30% of the cost of professional buildings on the basis of a maximum unit cost of 2,000 MAD/m2 (excluding taxes);
Acquiring new equipment goods: the Fund may contribute up to 15% of the purchase cost of new equipment goods (excluding import duties and taxes).
These contributions are limited to 15% of the investment amount and 30 million MAD.

The relevant sectors are:

Manufacturing equipment for the car industry
Manufacturing components for electronic assemblies and subassemblies
Manufacturing equipment for the aviation industry
Manufacturing activities related to nanotechnology, microelectronics and biotechnology
Manufacturing tools and mould for the car and the aircraft industry
Aeronautical maintenance and planes dismantling

The beneficiary projects are the new investment projects (creation or extension) with a total investment amount of more than 10 million MAD (excluding import duties and taxes) and under the condition that the amount of investment in equipment goods is above 5 million MAD (excluding import duties and taxes).

Specific treatment:

The projects in the aircraft industry which the investment amount in capital goods is upper to 200 million dirhams (except import duties and tax) can be realized in one or several phases considering each of the phases as eligible project for the Fund contribution.
The eligible investment projects in the manufacturing equipments activities for the car industry benefit from a maximal contribution of 15 % to the acquisition of the imported capital goods used in the deep-drawing activities, the plastic injection and tools and moulds manufacturing.

IMPORT DUTY EXEMPTION

Businesses that commit to making an investment of an amount equal to or greater than two hundred (200) million dirhams can benefit, as part of agreements to be concluded with the government, from exemption from import duty and the value added tax applicable to goods, materials and tools needed for their project and imported directly by the companies or on their behalf.

This exemption is also granted to the parts, spare parts and accessories imported at the same time as capital goods, machinery and equipment for which they are intended. The investment must be made within thirty-six (36) months from the date of the signature of the abovementioned agreement.

VAT EXEMPTION

Equipment goods, materials and tools needed to achieve investment projects involving an amount higher than or equal to MAD 200 million are exempt from VAT on imports within the framework of an agreement concluded with the State, in favor for the beneficiaries during a period of thirty six (36) months from the start of business. This exemption is also granted to parts, spare parts and accessories imported at the same time as the aforesaid equipment.

INVESTMENT ZONES

Three types of investment zones are available in Morocco

Integrated Industrial Platforms

Presentation

This program includes 3 types of platforms:

The General P2I : Open to all sectors, and can combine several sectoral areas

The Sectoral P2I: Although they are dedicated to a specific sector, they may contain areas reserved to sectors close to the main sector (e.g. electronics area in a car P2I)

The Regional/National P2I areas: general areas reserved for an industrial organization from the same region of a foreign country

The P2I program aims to progressively establish a network of 22 P2I, some of which are existing zones and which need to be upgraded according to the value proposition offered to investors.

Site selection

The final selection of sites for basing P2I is done on the basis of the following criteria:

Availability of manpower to meet the needs of the industry;

Logistics accessibility ensuring a good connection of the site for receiving suppling and exporting products;

Land availability

P2I value offer for investors is structured around the following offers:

Real-Estate offer

The P2I envisage providing 3 types of real estate offers to investors:

Rental or purchase of serviced land

Rental or purchase of ready buildings

Rental or purchase of customized buildings

Services Offer

A complete Services Offer for investors and their employees:

Services for exploiting the area: infrastructure maintenance, security, etc.

General services: telecoms, food, health services, banking, etc.

"Business" Services: business center, hiring support, travel agency, etc.

Advanced services specific to industrials: industrial maintenance, engineering, recycling and logistics areas, etc.

Training Offer

Offering the possibility of training within the area by creating, in the P2I, a specialized training institute or a public training center (OFPPT)

Logistics Offer

The zone is in an optimal logistics position in relation to the major national transport routes, according to the needs of the sector (maximum proximity to major ports and/or airports, highways ...)

One-stop-shop

There is a one-stop-shop bringing together the various key administrative departments for investors. Delegations of full-time staff of these authorities will be grouped in a dedicated area within the P2I. The main administrative services are:

ANAPEC: recruitment support services, allocation of public training assistance, issuing work permits, etc.Municipality services: Document Legalization

Regional Investment Center

Regional Investment Center (CRI): company creations, patents, etc.

National Social Security Fund - CNSS: employees' declaration, affiliation, etc.

Logistics connectivity

An optimal living framework and a link to the city, mainly through the selection of ideally-positioned land in relation to the city, and which is interconnected with the public transport network.

Status of free zones

The P2Is of Kenitra, Nouaceur, Tangier Oujda enjoy the status of free zones for exporting.

INDUSTRIAL ZONES

Alongside the development of P2I, a program for creating areas for economic activity is set up, besides the rehabilitation of several industrial zones. The main objective is to enable regions to strengthen their industrial potential.

Both programs aim at:
Developing land supply;
Providing entrepreneurs with quality services for carrying out their projects;
Optimal benefiting from regional industrial opportunities;
An annual budget of 100 Million MAD is reserved for these programs.

FREE ZONES

Instituted by Law 19-94 (Dahir No. 1-95-1 dated January 26, 1995), export processing zones are identified areas of the customs territory where they are authorized, exempted from customs regulations, foreign trade and exchange control, all industrial and commercial export activities as well as linked service activities. Each zone is created and defined by a decree which stipulates the nature and activities of the companies that can operate in the zone

The agent of the export processing zone provides the development and management of the zone and the submission of the investors folders for approval by the local Committee of Export Processing Zones. The company manager offers one stop service to the investor

Free Zones in Morocco:
Export Processing Zone of Tangier
Free Zones at Tanger Med Ksar el Majaz Mellousa 1 and 2
Free Zone in Dakhla and Laayoune:
Free Storage Zone of hydrocarbons: Kebdana and Nador
Export Processing Zone in Kenitra
Source: http://www.mce.gov.ma

MARKETING PRODUCTS AND SERVICES

Foreign goods are imported mainly through Casablanca by companies that distribute either directly to the public or to other wholesalers, distributors, or retailers. Mark-ups can be substantial, although current price controls tend to keep them lower for many market staples. Goods may also be imported through commission agents for delivery to wholesale and retail warehouses or to end-users. The agent's commission usually represents 5 percent of the cost, and can sometimes be even higher.

Ordinarily, locally manufactured products are distributed by the manufacturer directly to wholesalers, distributors and retailers. This system, driven by strong price competition, eliminates certain intermediaries and helps maintain competitive pricing. Manufacturers' mark-ups range between 20 and 30 percent depending on the product; those of distributors from 15-20 percent.

Most of the wholesale and retail commercial enterprises in Morocco are family-run businesses that perform a variety of commercial roles.

FINDING A PARTNER

All foreign manufacturers and exporters are represented in the market either through their own affiliate branch office or through authorized agent/distributors who import, install and service the equipment. These distributors customarily provide total technical support to end users. Certain locally registered agent/distributors with long-term relationships with foreign manufacturers have contractual arrangements with their principals under which the local importers provide in-bond warehousing. New-to-market U.S. exporters are urged to consider similar agreements.
Franchising

Franchising is a growing phenomenon in Morocco. The first franchise, Pizza Hut, started its operations in 1992. There are about 30 franchises in Morocco. Most of them are in fast food, clothing, furniture and cosmetics. Franchise holders are generally attracted by the image, notoriety and security brought by a famous product or brand. For example, McDonald=s, Pizza Hut, Dominos Pizza, Dunkin Donut, Subway, Scholtsky Dely and Dairy Queen, are doing very well and are now expanding their operations in Casablanca and in other major cities. The rapid growth in the sector stems from major economic and social changes in Morocco, particularly economic growth, higher disposable incomes and the increased number of women working outside the home.

DIRECT MARKETING

This selling method is allowed in Morocco. Avon and several other French companies employ Moroccans primarily for direct sales of cosmetics, toys and household goods.

JOINT VENTURES/LICENSING

Moroccans are increasingly interested in joint venture business. There are an estimated 1,500 joint ventures in manufacturing with French, Spanish, German and American partners. Licensing is a widely practiced form of doing business in Morocco. Over 250 U.S. pharmaceuticals are produced under license in Morocco, in addition to popular U.S. beverages and some snack foods. EU firms dominate the licensing market with vehicle assembly, clothing, pharmaceuticals and cosmetics.

ESTABLISHING AN OFFICE

The Commercial Code freely permits the establishment, extension or merger of firms. Formalities required to form a company consist of entering the statutes with the Secretariat of the Court of First Instance and in the Commercial Register kept by the Court. As in the United States, a person may create or purchase a business without incorporating. The owner of a such proprietorship has responsibility for all operations, transactions, and debts.

SELLING FACTORS/TECHNIQUES

Most local distributors of imported merchandise expect their suppliers to provide substantial advertising and promotional support, particularly when introducing a new product or brand name. Sales promotion material and technical documentation should be in French. Clear and simple

French-language operating instructions, displays of the product in use, sample handouts and frequent personal visits are vital for successful sales in Morocco.

ADVERTISING AND TRADE PROMOTION

While a number of advertising agencies operate in Morocco, most do not provide the number of services an American seller would expect. Media advertising is well developed. Newspaper and magazine advertising is most commonly used and French language papers have the most significant readership.

Leading daily papers published in Casablanca in French include "Le Matin", "l'Opinion" and "Al Bayane". "La Vie Economique" and "l'Economiste" are widely-read business economic weeklies. In addition, several local industry groups publish specialized trade and industry journals. Commercial time is available on the television channels in 10 to 60 second "spots" usually repeated 2 or 3 times daily.

The most common advertisement is the 30 second spot. Advertising is prohibited on the government-owned radio, but commercial time is available on Tangier-based French broadcasts that reach the entire Maghreb. Radio advertising has proven very effective and next to newspapers is the medium of choice for most consumer goods advertising. Direct mail is also becoming more common and a new firm now offers aerial-banner advertising. Street posters offer an important advertising medium for consumer goods in Morocco. Fast moving consumer product companies sometimes use sound trucks to advertise, particularly in remote areas.

PRICING PRODUCT

In most cases prices are freely determined by the market and there is little government involvement in price controls except for staple commodities such as gasoline, vegetable oil, sugar and subsidized flour. With the recently announced liberalization of imports of staple agricultural commodities, the government is expected to allow local prices of vegetable oil, flour and sugar to vary to encourage competition between various players.

Currently, vegetable oil, sugar, and a limited quantity of flour are subsidized at the retail level to make them affordable to the low income population. While the GOM policy is to phase out the retail subsidies, it may take a few years to do so because of the impact any abrupt price changes in sugar, vegetable oil, and flour might have on social stability. The GOM is also expected soon to announce the abolishment of the laws that preset the local retail prices for vegetable oil, sugar and standard flour. Retail prices will reflect the cost of production or imports and should be an effective tool to encourage competition between millers, refiners, and importers.

CUSTOMER SUPPORT

U.S. firms are urged to provide the following services to their local agent/distributors:

Readily available back-up service provided by manufacturer-trained local technicians and engineers and user-oriented products suited for local conditions.

Partnership agreements with local firms who provide expertise on local trading conditions, warehouse equipment, and spares.

Product information in French is vital in Morocco. The end users' support staff is often ill-trained and prone to mishandle equipment if they do not receive detailed instructions and are not provided with comprehensive manuals.

Major competitors often have agreements with local importers/distributors to share costs for local and factory technical training programs.

SELLING TO THE GOVERNMENT

Sales to the Government are made through direct negotiations or foreign government tenders. The most common method is through tenders. The public sector has three categories of projects: Minor, Medium and Major. Medium and Major projects are open to international firms. Major projects are usually guaranteed by an international financial entity.

There is no central purchasing bureau and no tendering authority. Ministries and state-owned enterprises issue their own tenders and deadlines vary from 30 to 90 days depending upon the complexity of the project. Different entities conduct their procurement activities differently, and procedures are sometimes opaque and irregular, with some suppliers being favored over others. Government tenders are published in local newspapers, with notices sent to embassies for distribution. Notices of tenders received are sent by cable to the U.S. Department of Commerce and are printed each day in the Commerce Business Daily.

All bidding documents are in French. They provide the technical requirements and the administrative clauses common to all government projects. A bidder's administrative package should include two copies of a statement of honor indicating the name, address, activity, current account number and bank guarantee. The technical package should include technical and human resources of the company and its references. The proposal must be in French and the metric system should be used.

PROTECTING PRODUCTS FROM IPR INFRINGEMENT

The legal system generally protects and facilitates acquisition and disposition of property rights, including intellectual property rights. Morocco has a relatively complete regulatory and legislative system for the protection of intellectual property. It is a member of the World Intellectual Property Organization (WIPO) and is a party to the Berne copyright, Paris Industrial Property, and Universal Copyright Conventions, the Brussels Satellite Convention, and the Madrid, Nice, and Hague agreements for the protection of intellectual property. Computer software is not explicitly covered by Morocco's copyright law. A quirk dating from the era of the French and Spanish protectorates requires patent and trademark applications to be filed in both Casablanca and Tangier for complete protection.

While Moroccan laws are generally adequate, enforcement is lacking. Counterfeiting of clothing, luggage, and other consumer goods is not uncommon; primarily for local consumption rather than for export.

NEED FOR A LOCAL ATTORNEY

New-to-market U.S. firms are strongly advised to obtain the services of one of the five major English speaking and U.S. business oriented law firms in Casablanca and Rabat. A complete list of recognized Moroccan law firms is available through the U.S. Commercial Service at the U.S. Embassy in Rabat or the Consulate General in Casablanca.

DUE DILIGENCE/CHECKING BONA FIDES OF BANKS/AGENTS/CUSTOMERS

All potential investors in Morocco, exporters of goods, and service providers are strongly recommended to perform due diligence on, and check the bona/fides of their Moroccan agents, partners and customers (when extending credit). Moroccan banks supply credit information to selected recipients, local certified public accountants and fiduciary firms will do likewise. U.S. firms especially those with no previous Moroccan experience should seriously consider U.S. Department of Commerce AInternational Company Profile, a service prior to signing any agreements with new partners.

TRADE AND PROJECT FINANCING

BANKING SYSTEM

Morocco is in the process of developing a relatively comprehensive banking system, originally modeled after the French system. There are 16 major banks in the country plus five government owned specialized financial institutions, about 15 credit agencies and about 10 leasing companies. Other elements of the financial infrastructure include insurance companies, pension funds, and the Casablanca stock exchange.

Until 1991, credit and money supply was controlled directly by the old French-style "encadrement system" allocating sectoral lending among banks based on historical patterns. Since financial liberalization, credit is supposed to be allocated freely, with the central bank using indirect methods to control the interest rate and volume of credit. The banking system is still used by the government, however, as a way to channel domestic savings to finance government debt, and the banks are required to hold a part of their assets in bonds paying below market interest rates.

A new bank reform law, promulgated in 1993, clearly laid out the parameters of banking activities, clarified oversight and control responsibilities, specified legal penalties for violations of banking regulations, and established a depositors guarantee fund.

FOREIGN EXCHANGE CONTROLS AFFECTING TRADING

Morocco maintains a system of foreign exchange controls, managed by a government agency, the Office de Changes, but the rules on transfers have been progressively liberalized to the point where the dirham is freely convertible according to the IMF definition for current account transactions. The value of the dirham is tied to a basket of hard currencies weighted according to Morocco's foreign trade. Because this basket is dominated by European currencies, variations in the dollar/franc or dollar/deutchmark rates are generally reflected in the dirham's dollar value.

Authority to buy and sell foreign exchange has been delegated to the banking system, which will carry out transactions on presentation of appropriate documentation justifying the transaction such as an invoice to pay for imports. Capital transactions require authorization from the "Office de Changes", which grants it routinely for business-related transactions. Under its investment code, the government offers a guarantee of repatriation of both invested capital and profits, provided that the initial investment was declared on the way into Morocco.

GENERAL FINANCING AVAILABILITY

Local financing is available for Moroccan investors and importers, but real interest rates are high by American standards, and Moroccan Banks generally require a high degree of security (e.g. collateral and personal signature) before committing themselves.

HOW TO FINANCE EXPORTS/METHODS OF PAYMENT

Most Moroccan imports are paid for by irrevocable confirmed letters of credit issued by major local banks with U.S. banking correspondence. Within the country, end-users are normally given up to 90 day credit by importers.

TYPES OF AVAILABLE EXPORT FINANCING AND INSURANCE

Exporters naturally want to get paid as quickly as possible, and importers usually prefer delaying payment at least until they have received and resold the goods. Because of the intense competition for export markets, being able to offer good payment terms is often necessary to make a sale. Exporters should be aware of the many financing options open to them in Morocco.

Five U.S. Government agencies provide financial consulting services to exporters through the Trade Promoting Coordinating Committee, a Washington based group that includes the Commerce Department, Ex-Im Bank, Small Business Administration, Overseas Private Investment Corporation, and the Trade Development Agency.

The Commerce Department's new office of Multilateral Development Bank Operations (MDBO) provides one-stop shopping services to U.S. firms interested in doing business with the MDBs. Its staff can help U.S. companies get a share of major contracts financed by the multilateral development banks. For more information on any of these services in the U.S., contact MDBO at (202) 482-3399 or fax (202) 273-0927.

Financing for U.S. exports in the form of loans or guarantees is available through Ex-Im Bank. However, a Moroccan guarantee, either from the government or from a private bank, may also be required. Ex-Im Bank has established a small bundling facility (a line of guaranteed credits of USD 10.0 million) with Credit du Maroc (CDM). Although other Moroccan banks have expressed some interest in this program, they have not overcome the reluctance of Moroccan importers to take on the foreign exchange risk of borrowing in dollars. The principal multilateral financial institutions such as the World Bank, the IFC, the African Development bank, and the European Investment Bank all lend to Morocco for infrastructure development.

The USDA Credit Guarantee Programs USD 100 million (GSM-102/3) are made available to Morocco to purchase various agricultural commodities from the US. The GSM-103 line, initially used by the GOM, has been made available to the Moroccan private sector importers through the BCM bank for fiscal year 1998. The list of eligble commodities has been extended to cover in addition to wheat and feed grains other commodities such as livestock, cotton, vegetable oil, oilseeds, and planting seeds. The private importers can benefit from up to 6 months financing and the GOM supports the exchange risk as the payment to the Moroccan bank are made in dirhams. The private sector GSM-102 line, provides $10 million for wheat, pulses, planting seeds, livestock, cotton, and dairy products. For more information about this program, please contact the office of the Agricultural Attache in Rabat at (212-7)765987/Fax:(212-7)765493.

Citicorp Structured Trade Finance, in cooperation with OPIC, now offers a new approach to African trade finance for U.S. exporters to Africa. The African Trade Finance Facility (ATFF) was developed jointly by Citicorp and OPIC to address the lack of availability of financing. To obtain more information, contact one of the following addresses.

A. Citicorp Structured Trade Finance
Tel: (212) 559-7998; Fax: (212) 793-2330
CITICORP
399 Park Avenue, 5/13
New York, N.Y. 10043

B. Overseas Private Investment Corporation (OPIC)
Tel: (202) 336-8576 or (202) 408-5142
Fax: (202) 408-5142
1100 New York Avenue, N.W.
Washington, D.C. 20527

Before proceeding with any international transaction, it is advisable to contact your local USDOC District Office for counseling and further information about the market.

The International Finance Assistance Section (which can be found under that topic heading on the NTDB), provides not only information on specific assistance available from USG financing agencies such as the U.S. Ex-Im Bank and OPIC, but also information on the Multilateral Development Banks.

The World Bank Group is a multilateral lending agency consisting of four closely related institutions: the International Bank for Reconstruction (IBRD), the International Development Association (IDA), the International Finance Corporation (IFC), and the Multilateral Investment Guarantee Agency (MIGA). The World Bank provides loans to developing countries to help reduce poverty and to finance investments that contribute to economic growth.

The International Bank for Reconstruction and Development (IBRD) provides funding for creditworthy developing countries with relatively high per capita income. It also provides technical assistance and policy advice. IBRD raises the money through the sale of AAA-rated bonds in international capital markets. Loans are made only to governments or to agencies that can obtain a government guarantee. The IBRD also provides partial risk or partial credit guarantees (with a counter-guarantee from their government) to private lenders on development projects. The interest rates are variable, set one half of a percentage point above the Bank's average cost of borrowing, or LIBOR. Repayment is usually over 12 to 15 years, including a grace period of three to five years. Opportunities for U.S. companies exist to supply goods and services in connection with these loans.

The International Finance Corporation (IFC) is an affiliate of the World Bank that provides project financing for private investment in developing countries. IFC offers long-term loans and equity investments, as well as other financing services. IFC will generally invest up to 25% of the total project cost. In addition to project finance, IFC also provides legal and technical assistance to private enterprises. Unlike the IBRD and IDA, the IFC does not require government guarantees. U.S. companies seeking direct investment funds should contact the IFC.

The Multilateral Investment Guarantee Agency (MIGA) was established in April 1988 to help investors'overcome the problems of political risk. Investors' concerns about political risk has the effect of slowing down the flow of foreign direct investment that in turn slowed the creation of jobs, and the transfer of modern technology. MIGA's purpose is to promote the flow of foreign direct investment commercial (political) risk and by providing promotional and advisory services to help member countries create an attractive investment climate. U.S. companies seeking investment guarantees should contact MIGA.

For further information and assistance contact the Commercial Service Liaison Staff, Office of the U.S. Executive Director, the World Bank, 1818 H Street NW, Washington DC 20433, USA. Tel (202) 458-0118 or 0120, Fax (202) 477-2967.

PROJECT FINANCING AVAILABLE

Financing for projects in Morocco comes primarily from the World Bank and the African Development Bank (AFDB), the European Investment Bank, the Kuwaiti Fund, the Saudi Fund and the Abu Dhabi Fund.

PROJECTS SCHEDULED FOR FINANCING BY THE WORLD BANK

INFRASTRUCTURE

Pilot Rural Infrastructure. The objective of the project is to provide satisfactory basic infrastructure services (water supply, electricity and access roads) to the rural population in six priority provinces. Appraisal mission is tentatively scheduled for June 1998. US$20.0 (IBRD).
-Ministry of Interior, Rabat, Morocco. Tel: (212-7) 73-44-65 ; Fax: (212-7) 73-45-63, Contact: Driss Guessab, Director of Rurales Affairs.

WATER SUPPLY/SANITATION

Water Resource Management. The project will assist the government in defining and implementing a comprehensive water resource management strategy. US$20.0 (IBRD).
-Ministry of Public Works, Administration de l=Hydraulique. Tel: (212-7) 77-90-08 ; Fax: (212-7) 77-86-96.

ENVIRONMENT

Protected Areas Management. The overall project objectives are to establish a system of protected areas in Morocco and promote sustainable conservation management with the participation of the local population in the ecosystems in the project areas. US$10.1 (IBRD).
-Administration des Eaux et Forets et de la Conservation des Sols, Ministry of Agriculture, Cite Administrative, Rabat, Morocco. Tel (212-7) 76-44-46, Contact: Dr. Abderrahmane Hanan, Directeur General de l=Administration.

POPULATION, HEALTH AND NUTRITION

Health Management. The project will support the development and implementation of new financing mechanisms, mainly health insurance; support hospital management reforms; and improve the quality of services provided through priority rehabilitation of health infrastructure, training of relevant personnel and maintenance programs. US$60.0 (IBRD).
-Ministry of Health, 335 Avenue Mohammed V, BP 812m Mechanar, Rabat, Morocco, tel (212-7) 76-16-75, fax: (212-7) 76-38-95.

SOCIAL SECTOR

Social Fund. The project will establish a fund to finance social investments and promote local community participation. Project preparation is under way. US$60.0 (IBRD).
-Consulting services and implementation agency is to be determined.

URBAN DEVELOPMENT

Fes Rehabilitation. The project will assist in the conservation and rehabilitation of the Fes Medina by expanding the ongoing conservation efforts, consolidating partnerships, empowering inhabitants in the self-rehabilitation process, and using this process to alleviate poverty. US$15.5 (IBRD).
-ADER-FES, 4 Ave. Zaid Ibn Harita, Fes, Morocco, tel (212-5) 65-34-69; fax (212-5) 65-38-83.

TRADE REGULATIONS, CUSTOMS AND STANDARDS

TRADE BARRIERS

The government has undertaken limited efforts to limit contraband, a significant competitor to U.S. products legally imported and to goods produced in Morocco by U.S. firms. Foreign companies have complained of irregularities in government procurement procedures, but the situation is improving.

CUSTOMS REGULATIONS

The stimulus to a competitive business environment provided by a liberalized trade regime can be offset by cumbersome customs administration and procedures that impose costs and delays on firms currently involved in international trade and defer others potentially interested in entering the trade area. The Government has therefore adopted a reform program to modernize customs administration. Work is underway to increase the use of computerization to manage critical information, such as the movement of goods, processing the declarations, assessment of tariffs in an integrated fashion, and payment of obligations. In parallel, it is streamlining the regime for temporary admissions, which allows exporters to import inputs free of duty. The reform program also calls for upgrading staff skills through on-the-job training and short-term courses. Progress has been documented by American Chamber of Commerce members who say that the waiting time has been cut from 1-2 weeks to 3-4 days and sometimes even 48 hours.

TARIFF RATES AND IMPORT TAXES

Import duties are generally high and considered as the main obstacle to higher imports. They vary from a minimum of 2.5 percent for many raw materials and equipment to a maximum of 349% for frozen lamb meat. Imports are also subject to a Value Added Tax (VAT), varying from 0 to 20%. VAT is not always paid on locally produced goods (e.g., corn). Food products are subject to an average 80 percent cumulated import taxes and duties, which makes the price of consumer oriented food products prohibitive for the average Moroccan consumer.

CUSTOMS VALUATION

The customs authorities will not give a binding ruling on customs classification in advance. An informal advisory opinion may be obtained from the Director General des Douanes (customs office), Avenue Hassan II, Rabat, Morocco, tele: (212-7) 26-90-01; fax: (212-7) 73-09-39; e-mail: addi@douane.msie.gov.ma..

EXPORT CONTROLS

Goods that are temporarily exported from Morocco for further processing abroad are only taxed on the value added outside of Morocco.

IMPORT/EXPORT DOCUMENTATION

A commercial invoice is required. No special invoice form is necessary, nor is a consular visa or consular certification required. The commercial invoice should fully describe the goods in French. Certification as to country of origin is required. Payments are made through bank-to-bank irrevocable letters of credit. Pro-forma invoices must be provided in most cases. Invoices, which should be on company letterhead, are required for both import licenses and foreign exchange transfers. "To order" bills are acceptable as bills of lading. When sending promotional material, and especially promotional videos, it is important to clearly state, in French, "Promotional use only", "No Commercial Value."

TEMPORARY GOODS ENTRY REQUIREMENTS

Goods imported under a temporary entry provision must be approved by decree of the Finance Ministry. Customs may authorize entry of goods on an individual basis. The limit for temporary entry is 6 months, renewable for up to one year.

LABELING REQUIREMENTS

No special regulations apply to the exterior marking of containers for shipments to Morocco. However, an indication on outer containers of the net weight in kilograms, together with other identification markings, will assist in locating goods on arrival and speed their clearance through customs.

Food labels can be in French or Arabic and must show country of origin. There is, however, a requirement for both local and imported canned foods and beverages to print the date of production and the expiration date.

The metric measurement is mandatory. Moroccans are not familiar with U.S. measurements and standards such as ounces, Lbs., cups, servings, etc. Metric measurements are common on both local and imported products. Also, unlike in Egypt and other Middle Eastern countries, most Moroccans use exclusively the same numbers (characters) as those used in the U.S. Also, when using the date format (xx/xx/xx), U.S. exporters should keep in mind that unlike in the U.S., the date format should be (dd/mm/yy). The Agricultural Attaché's office in Rabat has prepared a Food and Agricultural Import Regulations and Standards (FAIRS) report for U.S. exporters.

PROHIBITED IMPORTS

Import restrictions apply only to firearms, explosives, used clothing and used tires.

Warranty and non-warranty repairs:
Usually in Morocco a one-year warranty is given to end-users for products or equipment purchased.

EXPORT CONTROLS

In general, Morocco does not require authorization from the Exchange Office for the export of goods. However, certain restrictions apply to the following:
-Goods exported on consignment to be sold on commission: fruits, vegetables, flowers and handicraft goods are exceptions and do not require authorization for export.
-Good exported by individuals not registered with the Trade Registration authority.
-Goods valued at more than $300 that are not exported for sale.
-Samples valued at more than $1.000 that are exported without payment.
-Exports whose payment period exceeds 150 days.

The following goods require export licenses from the Ministry of
Foreign Trade:
- Antique articles older than 100 years
- Archeological, ethnographical, historical and paleontological products, and specimens of

anatomy, botany, mineralogy and zoology.
- Charcoal and flour made from cereals, except for ground rice.

STANDARDS

The Government does not require locally registered firms to apply ISO 9000 usage. However most multinational firms operating in Morocco currently use the ISO, primarily as a marketing tool. Except for few bulk commodities, Most Moroccan importers are not familiar with the USDA and US industry commodity grading systems and standards.

FREE TRADE ZONES/WAREHOUSES

Foreign investors and businesses are operating in the Free Zone established in Tangier. Companies operating in the Free Zone have the right of 100 percent duty-free imports and exemption from most taxes for export production. Warehouse storage allows storage of goods in public or private warehouses controlled by the Customs Administration.

MEMBERSHIP IN FREE TRADE AGREEMENTS

In an effort to broaden the geographic scope of its exports, Morocco has signed free trade arrangements with members of the Maghreb Arab Union (UMA). However, for all practical purposes, the UMA is dormant and regional economic integration has stalled. A free trade arrangement has also been established with Saudi Arabia. Import tax (PFI) and TVA are applied in these agreements.

The 1995 Morocco-EU Free Trade Agreement gives preferential treatment to Moroccan goods exported to the EU. Moroccan industrial products are thus exported to the EU duty-free and without quantitative restrictions. Several agricultural or agri-business products are subject to quotas or seasonal restrictions. Tariff reductions went into effect in March 2004 with the result that tariffs will be phased out completely on EU industrial goods, and substantially on raw materials by 2012. Negotiations have begun on a free trade agreement between Morocco, Tunisia, Egypt and Jordan.

CUSTOMS CONTACT INFORMATION

For more information on import duties for specific products, U.S. exporters should contact the Director General des Douanes (customs office), Avenue Hassan II, Rabat, Morocco, tele: (212-7) 26-90-01; fax: (212-7) 73-09-39; e-mail: addi@douane.msie.gov.ma..

BASIC COSTS FOR CONDUCTING BUSINESS

INDUSTRIAL WAGE RATES

SMIG (i.e. legal minimum wage for industry and commerce)DH 7.26/hour
Examples of Average Wages (as an illustration only, inclusive of productivity bonus, seniority, fringe benefits) :

. Unskilled worker	DH 7.40 - 7.88 per hour
. Specialized worker	DH 8.34 - 9.19 per hour
. Semi-skilled worker	DH 9.15 - 9.79 per hour
. Skilled worker	DH 10.56 - 11.70 per hour
. Team leader	DH 13.01 - 14.78 per hour
. Ganger (Foreman)	DH 2.489 - 3.293 per month
. Engineers and professional staff	DH 6,588 - 10,980 per month

To these wage costs which vary from one industrial sector to another, shall be added social security charges corresponding to about 34 percent of the overall wage rate.

PRICE OF INDUSTRIAL WATER

CITIES INDUSTRIAL RATES DH/PER TONNE TAX INCLUDED

Casablanca	4.839	
Rabat, Salé, Témara, Skhirat, Bouknadel	4,618	
Kénitra		3,270
Tétouan, Larache, Ksar El Kébir		2,249
Méknès		1,256
Fèz		2,921
Nador		3,544
Oujda		2,307
Béni Mellal, Kasba Tadla, Fquih Ben Salah	3,756	
Marrakesh	3,541	
El Jadida		4,305
Agadir		4,119
Tangier, Azilah	3,763	
Settat		2,910
Safi		4,679
Khouribga	4,603	
Taza		1,854
Smaller townships	4,728	

The amount of the fixed charge is as follows :

. Casablanca - Rabat	DH 84.00/year
. Other cities listed above	DH 74.00/year

OIL PRODUCTS

- Extra gasoline DH 7.41 per liter- Fuel oil No 1 DH 2,123/Metric Ton
- Regular DH 7.15 - Fuel oil No 2 DH 1,875.50/MT
- Kerosene DH 3.58/l - Fuel oil No 3 DH 2,387/MT
- Gaz-Oil DH 14.23 - Gas in bulk DH 2,800/MT

The VAT rates applied to oil products are :

- 7% for fuels;
- 14% for fuel transport;
- 19% for oils and greases.

The mode of payment granted to clients is either by cash for the network and individuals, or it is 15, 30, 45 or 60 days based on the importance of the clients concerned.

The tank installation price is billed based on the cost price :

- 20 m3 : 30,000 DH (HT)
- 10 m3 : 19,500 DH (HT)
- 5 m3 : 9,950 DH (HT)

For large consumers, storage equipment and pumps are installed on loan.

For ordinary consumers, gas reservoirs are installed on consignment at the following prices :

- 20 m3 : 230,00 DH
- 10 m3 : 100,00 DH
- 5 m3 : 35,00 DH

For large consumers, gas reservoirs are installed on loan.

ELECTRIC POWER

Maximum base rate for medium, high and very high voltages in Dirhams, tax included

Base Rate	HV and VHV Power and Consumption Charge (DH)	MV Power and Consumption Charge (DH)
Power Charge	280.00	291.00(DH xKWAxYR)
Consumption Charge(DH x KWH)		
. Full and Peak	0.80566	1.00073
. Off-Peak Hours	0.64453	0.80061

The installation cost for a 630 KVA station amounts to 350,000 DH. Moreover, the National Office of Electricity (ONE) is ready to provide an estimate of the installation cost of one/several electricity lines. Regarding the subscription fees and the rental charges to be paid to the state-owned Water/Electricity Distribution Company (RAD), the tariffs in force are the following :

- Cost of first establishment (power transformer): 300 DH/KVA installed (inclusive of tax);
- Cost related to lines connection : 30,000 DH to 40,000 DH;

- The provision or guarantee deposit to be paid to RAD when establishing the subscription contract is estimated at 3 months of the expected consumption.

COAL

Local coal / Anthracite of Jerada
. Crude coal DH 772 T
. Seed 6/10, 10/20 DH 944/T
. Class 20/30, 30/50 and 50/80 DH 994/T

TAX SYSTEM

CAPITAL REGISTRATION FEES

When forming or increasing capital, registration tax is fixed at 0.50 percent.

Capital registration is reduced to 0.25 percent for deeds of partnership or capital increase of investment banks and companies the main purpose of which is either stocks and shares management or application for other companies capital on joint account.

Formalities for the acquisition of investment land : complete exoneration. -

STAMP DUTY

Corporate stocks, founder's shares and bonds issued by companies are all free from both stamp duty and formalities.

NOTARIAL TAX

The basis of assessment is the capital stock

Up to DH 5,000 1%
From DH 5,000 to 10,000 0.5%
Over DH 10,000 0.2%

TAXATION ON IMPORTED PRODUCTION MATERIALS AND OTHER PRODUCTS

CUSTOMS DUTIES

The rates of import dues vary between 2.5 pc and 10 pc for equipment, materiels, spare parts and accessories.

. Tools : hedge cutters, hand saws, chain saws, etc;
. Kitchen appliances or food industry machinery;
. Vechicle spare parts; . Watches and children's toys
. Cameras

- Exemption

Among materials exempted are :

. Materials and products imported under the investment Code;
. Materials and products imported under customs economic systems;
. Materials using renewable energies.

IMPORT TAX LEVY (PFI)

The PFI is on imported commodities. The PFI is fixed at 15%. However it is reduced as follows :

. to 12.5% for pharamaceuticals or raw materials used in the manufacturing of pharmaceuticals.

- Exoneration

. Exoneration for the import of equipment,materiels,spare parts and accessories;

. Exoneration for enterprises which engage in research activities involving mineral substances;

. Exoneration for materials using renewable energies;

. Exoneration for fertilizers, potassium nitrate for fertilizer usage, potassium phosphate for fertilizer usage and other nitrates;

. Exoneration for certain antibiotic medical products.

VALUE ADDED TAX-VAT

VAT applies to industrial, commercial and handicraft-type business or to operations related to professional activities carried out in Morocco.

It also applies to imported products except those which are exempted.

- Exoneration

Among the materials and products exempted :

. Equipment, materiels and tools acquired locally or abroad;

. Agricultural materials and products;

. Materials and products imported within the framework of the customs economic system;

. Materials used in research and exploitation of mineral substances;*

. Materials using renewable energies.

- Applicable Rates :

. 7% : for basic products of prime necessity, credit operations, occupations such credit lawyers, etc; . 14% : for enterprise business related to real estate sales and involving coffee and other products; . 19% : normal rate.

DOMESTIC CONSUMER TAXES

These rates apply to certain categories of commodities imported or produced locally such as lemonades, mineral water, wines, beers, oil products, etc.

PARAFISCAL TAX AT IMPORTATION

This tax applies to imported commodities. Rate : 0.25% ad valorem.

The following are not subject to the tax :

- imports benefitting from the customs economic systems;
- imports of materials, tools and equipment goods cited in an investment program having received a conformity approval or being the subject of a convention.

INTERNATIONAL ADOPTION - MOROCCO

GENERAL ADOPTION INFORMATION

The adoption of a Moroccan child by United States citizens who wish to raise the child in the United States is a complex project, largely because it involves satisfying the requirements of several government agencies, both in the U.S. and in Morocco. We suggest that U.S. citizens wishing to adopt begin by contacting the U.S. Immigration and Naturalization Service (INS) District Office for their area. INS can provide you with detailed information concerning the requirements and procedures involved in adopting a child from overseas. At the same time, we encourage you to familiarize yourself with the adoption laws in your state. Once it is clear to you that your family can meet the requirements of both INS and your state of residence, you may begin the process of identifying a child you would like to adopt.

LEGAL "ADOPTION" IN MOROCCO

In can be quite difficult to adopt a child in Morocco. However, there are several orphanages in Morocco that have a record of arranging for the adoption by non-Moroccans of Moroccan children. These orphanages issue specially worded adoption decrees to foreigners that allow the child to be raised by the "adoptive" parents and to be taken out of Morocco.

In order to adopt a child in Morocco, you must become officially Moslem and obtain a document to that effect from the appropriate religious authorities in Morocco. Statements asserting that Moslem beliefs are held by an American from any religious authorities outside Morocco will not be honored. You must also demonstrate to the satisfaction of the Moroccan authorities that you were resident in Morocco prior to your adoption of a Moroccan child. There is no set time period for residence, which means that Moroccan authorities can essentially decide at will who is and who is not a qualified resident.

The paperwork involved in Moroccan adoption is extensive and time-consuming to obtain. Documents required include birth certificates, marriage certificates, and divorce decrees, which should all be either original documents or certified copies.

Employment attestations and bank statements may also be requested. Other documents may be requested as well, and requirements may change without notice and from one case to the next. Translation of documents requires both time and significant expense, especially for lengthy legal documents such as divorce decrees. All translations must be performed in Morocco.

Once the adoption decree is obtained, it can serve as the basis for requesting the Moroccan government to issue the child a Moroccan passport. Obtaining a Moroccan passport takes a minimum of six weeks, and can take even longer.

The adoption decree can also serve as the basis for filing a petition with the INS requesting their clearance for the child to enter the U.S. as an immigrant. This petition should be filed in the United States at the office of the INS having jurisdiction over the petitioner's place of residence. If the petitioner is residing inside Morocco, the petition can be filed at the U.S. Consulate General in Casablanca. Since the petition is mailed to the INS regional office in Madrid, Spain, processing time for this petition is at least two months, and can be even longer.

If the petition is approved by INS, it will be forwarded to the Consulate-General in Casablanca, the only U.S. immigrant visa issuing post in Morocco. The consular officer in Casablanca will explain the requirements for obtaining a U.S. immigrant visa, which if issued will allow the child to travel to the U.S. for permanent residence.

Please Note: A foreign country's determination that the child is an orphan does not guarantee that the child will be considered an orphan under the U.S. Immigration and Nationality Act. For more specific information on adoption in Morocco, please contact an attorney familiar with Moroccan laws or the Embassy of the Kingdom of Morocco.

Specific questions regarding child custody in Morocco may be addressed to:

Embassy of the Kingdom of Morocco
1605 21st Street, N.W.
Washington, D.C. 20049

Phone: (202) 462-7979 to 7982
Fax Number: (202) 265-0161

U.S. Consulate General

Consular Section
8 Boulevard Moulay Youssef
Casablanca, Morocco

Phone: [212] (2) 26-45-50
Fax Number: [212] (2) 20-41-27

or

Consular Section
U.S. Consulate General
PSC 74
Box 24
APO AE 06718

For further information on international adoption, contact the Office of Children's Issues at 202-736-7000, visit our home page on the Internet at http://travel.state.gov, or send a nine-by-twelve-inch, self-addressed envelope to:

Office of Children's Issues
2401 E Street, N.W.
Room L127
Washington, D.C. 20037
Phone: (202) 736-7000
Fax: (202) 312-9743

In addition, the State Department publishes Consular Information Sheets for every country in the world, providing information such as location of the U.S. Embassy, health conditions, political situations, and crime reports. When situations in a country are sufficiently serious, the State Department issues Travel Warnings which recommend U.S. citizens avoid traveling to a country. These documents are available on the Internet at http://travel.state.gov or by calling the State Department's Office of Overseas Citizen Services at (202) 647-5225.

Information on immigrant visas is available from the State Department's Visa Office, at (202) 663-1225. This 24 hour automated system includes options to speak with consular officers during business hours for questions not answered in the recorded material. Application forms and petitions for immigrant visas are available from the U.S. Immigration and Naturalization Service, the nearest office of which is listed in the federal pages of your telephone book, under U.S. Department of Justice.

BUSINESS TRAVELING

US STATE DEPARTMENT SUGGESTIONS

ENTRY/EXIT REQUIREMENTS: Travelers to Morocco must possess a valid passport. Visas are not required for American tourists traveling in Morocco for less than 90 days. For visits of more than 90 days, Americans are required to obtain a residence permit and a return visa should they wish to return to Morocco for extended periods.

A residence permit and return visa may be requested and obtained from immigration authorities (Service d'Etranger) at the central police station of the district of residence. For additional information concerning entry requirements for Morocco, travelers may contact the Embassy of Morocco at 1601 21st St. N.W., Washington, D.C. 20049, telephone (202) 462-7979 to 82. The Moroccan Consulate General is located at 10 E. 40th St., New York, N.Y. 10016, telephone (212) 758-2625.

DUAL NATIONALITY: In addition to being subject to all Moroccan laws affecting U.S. citizens, dual nationals may also be subject to other laws that impose special obligations on Moroccan citizens. Regardless of which passport is used to enter Morocco, persons with dual nationality are normally treated by Moroccan authorities as Moroccan citizens. U.S. consular protection to dual nationals cannot be assured. For additional information, please see the Consular Affairs home page on the Internet at http://travel.state.gov for our flyer on Dual Nationality.

SAFETY/SECURITY

Area of Instability: The sparsely settled Western Sahara (formerly Spanish Sahara) was long the site of armed conflict between Government forces and the Polisario Front which has demanded independence. A cease-fire has been in effect since 1991 in the UN administered area. There are thousands of unexploded mines in the Western Sahara and in areas of Mauritania adjacent to the Western Sahara border. There have been occasional clashes between police and protesters in the region of Laayoune. Exploding mines are occasionally reported, and they have caused death and injury. Transit to the Western Sahara remains restricted; persons planning to travel in the region may obtain information on clearance requirements from the Moroccan Embassy.

Although rare, security personnel in Morocco may at times place foreign visitors under surveillance. Taking photographs of anything that could be perceived as being of military or security interest may result in problems with authorities. There is no ongoing terrorist threat in Morocco, but the potential for transnational terrorism remains high in the region, and appropriate precautions should be taken. When tensions rise in the Middle East region, the U.S. Embassy sometimes receives threatening calls and letters. Travelers should be cognizant of the current levels of tension in the region and remain alert to their surroundings.

CRIME INFORMATION: Morocco has a high crime rate in urban areas. Criminals have targeted tourists for robberies, assaults, muggings, thefts, purse snatching, pick-pocketing, and scams of all types. Most of the petty crime occurs in the medina/market areas, parks and beaches. Commonly reported crimes include falsifying credit card vouchers and shipping inferior rugs as a substitute for the rugs purchased by the traveler. The U.S. Embassy and Consulate have also received reports of thefts occurring in the vicinity of ATM machines. Aggressive panhandling is common.

Some travelers have been befriended by persons of various nationalities who have offered them food, drink, or cigarettes that are drugged. Harassment of tourists by unemployed Moroccans posing as "guides" is a common problem. Prudent travelers hire only official tour guides through hotels and travel agencies. Traveling alone in the Rif Mountain area is risky because tourists have fallen victim to schemes involving the purchase and/or trafficking of hashish. Unescorted women in any area of Morocco may experience verbal abuse. The best course of action is to ignore such abuse because women who have responded have come under physical attack. Thieves sometimes bump cars from behind and then rob their victims when they get out of the car to inspect the damage. Taxis and trains in Morocco are generally crime-free; buses are not.

MEDICAL FACILITIES: Adequate medical care in Morocco is available, particularly in Rabat and Casablanca, although not all facilities meet high quality standards, and specialized care or treatment may not be available. Medical facilities are adequate for non-emergency matters, particularly in the urban areas, but the medical staff will probably not be able to communicate in English. Travelers planning to drive in the mountains and other remote areas may wish to carry a medical kit and a Moroccan phone card for emergencies. In the event of car accidents involving injuries, immediate ambulance service usually is not available.

MEDICAL INSURANCE: U.S. medical insurance is not always valid outside the United States. U.S. Medicare and Medicaid programs do not provide payment for medical services outside the United States. Doctors and hospitals in Morocco often expect immediate cash payment for health services. Uninsured travelers, who require medical care overseas, may face extreme difficulties.

Please check with your own insurance company to confirm whether your policy applies overseas, including provision for medical evacuation and for adequacy of coverage. Serious medical problems requiring hospitalization and/or medical evacuation to the United States can cost tens of thousands of dollars. Please ascertain whether payment will be made to the overseas hospital or doctor or whether you will be reimbursed later for expenses that you incur. Some insurance policies also include coverage for psychiatric treatment and for disposition of remains in the event of death.

Useful information on medical emergencies abroad, including overseas insurance programs, is provided in the Department of State's Bureau of Consular Affairs brochure Medical Information for Americans Traveling Abroad, available via the Bureau of Consular Affairs home page or autofax: (202) 647-3000.

OTHER HEALTH INFORMATION: Visitors to Morocco should exercise common sense and caution when purchasing food from street vendors or stalls. The beaches as well as the ocean in the immediate vicinity of Casablanca are polluted and considered unsafe for swimming, although other coastal areas are safe. Information on vaccinations and other health precautions may be obtained from the Centers for Disease Control and Prevention's hotline for international travelers at 1-877-FYI-TRIP (1-877-394-8747); fax 1-888-CDC-FAXX (1-888-232-3299), or via the CDC's Internet site at http://www.cdc.gov.

TRAFFIC SAFETY AND ROAD CONDITIONS: While in a foreign country, U.S. citizens may encounter road conditions that differ significantly from those in the United States. The information provided below concerning Morocco is provided for general reference only, and it may not be totally accurate in a particular location or circumstance.

Safety of Public Transportation: Poor
Urban Road Conditions/Maintenance: Fair

Rural Road Conditions/Maintenance: Poor
Availability of Roadside Assistance: Poor

Traffic accidents are a significant hazard in Morocco. Driving practices are poor and have resulted in serious injuries and fatalities to U.S. citizens. This is particularly true at dusk during the Islamic holy month of Ramadan, when adherence to traffic regulations is lax, and from July to September, when Moroccan residents abroad return from Europe by car in large numbers.

Urban driving is characterized by congested streets. Traffic signals do not always function and are sometimes difficult to see. Modern freeways link the cities of Tangier, Rabat, Fez and Casablanca. Other major cities are linked by two-lane highways.

Secondary routes in rural areas are often narrow and poorly paved. Roads through the Rif and Atlas Mountains are steep, narrow, winding, and dangerous. Maximum caution should be exercised when driving in the mountains. During the rainy season (November-March), flash flooding is frequent and sometimes severe, washing away roads and vehicles in rural areas.

Pedestrians, scooters, and animal-drawn conveyances are common on all roadways, including the freeways, and driving at night should be avoided if possible. Often Moroccan police officers pull over drivers for inspection within the city and on highways. In the event of a traffic accident, including accidents involving injuries, the parties are required to remain at the scene and not move their vehicles until the police have arrived and have documented all necessary information. This procedure may take several hours.

While public buses and taxis are inexpensive, drivers typically exhibit poor driving habits, and the buses are frequently overcrowded. For specific information concerning Moroccan driver's permits, vehicle inspection, road tax and mandatory insurance, please contact the Moroccan Embassy in Washington, D.C.

AVIATION SAFETY OVERSIGHT: The U.S. Federal Aviation Administration (FAA) has assessed the Government of Morocco's Civil Aviation Authority as Category 1 -- in compliance with international aviation safety standards for oversight of Morocco's air carrier operations. For further information, travelers may contact the Department of Transportation within the U.S. at telephone 1-800-322-7873, or visit the FAA's Internet web site at http://www.faa.gov/avr/iasa/iasa.pdf. The U.S. Department of Defense (DOD) separately assesses some foreign air carriers for suitability as official providers of air services. For information regarding the DOD policy on specific carriers, travelers may contact the DOD at telephone (618)-229-4801.

CUSTOMS REGULATIONS: Moroccan customs authorities may enforce strict regulations concerning temporary importation into or export from Morocco of items such as firearms, religious materials, antiquities, business equipment, and large quantities of currency. It is advisable to contact the Embassy of Morocco in Washington, D.C. or the Moroccan Consulate General in New York for specific information concerning customs requirements. Moroccan customs authorities encourage the use of an ATA (Admission Temporaire/Temporary Admission) Carnet for the temporary admission of professional equipment, commercial samples, and/or goods for exhibitions and fair purposes. ATA Carnet Headquarters, located at the U.S. Council for International Business, 1212 Avenue of the Americas, New York, NY 10036, issues and guarantees the ATA Carnet in the United States. For additional information, please call (212)354-4480, or send an e-mail to atacarnet@uscib.org, or visit http://www.uscib.org for details.

CURRENCY REGULATIONS: Travelers' checks and credit cards are accepted at some establishments in Morocco, mainly in urban areas. Travelers' checks may be cashed at most banks, although some require the bearer to present both the check and the receipt. ATM machines are available in Casablanca and Rabat, and some American bank cards may be used to withdraw local currency from an account in the United States. Current Moroccan customs procedures do not provide for the accurate or reliable registration of large quantities of American dollars brought into the country by tourists or other visitors. As a result, travelers encounter difficulties when they attempt to depart with the money. In particular, American citizens with dual Moroccan nationality have been asked to provide proof of the source of the funds and have incurred heavy fines. Moroccan currency can not be converted back into U.S. dollars prior to departure.

CRIMINAL PENALTIES: While in a foreign country, a U.S. citizen is subject to that country's laws and regulations, which sometimes differ significantly from those in the United States and may not afford the protections available to the individual under U.S. law. Penalties for breaking the law can be more severe than in the United States for similar offenses. Persons violating Moroccan laws, even unknowingly, may be expelled, arrested or imprisoned. Penalties for possession, use, or trafficking in illegal drugs in Morocco are severe, and convicted offenders can expect long jail sentences and heavy fines.

PROSELYTIZING: Islam is the state religion of Morocco. The Moroccan Government does not interfere with public worship by the country's Christian or Jewish minorities. However, while Christians are allowed to practice freely, some activities, such as proselytizing or encouraging conversion to the Christian faith -- both considered legally incompatible with Islam -- are prohibited. It is illegal for a Muslim to convert to Christianity. In the past, American citizens have been detained or arrested and expelled for discussing or trying to engage Moroccans in debate about Christianity.

WOMEN AND CHILDREN'S ISSUES: For information on international adoption of children and international parental child abduction, please refer to the Office of Children's Issues Internet site at http://travel.state.gov.children's_issues.html or telephone (202) 736-7000. The government of Morocco considers all children born to Moroccan fathers to be Moroccan citizens. Even if the children bear American passports, immigration officials may require proof that the father approves their departure before the children will be allowed to leave Morocco. Although women are normally granted custody of their children in divorces, regardless of nationality, the children's departure from Morocco must be approved by their father. Women must obtain permission to move the children more than 100 kilometers (about 60 miles) from their last residence before the divorce. American women married to Moroccans do not need their spouse's permission to leave Morocco.

REGISTRATION/U.S. EMBASSY AND CONSULATE LOCATIONS: U.S. citizens living in or visiting Morocco are encouraged to register at the Consular Section of the U.S. Consulate General in Casablanca. Updated information on travel and security within Morocco (or elsewhere) may be obtained at the U.S. Embassy or Consulate.

The U.S. Embassy is located at 2 Avenue de Marrakech in the capital city of Rabat, telephone (212)(3) 776-2265. The American Consulate General in Casablanca is located at 8 Boulevard Moulay Youssef, telephone (212)(2) 226-4550. Please note that all consular matters are handled at the U.S. Consulate General in Casablanca. The Consular Section's American Citizens Services hotline is (212)(2) 243-0578. The fax number is (212)(2) 220-4127. The Internet web site is http://www.usembassy-morocco.org.ma/.

GETTING THERE

Air

Morocco's national airline is *Royal Air Maroc (AT).* Airlines serving Morocco include *Air France, Alitalia, British Airways, KLM, Sabena Belgian World Airlines, Lufthansa* and *Swissair.* There are frequent direct flights from all major European cities, from North America and from the Middle East.

Approximate flight times

From Casablanca to *New York* is 6 hours and 30 minutes. From Casablanca to *London* is 3 hours; from Tangier is 2 hours 30 minutes.

International airports

Casablanca (CAS) (Mohammed V) is 30km (19 miles) south of the city (travel time - 35 minutes). Airport facilities include outgoing duty-free shop (closed after last arrival), post office, banking and currency exchange facilities (open 24 hours), restaurant and bar (0800-2300) and car hire (*Avis, Hertz* and *Europcar*). There are taxi services into Casablanca and train services available to Rabat.
Tangier (TNG) (Boukhalef Souahel) is 12km (7.5 miles) from the city (travel time - 20 minutes). Airport facilities include outgoing duty-free shop, banking and currency exchange facilities, restaurant and bar, car rental facilities (*Avis, Omnium, Starc-Hertz* and *Moroccan Holidays*). Bus and taxi services are available into Tangier.

Sea

Principal ports are Tangier, Casablanca and Ceuta. Lines serving these ports are *Transtour, Compañía Trasmediterránea, Limadet, Bland Line* (from Spain and Gibraltar), *Polish Ocean Lines* and *Nautilus* (from Spain and the USA), and *Comanav.*

Car/passenger ferries

There are cheap and regular car- and passenger-ferry links between southern Spain and Tangier and the Spanish enclaves on the north Moroccan coast. Most links are roll-on, roll-off car ferries except where shown. The routes are from Algeciras to Ceuta (Sebta) (car ferry); Algeciras to Tangier (hydrofoil and car ferry); Tarifa to Tangier (hydrofoil only); Gibraltar to Tangier (hydrofoil and car ferry); Almería to Melilla (car ferry); Málaga to Melilla (car ferry) and Almeria to Nador (car ferry). There are also car ferries between Sète on the French coast (between Béziers and Montpellier on the Golfe du Lyon) and Tangier run by *Compagnie Marocaine de Navigation.*

Train

Rail links between Morocco and Algeria are currently suspended. The main international routes are from Oujda to Algiers or from Oran to Algiers.

Road

The best road link is from southern Spain or France via passenger/car ferries. The road link on the north Algerian border is currently closed.

GETTING AROUND

Air

Royal Air Maroc (AT) operates regular services from Casablanca airport to Agadir, Al Hoceima, Dakhla, Fès, Marrakech, Ouarzazate, Oujda, Rabat, Tangier and Tetouan. There are cheaper deals for those under 26 years of age depending on their destination in Morocco. Contact *Royal Air Maroc* for further details. There is also a new airline company (*Regional Airlines*).

Train

The Moroccan rail system is all standard gauge and, though limited, provides regular and cheap services with first-class travel available between major centres. Rail fares are amongst the cheapest in the world, although a supplement must be paid for air-conditioned trains. Sleeping cars and restaurant cars are available. The network runs from Oujda in the northeast to Casablanca on the west coast, Tangier on the north coast and Fès and Marrakech in the interior. The main routes include (a) Marrakech-Casablanca-Rabat-Meknes- Fès-Oujda; (b) Marrakech-Casablanca-Rabat; (c) Marrakech-Casablanca-Meknes-Fès and Casablanca-Rabat-Tangier. The most useful route is from Fès to Rabat and Casablanca, with five daily and two overnight trains. There are also two daily trains and one overnight train (without sleepers) which run from Casablanca to Marrakech. Also, from Monday to Friday, a train runs every half an hour from Kenitra to Rabat.

Cheap fares

Children under 4 travel free and children from 4-10 may travel for half-fare. The European Inter-Rail pass is valid in Morocco; holders may be entitled to a discount on the fare of a ferry ticket - check with the company concerned for details. Discounts of up to 30% are available for groups of more than ten. First- and second-class seats can be reserved in advance. Trains can also be chartered.

Road

Traffic drives on the right. The major Moroccan roads, particularly those covering the north and northwest of the country, are all-weather highways. In the interior, south of the High Atlas Mountains, road travel becomes much more difficult, especially across the Atlas Mountains in winter.

Coach

The main centres are connected by a wide variety of coach services, many of which are privately run. The two largest firms are *CTM* (covering the whole country) and *SATAS* (between Casablanca, Agadir and south of Agadir).

Bus

Connections between most major towns and villages are regular and frequent, although buses can be very crowded and it may be wise to buy tickets in advance and arrive well before departure to secure a seat. The price of tickets is very low, especially with some of the smaller local bus companies. It is customary to tip the guard for loading luggage. For charter purposes, air-conditioned motor coaches are available from several companies.

Taxi

Those available in major towns, the *petits taxis*, are metered (see below under *Urban*). Other larger taxis, usually Mercedes cars, are used for travel to areas outside towns. These can be shared, but fares should be agreed before departure.

Car rental

Avis and *Hertz* can deliver cars to Gibraltar or Tangier from London. Major hire companies have offices in Tangier, Casablanca and Agadir. Car hire is generally expensive.

Documentation

Foreign driving licenses are accepted, as well as International Driving Permits. Third Party insurance is required. A Green Card is also necessary. Insurance can be arranged locally.

Urban

There are extensive bus services in Casablanca and other main towns. Pre-purchase tickets are sold. Urban area *petits taxis* are plentiful and have metered fares. Taxi drivers expect a 10% tip.

Journey Times

The following chart gives approximate journey times (in hours and minutes) from Casablanca to other major cities/towns in Morocco.

	Air	**Road**	**Rail**
Rabat	0.30	1.30	1.00
Marrakech	0.30	4.00	4.00
Agadir	0.55	9.00	-
Fès	0.40	5.00	5.00
Meknès	-	2.30	4.00
Tangier	0.50	6.00	6.00
Oujda	1.05	12.00	12.00
Laayoune	1.30	20.00	-
Er Rachidia	1.35	12.00	-

Note: These represent times by the main air link from Casablanca.

ACCOMMODATION

HOTELS

Morocco has 100,000 hotel beds to cater for its thriving tourist market. In all sizeable centers there is quite a wide choice. The upper end of the market is represented by internationally known hotels in most main towns, notably Agadir, Marrakech and Tangier. For more information contact the Fédération Nationale de l'Industrie Hôtelière, Angle avenue Nador et rue 3, Quartier Polo, 20550 Casablanca, Morocco (tel: (2) 800 487; fax: (2) 800 315), e-mail: fnih@iam.net.ma.

Grading: Hotels are rated from 1 to 5 stars.

Self-Catering

Self-catering apartments are available in Agadir, Marrakech and Tangier. Full details are available from the National Tourist Office.

Camping

There are established campsites with good facilities in many parts of Morocco. Full details are available in a brochure from the National Tourist Office.

Youth Hostels

There are hostels in Asni, Azrou, Casablanca, Fès, Ifrane, Meknes and Rabat. Up-to-date information is available from the Fédération Royale Marocaine des Auberges de Jeunes, BP 15998, Casa Principale, Parc de la Ligue Arabe, Casablanca 21000 (tel: (2) 470 952; fax: (2) 227 677).

MONEY

Currency

Moroccan Dirham (Dh) = 100 centimes. Notes are in denominations of Dh200, 100, 50, 20 and 10. Coins are in denominations of Dh10, 5 and 1, and 50, 20, 10 and 5 centimes.

COSTS

Budget meal: US$5-10
Mid-range meal: US$10-15
Top-end meal: US$15-30
Budget hotel: US$15-25
Mid-range hotel: US$25-50
Top-end hotel: US$50-80

Reckon on about US$40-50 per day if you want to travel in comfort. Budget travelers prepared to camp or stay in hostels could happily survive on about US$15-20 a day. Expect to pay dearly for the pleasure of beer (around US$3) and other heady imports. Getting around is relatively cheap and there are plenty of options, one of the cheapest (and most rewarding) is cycling.

There's a wide range of banks available for changing money and cashing travelers' checks and credit cards. Generally, it's quick and easy with rates varying little from bank to bank. Probably the best of the banks is the Banque Marocaine du Commerce Extérieur (BMCE). Cash advances on credit cards and ATM carry a charge of about 1.5%.

Tipping is expected in the fancier eateries. Around 10-15% of your bill is usual. A dirham or two should suffice at the more humble restaurants and cafes. A whole range of other services, some of which you may not notice or want, are also performed with the aim of pocketing a few dirhams. Remember that for many porters, guides, bus stop spruikers (a particularly pesky species of hustler endemic to Tangier) and the like, this is how they make a living. On the other hand, aggressive hustling shouldn't be rewarded.

CURRENCY EXCHANGE

Moroccan Dirhams can only be obtained in Morocco. National currencies should be exchanged at official bureaux de change only (identified by a golden sign); changing money in the streets is illegal. There is no commission charge and visitors will be issued with a receipt which they must keep in order to exchange Moroccan currency back into the original national currency at departure. Money can be withdrawn in banks with a credit card and a cheque book or directly from a cash dispenser in some larger towns.

Credit cards

Some credit cards are accepted. Check with your credit card company for details of merchant acceptability and other services which may be available.

Exchange rate indicators

The following figures are included as a guide to the movement of the Moroccan Dirham against the US Dollar:

Date	Oct '99	Nov '99	May'99	Aug '00
$1.00=	9.75	9.85	10.82	10.63

Currency restrictions

The import and export of local currency is prohibited; all local currency must be reconverted prior to departure. The import and export of foreign currency is unlimited but must be declared if in excess of the equivalent of Dh15,000. Upon production of bank vouchers, half the Moroccan currency purchased during a visitor's stay may be re-exchanged for foreign currency (subject to some limitations) and all of it if the stay is less than 48 hours.

Banking hours: 8.30 AM-11.30 AM and 2.15 PM-4.30 PM Monday to Friday.

PUBLIC HOLIDAYS

Jan 1 2001 New Year's Day.
Jan 11 Manifesto of Independence.
Mar 3 Aïd al-Adha (Feast of the Sacrifice).

Mar 22 Fatih Mouharram (Muslim New Year).
May 1 Labour Day.
May 23 National Day.
Jun 13-14 Aïd al-Mawlid (Prophet's Birthday).
Jul Feast of the Throne.
Aug 14 Fête Oued Eddahab (Oued Eddahab Allegiance Day).
Aug 20 Révolution du Roi et du Peuple (The King and the People's Revolution Day).
Nov 6 Marche Verte (Anniversary of the Green March).
Nov 18 Fête de l'Indépendence (Independence Day).

Dec 16-17 Aïd al-Fitr (End of Ramadan).

SUPPLEMENTS

STRATEGIC STATISTICTS & DATA

Population: 28 million
Population Growth Rate: -2 percent
Religion: Islam, Judaism (less than 1%)
Government System: Constitutional Monarchy. King Hassan II has reigned since 1961.
Languages: French (business), Arabic (official), Berber dialects, Spanish (in north)
Location: On the northwest corner of Africa, less than 20 kms across the Straits of Gibraltar from Spain.
Area: 280,000 square miles, about the size of Oregon and Washington
Combined Coastline: 2,120 miles; Mediterranean Sea and Atlantic Ocean
Climate: Mild Mediterranean climate
Work Week: Monday - Friday, generally 8:30 a.m.-12:30 p.m. and 2:00-6:30 p.m., with summer variation

Direct Dial Country Code 212

Major Cities codes

Rabat 7 Agadir 8
Casablanca 2 Fes/Meknes 5
Tangier 9 Marrakech 4

ECONOMY STATISTICS

USD millions, except where noted

	1997	1998 (e)	1999 (e)
Gross Domestic Product	33,473	35,733	38,234
Real GDP Growth (percent change)	-2.2	+6.8	+4.0
GDP Per Capita ($)	1,220	1,287	1,323
Government Spending (percent of GDP)	20.7	20	19.5
Inflation(Dec/Dec CPI pct change)	1.0	3.1	3.0
Unemployment (urban, percent)	16.9	18.5	18.0
Foreign Exchage reserves (year-end)	4,323	4,500	4,600
Average exchange rate (dirhams/$)	9.5	9.7	9.7
Foreign Debt	18,983	18,900	18,000
Foreign Debt Service (as pct. of foreign inc.)	25.4	25.0	24.5
U.S Economic Assistance	N/A	N/A	N/A

Source: 1997 - Moroccan government data

1997 and 1998 - U.S. Embassy projections. (1999 economic performance will depend on future exogenous factors, notably rainfall during the winter of 1998/1999).

TRADE STATISTICS

USD Millions, except where noted.

	1997	1998 (e)	1999 (e)
Total Country Exports	5,900	5,700	6,300
Total Country Imports	8,500	9,700	10,000
U.S. Exports	590	650	700
U.S. Imports	220	280	350

INVESTMENT STATISTICS

FOREIGN DIRECT INVESTMENT STATISTICS

The Moroccan foreign exchange office maintains balance of payments statistics which include annual foreign exchange inflows for private foreign investment. Historically, these statistics do not correspond exactly to foreign direct investment (e.g., they include portfolio investment). In 1994, the office started to separate portfolio and direct foreign investment. There are no statistics on the stock of foreign investment in Morocco. However, foreign direct investment totaled $4.07 billion from 1967-1997, including portfolio investment until 1994. The following tables are based on the balance of payments statistics.

Foreign direct investment in Morocco
($ millions)

Year	Total FDI	% of GDP
1992	386.7	1.4%
1993	433.5	1.6%
1994*	213.6	0.7%
1995*	211.1	0.7%
1996*	235.0	0.7%
1997*	800.9	2.5%

** Does not include portfolio investment

FOREIGN INVESTMENT INFLOWS BY COUNTRY OF ORIGIN

($ million)

Country	1994	1995	1996	1997
Sweden	--	--	--	366.2
United States	59.9	50.8	35.3	351.2

France	190.6	108.4	111.2	137.7
Japan	1.5	11.1	2.4	81.0
Germany	11.0	11.0	7.3	61.8
Spain	28.3	29.0	18.8	50.1
United Kingdom	140.1	37.2	96.4	32.2
South Korea	--	--	--	29.4
Netherlands	0.4	20.0	24.0	25.7
Libya	--	--	17.3	24.3
Benelux	--	--	17.7	8.5
Sauid Arabia	31.1	18.1	19.8	7.9
Switzerland	35.3	45.1	8.3	7.9
U.A.E.	5.3	16.2	1.4	3.9
Bahrain	1.6	22.8	1.7	--
Ireland	8.2	18.0	1.4	--
Portugal	--	--	73.8	--
Others	41.6	31.0	12.8	17.9
Total	554.9	418.7	449.8	1205.7

N.B.	1994	1995	1996	1997
Exchange rate (dh/$)	9.2	8.5	8.7	9.8
GDP ($ Billions)	30.3	32.4	36.8	32.5

FOREIGN INVESTMENT INFLOWS BY SECTOR

(USD millions)

Sector	**1994**	**1995**	**1996**	**1997**
Other Industry	113.9	110.3	154.7	153.1
Banking	97.7	109.3	118.8	211.2
Energy & Mining	3.1	19.0	10.0	654.1
Holding Companies	93.2	51.5	34.6	41.8

Tourism	23.9	9.1	3.7	48.0
Real Estate	18.3	31.0	42.6	28.4
Commerce	53.4	27.1	16.8	18.6
Textiles	7.0	10.9	17.2	9.3
Other Services	2.7	11.8	5.7	2.7
Agriculture	2.2	1.7	1.0	2.2
Transport	1.5	.2	2.4	1.2
Public Works	3.0	3.8	11.8	34.8
Fishing	4.9	11.3	.4	.3
Others	30.1	15.7	30.2	12.5
Total	554.9	418.7	449.8	1205.7
N.B.				
Exchange rate (dh/$)	9.2	8.5	8.7	9.8
GDP ($ billions)	30.3	32.4	36.8	32.5

MARKET RESEARCH

Market Research
- Safety Equipment
- Passenger Automobiles

- Solid Waste
- Electrical Energy

LIST OF USDA/FAS/COMMODITY REPORTS & BRIEFS

Report	(Yearly)
Oilseeds & Products	February 1
Grain & Feed	March 6
Sugar	April 10
Citrus	November 1
Almonds	August 20
Agricultural Situation	September 30
Seafood Report (Squid)	September 15
High Value Food Products	July 31

U.S. AND COUNTRY CONTACTS

COUNTRY GOVERNMENT AGENCIES

CUSTOMS AND INDIRECT TAXES ADMINISTRATION
Noureddine Omary, General Manager
Place Mohammed V
Casablanca, Morocco
Phone: (212) (2) 22-41-16
Fax: (212) (2) 26-07-06

DIRECTION DES STATISTIQUES
Toufik Charkaoui, General Manager
Rue Mohamed Belhassan El-Ouzani
Agdal-Rabat, Morocco
Phone: (212) (7) 77-36-06
Fax: (212) (7) 77-30-42

MINISTRY OF FINANCE AND ECONOMY
Fathallah Oulalou, Minister
Ancien Quartier Administratif
Rabat, Morocco
Phone: (212) (7) 76-22-21
Fax: (212) (7) 76-15-75

MINISTRY OF TRADE AND INDUSTRY
Alami Tazi, Minister
Quartier des Ministeres
Rabat-Chellah, Morocco
Phone: (212) (7) 76-18-78
Fax: (212) (7) 76-62-65

OFFICE NATIONAL DE L'ELECTRICITE (ONE)
Driss Benhima, General Manager
65, Rue Othman Ben Affane -ex Lafuente
Casablanca, Morocco
Phone: (212) (2) 22-41-65
Fax: (212) (2) 22-00-38

AGENCE NATIONALE DE REGLEMENTATION DES TELECOMMUNICATIONS (ANRT)
Mustapha Terrab, General Manager
Rue Al Khalil, Imm. A, 3rd floor
Rabat, Morocco
tel: (212-7) 20-38-69
fax: (212-7) 30-38-62

ITTISSALAT AL MAGHRIB (IAM)
Abdeslam Ahizoune, General Manager
Hay Riad, Avenue El-Nakhil
Rabat, Morocco
Phone: (212) (7) 71-41-41
Fax: (212) (7) 71-33-00

OFFICE NATIONAL DE L'EAU POTABLE (ONEP)
Lahoucine Tijani, General Manager
6, Bis Rue Patrice Lumumba
Rabat-Chellah, Morocco
Phone: (212) (7) 72-65-15
Fax: (212) (7) 72-67-07

OFFICE CHERIFIEN DES PHOSPHATES (OCP)
Mourad Cherif, General Manager
Route d'El Jadida
Casablanca, Morocco
Phone: (212) (2) 23-01-25
Fax: (212) (2) 25-09-99

OFFICE D'EXPLOITATION DES PORTS (ODEP)
Mohamed Halab, General Manager
175, Blvd. Mohamed Zerktouni
Casablanca, Morocco
Phone: (212) (2) 23-23-24
Fax: (212) (2) 25-81-58

COUNTRY TRADE ASSOCIATIONS/CHAMBERS OF COMMERCE

A.F.A.C.
(Feed Millers Association)
TOUZANI, Idrissi Abbes; President
c/o INAM-PROVIMI,151 Route Ouled Ziane;CASABLANCA(05); MOROCCO
Phone: (212) (2) 311249/442276
Fax: (212) (2) 311249/442276

AMERICAN CHAMBER OF COMMERCE
Dominic Demme, President
Hyatt Regency Hotel
Place Mohammed
Casablanca, Morocco
Phone: (212) (2) 29-30-28
Fax: (212) (2) 48-15-97

APEBI
(Telecom/Computers)
Fouad Brini, President
Place Zellaqua, Tour Atlas
Casablanca, Morocco
Phone: (212) (2) 45-00-54
Fax: (212) (2) 45-00-60

ASSOCIATION DES INDUSTRIES MINIERES
Abdelaziz Abarro, President
1, Place de l'Istiqlal
Casablanca, Morocco
Phone: (212) (2) 30-68-98
Fax: (212) (2) 31-99-96

ANCL
(Wheat Importer=s Association)
Azzedine Bennani, President
c/o COPRAGI, km 6,3, Boulevard Moulay Ismail
Ain Sebaa, CASABLANCA
Phone: (212) (2) 353141/352489
Fax: (212) (2) 350869

ASSOCIATION DES MARCHANDS ET IMPORTATEURS DE MATERIEL AGRICOLE
Abdellatif Ouazzani, President
Comicom, 9 Boulevard d'Oujda
Casablanca, Morocco
Phone: (212) (2) 30-22-11
Fax: (212) (2) 30-60-82

ASSOCIATION MAROCAINE DU CONSEIL ET DE L'INGENIERIE
(Engineering)
Rachid Balafrej, President
Charii Maryniyines, Secteur 22 Hay Ryad.
Rabat, Morocco
Phone: (212) (7) 75-61-01
Fax: (212) (7) 75-61-00

LESIEUR
(Oilseed Crusher, Vegetable Oil Refiner)
Drissi, Amar, CEO
1, Rue Caporal Corbi, CASABLANCA
Phone: (212) (2) 354636/354327
Fax: (212) (2) 268957/354097

FEDERATION NATIONALE DE LA MINOTERIE (FNM)
(Wheat Millers Association)
SEBTI, Ghali; President
Angle Boulevard Girardot et Rue du Havre;
CASABLANCA; MOROCCO
Phone: (212) (2) 301801/301158
Fax: (212) (2) 305924

CONFEDERATION GENERALE ECONOMIQUE MAROCAINE (CGEM)
(Moroccan Employers Association)
Abderrahim Lahjouji, President
Rue de la Plage avenue des Far
Casablanca, Morocco
Phone: (212) (2) 25-26-96
Fax: (212) (2) 25-38-39

OFFICE DES FOIRES ET EXPOSITIONS DE CASABLANCA
Abdelkader Berbache, General Manager
11, Rue Boukraa -ex Jules Mauran
Casablanca, Morocco
Phone: (212) (2) 22-28-16
Fax: (212) (2) 26-49-49

U.S.- MOROCCO COUNCIL ON TRADE & INVESTMENT
c/o Banque Marocaine du Commerce Exterieur
140, Avenue Hassan II
Casablanca, Morocco
Phone: (212) (2) 26-27-30
Fax: (212) (2) 47-14-17

COUNTRY MARKET RESEARCH FIRMS:

M.T.D.S.
Karl Stanzick, General Manager
43, Rue Oukaimeden, No. 2
Rabat-Agdal, Morocco
Phone: (212) (7) 67-48-61
Fax: (212) (7) 67-48-63

MAJOR COUNTRY COMMERCIAL BANKS

BANQUE CENTRALE POPULAIRE
Rachid Bennani-Smires, Director Int'l Affairs
101 Blvd. Mohammed Zerktouni
Casablanca, Morocco
Phone: (212) (2) 20-25-33
Fax: (212) (2) 20-19-32

BANQUE COMMERCIALE DU MAROC
Ali Kadiri, Head of Int'l Department
2, Blvd Moulay Youssef
Casablanca, Morocco
Phone: (212) (2) 47-64-39
Fax: (212) (2) 47-64-29/30

BANQUE MAROCAINE DU COMMERCE EXTERIEUR
Farid Arfaoui, Head of Int'l Department
140, Blvd. Hassan II
Casablanca, Morocco
Phone: (212) (2) 20-04-20
Fax: (212) (2) 26-49-20

BANQUE MAROCAINE POUR LE COMMERCE ET L'INDUSTRIE
Mustapha Faris, President
26, Place Nations Unies
Casablanca, Morocco
Phone: (212) (2) 22-41-61
Fax: (212) (2) 20-89-78

CITIBANK-MAGHREB
Reza Ghaffari, Managing Director
52, Avenue Hassan II
Casablanca, Morocco
Phone: (212) (2) 22-41-68
Fax: (212) (2) 20-57-23

CREDIT DU MAROC
Jamal Lemridi, Director Int'l Affairs
48-58 Blvd. Mohammed V
Casablanca, Morocco
Phone: (212) (2) 22-41-42
Fax: (212) (2) 27-71-27

INTERNATIONAL FINANCE CORPORATION
Mansour Kellada Antoun, Regional Representative for North Africa
8, rue Kamal Mohamed -ex 30, Avenue des F.A.R.
12eme etage.
Casablanca, Morocco
Phone: (212) (2) 48-46-87
Fax: (212) (2) 48-46-90

SOCIETE GENERALE MAROCAINE DE BANQUES
Omar Tazi, General Manager
55 Blvd. Abdelmoumen
Casablanca, Morocco
Phone: (212) (2) 27-92-69
Fax: (212) (2) 20-09-52

WAFABANK
Larbi Aouad, Head of Int'l Department
163, Avenue Hassan II
Casablanca, Morocco
Phone: (212) (2) 22-41-05
Fax: (212) (2) 29-72-72

U.S. MISSION TRADE PERSONNEL

AMERICAN CONSULATE GENERAL CASABLANCA
The Commercial Office
Kathy Kriger, Senior Commercial Officer
Address: 8, Blvd. Moulay Youssef
Casablanca, Morocco
Phone: (212) (2) 26-45-50
Fax: (212) (2) 22-02-59

AMERICAN EMBASSY RABAT
2, Avenue de Marrakech
Rabat, Morocco
Phone: (212) (7) 76-22-65
Fax: (212) (7) 76-56-61

-Economic Section
Richard Johnson, Economic Counselor
Douglas Griffiths, Economic Officer

-Agricultural Section
Quintin Gray, Agricultural Attache

-U.S.Agency for International Development
James Bednar, Director USAID

WASHINGTON-BASED USG COUNTRY CONTACTS

U.S. Department of Commerce
Robert Marro, Regional Director
OIO/ANESA, US&FCS
U.S. Department of Commerce
Washington, D.C.
Phone (202) 482-4836; Fax 482-5179

Tom Parker, Regional Director IEP/ONE
David Guglielmi, Morocco Desk Officer
U.S. Department of Commerce
Washington, D.C.
Phone: (202) 482-5545; Fax 482-5179

Multilateral Development Bank Office
Department of Commerce
14th and Constitution, N.W.

Washington, D.C. 20047
Phone: (202) 482-3399; Fax: 482-5179

TPCC TRADE INFORMATION CENTER
Washington, D.C.: 1-800-USA-TRADE

U.S. Department of State
Morocco Desk Officer: Laura Byergo, NEA/ENA Washington, D.C.
Phone (202) 647-4675; Fax: 736-4458

Office of the Coordinator for Business Affairs
Phone (202) 746-1625; Fax: (202) 647-3953

U.S. Department of Agriculture
Foreign Agriculture Service (FAS), Trade Assistance and Promotion Service
Director Grain & Feed Division: Robert Riemenshneider, Washington D.C.
Phone: (202) 720-6219; Fax: 720-0340

U.S. Trade Development Agency
Regional Director Africa/Middle East: John Richter
Country Director: Danielle Camner
Phone: (703) 875-4357; Fax: 875-4009

U.S. Export Import Bank (Ex-Im)
Country Loan Officer: Tony DiStefano
Africa and Middle East Division
811 Vermont Avenue, NW, Washington D.C. 20571
Phone: (202) 565-3900; Fax: 565-3931

Office of Private Investment Corporation (OPIC)
1100 New York Avenue, NW
Washington, DC 20527
Phone: (202) 336-8799
Toll-free: (800) 424-OPIC (6742)

U.S.-BASED MULTIPLIERS RELEVANT FOR COUNTRY

Morocco-U.S. Council on Trade & Investment
Allan Gerson, Executive Director
Watergate Building
600 New Hampshire Ave., NW
6th Floor
Washington, D.C. 20037
Phone: (202) 965-2380
Fax: (202) 337-0301

U.S.-Morocco Council on Trade & Investment
Barbara Lewis, Executive Director
Rockfeller Plaza, 8th floor
New York, N.Y. 10020
Phone: (212) 218-5750
Fax: (212) 218-5751

Moroccan Embassy
1601 21st Street NW
Washington, D.C. 20049-1002
Phone: (202) 462-7979
Fax: (202) 265-0161

BANKS WITH CORRESPONDENT U.S. BANKING ARRANGEMENTS

Among the leading commercial banks in Morocco, the following deal with major U.S. correspondent banks:

BANQUE MAROCAINE DU COMMERCE EXTERIEUR
Bank of New York
Bank of America
Bankers Trust
Chase Manhattan
Chemical Bank
Citibank

BANQUE CENTRALE POPULAIRE
Arab Banking Corporation
Bank of New York
Bank of America
Chemical Bank
Citibank

BANQUE MAROCAINE POUR LE COMMERCE ET L'INDUSTRIE
American Express
Bank of New York
Citibank
First American Bank Inc.

BANQUE COMMERCIALE DU MAROC
American Express
Arab-American Bank of New York
Bank of New York

Chase Manhattan Bank
Chemical Bank
Citibank
First National Bank of Chicago
First Bank of America
National Bank for Cooperatives
State Street Bank & Trust Company

CITIBANK-MAGHREB
Citibank

CREDIT DU MAROC
American Express Bank
Bank of New York
Chemical Bank
Credit Lyonais of New York
USEXIM Export Credit Program

SOCIETE GENERALE MAROCAINE DE BANQUES
Chase Manhattan
Citibank
Societe Generale

WAFABANK
Arab Banking Corporation (ABC)
Bank of New York
Bank of America
Bankers Trust Co.
Chase Manhattan
Citibank
Continental Bank
Manufacturers Hanover Trust Co. Ubaf

SELECTED GOVERNMENT AGENCIES

OFFICE	ADRESSE	VILLE	TEL	FAX
BUREAU DE RECHERCHES ET DE PARTICIPATIONS MINIERES	5 Avenue My Hassan	RABAT	(212)(7) 70 50 05	(212) (7) 70 94 11
CENTRE MAROCAIN DE PROMOTION DES EXPORTATIONS	Rue Ibnou Majid Al Bahhar	CASABLANCA	(212)(2) 30 22 10	(212)(2) 30 17 93
OFFICE NATIONAL DE L'EAU POTABLE	6, Rue Patrice Lumumba	RABAT	(212)(7) 72 12 81	(212)(7) 72 65 33
OFFICE NATIONAL DES TRANSPORTS	Rue Al Fadila, Quartier Industriel B.P 596	RABAT	(212)(7) 79 78 42	
OFFICE DES CHANGES	Place My Hassan - B.P 71	RABAT	(212)(7) 73 19 72	(212)(7) 72 12 85
OFFICE DE COMMERCIALISATION ET D'EXPORTATION	45, Avenue des FAR - B.P 13259	CASABLANCA	(212)(2) 31 41 03	(212)(2) 31 30 79
OFFICE NATIONAL D'ELECTRICITE	65, Rue Othmane Bnou Affane - B.P 13498	CASABLANCA	(212)(2) 22 33 30	(212)(2) 22 00 38
OFFICE NATIONAL DES PECHES	13, Rue du Lieutenant Mahroud Md	CASABLANCA	(212)(2) 24 05 51	(212)(2) 24 23 05
OFFICE CHERIFIEN DES PHOSPHATES	Boulevard de la grande ceinture,Route d'El Jadida	CASABLANCA	(212)(2) 23 00 25	(212)(2) 23 06 35
OFFICE NATIONAL DE RECHERCHES ET D'EXPLOITATION PETROLIERES	Avenue Michlifen Agdal	RABAT	(212)(7) 67 02 95	(212)(7) 317 15

OFFICE NATIONAL DES CHEMINS DE FER	Rue Abderrahmane Ghafiki, Agdal	RABAT	(212)(7) 77 47 47	(212)(7) 77 43 76
OFFICE NATIONAL DES POSTES ET TELECOMMUNICATIONS	Avenue Nakhil, Hay Riyad	RABAT	(212)(7) 71 91 37	(212)(7) 71 33 00
OFFICE DES FOIRES ET EXPOSITIONS DE CASABLANCA	11,Rue Boukrâa	CASABLANCA	(212)(2) 22 28 13	(212)(2) 26 49 49
OFFICE MAROCAIN DE LA PROPRIETE INDUSTRIELLE	8, Rue Essanaoubar	CASABLANCA	(212)(2) 30 16 31	(212)(2) 30 16 31
OFFICE D'EXPLOITATION DES PORTS	2, Bd des Almohades	CASABLANCA	(212)(2) 23 23 24	(212)(2) 25 81 58
OFFICE POUR LE DEVELOPPEMENT INDUSTRIEL	10, Rue Ghandi - B.P 211	RABAT	(212)(7) 70 84 60	(212)(7) 70 76 95
DELEGATION A PARIS DE L'OFFICE POUR LE DEVELOPPEMENT INDUSTRIEL	76, Avenue des Champs Elysé	PARIS	(33 1) 43 59 22 39	(33 1)43 59 00 30
OFFICE DE LA FORMATION PROFESSIONNELLE ET DE LA PROMOTION DU TRAVAIL	231, Bd Ibn Tachfine BP 2119	CASABLANCA	(212)(2) 40 22 50	(212)(2) 40 3650
OFFICE NATIONAL DES AEROPORTS	Aéroports Mohamed V20250 Nouasseur BP 8101	CASABLANCA	(212)(2) 33 90 40	(212)(2) 33 99 01
OFFICE NATIONAL MAROCAIN DU TOURISME	Rue Oued Fès Angle Abtal- Agdal	RABAT	(212)(7) 77 74 36	(212)(7) 77 74 47
OFFICE NATIONAL DU THE ET DU SUCRE	Route Tit Mellil, Bd Ahl Loghlam BP 13618 Ainsebâa	CASABLANCA	(212)(2) 35 08 73	(212)(2) 35 09 11

ECONOMIC DEVELOPMENT OFFICES

VILLE	ADRESSE	TEL (212)	FAX (212)
AGADIR	RUE DES ADMINISTRATIONS PUBLIQUES.BP.182	(8) 84 08 66	((8) 84 73 60
BENI MELLAL	QUARTIER ADMINISTRATIF B.P 182	(3) 48 20 22	((3) 42 07 81
BENSLIMANE	AVENUE HASSAN II N°71-73 B.P.14	(3) 29 11 90	(3) 29 83 30
BOUJDOUR	69, Bd Hassan II	(8) 89 62 50	(8) 86 62 49

CASABLANCA	Km, 9.500 Route Nouasseur	(2) 33 54 81	(2) 33 54 86
DAKHLA	18, RUE 18 JUILLET OUED EDDAHAB	(8) 89 70 87	(8) 89 86 58
EL HOCEIMA	BD, MOULAY DRISS AL AKBAR N°6/B.P.48	(9) 98 29 28	(9) 98 15 09
EL JADIDA	AV.JAMIA AL ARABIA	(3) 34 32 20	(3) 35 48 20
ERRACHIDIA	15 RUE EZZERKTOUNI	(5) 57 21 75	(5) 57 38 38
ESSAOUIRA	183.CA 4 HAY LALLA AMINA	(4) 78 42 97	(4) 78 41 98
ES SEMARA	AVENUE HASSAN II B.P.71	(8) 89 95 61	(8) 89 95 12
FES	38, AVENUE LALLA HASNAA FES	(5) 62 37 55	(5) 93 16 40
KENITRA	IMMEUBLE EL HARRATI RUE IBN ABI ZARAA B.P.234	(7) 37 13 23	(7) 37 15 44
KHEMISSET	B.P 675 LOTISSEMENT ENAJAH N°7	(7) 55 00 53	(7) 55 60 54
KHOURIBGA	1,ANGLE MY ABDELLAH PLACE ISTIQLAL	(3) 49 23 78	(3) 49 33 65
LAAYOUNE	PROVINCE DE LAAYOUNE B.P.529	(8) 89 44 33	(8) 89 08 60
MARRAKECH	CITE MOHAMMEDIA DAOUDIAT BP 1482	(4) 30 75 23	(4) 30 75 23
MEKNES	PLACE DE L'UNITE AFRICAINE BP.S.44	(5) 52 28 70	(5) 52 48 94
MOHAMMEDIA	LOTISSEMENT DEMNATE RUE EL JAHID N°15	(3) 31 43 84	(3) 32 98 58
NADOR	170 BD KHALID IBNOU OUALID B.P 317	(6) 60 60 96	(6) 33 54 62
OUARZAZATE	75, HAY EL HASSANI GASTOR	(4) 88 26 22	(4) 88 34 20
OUJDA	28 AV.OMAR ERRIFI B.P.529	(6) 68 22 21	(6) 68 67 90
RABAT	1 PLACE SEFROU HASSAN	(7) 20 15 58	(7) 73 60 95
SAFI	PLACE DE LA MARNE B.P.248	(4) 46 46 25	(4) 63 06 03
SETTAT	QUARTIER ADMINISTRATIF BP.622	(3) 40 36	(3) 40 36

		78	78
TANGER	40, AVENUE MOHAMMED V	(9) 94 44 50	(9) 94 29 54
TAZA	LOTISSEMENT LA SABLI7RE N°13 ROUTE PRINCIPALE	(5) 67 35 09	(5) 67 26 15
TETOUAN	AV. MOHAMMED V IMMEUBLE TRAVAUX PUBLICS BP 24	(9) 96 45 40	(9) 96 67 89
TIZNIT	QUARTIER YOUSSOUFIA B.P. 419.	(8) 86 29 48	(8) 86 64 82

CHAMBERS OF COMMERCE

CCIS	*PRESIDENT*	*DIRECTEUR*	*EMAIL*	*TELEPHONE*	*FAX*	*ADRESSE*
FCCISM	**Abdellah ZOUHIR**	**Hassan ouslim**	ccisa@agadirnet.net.ma	**(037) /76.70.51/ 76.78.81/ 76.70.78**	**76.70.76**	**RUE ARFOUD, N° 6 - RABAT-**
Agadir	**Said DOUR**	**Ali BADOUH**		**(048) 84.71.41/ 84.71.24**	**84.54.55**	**B.P.240/ Bd.HASSAN II - AGADIR- C.P 80001**
Al Hoceima	**Abdesselam AGHARBI**	**Ali FARISSI**		**(039) /98.21.29/ 98.37.98**	**98.49.04**	**97,Bd.MOHAMED V- AL HOCEIMA- C.P 32004**
Benni Mellal	**Salah EZZOUINE**	**Lahcen BIDANI**	**ccisbma@iam.net.ma**	**(023) 48.24.34/ 48.90.54**	**48.90.54**	**BP.271 - BENI MELLAL- C.P 23001**
Casablanca	**Abdellatif BELMADANI**	**Chafiq BERRADA (P.I)**		**(022) 26.44.38/ 26.43.27/ 26.86.15**	**26.84.36**	**BP.423/ Bd.MOHAMED V N 98 - CASABLANCA- C.P 20041**
El Jadida	**Jamal BENRABIA**			**(023) 34.37.85/ 34.23.02/ 34.10.04**	**34.10.04**	**BP.53/AV.FKIH M.HAMED**

						ERRAFII-EL JADIDA-C.P 24001
El Kelaa	Mounir BEN CHLIKHA	Touhami MOUHIB		(044) 41.20.56/ 41.28.87	41.28. 74	IMM.7 ESC.2/1 ERRAHA-EL KELAA DES SRAGHNA-C.P 43001
Errachidia	Bassidi AGOUMI	Mohamed SAAIDI (PI)		(055) 57.35.13/ 57.31.06	57.04.48	BP.6/ Bd.DE L'OCEAN N 4 - ERRACHIDIA- C.P 52001
Essaouirra	Mouly Said ABBARY	Abdelhafid KARIMI		(044) 78.46.66	78.59-32	10, RUE EL KAHIRA - ESSAOUIRA- C.P 44000
Fes	Boubker EL AMRANI JOUTEY	Mohamed TAZI	ccis.fes@fesnet.net.ma	(055) 62.31.83/62.28.32/ 93.25.65	62.68.84	BP.2203/ Bd.ABDELLAH CHEFCHAOUNI FES V.N - PLACE ABDELMOUMEN- C.P 30001
Kenitra	Ahmed M.RABET	Hamid ETTADLAOUI		(037) 37.10.80/ 37.10.81/ 37.25.75/ 37.25.76	37.15.44	BP.151/PLACEADMINISTRATIVE - C.P.TTEL:37.17.73-C.P14001
Khemisset	Adelhamid BELFIL	Hassan MISSOUR		(035) 55.21.13/ 55.70.76	55.16.94	BP.206/RUECADIAYA DN21-KHEMISSET-C.P15001

Khenifra	Mly Mahdi BADRI	Charki EL HABCHI		(055) 58.64.83	38.45.83	BP.1/ KHENIFRA - C.P 54001
Khouribga	Mohamed GOURRAM	Mohamed SFA		(023) 56.34.34/ 56.42.15/ 56.20.04	56.20.04	BP.67 - KHOURIBG A- C.P 25001
Laayoune	Brahim AHL HOUMMAD	Ahmed BAGHDADI		(048) 89.49.71	89.49.72	BP.265/45, AV.MOHA MED SALEM BEIDE - LAAYOUN E- C.P 70001
Marrakech	Mohamed El Habib EL BERDAI	Tayeb GUEMOURI A		(044) 43.19.51/ 43.05.50/ 43.61.91/ 43.52.56	43.52.56	BP.529/ JENANE EL HARTI- GUELIZ- MARRAKE CH- C.P 40001
Meknes	Alami TAZI	Fouad AMINE'		(055) 52-11. 10/ 52. 12- 72/ 51.09.37	51.09.51	BP .325/ PLACE ABDELAZI Z BEN DRISS - MEKNES- C.P 50001
Mohammed ia	Abdellah ZOUHEIR	Abdehadi BAYOUDA		(023) 31.43.30	31.43.32	BP.164/ 25 Bd. MOHAMED V - MOHAMMA DIA- C.P 20650
Nador	Abdelhafid JARROUDI	Houcine HAMOUTI	danti@ia m.net.ma	(056) 60.38.57/ 60.35.49	33.15.48	Bp.37/- Nador- C.P62001
Ouarzazate	Omar Bouaida	Moha SANI	ccisozte @iam.net .ma	(044) 88.23.28/ 88.28.32	88.54.00	Bp 51/AV.MOH AMEDV RUE

						OURIZEN - OUARZAZATE C.P 45001
Oued Eddahab	Brahim BOUIGHDEN	Mostafa ERRQUIZI		(048) 93.04.20	93.04.21	IMMEUBLE AL BARAKA QUARTIER MOULAY RACHID BP:111 DAKHLA
Oujda	Driss HOUAT	Rachid SLISLI	cciso@espacenet.net.ma	(056) 68.24.11/ 68.24.12/ 74.93.03	68.24.12	BP.413/ Bd. ALLAL BEN ABDELLAH N° 12 - OUJDA- C.P 60001
Rabat	Omar SENTISSI	Najib AFFANE		(037) 70.64.44/ 70-64.66/ 70.64.42/ 70.31.95	70.67.68	BP.131/ RUE GHANDI - RABAT- C.P 10000
Safi	Mounir IDHALOUMAL	Khalid ERRACHDI		(044) 62.30.34/ 62.26.47/ 61.06.27	62.65.82	BP.224/- SAFI- C.P 46001
Settat	Haj Ahmed ABOU LAHCEN	JelloulL SEMESEME		(023) 40.26.58/ 40.33.86	40.38.68	BP.161/ Bd. DES F.A.R N° 19 -SETTAT. C.P 26001
Tanger	Taha ABAAKIL	Mohamed SERRIFI	cciswig@iam.net.ma	(039) 94.63.37/ 94.63.77	94.63.78	BP.411/ Bd. PASTEUR N° 41 - TANGER- C.P 90001
Tantan	M'bar.k EL BETTAH	Aziz DOUBI	ccitantan@iam.net.ma	(048) 87.89.49/ 87.89.59	87.89.59	Avenue Hassan II BP: 583
Taza	Abdelwahed	Hamid	ccistz@ia	(055) 67.35.83/	67.11.94	BP 203-

	MESSAAOU DI	TLAMTI	m.net.ma	67.36.76/ 67.29.96		TAZA - C.P35001
Tetouan	Abd.lhadi BENALLAL	Moham.d SOTTOU				

CHAMBRE	ADRESSE	VILLE	TEL	FAX
AMERICAN CHAMBER OF COMMERCE	American Chamber of Commerce in Morocco Hyatt Regency Hotel, Place des Nations Unies Casablanca, Morocco	CASABLANCA	(212) 22 29 30 28 / 29 49 49	(212) 22 49 18 88
BRITISH CHAMBER OF COMMERCE FOR MOROCCO	65, Avenue Hassan Sghir	CASABLANCA 20040	(212) 22 44 88 60	(212) 22 44 88 68
CHAMBRE ESPAGNOLE DU COMMERCE ET D'INDUSTRIE AU MAROC	6, Rue Hsain Ramdan (ex-rue de l'Eglise)	CASABLANCA 01	(212) 22 30 31 65	(212) 22 30 31 65
CHAMBRE FRANCAISE DU COMMERCE ET D'INDUSTRIE AU MAROC	15, Av Mers Sultan	CASABLANCA 01	(212) 22 22 23 99	(212) 22 20 01 30
CHAMBRE ITALIENNE DU COMMERCE ET D'INDUSTRIE AU MAROC	Rue Amine Kacem	CASABLANCA 01	(212) 22 27 82 17	(212) 22 27 86 27
CHAMBRE SUISSE DU COMMERCE ET D'INDUSTRIE AU MAROC	305, Bd Bir ANZARANE, Romandie II, Tour Koweit	CASABLANCA	(212) 22 36 27 93	(212) 22 36 49 66
CHAMBRE BELGO-LUXEMBOURGEOISE	124, Avenue My Hassan 1èr	CASABLANCA	(212) 22 20 00 61	(212) 22 20 33 83
FEDERATION ALLEMANDE DU COMMERCE ET DE L'INDUSTRIE	C/O Bayer Maroc, 3 Bd Zerktouni	CASABLANCA	(212) 22 76 70 51	(212) 22 76 70 76
CHAMBRE DU COMMERCE CANADIENNE AU MAROC	Rond-point Hassan II, Hotel Holiday IMM Suite 207	CASABLANCA	(212) 22 29 50 37	(212) 22 29 50 28
FEDERATION DU COMMERCE DU L'UNION EUROPEENNE AU MAROC	Tours Atlas, Place Zellaqua	CASABLANCA		

PROFESIONAL ASSOCIATIONS

ASSOCIATION	ADRESSE	VILLE	TEL (212) 2	FAX (212) 2
CONFEDERATION GENERALE DES ENTREPRISES DU MAROC (CGEM)	Angle Avenue des FAR et rue Arrachid Mohamed	CASABLANCA	25 26 96	25 38 39
FEDERATION NATIONALE DE L'AGRO-ALIMENTAIRE (FENAGRI)	77, Rue Mohamed Smiha	CASABLANCA	30 39 53	30 35 34
FEDERATION DES INDUSTRIES DE LA CONSERVE AU MAROC (FICOMA)	7, Rue El Yarmouk Longchamp	CASABLANCA	36 50 42	36 61 54
FEDERATION DES INDUSTRIES DE LA CONSERVE DES PRODUITS AGRICOLES AU MAROC (FICOPAM)	77, Rue Mohamed Smiha	CASABLANCA	30 39 53	30 35 34
UNION NATION. INDUS.DE CONSERV.DE POISSON."UNICOP	RUE 5 N° 7 LONGCHAMP	CASABLANCA	36 50 42	36 61 54
FEDERATION DES INDUSTRIES METALLURGIQUE, MECANIQUE, ELECTRIQUE ET ELECTRONIQUE (FIMME)	147, RUE MOHAMED SMIHA	CASABLANCA	30 16 83	94 05 87
ASSOCIATION DES INDUSTRIES DE LA CONSTRUCTION METALLIQUE ET CHAUDRONNERIE-TOLERE (COMECH)	147, RUE MOHAMED SMIHA	CASABLANCA	30 16 83	30 92 63
ASSOCIATION DE LA MECANIQUE GENERALE INDUSTRIELLE ET RECTIFICATION (ASMIR)	147, RUE MOHAMED SMIHA	CASABLANCA	30 16 83	30 92 63
FEDERATION DES INDUSTRIES CHIMIQUES ET PARACHIMIQUES"F.I.C.P"	36, RUE CHAOUIA (ex-Cobert)	CASABLANCA 20040	22 92 15	22 56 13
ASSOCIATION DES FABRICANTS ET IMPORTATEURS DE PEINTURES ET DE PRODUITS DE DROGUERIE AU MAROC (AMFIP)	Chemin des Giroflées, Beausite Ain Sebâa	CASABLANCA	35 07 27	35 25 75

ASSOCIATION MAROCAINE DE L'INDUSTRIE PHARMACEUTIQUE (AMIP)	Résidence Amir, Place Division Leclerc, Bd Jerrada , Oasis	CASABLANCA	23 36 90	23 40 90
ASSOCIATION MAROCAINE DES INDUSTRIE DU CUIR "FEDIC"	47 Rue Planquette, Bélvédère	CASABLANCA	40 39 87	40 15 00
ASSOCIATION MAROCAINE DES TANNEURS (AMT)	47 Rue Planquette, Bélvédère	CASABLANCA	40 39 87	40 15 00
ASSOCIATION MAROCAINE DES INDUSTRIES DU TEXTLE ET DE L'HABILLEMENT (AMITH)	92, BD MOULAY RACHID	CASABLANCA	94 20 84	94 05 87
ASSOCIATION PROFESSIONNELLE DES CIMENTIERS (APC)	239, Bd Moulay Ismail	CASABLANCA	40 13 42	24 82 08
ASSOCIATION MAROCAINE POUR L'INDUSTRIE ET LE COMMERCE DE L'AUTOMOBILE (AMICA)	625, Bd Mohamed V	CASABLANCA	24 28 82	28 85 81
ASSOCIATION MAROCAINE DES EXPORTATEURS (ASMEX)	36, Résidence Anfae Bd Anfa, 14 eme étage	CASABLANCA	26 10 33	48 41 91
FEDERATION DES ASSOCIATIONS DES JEUNES ENTREPRENEURS DU MAROC (FAJEM)	64, Rue Allal Benabdellah	CASABLANCA	22 89 67	22 89 67

MAROCCO EMBASSIES

COUNTRY	ADRESSE	TEL	FAX
ABOU-DHABI (EMIRATS ARABES UNIS)	Avenue Al Nahyan al Manassir BP 4066 - ABOU-DHABI	(9712) 43 39 63	43 39 17
ALGER (ALGERIE)	8, Rue des cèdres - ALGER	(2132) 69 26 39	69 29 00
AMMAN (JORDANIE)	Jabal Amman, 4 th circle, Fawzi El molqi street BP BOX 2175	(9626) 86 60 69	86 51 85
Ankara (TURQUIE)	Resit Galip Caddesi Rabat Sokak n° 11 Gaziomanpasa	(312) 437 60 20	446 84 30
Athenes (GRECE)	14, Rue Mousson Paleo Psychico, ATHENES 15452	(301) 674 42 09	674 94 80
BAGHDAD (IRAQ)	Mansour 601/11/27 , P.O BOX 6039? BAGHDAD	(9641) 86 17 71	86 51 85
BANGKOK (THAILANDE)	Ban Chang Glas Haus Building, 1 Soi Sukhumvit 25, Klongtoey	(66 2) 260 64 10	260 64 12

BELGRADE (YOUGOSLAVIE)	Sanje Zivanovica 4, 11000 BELGRADE	(38 111) 651 775	647 296
BERNE (SUISSE)	42 HELVETIASTRASSE - CH - 3005 - BERNE -	(4131) 351 03 62	351 03 64
BEYROUTH (LIBAN)	Ain Tinna Verdun Bd 54 n° 8 - 5eme étage - BP 5920	(9611) 862 966	865 194
BONN (R. F. A.)	Gotenstr. 7-9 53175 BONN	(49228) 35 50 44	35 78 94
BRASILIA (BRESIL)	S.E.N., Avenida das Nacoes, lote 02 - Cep 70432-900	(5561) 226 22 88	321 07 45
BRUXELLES (BELGIQUE)	29 Bd Saint Michel - 1040 BRUXELLES	(322) 732 65 45	734 64 68
BUCAREST (ROUMANIE)	75, Bd Dacia Secteur 2 - BUCAREST	(401) 210 29 45	210 27 67
BUDAPEST (HONGRIE)	12, Torokvész lejto, BUDAPEST	(361) 175 54 86	275 14 37
BUENOS-AIRES (ARGENTINE)	Mcal. Ramon Castilla 2952 - C.P. 1425 Capital	(541) 801 81 54	802 01 36
COPENHAGUE (DANEMARK)	Oreggards Allé 19, 2900 Hellerup	(45) 39 62 45 11	39 62 24 49
DAMAS (SYRIE)	Mezzah Villas Est Rue Farabi - DAMAS	(96311) 662 08 39	662 44 95
DJAKARTA (INDONESIE)	Kuningan Plaza South Tower suite 512 Jl HR Rasuna Said KAV	(6221) 520 09 56	520 05 86
DOHA (QATAR)	DIPLOMATIC Area - P.O. BOX 3242	(0974) 83 18 84	83 34 16
DUBLIN (IRLAND)	53 Raglan Road, Ballsbridge - DUBLIN 4	(3531) 660 94 49	660 94 68
KUALA-LAMPUR (MALAISIE)	BOX 9 Wisma Selamgor Dredging, 7 th Floor, Est Block 142-B Jalan Ampang -50450- K. LUMPUR	(603) 261 07 01	262 30 81
LE CAIRE (EGYPTE)	10, Rue Salah Eddine Zamalek	(202) 340 96 77	341 19 37
LIMA (PEROU)	Av. Javier PRADO Oeste 2108 - SAN ISIDRO	(5114) 41 77 62	41 77 62
LISBONNE (PORTUGAL)	Rue Alto DO DUQUE N° 21 - 1400 LISBOA	(3511) 30 20 842	30 20 935
LONDRES (GRANDE-BRETAGNE)		(44171) 581 50 01	225 38 62
MADRID (ESPAGNE)		(341) 563 10 90	561 78 87
MEXICO (MEXIQUE)		(525) 245 17 86	245 17 91

MOSCOU (RUSSIE)	8 PRETCHISTENSKI PEREOULOK MOSCOU	(7095) 201 73 95	230 20 67
NEW DELHI (INDE)	33 GOLF LINKS, NEW DELHI - 110003 INDIA	(9111) 46 36 920	46 36 925
NOUAKCHOTT (MAURITANIE)	TEVRAGH ZEINA N° 634 BP 621	(222) 25 14 11	25 48 75
OTTAWA (CANADA)	38, Range Road, Ottawa ontario KIN 8J4	(1613) 236 73 91	236 61 64
PARIS (FRANCE)	5, RUE LE TASSE - 75116 PARIS	(331) 45 20 69 35	45 20 22 58
PEKIN (CHINE)	16 SAN LI TUN LU Beijing	(8610) 653 21 796	653 21 453
PRAGUE (REPUBLIQUE TCHEQUE)	Ke Staremu bubenci 4, 160 00 PRAGUE 6	(422) 32 47 92	32 17 58
PRETORIA (AFRIQUE DU SUD)	799 Schoeman Street Arcadia 0083 - PRETORIA -	(2712) 34 30 230	34 30 613
RIYAD (ROYAUME D'ARABIE SAOUDITE)	Quartier diplomatique B.P. 94392 RIYAD 11693	(9661) 48 11 858	48 27 016
ROME (ITALIE)	Via lazzaro Spallanzani, 8/10 - 00161 ROME	(396) 440 25 06	440 26 95
SEOUL (COREE DU SUD)	S-15, UN Village, 270-3, Hannan -Dong yongsan-Ku, Seoul	(822) 793 62 49	792 81 78
SOFIA (BULGARIE)	129 BOULEVARD EVLOGUI GUEORGUIEV SOFIA	(3592) 943 30 90	946 10 43
STOCKHOLM (SUEDE)	Kungsholmstorg 16 - 112 21 - STOCKHOLM	(468) 654 43 88	651 97 96
TEHERAN (IRAN)	Ave Africa (Jordan) Rue Armaghan sharghi n° 47	(9821) 205 97 07	205 18 72
TEL AVIV (ISRAEL)	67 WEIZMAN STREET KIKAR HAMEDINA TEL AVIV	(9723) 54 64 007	54 64 263
TOKYO (JAPAN)	SILVA KINGDOM BLDG 3-16-3, SENDAGAYA, SHIBUYA-KU	(813) 3478-3271	3402-0898
TRIPOLI (LIBYE)	Avenue Ben Achour B.P. 908 - TRIPOLI	(2182) 16 00 110	44 45 757
TUNIS (TUNISIE)	39, Rue du 1er juin Mutuelleville TUNIS	(2161) 783 801	787 103
VARSOVIE (POLOGNE)	ul STAROSCINSKA 1/11, 12 02-516 VARSOVIE	(4822) 49 63 41	48 18 40
VIENNE (AUTRICHE)	OPERNING 3-5 1010 WIEN	(431) 586 66 50	586 76 67
WASHINTON (U. S. A)	1601 21 ST STREET N.W., WASHINGTON D.C. 20049	(202) 462 79 79	462 76 43

LEADING RESTAURANTS

As an indication, listed below is the list of some restaurants in the large cities of the Kingdom.

CASABLANCA

French Specialities :
- A MA BRETAGNE : Bd de la Corniche Tel : (212) (02) 36 21 12
- LE CABESTAN : Phare d'El Hank Tel : (212) (02) 39 11 90
- AU PETIT ROCHER : Phare d'El Hank Tel : (212) (02) 39 57 48

Fish Specialities :
- RESTAURANT DU PORT : Port de pêche Tel : (212) (02) 31 85 61

Asian Specialities :
- LA TONKINOISE : Av. de la Côte d'Emeraude Tel: (212) (02) 39 11 87
- DELICES D'ASIE : 140, Rue Ibnou Mounir Maârif Tel: (212) (02) 23 79 82

Moroccan Specialities :
- AL MOUNIA : Rue Prince My Abdellah Tel : (212) (02) 22 26 69
- IMILCHIL : Rue Vizir Tazi Tel : (212) (02) 22 02 99

Indian Specialities :
- NATRAJ : 13, Rue Chenier Tel : (212) (02) 22 28 86

Italian Specialities :
- IL VENEZIANO : 90, Rue Jean Jaurés Tel : (212) (02) 29 50 03
- DON CAMILLO : 13, Rue Verdun Tel : (212) (02) 31 16 44

MARRAKESH

- AL FASSIA : 232, Bd Mohammed V Tel : (212) (04) 43 40 60
- LA TRATTORIA : 179, Rue Med El Bequal Tel : (212) (04) 43 26 41
- LE JACARANDA : 32, Bd Med Zertouni Tel : (212) (04) 44 72 15
- CHEZ JACK'LINE : 63, Bd Mohammed V Tel : (212) (04) 44 75 47
- LE PAVILLON : Bab Doukkala, Dar Zaouia N°67 Tel : (212) (04) 44 37 47
- LE DRAGON D'OR : 10 bis, Bd Zerktouni Tel : (212) (04) 43 33 41
- KSAR ESSAOUSSAN : N°3 Derb Chorfa El Messaoudyenne

MEKNES

- LA COUPOLE : Av. Hassan II Tel : (212) (05) 52 24 38
- METROPOLE : Angle Av. Hassan II Tel : (212) (05) 52 25 76
- LE DAUPHIN : 5, Av. Mohammed V Tel : (212) (05) 52 34 23
- NOVELTY : Av. de Paris Tel : (212) (05) 52 21 56
- L'HACIENDA : Route de Fès Tel : (212) (05) 52 10 92
- BELLEVUE : Quartier Bellevue Tel : (212) (05) 52 08 26

RABAT

- KANOUN GRILL : 2, Rue d'Ifni Tel : (212) (07) 76 02 09
- BORDJ EDDAR : Plage de Rabat Tel : (212) (07) 70 15 00
- L'ENTRECOTE : 74, Bd Fal Ould Oumeir Tel : (212) (07) 67 11 08
- LE PROVENCAL : Temara Tel : (212) (07) 74 11 11
- LES DELICES D'ASIE : 17, Rue Oqbah Tel : (212) (07) 77 94 79
- LA PAGODE : 13, Rue Baghdad Tel : (212) (07) 70 93 81

LEADING HOTELS

Some hotels (**5* et 4***) located on Moroccan major cities.

AGADIR

- SAFIR (5*) : Bd 20 Août Fax : (212) (08) 84 34 35
-SHERATON (5*) : Bd Mohammed V Fax : (212) (08) 84 43 79
-ADRAR (4*A) : Bd Mohammed V Fax : (212) (08) 84 05 45
-ANEZI (4*A) : Bd Mohammed V Fax : (212) (08) 84 07 13
-AMADIL (4*A) : Route Oued Souss Fax : (212) (08) 84 22 48
-SAHARA (4*A) : Bd Mohammed V Fax : (212) (08) 84 07 38
-TAFOUKT (4*A) : Bd 20 Août Fax : (212) (08) 84 09 71
-ALMOHADES (4*B) : Bd 20 Août Fax : (212) (08) 84 01 30
- MARHABA (4*B) : Bd Mohammed V Fax : (212) (08) 84 35 29
- OASIS (4*B) : Bd Mohammed V Fax : (212) (08) 84 42 60
- SUD BAHIA (4*B) : Rue des Adm. Publiques Tél : (212) (08) 82 48 63
- TAGADIRT (4*B) : Bd 20 Août Fax : (212) (08) 84 12 12

CASABLANCA

- ROYAL MANSOUR (5* Luxury) : 27, Av. des FAR Fax : (212) (02) 31 25 83
- HYATT REGENCY (5*) : Place des Nations Unies Fax : (212) (02) 26 95 35
- SHERATON (5*) : 100, Av. des FAR Fax : (212) (02) 31 51 36
- HOLIDAY INN (5*) : Rond point Hassan II Fax : (212) (02) 29 30 29
- SAFIR (5*) : 160, Av. des FAR Fax : (212) (02) 31 65 14
- RIAD SALAM (5*) : Bd de la Corniche Fax : (212) (02) 39 13 45
- IDOU ANFA (4*A) : 85, Bd Anfa Fax : (212) (02) 20 00 29
- EL KANDARA (4*A) : 44, Bd d'Anfa Fax : (212) (02) 26 06 17
- ATLANTIS (4*A) : Bd de Biaritz Fax : (212) (02) 39 15 57
- AL MOUNIA (4*B) : Bd de Paris Fax : (212) (02) 22 23 14
- BASMA (4*B) : Av. My Hassan 1er Fax : (212) (02) 26 89 36
- DAWLIZ (4*B) : Bd de la Corniche Fax : (212) (02) 39 14 29
- SUISSE (4*B) : Bd de la Corniche Fax : (212) (02) 36 77 58
- TARIK (4*B) : Bd de la Corniche Fax : (212) (02) 36 75 93
- WASHINGTON (4*B) : 26, Bd Rahal El Meskini Fax : (212) (02) 27 59 95
- LES ALMOHADES (4*B) : Av. My Hassan 1er Fax : (212) (02) 25 05 05
- LA CORNICHE (4*B) : Bd de la Corniche Fax : (212) (02) 39 11 10
- TROPICANA (4*B) : Bd de la Corniche Tél : (212) (02) 36 75 95

FEZ

- JNAN PALACE FES (5*) : Av. Ahmed Chaouki Fax : (212) (05) 65 19 17
- PALAIS JAMAI (5*) : Bad El Guissa Fax : (212) (05) 63 50 96
- LES MERINIDES (5*) : Borj Nord Fax : (212) (05) 64 52 25
- DE FES (4*A) : Av. des FAR Fax : (212) (05) 62 04 86
- BATHA (4*A) : Place Batha Tel : (212) (05) 63 37 73
- PLM SIDI HARAZEM (4*A) : Sidi Harazem Tel : (212) (05) 64 55 22
- SOFIA (4*A) : 3, Rue du Pakistan Tel : (212) (05) 62 42 65
- PLM VOLUBILIS (4*A) : Rue Allal Ben Abdellah Fax : (212) (05) 54 43 69

LAAYOUNE

- AL MASSIRA : Rue de la Mecque Tel : (212) (08) 89 44 11
- PARADOR : Rue Okba Ibn Nafih Fax : (212) (08) 89 45 13
- NAGJIR (4*) : Place Nagjir Fax : (212) (08) 89 41 69

MARRAKESH

- LA MAMOUNIA (5*Luxury) : Av. Bab Jdid Fax : (212) (04) 44 46 60
- GOLF PALACE (5*Luxury) : Circuit de la Palmeraie Fax : (212) (04) 30 20 20
- SHERATON (5*) : Av. de la Menara Fax : (212) (04) 44 89 72
- ES SAADI (5*) : Av. Kadissia Fax : (212) (04) 44 76 44
- FARAH SAFIR (5*) : Av. Président Kennedy Fax : (212) (04) 44 87 30
- MERIDIEN (5*) : Av. de Casablanca Fax : (212) (04) 44 71 27
- MANSOUR EDDAHBI (5*) : Av. de France Fax : (212) (04) 44 81 68
- IMPERIAL BORG (5*) : Av. Echouhada Fax : (212) (04) 44 62 06
- LES ALMORAVIDES (4*A) : J'nane Lakhdar Fax : (212) (04) 44 31 33
- ATLAS ASNI (4*A) : Av. de France Fax : (212) (04) 44 33 08
- PLM N'FIS (4*A) : Av. de France Fax : (212) (04) 44 74 46
- CHEMS (4*B) : Av. Houmane Fetouaki Fax : (212) (04) 44 05 47
- SAHARA INN (4*B) : Av. de Casablanca Tél : (212) (04) 43 43 88
- LA MENARA (4*B) : Av. des Remparts Fax : (212) (04) 44 73 86

MEKNES

- TRANSATLANTIQUE (5*) : Rue Al Mariniyine Fax : (212) (05) 52 00 57
- RIF (4*A) : Zankat Accra Fax : (212) (05) 52 44 28
- ZAKI (4*A) : Bd Al Massira Fax : (212) (05) 52 48 36

RABAT

- HYATT REGENCY (5*) : Souissi Fax : (212) (07) 77 24 92
- SAFIR (5*) : Place Sidi Makhlouf Fax : (212) (07) 72 21 55
- TOUR HASSAN (5*) : 22, Av. Abderahman Anagai Fax : (212) (07) 72 54 08
- CHELLAH (4*A) : 2, Rue d'Ifni Fax : (212) (07) 70 63 54
- BELERE (4*A) : 33, Av. My Youssef Fax : (212) (07) 70 98 01
- LES OUDAYAS (4*B) : 4, Rue Tabrouk Fax : (212) (07) 70 82 35

TANGIER

- EL MINZAH (5*) : 85, Rue de la Liberté Fax : (212) (09) 93 45 46
- LES ALMOHADES (4*A) : Av. des FAR Fax : (212) (09) 94 63 71

- INTERCONTINENTAL (4*B) : Park Brooks Fax : (212) (09) 93 79 45
- FLANDRIA (4*B) : 6, Bd Mohammed V Fax : (212) (09) 93 43 47
- RIF (4*B) : Av. d'Espagne Fax : (212) (09) 94 17 94
- SOLAZUR (4*B) : Av. des FAR Fax : (212) (09) 94 52 86

PRESIDENTIAL INITIATIVE ON INTERNET FOR ECONOMIC DEVELOPMENT:

Assessment for USAID/Morocco

PART I—GOVERNMENT POLICY CONSIDERATIONS IN THE IT SECTOR

The Internet and electronic commerce is a broad and complex amalgam of technology, practice, and protocols that affect the way the private and public sectors do business. The Internet and electronic commerce are evolving rapidly and – to a great degree – unpredictably. Governments around the world are not blind to these trends. They are increasingly aware of both the benefits and challenges of the Internet and electronic commerce. The benefits of new jobs, products, industries, and greater efficiency within many existing industries surely outweigh concerns about tax-base erosion and national integrity and sovereignty over telecommunications networks and financial intermediaries. But the benefits cannot be enjoyed unless the challenges are managed.

The challenges that the Internet and electronic commerce present in the government domain leave policymakers scrambling to find the right recipe for managing change. On the one hand, since the Internet is so fluid, a laissez-faire approach is necessary. Private-sector initiatives should lead the development of the Internet/electronic commerce. On the other hand, a clear and consistent statement of the government's objectives will give guidance to the private sector and allow it to proceed with confidence. Government policies and regulation should be focused on the ultimate objective, and maintain a flexible, forward-looking, and technologically neutral stance towards solutions that achieve these objectives. Government intervention to enhance competition is appropriate when the private sector delivers not competitive results but rather collusion and restraints to competition.

A third dimension where the government and the private sector interact is in fostering familiarity with the Internet. The GOM can play a key role in helping private enterprise learn what other businesses and consumers are doing with Internet and electronic commerce, both within Morocco and around the world. The promise of the Internet and electronic commerce cannot be learned from a textbook or in a vacuum. The Internet is best experienced by actually participating and seeing how other market participants are using it. This learning process is very interactive. The GOM needs to enhance and encourage the use of the Internet to prepare businesses to launch their own inventions that meet best the needs of Morocco's consumers and businesses at home and Morocco's markets-to-be abroad. The full benefits from electronic commerce and the Internet will come only when the private sector can see its benefits, and starts to innovate in ways that neither they nor the government can now imagine. Consequently, demonstration projects used to create a foundation of familiarity and learning are critical.

A. GOVERNMENTAL POLICY CONSIDERATIONS

The U.S. and the European Union (EU) offer two approaches for what role government might play in the development of an environment conducive to the use of the Internet and electronic commerce. The U.S. policy approach can be described as "the private sector leads, market forces guide, and the government generally stays out of the way."

The EU approach can be described as "the government guides, and the private sector responds using market forces." While much has been made of these differences, the similarities are greater than the differences. In both cases, it is presumed that there is a relatively well-developed private sector of businesses capable of using information technology to enhance existing business functions and to create new businesses. Also in both cases, it is presumed that there is a well-developed, transparent, and open marketplace. While this may be truer in the U.S. than the EU, the two markets differ little in comparison to an emerging economy such as Morocco, where the private sector accounts for a smaller percentage of GDP. Nevertheless, articulating these goals helps assess the current policy options and guide recommended changes.

The GOM, has four challenges to engage Morocco in information technology generally and electronic commerce more specifically:

> First, the GOM might be wise to dismantle that segment of the administration unfriendly to the market, e.g., streamline and make more transparent business regulations that discourage the development of a vibrant private sector;
>
> Second, the GOM should be encouraged to actively promote competition in infrastructure that is key to development of the Internet and electronic commerce, namely, telecommunications and the financial system. (These two objectives, while perhaps stimulated by the goal of promoting information technology growth, would have the salutary effect of enhancing economic activity more generally);
>
> Third, the GOM is encouraged implement a transparent, equitable tax system that encourages the use of information technology, as well as the profit-making potential of private businesses active in the information technology sector; and
>
> Fourth, because the Moroccan public and the private sector may remain unfamiliar with the potential of the Internet and electronic commerce, the GOM is encouraged to actively promote access and uptake of information technologies and the Internet through information dissemination, education, and pilot projects.

A key aspect of Internet and electronic commerce is the synergies among the challenges to government policies. Making progress on one of set of policies (e.g., business regulation), but little on another (e.g., telecommunication liberalization), will yield much smaller benefit and less progress than hoped for toward an Internet-enabled business and society. This is because Internet and electronic commerce are like an organism—complex, with internally interdependent systems. Many businesses originally believed that the Internet would only change their internal (back-office) operations, or only the way they market to customers. Business now understands that the Internet completely changes the business that they do, as well as the way they do it. Government policy is exactly the same. Government policymakers have often argued that they can only change certain policies at a time, and only step-by-step. The challenge to policymaking in the Internet area is to make fundamental policy changes on all fronts at once—to completely remake the business of government policy making. While the government will not "go out of business" if it fails in this policy challenge, it will forgo tremendous benefits of economic development for its citizenry.

BUSINESS REGULATION AND PROMOTING A MARKET-FRIENDLY ENVIRONMENT

1. FINDINGS

A recent report by USAID/Morocco (Investor Road Map) as well as other reports by the Economist Intelligence Unit and anecdotes gathered during the assessment noted the difficult and *ad hoc* nature of the Moroccan business environment. Facilitators help companies through the opaque nature of initiating a company (domestic or foreign), but that company can still fall prey to frequent and capricious regulatory changes. Use of electronic commerce and the Internet by government generally results in greater transparency, consistency, and harmonization on regulations because the government usually puts such information up on a web site.

In a recent program by the Secretary of Post and Information Technology (SEPTI), the GOM is working to place information about all government ministries and departments online, including all business regulations. The GOM is also setting up public access to this information in regional and district government offices so that people without computers can use this site. The Wali of the Souss-Massa area is also interested in connecting his regional headquarters in Agadir to each of the region's five provinces and to two prefectures to give more remote government officials Internet access.

2. Assessment

Although use of electronic commerce and the Internet by government generally promotes transparency, not all ministries at all levels of government are convinced of the benefits of information sharing (and indeed, an individual bureaucrat's power could be constrained by the availability of information on the Internet). As an example, during the last week of September 1999 SEPTI scheduled another workshop on IT in Morocco, but it was unclear just a week prior to the event whether an important player (ANRT) would attend. In addition, small- and medium-sized enterprises, on which the burdens of *ad hoc* business regulation fall most heavily, often will not have a computer to check the consistency of laws and applications.

Moreover, not all problems with business regulation can be solved through transparency. Business regulation is also being used to support inefficiencies in the financial system. Under the current system, funds are deposited during the incorporation procedure and cannot be accessed to pay for the various fees required of the incorporation process. This effectively is a tax on the incorporation of a business and disproportionately impacts small- and medium-sized enterprises.

A final aspect of business regulation, which cannot be solved by transparency (and which will be addressed more completely in the section on financial system readiness) is the inconvertibility of the Dirham on capital accounts and the retention of 80 percent of export proceeds by the bank. Both of these regulations act as a tax on external transactions, with the retention requirement for exporters being the most obviously onerous, and with little or no benefit to the country.

C. THE FINANCIAL SYSTEM

1. Findings

The use of the Internet for electronic commerce poses two sets of issues for the financial system: 1) issues relating to the official role of the central bank and supervisory agency, including the interbank clearing system and management of foreign exchange reserves; and 2) issues relating to the commercial relationships between financial intermediaries and their customers, including the presence of domestic cartels.

2. Assessment

On the official side of the banking system, there are several weak spots in central bank operations and regulation that might be exacerbated by electronic commerce. The first is in the inter-bank clearing procedure. A bank that borrows substantial funds in the inter-bank market will develop "day-light overdrafts" to other banks. If this overdraft persists at the end of the day, the borrowing bank would need to access the central bank's "window" borrowing facility to avoid causing spillover effects on the lending banks and throughout the financial system. Because electronic commerce should enable more rapid buying and selling between businesses during the course of the day, the inter-bank market will have to support more transactions flow, and daylight clearing (also called real-time gross settlement), which would help prevent instability of the inter-bank market during the course of the day.

This problem is more acute for crossborder clearing. Because the Dirham is inconvertible, purchase and sale "invoices" probably cannot be consummated in real time. That is, a cross-border "purchase" transaction that requires foreign currency probably will not clear until night-time, so the seller cannot send the product until the next day, after the payment has cleared. When the "product" is, for example, downloaded software, clearly one of the benefits of electronic commerce—rapid business response—will be undermined.

Second, electronic commerce could create excess demands on foreign reserves. Just as in the case of a "daylight overdraft " in the domestic interbank markets, foreign exchange exposure could build up during the day on account of transactions made but not cleared in real time. For example, suppose that large purchases are made during the day by an importer, who needs to pay in a hard currency, such as in Euros or US dollars. Such purchases could create an excessive demand for hard currency, beyond what the central bank has available or wishes to make available. The central bank could find itself exposed to excessive demands on their foreign currency reserves when the batch of external transactions is cleared.

Electronic commerce opens the possibility for more rapid and monetarily more significant crossborder trade, thus making central bank management of foreign exchange more challenging. The Office de Change recognizes the possible constraint on importation, and believes that stored-value-card technology could solve the problem of daylight exposures. An importer would be allowed to place a certain amount of foreign exchange on a smart card, and then would be able to debit the card during the day as needed. The technology of using a stored-value-card on the Internet is being tested, but is not yet on the market. Nevertheless, this technique could make crossborder transactions more fluid than at present.

A third issue is that the central bank retains 80 percent of the foreign exchange earned by exporters when they return their earnings for deposit in domestic banks. This retention provides the central bank with working foreign exchange reserves. To the extent that electronic commerce makes it easier for exporters to deposit funds into banks outside Morocco, the funding of these official foreign exchange reserves could be undermined. While there are numerous well-established means for keeping export earnings out of a country with such a retention requirement (under-invoicing of exports), electronic commerce could make it easier and more difficult for the government to track currency flows. Regardless of the rationale for this retention, it simply does not recognize that exporting often requires substantial importing costs—more than 20 percent of the value-added process. Further integration into the global process of value-added creation will require elimination of the retention arrangement.

Fourth, to avoid undue and potentially volatile demands on the foreign exchange reserves, the Moroccan capital account is not "open," meaning that individuals or businesses cannot freely buy foreign currency in order to make financial investments abroad. Electronic commerce makes it difficult, if not impossible, for the central bank to "tell" which of the transactions it is clearing for trade in goods, for which foreign exchange is made available, versus trade in financial products, for which foreign currency is not available. For example, if a firm makes a purchase using its stored-value card, its ISP (or the ISP of the firm running the financial element of the Web site) is the conduit for transactions abroad, first connecting to a domestic bank that then clears through the central bank. The ISP will not know whether the transaction going through its network is for purchases of a computer from abroad or to buy a US Treasury bond. So, electronic commerce might make it more difficult to keep the capital account of the balance of payments "closed."

The commercial bank environment appears to be insufficiently competitive and not yet technologically prepared to use electronic commerce. Moroccan law mandates that all commercial banks belong to one bankers' association, the Groupement Professionnel des Banques du Maroc (GPBM), which meets regularly and presents policy positions collectively (after a consensus vote) before the Moroccan government. For the last five years this association has not voted on interest rates or lending requirements, but opportunities for more informal collusion on these issues through GPBM still exist. Moreover, there seems to be relatively little lending activity, suggesting a sleepy, protected set of financial institutions. This is not an environment where financial institutions actively promote electronic commerce either as a tool to reduce their costs or as a way to compete for customers and increase their competitive edge in the marketplace.

Electronic commerce cannot flourish in Morocco without the ability to buy products and services online. The vehicle commonly used for making online purchases is a credit or debit card; the technology for using stored-value cards is only in the testing stage (the card plugs into an attachment to the CD drive). Credit and debit card penetration is relatively low in Morocco. Currently, four Moroccan banks issue credit/debit cards with Visa or MasterCard logos (BMCE, Wafabank, Interbank, BCP), but in the future these banks will only offer cards through GPBM and not individually. This will tend to eliminate interest-rate competition between different credit cards in Morocco, which again is evidence of a non-competitive banking sector. Moreover, the credit cards do not guarantee cardholders protections that similar cardholders have in the United States (such as limited liability for lost or stolen cards). Stored-value cards are more prevalent, in part because the need for physical presence suggests better security features (although if such cards can be "topped-up" with money from an automatic teller machine (ATM) they do offer a different type of security problem. Moreover, in Morocco the cards still are principally single purpose (e.g., Afriquia's gas station cards). Therefore the stored-value card is not yet a viable tool for e-commerce transactions. Nonetheless, one company responsible for creating electronic means of payment, S2M, thinks that electronic commerce in Morocco can flourish with the widespread dissemination of stored-value cards.

The GOM's approach to the structure, conduct, and performance of institutions in the financial marketplace will be important for whether this sector initiates a virtuous or vicious cycle of electronic commerce development. On the one hand, uptake of electronic commerce creates a positive synergy whereby firms actively embracing electronic commerce will become more competitive, gain market share, and improve the functioning of the financial system, with ongoing gains to the whole economy. Studies on industrial country banks show that the cost of banking transactions over the Internet are one-tenth the cost of transactions using bricks, mortar, and paper.

Moreover, the ability to use the Internet to advertise services and offerings, as well as to collect and process information on a borrower enhances the efficiency by which a financial sector transforms savings into investment in an economy. Reducing these costs is essential to enabling small- and medium-sized enterprises (SMEs) to obtain finance. Finally, the institutions themselves can use the Internet to upgrade their capacity to offer electronic banking services (e.g., bill payment) to their borrowers. The institutions that utilize electronic commerce will have lower costs of funds and a greater diversification of the lending assets. In addition, these firms can gain technical assistance from institutions abroad that are also using electronic commerce technology. While Morocco's financial institutions are a long way from these goals, the direction of movement correlates with the benefits to be obtained.

On the other hand, if cartel behavior is maintained, then banks will be a stumbling block for electronic commerce development. The cost of finance to firms and the range of financial offerings will be lower than in the environment of competition. One approach to competition policy is to inject competition by allowing foreign institutions to compete through new facilities, or, alternatively, by allowing majority shareholding in financial institutions. Foreign ownership of financial institutions is currently limited to 49 percent. It is well known that such limited ownership does not lead to active foreign investment or the adoption of new management styles.

The GOM is planning to privatize two banks, Banque Centrale Populaire (BCP), and Credit Immobilier et Hotelier (CIH). These two institutions, BCP and CIH, are retail and for a specific purpose, respectively. In the first case, majority foreign participation is unlikely because retail banking is primarily a local business (although Citibank might attempt it). A foreign real estate conglomerate might buy CIH. Neither is likely to invigorate Moroccan finance or change the sector's attitude toward electronic commerce.

A key additional issue, however, inhibiting greater use of technology by banks, is labor law. For firms to get the full benefit of technology, they need to restructure labor within the organization. Labor laws are a very important impediment to accomplishing such restructuring. This issue points out the cross-cutting nature of the policy issues facing the GOM where the common thread is technology.

Non-bank financial institutions, particularly the operations of the Moroccan stock exchange in Casablanca, also will be significantly affected by electronic commerce. Indeed, with electronic quotation, centralized settlement and clearing, and an oversight agency (CDVM) committed to increased transparency of operations, the Casablanca Stock Exchange (CSE) could become the exemplar of electronic technology and perhaps of openness as well to the rest of the Moroccan private sector. Since 1998, all trading on the CSE has been completely electronic, and Moroccan and foreign investors can purchase shares from a broker over the Internet. However, brokers then take all orders to the CSE and place them over a special computer terminal in the CSE building. There is a plan underway to allow brokers to buy and sell directly from the computers in their offices, and the next step could be fully integrated online trading.

Nonetheless, the CSE has yet to become a viable vehicle for raising equity for the Moroccan private sector. Only 56 companies are now traded on the CSE, and capitalization requirements and audited financial statements bar many newer and smaller companies (such as those in the IT sector) from taking advantage of equity-raising through initial public offerings (IPOs). While the requirement that listed companies have three years of audited financial statements contributes importantly to improved accounting procedures and much needed corporate transparency, there should be a way to use the equity markets as a funding vehicle for SMEs.

One possibility proposed by market participants is to create a "second tier" market where stocks of companies with less of a corporate history could be officially recognized. If such companies were in some way vetted by CDVM (for example, as regards to their audited statements), then mutual funds could develop that could create a portfolio of the "recognized" firms. The concept of the mutual fund was just developed in 1995, yet already there are 103 mutual funds managed by

15 brokers that offer different combinations of all stocks, all bonds, and diversified instruments. So the mutual fund is a popular investment vehicle for Moroccans.

Adding a further diversification possibility of "second tier" companies would offer more funding possibilities to emerging companies, as well as give investors new opportunities to invest in Morocco. The representative of the Office de Change noted that one reason for the convertibility law is to "keep Moroccan savings at home." If good investments are available at home, Moroccans will invest domestically regardless of the currency's convertibility. Representatives of CDVM noted that many bond and stock issues are 10 and 15 times oversubscribed, and that people often pay with cash. Thus suggests a great demand for non-bank financial assets on the part of the population (it also suggests, further, a non-competitive banking system).

There is no limit on foreign participation in the stock exchange, yet foreign participation has been relatively thin—only about 5-8 percent of market capitalization—perhaps because it is difficult to buy into Moroccan firms. The privatization program has used the stock exchange to raise funds, and a revitalization of the privatization program could engage new foreign investors to the exchange. Moreover, the International Finance Corporation (IFC) lists Morocco in its composite index, which has promoted investor interest.

In the future, electronic commerce (combined with capital risk insurance) can underpin a new approach to lending to SMEs that brings together the bank and non-bank financial sectors. Often lending to SMEs is viewed as too risky and too costly (too much hard work) for banks, so lending to these companies often lags without directed credit from the government. A new approach that uses the power of electronic commerce is the securitization of small-business assets (securitization is the packaging of SME loans into securities that then can be sold as shares in a mutual fund). Electronic commerce reduces the cost of servicing SME loans, and securitization is a way to diversify risk. Both the bank and the non-bank sectors become involved—the bank to originate and service the loan and the non-bank firm to package and sell the asset.

D. THE TAX SYSTEM

1. Findings

The current structure of Morocco's tax system is quite fragmented, which raises administrative costs and reduces transparency. Moreover, the current system depends on revenue sources that can be undermined by the growth of electronic commerce, particularly the value-added tax (VAT) and tariffs. Indirect taxes via the VAT account for 30 percent of revenues, which is about the average typical for a EU country. Revenues are highly dependent on trade taxes (tariffs), which account for 15 percent of revenues. Direct taxes, which electronic commerce will affect as well (although in somewhat different ways than the VAT), account for 25 percent of revenues. Finally, the fragmented nature of the tax system is evident from the observation that the rest of revenues are raised through a hodgepodge of sources and transactions: 11 percent from energy and 4.5 percent each from stamp and excise taxes, SOEs, and "other."

2. Assessment

Greater use of the Internet and promotion of electronic commerce will challenge the GOM's current tax and tariff system as well as the administration of the systems. However, more streamlined systems that use the Internet will greatly enhance the efficiency and transparency of generating government revenue, which will also improve the environment for business and trade.

Taxes on electronic commerce transactions raise three issues: 1) jurisdiction of the tax authority, 2) identity of a taxpayer, and 3) appropriate categorization and coverage of goods vs. services (in the case of VAT) and of income and capital (in the case of direct taxes). Electronic commerce promises to blur the international borders of transactions, blur who engages in the transactions, and blur what kind of transaction it is. These questions have fully engaged the tax authorities in the most advanced nations, so in no sense is Morocco "behind" in its treatment of these issues. Indeed, the GOM has the potential to benefit from the analysis of other groups (OECD, EU), leap-frog intermediate stages of tax development, and use electronic commerce to bring its tax administration into compliance with Model Tax Laws as they are developed. Moreover, GOM has already implemented Internet systems for the administration of import tariffs, although how well those systems operate in fact is somewhat unclear.

Several ongoing changes in the Moroccan economy, particularly when combined with electronic commerce put a premium on having tax treaties with other countries, or at minimum having close collaboration among tax authorities. First, as Morocco privatizes state-owned operations and as they increasingly become part of the value chain of multinationals (e.g., autos, apparel), crossborder trade will increase, as will the issues associated with location of value-added and transfer-pricing. VAT rules have always been difficult to apply when transactions cross the border, and electronic commerce offers easier ways to engage in transfer-pricing that arbitrage tax differences, particularly when tariffs are the type of tax involved.

Second, electronic commerce blurs the distinction between trade in goods and services. The EU has proposed that all electronic commerce should be taxed as a service based on the location of the consumer (instead of the "place of supply"). This may or may not be workable in the future as bundling of services, as well as the provision of near-goods (for example, downloadable software), through the ISP become more prevalent. Indeed, the representatives of the Office de Change noted a test case ongoing with the Customs department on the issue of whether downloaded software was a good or a service.

Third, the privatization and development of a vibrant private sector of SMEs in Morocco means that tax efficiency is critical. VAT requires a taxpayer ID for all transactions, "double-entry" accounting for inputs and outputs, and special treatment for imports and exports. It is an administratively intensive system that depends on computerization to keep the tax rates low. Low tax rates are critical to minimize distortions and evasion. In contrast, Morocco's current system of fragmented and specific taxes invite evasion and promote distortion, leading to tax inefficiency.

The GOM's high dependence on tariff revenue deserves special attention. Although the Customs department has a computerized administrative system (the SADOC system) it apparently has not done very much to streamline the administrative process. More generally, the very high average tariff rate of 24 percent (ranging from 2.5 to 35 percent) invites transfer-pricing and distorts economic development. While transfer-pricing is one way of avoiding tariffs (and apparently it is widely used), it is not legal. Furthering an environment where flouting legal requirements as the way to efficient business practices should not be an accepted as the way to encourage trade and development.

A representative of the Customs department indicated that e-commerce only changes the location of taxation – from the border to inside the border, and from application on the good or service, to the application on the earnings of the corporation in question. It is interesting to note that most Customs departments around the world have shown much greater concern about how e-commerce will potentially erode tariff revenues.

The prospects for a Euro-Med free trade zone will give preferential treatment to Morocco-EU trade. This should increase trade flows but will likely reduce overall tariff revenues. The GOM should be wary of responding to this potential shortfall by raising tariffs on trade with other countries. Introducing distortions in trade across different regions can be particularly distortionary and inefficient.

To encourage information technology, the Internet, and electronic commerce, the GOM should immediately sign the *Information Technology Agreement I* and commit to zero tariffs on information technology products by 2002.

Electronic commerce, while presenting the GOM with tax administration challenges, also offers solutions. It is much cheaper to keep track of taxpayers electronically. Electronic identifiers, audit trails, and value-added accounting are significantly eased by information technology. The World Customs Organization is working with business and governments to use information technology to streamline and make electronic information on trade flows as well as trade taxes. As the character of Morocco's economy changes, the GOM should not squander the opportunity to use the power of information technology to extend tax coverage, reduce tax rates, and increase tax efficiency.

The tax authority recognizes that the administrative costs of this regime are quite high. It also recognizes that use of the Internet in its internal operations would significantly improve tax administration. Finally, it is quite responsive to the possibility of online filing of taxes by corporations and business. The authority is so convinced of the administrative benefits of the Internet that it might even consider giving a small tax rebate to people filing taxes on-line. Of course there are two impediments to greater use of the Internet in the tax administration. First, those inside the tax administration are unfamiliar with the computer and training is needed. Second, online filing presumes that a credit/debit/or SVC can be used.

PART II—TELECOMMUNICATIONS INFRASTRUCTURE

Introduction

Over the past few years, the Government of Morocco (GOM) has undertaken a number of reform initiatives aimed at liberalizing its telecommunications, post, and information technology sectors. These largely sprang out of Law 24-96, which was passed in August of 1997. A Letter of Sector Development Policy, which resulted from Law 24-96, articulates the Kingdom of Morocco's reform program in the Telecommunications, Post, and Information Technology Sectors and serves to inform the reader of key strategies, objectives, and progress already achieved—and the in-country setting upon which the IED Assessment took place.

Assessment and Findings

One of the major reasons for Morocco's success in liberalizing its Telecommunications Sector has been financial assistance from the World Bank. For the past several years the Private Sector Development and Finance Department, Middle East and North Africa Region of the World Bank has been working with the government of Morocco in an effort to liberalize their telecommunications sector. This has included making a US$ 101 million Telecommunications, Post, and Information Technology Adjustment Loan (TPI-TAL) to assist in this transition. Quoting from the World Bank's report:

"The TPI-TAL is aimed at supporting the overall objective of the Government reform program to accelerate Morocco's integration into the global information economy. Access to competitively priced and efficient communications services and information technology (IT) determines to a large extent the ability of economies to grow, create jobs, and reduce social disparities. The service sector, which is heavily dependent upon communications and IT, accounts for an increasing share of GDP inmost economies, while the IT industry itself is emerging as a major source of growth, job creation, and export earnings in those economies. Adequate provision of telecommunications, postal, and IT services to poor and remote households also constitutes a powerful means to reduce social exclusion and to broaden the scope of economic opportunities provided outside of the main cities."

The "...operation supports the adoption of measures in six specific areas:

telecommunications liberalization;
telecommunications regulation;
(iii) privatization of the incumbent telecommunications operator;
(iv) access to telecommunications services by poor and remote households,
(v) competitiveness of postal services; and (vi) development of a national IT strategy."

The objectives of the loan are to "...support the implementation of a comprehensive package of pro-competitive reforms in the telecommunications, post, and information technology (IT) sectors designed to increase the competitiveness of the Moroccan private sector, to broaden access to communications services to the poor, particularly in rural areas, and to facilitate Morocco's transition to a global, information-based economy. In telecommunications, the primary objective of the load is to promote increased competition, greater private participation and investment, and autonomous regulation. With respect to postal services, the operation seeks to increase the competitiveness of service provision and to ensure that the public service obligations are adequately defined, financed, and met. The law also supports the development of a national strategy aimed at facilitating Morocco's integration into the global information society."

The target benefits of the loan state that, "[t]he Moroccan private sector will be the major beneficiary of competitive telecommunications, post, and IT services. The service industry, in particular, which accounts for an increasingly important share of the GDP in most developing economies, stands to benefit from a broader array of competitively priced communication and IT services. The project will address some of the needs of the poor and remote households by increasing their access to communications and IT services, a critical factor for developing local economic activities. In addition, the reforms supported by the loan will bring substantial revenues to the Treasury (higher taxes levied on enlarged telecommunications and IT sectors, the ward of a new telecommunications licenses and the privatization of the incumbent telecommunications operator)."

1. Current Status

Whereas the above reflects the plans, at the time of this assessment, many of these plans have already been implemented. In July of 1999 a second GSM license was issued, bringing a price of US$1.1 billion to the GOM, US$0.7 billion more than originally estimated. Current regulatory schedules are to issue the VSAT tender in the latter part of CY 1999. Privatization of Itissalat al-Maghrib (IAM), the incumbent operator, is currently scheduled for summer of 2004.

Teledensity—Regarding telecommunication coverage in Morocco, here, too, the pace of expansion has been considerable, recognizing the low base from which these increases are taking place. A recent publication from the International Telecommunications Union (ITU), "Challenges to the Network, Internet for Development" outlines the following picture in Morocco (1997 data).

Total population: 27.52 million

Population density (per square km): 42

Total GDP: US$36.7 billion

Per capita GDP: US$1,350

Total phone lines: 1.375 million

Teledensity: 5 (per 100 population)

Number of Internet Hosts: Jan96=230; Jan97=470; Jan98=1,409; Jan99=1,994 (Change 1997-1999: 41.5%)

Internet Host Density: Jan96=0.09; Jan97=0.17; Jan98=0.51; Jan99=0.72 (CAGR 1994-1998=526.8%; Change 1997-1999=41.5%)

Main Telephone Lines: 1990=.403B; 1997=1.375B (CAGR 1970-1997=19.2%; Change 1996-1997=8%)

Main Telephone Lines Teledensity: 1990=1.65; 1997=5.0 (CAGR 1990-1997=17.2%; Change 1996-1997=8.5%)

With respect to the number of PCs in Morocco, the ITU report does not provide data for Morocco. It is estimated that there are approximately 70,000 PCs sold in 1999, with 14 percent being replacement PCs. An estimated 50 percent of these PCs are assembled incountry by a number of small local original equipment manufacture (OEM) firms.

Discussions with a wide array of both private and public sources during the course of this Assessment reflect a total Internet user community in Morocco of somewhere between 40,000 and 50,000. Estimated number of actual Internet accounts is thought to be substantially lower at around 20,000 to 30,000. These are provided by a number of independent ISPs providing value-added services from IAM's infrastructure. It is estimated there are between 130-300 ISPs.

Itissalat al-Maghrib (IAM)—Until recently, the monopoly provider, IAM, did not provide its customers with ISP services. Instead, it encouraged and supported these value-added services by the private ISP community in Morocco. This arrangement was typically carried out via a series of informal arrangements that dated back to when there was a single Postal Telegraph and Telephone (PTT)—ONTP. With the move toward privatization it is clear the new IAM views the ISP market as something in which they wish to enter. In entering this market, IAM has leveraged their monopoly position to lower prices to a level that is below their costs in order to gain market share. In addition, they also have reversed an earlier agreement with the ISP community whereby a local call rate was available to all ISPs for accessing the Internet throughout Morocco. This is now available only to IAM customers. On the current track, IAM has the potential to severely restrict the growth of the private-sector ISP sub-sector by unfairly leveraging its monopoly position. At present there is no law or regulatory capability to prohibit such actions.

Agence Nationale de Reglementation du Secteur des Telecommunications (ANRT)—With the breakup of ONTP, an independent regulatory agency was put into place—ANRT. This Agency has aggressively led the charge to bring about a competitive telecommunications market in Morocco. The ANRT has grown from approximately 30 to over 150 personnel during this last year. Because the breakup of ONTP was largely crafted by what later became IAM, the legislation creating ANRT has restrictions as to how much it can restrict IAM's behavior relative to limitations on its leveraging its dominant and monopoly position. As a result, the ANRT's first priority is to introduce competition into the marketplace (e.g., the second GSM license, near-term VSAT tender and licensing, GMPCS, etc.). This strategy leverages the marketplace and extends the scope of influence ANRT can exert in the telecommunications sector as it has full authority over the new entrants. ANRT's plans are to focus on seeking to revise legislative authorities with respect to IAM, once it has completed its major efforts to introduce competition into the marketplace in Morocco.

2. Missing Pieces

A tremendous amount of progress has been made in recent years in Morocco; the Telecommunications Sector has been liberalized in record time. While there continue to be privatization efforts underway, the real work is in the infrastructure build-out itself and the subsequent expanded use. The current community of up to 50,000 Internet users in a population of nearly 30 million is small even though growth rate is encouraging. While the second GSM operator will expand telephony, these technologies are not adequate for Internet other than simple e-mail use. The upcoming VSAT tender could open this market up considerably, but there are a number of questions regarding local access to these services, as IAM will still control the local loop. Also, the population of PCs simply needs to grow more before critical mass will likely be reached in country.

Conclusion

Morocco's Telecommunications Sector is undergoing rapid transformation under the direction of ANRT. This started with the breakup of the PTT (ONTP) into three separate units (regulatory, telecommunications and post), and has progressed such that competition has been, and is increasingly being brought into the market place—first via the licensing of the second GSM operator, and second in the near-term with the granting of licenses for VSAT operators. The privatization of the IAM is scheduled for the year 2004, with efforts already underway. The speed and comprehensiveness of this liberalization effort is perhaps unparalleled and could well become a model for other developing

PART III—LEGAL AND REGULATORY REFORM INTRODUCTION

Countries wishing to fully realize the full potential of e-commerce generally have a predictable legal and regulatory environment that governs transactions. In addition, a country's legal and regulatory framework should be encouraged to achieve a balance between a nonregulatory, market approach that encourages e-commerce transactions and regulatory approach designed to protect those involved in e-commerce.

This section of the assessment provides an overview of Morocco's current legislative system, highlights those areas of Moroccan law and regulation that currently affect the development of e-commerce in Morocco, and provides recommendations based upon interviews with various representatives of Morocco's private and public sectors.

A. The Legal System in Morocco

Morocco has a democratic, constitutional monarchy. The legal system is based on Islamic law and French and Spanish civil law systems; judicial review of legislative acts takes place in a Constitutional Chamber of Supreme Court.

B. Information Technology and Legal Reform

Electronic commerce is the fastest growing segment of the world's economy. Commerce on the Internet could total tens of billions of dollars by the turn of the century. For this potential to be realized fully, governments will need to adopt a nonregulatory, market-oriented approach to electronic commerce, one that facilitates the emergence of a transparent and predictable legal environment to support global business and commerce. Official decision-makers do well to respect the unique nature of the medium and recognize that widespread competition and increased consumer choice should be the defining features of the new digital marketplace.

However, many businesses and consumers are still wary of conducting extensive business over the Internet because of the lack of a predictable legal environment governing transactions. This is particularly true for international commercial activity where concerns about enforcement of contracts, liability, intellectual property protection, privacy, security and other matters have caused businesses and consumers to be cautious.

As use of the Internet expands, many companies and Internet users are concerned that some governments will impose extensive regulations on the Internet and electronic commerce. Potential areas of problematic regulation include taxes and duties, restrictions on the type of information transmitted, control over standards development, licensing requirements and rate regulation of service providers. It is important to preempt these harmful actions in governmental regulation before they take effect and become imbedded into the regulatory system.

The promise of the Internet and its contribution to the growth of the world's economy can only be sustained if governments create legal structures that nurture, rather than inhibit, the growth of electronic commerce.

Morocco can have a profound effect on the growth of its commerce on the Internet. By its actions, it can facilitate electronic trade, both internally and externally, or inhibit it. Knowing when to act and – at least as important – when not to act, will be crucial to the development of electronic commerce in Morocco.

C. Legal Reform Underway in Morocco: Findings and Conclusions

From the date that the Moroccan government inaugurated its first Web site in July 1996, the Moroccan government has recognized the profound affect that information technology has had and will have upon the world as a whole and that information technology will affect all of the important aspects of society such as culture, education, public services, employment, and the economy. As such, the government of Morocco, in August 1997, created the National Agency of Telecommunication Regulation (ANRT), which has been granted the authority to promulgate regulations on telecommunications and encryption. This agency reports to the Prime Minister and views itself as a "think tank" for all other aspects of information technology and e-commerce that are not contained within its specific enabling statute.

In addition, the Secretary of the Post and Information Technology (SEPTI) has established a commission that reports directly to the Prime Minister to guide and advise the Government on the various legal and regulatory reforms that may be needed so that Morocco may participate more fully in e-commerce and information technology. This commission is in the process of developing an information technology plan for Morocco that will include:

-- Preparation of a regulatory framework relative to electronic commerce, domain names and encryption;

-- Development of a national system of assigning domain names;

-- Commencement of a tele-education project with UNESCO, UIT and other ministerial departments;

-- Participation of Morocco in ITU's Electronic Commerce for Developing Countries;

-- Commencement of Morocco's current utilization of information technology;

-- Participation of Morocco in the EUMEDIS initiative;

-- Participation of Morocco in the Governmental Advisory Committee on Internet domain names; and

-- Organization of a September 1999 workshop for government and industry on barriers to e-commerce.

Finally, Morocco's Ministry of Industry, Commerce and Artisans' Department of International Trade Relations has also created an Information Technology committee made up of private and public sector representatives to evaluate those changes required for Morocco's full participation in e-commerce.

1. Leadership of the Private Sector

Morocco should encourage industry self-regulation wherever appropriate and support the efforts of private sector organizations to develop mechanisms to facilitate the successful operation of the Internet. Even where collective agreements or standards are necessary, private entities should, where possible, take the lead in organizing them. Where government action or intergovernmental agreements are necessary, on taxation for example, private sector participation should be a formal part of the policy making process.

Morocco's private sector recognizes the benefits to be derived from Morocco's full participation in e-commerce. Many representatives of the high technology industry accept that the Moroccan government is moving in the right direction with regard to the Government's re-evaluation and reform of existing laws and the Government's creation of new agencies (ARNT) and commissions. But the private sector does not believe that Morocco is making the necessary changes and adaptations fast enough.

For example the Moroccan chapter of the Business Software Alliance (BSA) has drafted a revision to the current copyright law that was last modified in 1970 and does not currently encompass software protection. As part of the currently proposed draft legislation, BSA addressed the issue of software protection. BSA presented this draft to the Government in 1998. To date, this law has not been passed.

The private sector in Morocco cited another example of slow progress in the area of telecommunications. Although the Moroccan government has undertaken a number of reform initiatives aimed at liberalizing telecommunications, post and information technology, a number of Internet service providers (ISPs) may be forced out of business in the immediate future due to the IAM's current monopolistic practices. It is obvious from the interviews conducted that IAM is attempting to gain as much market share as possible prior to the completion of the privatization process.

The private sector has taken the initiative to create associations that provide guidance to the private sector in the area of best management practices and the retraining of managers in areas of new technology. In addition, these associations are responsible for lobbying the government for legislative reforms that the private sector views as required for Morocco to successfully participate in the high technology industry and e-commerce.

On the whole, the initiative and actions taken by private industry in Morocco are positive steps towards Morocco's full participation in e-commerce. Based upon various interviews, however, it became apparent that many of these associations were not aware of the existence of other such organizations or the government commission that had been created to address information technology issues.

2. Government Restrictions on E-Commerce

As in other parts of the world, Moroccans should be able to enter into legitimate agreements to buy and sell products and services across the Internet with minimal government involvement or intervention. Unnecessary regulation of commercial activities will distort development of the electronic marketplace by decreasing the supply and raising the cost of products and services for consumers the world over. Business models must evolve rapidly to keep pace with the breakneck speed of change in the technology; government attempts to regulate are likely to be outmoded by the time they are finally enacted, especially to the extent such regulations are technology-specific. Accordingly, Morocco should refrain from imposing new and unnecessary regulations, bureaucratic procedures, or taxes and tariffs on commercial activities that take place via the Internet.

As stated above, the Moroccan government recognizes the importance of the high technology industry and e-commerce to Morocco. However, government officials are approaching legislative reform cautiously. In some cases, such as encryption, such caution may be necessary as international standards for encryption are currently being developed by international organizations such as the United Nations Center for International Trade and Development and others.

Based upon the interviews conducted with both private and public sector representatives, the assessment team is unaware of any pending or proposed legislation that would place restrictions on e-commerce.

3. The Moroccan Legal and Regulatory Environment

Regulation should be imposed only as a necessary means to achieve an important goal on which there is a broad consensus. Existing laws and regulations that may hinder electronic commerce should be reviewed and revised or eliminated to reflect the needs of the new electronic age.

Based upon the interviews conducted, it is apparent that the Moroccan government's intervention is needed in a number of areas to support and enforce a simple legal environment for e-commerce.

E-Commerce Definitions

In accordance with the manner in which Morocco's Law No. 24-96 (the 1997 reform of Morocco's telecommunications and post office regulations) was drafted, the first step towards a predictable, minimalist, consistent and simple legal framework for e-commerce will be to define the various steps and participants involved in an e-commerce transaction. Such definitions may be as simple as defining an "agreement" to be "the bargain of the parties in fact found in their language or inferred from other circumstances..." to a more complex concept such as the definition of an "automated transaction."

Intellectual Property Protection

The ability to transmit and receive large amounts of information electronically makes copying simple and cost-free. Authors and creators of intellectual property may not be compensated when their works are copied. Morocco's law needs to implement the protections contained in the World Intellectual Property Organization Copyright Treaty and Performances of Phonograms Treaty. Protection of intellectual property is necessary to encourage further creative acts and the disbursement of such acts through e-commerce.

During the course of the assessment, it became clear that that Morocco's current copyright law provides insufficient protections for the private sector and did not address the protection of software. Although companies such as Microsoft have taken court action to enforce their rights in their property through Morocco's trademark laws and been successful, the penalties contained in Morocco's current cadre of intellectual property law are insufficient to provide long-term, effective deterrence of the theft of intellectual property. Morocco needs to reform its intellectual property protection to be in accordance with international standards so that the high technology industry will look more favorably upon Morocco as a country in which to set up business.

Contract Law and E-Commerce

Both the private and government sector expressed an opinion that Morocco's current laws relative to contract formation and performance were adequate if e-commerce were not part of the equation. Morocco has recently established a new commercial court system and is providing training to judges on commercial law. Lawsuits in this area are now being processed through the Moroccan legal system in an expeditious manner.

However, Morocco's current law does not recognize electronic signatures therefore the validity of any contact entered into electronically is questionable. In addition, electronic payment is currently impossible in Morocco. For a supplier to receive payment on a credit card transaction, the supplier is required have the customer sign an invoice and provide the bank with a paper copy of this invoice prior to receiving payment. To successfully participate in e-commerce, the Moroccan government will have to reform these laws to provide for legally recognizable electronic signatures and electronic payment.

ENCRYPTION

Encryption is a necessary tool to achieve better protection of confidential information that is sent over the Internet. It is also necessary to provide security for payments made through electronic commerce. The ability to provide encrypted information over the Internet is required in order to provide greater confidence in the confidentiality and security of electronic transactions.

When Morocco established the ANRT it gave to the ANRT, as part of its of its charter, the responsibility for drafting Morocco's encryption laws. The ANRT is currently drafting this law such that the draft legislation submitted to the government will agree with internationally accepted parameters.

PRIVACY

The ability to gather and disseminate information electronically has risks as well as benefits. Children are particularly susceptible to requests for information.

Individuals are not likely to participate in e-commerce when personal information may be acquired and disseminated without restriction. Information circulated on the Internet is reasonably accessible to anyone. Whenever an individual visits a Web site, software allows the web site to collect data without the individual being aware of the collection. In addition, the collection and exchange of certain types of personal information may be necessary for various commercial purposes. However, this information may be accessible by others, and unauthorized access to personal information may result in the receipt of many unwanted e-mails (SPAM) or the theft of an individual's identity.

To encourage Morocco's participation in e-commerce, Morocco needs to enact legislation that will protect the personal information of those individuals who choose to participate in e-commerce.

CONTENT

Content is generally defined as the collection of information found on a Web site. This information may originate either at the Web site or on the machines of individual users. A question to be addressed is who is legally responsible when the information displayed may be illegal or immoral? Similarly, who will be legally responsible for the violation of an intellectual property owner's copyright?

Morocco does not currently have laws that limit content or assign liability.

TECHNOLOGY CRIMES

The Internet is accessible to millions of people worldwide. It is used by the public and private sector to transmit confidential and privilege information, both internally and externally. Acts of fraud, piracy, sabotage, espionage, and vandalism occur on a frequent basis. To address such issues, Morocco is encouraged to draft legislation that defines rights and responsibilities as well as provides sanctions against those who engage in such crimes over the Internet. Such a law would provide for government intervention when necessary to reach the criminal responsible for such acts.

Monopolistic Practices

As one final barrier, the monopolistic practices of Morocco's former government-owned telephone company (IAM) and other such businesses whose goal may be to capture the Moroccan market through anti-competitive practices should be examined. Based upon the information collected during our interviews, it appears that IAM is currently grabbing for market share at the expense of ISPs that previously were regulated by IAM. IAM has arbitrarily changed the terms and conditions of contracts it entered into with ISPs and is now competing directly with the ISP's it originally regulated on more favorable terms than those granted to the ISPs. If IAM continues with this type of behavior, the most likely result will be that Morocco's 200 ISP's will be reduced to one ISP, which in turn will be IAM.

4. The Unique Quality of the Internet

Government regulation is appropriate to foster transparency, support commercial transactions, and encourage dispute resolution. In some areas, government agreements may prove necessary to facilitate electronic commerce and protect consumers. In these cases, governments should establish a predictable and simple legal environment based on a decentralized, contractual model of law rather than one based on top-down regulation. Where Moroccan governmental intervention is necessary to facilitate electronic commerce, its goal should be to ensure competition, protect intellectual property and privacy, prevent fraud, foster transparency, support commercial transactions, and facilitate dispute resolution.

As early as July 1996, King Hassan II recognized the unique qualities of the Internet. As discussed above, Morocco has taken steps to review existing laws and regulations and revise or eliminate those laws that may hinder Morocco's full participation in e-commerce. SEPTI anticipates that it will be able to provide the government with draft regulations on e-commerce within the next eight months.

As discussed above, Morocco's banking laws need to be reviewed and revised in order to allow for paperless electronic payment systems. If corporations and individuals cannot be paid for an item purchased electronically without providing the signed invoice as validation of the transaction, corporations and individuals will not make full use of e-commerce.

As the Internet is unique, just as Morocco has created new commercial courts and provided training to its judges in the area of commercial law, Morocco will need to provide its judiciary with training to understand e-commerce and the high technology industry.

One last point for Morocco to consider vis-à-vis high technology corporations and Morocco's desire to appeal to such corporations to invest in Morocco is the unique employment characteristics of such high technology corporations. Such corporations would be better served if they were able to adapt quickly to changes in the business climate. Currently, Morocco's laws make it extremely difficult for a corporation to change the size of its labor force to meet short-term requirements or a sudden upsurge in work. Morocco's labor laws present numerous hurdles that make it extremely difficult to terminate an individual's employment. As such, any corporation will hesitate before hiring new employees to meet what may only be a temporary change in the business climate. As a result of this, business opportunities will be lost both for the corporation and for the individuals who could have been employed.

5. Facilitation of Global Commerce

The Internet is emerging as a global marketplace. Moroccan law should facilitate not only the development of the nation's domestic electronic commerce, but also the growth of global commerce. The legal framework supporting commercial transactions on the Internet should be governed by consistent principles across state, national, and international borders that lead to predictable results regardless of the jurisdiction in which a particular buyer or seller resides.

Morocco is currently reviewing and proposing reforms relative to e-commerce. Morocco is looking to the laws of other countries and international organizations as models for the laws it may enact such that e-commerce will be able to facilitate not only the development of Morocco's domestic electronic commerce, but also the growth of global commerce. However, other aspects of Moroccan law that are discussed elsewhere in this assessment, such as the convertibility of the Dirham, present a substantial barrier to Morocco's full participation in global commerce.

PART IV—E-COMMERCE AND BUSINESS DEVELOPMENT

In supporting the development of the Internet and electronic commerce in Morocco through policy reform and pilot projects, the GOM will concurrently encourage the creation and development of private enterprise. Private sector growth, especially that of SMEs, will in turn fuel the growth of the Moroccan economy.

Electronic commerce and information technology more generally can help the GOM diversify the economy away from agriculture and toward value-added services and industrial production. As electronic commerce begins to flourish in Morocco, a whole host of new businesses centered in the IT sector will start to emerge. These businesses are being created in Morocco even today. Last year, there were 83 private Internet service providers (ISPs) in Morocco, now there are more than 230. Each one of these ISPs is responsible for much-needed job creation and revenue generation.

There are other kinds of businesses being created that are specifically designed around electronic commerce, including Web design and Internet/electronic commerce consulting. Indeed, Arthur Andersen in Casablanca recently added four new consultants to assist Moroccan businesses with how to reconfigure back-office operations as well as sales and marketing to make the best use of the Internet. There are also new retail service operations like cyber cafes, prevalent today in Rabat and Casablanca, that depend directly on the Internet. Supporting the creation of these new businesses is important because IT-sector companies tend to pay their employees higher-than-average salaries. Moreover, the IT sector, once developed, contributes more to economic growth than other more mature industries like commodities.

The Internet and electronic commerce also help existing businesses increase efficiency and profits, thereby generating economic growth. Key entry points to the Internet, e-mail and Web "surfing," serve as important sources of information exchange and idea generation for the private sector. All of the Moroccan businesses spoken to over the two-week period had e-mail accounts and were connected to the Internet, although some businesses integrated these services into their day-to-day operations more fully than others. For instance, only about half of the companies printed e-mail accounts on their business cards, suggesting that the telephone and facsimile are still the primary modes of communication for many Moroccan businesses.

Also, the vast majority of those businesses with Web sites used their sites exclusively for "brochureware," or marketing purposes. Generating two-way communication through the use of e-mail or live Internet links on the company's Web site, engaging in electronic transactions over the Internet, or linking the site to back-office operations is still relatively rare in Morocco. It is in the integration of these types of activities that will generate the most productivity gains for Morocco's private sector. Fully integrated use of the Internet, however, depends on cheaper telecommunications costs and a facilitative financial system, as discussed above. In fact, the high cost of connecting to the Internet and impediments present in Morocco's financial system were the problems most-often cited in interviews with Moroccan companies.

As in the U.S., initially business-to-business electronic commerce will be more important for the development of the Moroccan economy than electronic commerce that flows from business to consumer. While most people think of buying books from Amazon.com or airplane tickets from Microsoft's Expedia as examples of electronic commerce, over 80 percent of electronic commerce in the U.S. flows between businesses. Similar patterns are emerging in other industrialized countries.

There are several ways in which business-to-business electronic commerce can spur private sector growth and economic development in Morocco. Most generally, electronic commerce over the Internet increases efficiency across the value-added chain, from input sourcing, to production, to packaging, to marketing/sales, to distribution, creating higher quality products and services at lower prices. The more intricate the value-added chain, the more benefits the sector will experience in integrating electronic commerce into its day-to-day operations. These benefits can be seen in commodity sectors, like www.esteel.com, where buyers and sellers of steel can trade privately and securely over the Internet, and service sectors, like www.eloan.com, where individuals and business can receive approval on mortgage applications in less than 24 hours.

A key inhibitor of greater use of technology by private sector entities is labor law. For firms to get the full benefit of technology, they need to restructure labor within the organization. Labor laws are a very important impediment to doing this. That is, the decision to upgrade information technology is usually associated with the potential efficiency gains and cost reductions. Some of those benefits come from reducing labor inputs in some areas of ongoing operations. If labor cannot be restructured, the firm is left with no efficiency gains and only additional costs. This issue points out the crosscutting nature of the policy issues facing the GOM where the common thread is technology.

A. Development of Trade Associations

Trade associations in Morocco are a key locus for information exchange, technology uptake, and diffusion. These associations can serve as a conduit for awareness education for Moroccan companies in both business-to-business and business-to-consumer electronic commerce applications. For example, a trade association can get the word out to people about the possibilities of electronic commerce. Similar public relations and information campaigns have had good success in the U.S., Europe, and emerging economies like Brazil.

Educational approaches used by trade associations like the American Chambers of Commerce include product seminars and demonstration kiosks. Seminars sponsored through trade associations (possibly at annual conventions or trade shows) would allow companies already active in electronic commerce the opportunity to demonstrate and explain electronic commerce products and services to the Moroccan business community. Such interaction is vital to developing a widespread mindset for new ideas like electronic commerce. In addition, kiosks sponsored through trade associations can be set up for access and information in public areas. The kiosk contains a monitor and mouse and is connected to a local server, with access to limited Web sites. Rather than being full and free Internet access devices, kiosks are rather places where people can gain a preliminary insight into the power of the Internet generally, and electronic commerce more specifically.

Trade associations can also serve as important conduits for electronic commerce success stories. Often, what businesses need most in approaching electronic commerce is to see how a business similar to their own has succeeded with the use of this (relatively) new technology. In addition, linkages across borders to international groups can further the outward orientation and rapid uptake of the more advance uses for electronic commerce.

B. SMEs and Micro-enterprise Development

Micro-enterprises employ the majority of Morocco's poorer citizens. USAID/Rabat and Volunteers in Technical Assistance (http://www.vita.org) are working with Al Amana of Morocco to lend start-up and expansion monies to Morocco's micro-enterprises. As of June 1999, $5.16 million was loaned to Moroccan companies, with a 99 percent repayment rate. Fifty-three percent of VITA's clients in Morocco are women. VITA relies on the Internet to help gather information on its clients; the organization also conducts many of its conferences over the Internet. Al Amana is moving quickly to integrate the Internet into its back-office operations. The greater efficiency of the Internet will improve its cost structure so that even more funds are available for lending.

SMEs are a fertile ground for electronic commerce. In the US, 40 percent of SMEs use the Internet, up from 20 percent in 1996. SMEs usually focus on a core business, which might or might not be related to information technology. Back-office operations, from accounting to order fulfillment, often receive little attention from top management, which can lead to resource misallocation, cost overruns and the demise of the firm. Electronic commerce makes it easier and cheaper to outsource these activities so that the SME can focus on their core competencies. Growth of electronic commerce business in order fulfillment is staggering; about 25 percent of firms in the US outsource order fulfillment. This outsourcing has the added benefit of creating new markets for new firms.

Electronic commerce may enable a new form of finance for SMEs and micro-enterprises. Offering financial services to these groups is costly and risky. Yet they cannot bear the relatively higher interest rates that go along with cost and risk. Consequently, these firms often are ignored and left out of financial intermediation. Electronic commerce may reduce the cost of obtaining information, particularly if the enterprises can use a local IT center to input pertinent information. In addition, electronic commerce certainly will reduce the cost of administration and communication with borrowers, through use of interactive spreadsheets and e-mail. Through securitization of assets, electronic commerce might open the door to a new source of finance that has not been available for individual borrowers, but which is available for shares in an assets that is backed by a package of loans to small borrowers. While this is still a high-risk asset, between new sources of funds and lower costs, the financing rate might be accessible for small borrowers.

C. Sector-specific Business Development

There are several sectors important to Moroccan industrial development where electronic commerce is becoming more prevalent in global relationships. Morocco's overall development could be stifled if these sectors lag in the uptake of the Internet and electronic commerce.

1. Textiles and Apparel

Textiles and apparel are a key component of Morocco's industrial production (14.5% of total industrial production, comparable to mining or energy). Currently the sector is at the forefront of the country's export-led industrial growth. For example, from the early 1980s to the early 1990s net exports of textiles and clothing expanded almost fivefold, from $120 million to $570 million.

There are several U.S.-based multinational apparel companies operating in Morocco: Fruit of the Loom, Jordache, and Sara Lee Haynes. Electronic commerce can help these MNCs to overcome two of the industry's greatest growth challenges: a large number of steps/variables along the value-added chain and a fluctuating/seasonal demand cycle. By bringing up Moroccan textile mills, cutters and sewers, and wholesale buyers, as well as internationally-based retail suppliers, onto the Internet, significant improvements can be made to communication and just-in-time inventory and distribution systems.

Electronic commerce can also allow Moroccan textile mills to communicate directly with internationally based buyers of wholesale fabrics. For example, Phoenix Textiles (http://www.fabric.com), a U.S.-based buyer and distributor of textiles, uses the Internet to purchase its fabrics from mills around the world. Then, through its Web site, Phoenix Textiles sells to individuals and small and medium-sized enterprises as well as large corporations. The company relies on the Internet to replenish its inventory as needed.

Supplying international buyers of wholesale textiles will become increasingly important for Moroccan textile mills as World Trade Organization (WTO)-member countries phase out the quotas in the Multi-Fiber Arrangement by the year 2005.

Recognizing the importance of electronic commerce in the textile sector, many countries have started implementing electronic commerce pilot projects specifically targeted toward the textile industry. The European Union, for example, is launching Texconnect, an EDI/Web EDI (Electronic Data Interchange) interface to allow smooth communication for all companies in the textile supply chain.

A potential problem lies in that some Moroccan firms, in textiles and other sectors as well, are turning to EDI as the form of electronic interconnection. EDI is about five times more expensive than connectivity through the Internet, and is a much less flexible electronic transmission mechanism. EDI cannot be interactive, cannot be multimedia, and most importantly, does not support a competitive environment between buyer and seller.

2. Services-based Trade: Tourism

Tourism is a significant foreign-exchange earner in Morocco ($1.2 billion in 1997), as well as an important source of employment. Tourism accounted for nearly 10 percent of GDP last year. The GOM's plan to double tourist numbers and raise gross receipts to $6 billion by the end of the year, while ambitious, can be assisted by the use of electronic commerce and the Internet more generally. Indeed, if Morocco lags in the uptake of electronic commerce, it will lose its international standing as a tourist destination.

At a minimum, the Internet can serve as an important vehicle for the distribution of brochure-ware (information, photographs, video clips, etc.) to potential tourists planning a vacation in Morocco. The Internet can also offer potential tourists the convenience of researching and booking their entire vacation online, from airplane tickets, to hotel accommodation, to auto rental, etc. Currently, few of the tourist activities in Morocco use the Internet to reach international audiences. Moreover, none have the capacity to take reservations, pre-payment of other common and increasingly valued services. Because of this, Moroccan businesses cannot reach the traveler directly, and thus are required to pay a reservations agent a portion of the profits to be earned on the client. The process of putting tourist operations online itself creates new businesses, so the Internet becomes part of a virtuous circle of development.

3. Computers and Software

Morocco is emerging as an African hub for software production. In early 1998, for example, Microsoft set up its regional headquarters in Casablanca. Compaq and Oracle have also decided to set up regional bases in Morocco. By locating their production in Morocco, software MNCs can benefit from the relatively inexpensive labor costs, an investment-friendly environment, and Morocco's trade association with the EU. The Internet can help these companies communicate with headquarters. It can also serve as an important distribution channel for software, allowing the companies to bypass Africa's physical infrastructure challenges.

4. Resource-based Trade: Phosphates

Morocco holds approximately three-quarters of the world's phosphate reserves; it is also the largest exporter of phosphate rock. Morocco can use the Internet to secure outside funding to expand exploration and extraction activities, or to develop relationships with downstream processors in Europe and Asia.

The state-owned Office Chérifien des Phosphates (OCP), for example, is marketing partnership opportunities through its Web site at http://www.ocpgroup.com. The site displays pictures and data of the OCP Group's mines in Oulad Abdoun, Gantour, and Ouad Eddahab, and gives contact information for OCP Group headquarters in Casablanca.

Recently there have been movements toward moving commodity trade to electronic media. For example, on the previously-cited Web site http://www.esteel.com, producers and buyers of steel can post offers and bids over the Internet confidentially and securely. Similar trade with phosphates over the Internet might be a possibility in the short-term future.

5. High-value Agriculture-based Trade: Fruits and Vegetables

The agricultural sector–including cereals, export crops like citrus fruit and tomatoes, forestry, fishing, and livestock–employs approximately 40 percent of the Moroccan labor force and accounts for approximately 15 percent of GDP. As a result, climate changes can have a significant impact on the Moroccan economy. For example, this year a poor harvest is causing the GOM to miss its budget targets.

The Internet can help both farmers and the government better plan for these climate changes. In the United States, for example, a Weekly Weather and Crop Bulletin–sponsored by the U.S. Department of Commerce, the U.S. Department of Agriculture, and the National Oceanic and Atmospheric Administration–is posted over the Internet (see http://www.usda.gov) to give farmers detailed information on many issues, including temperature changes and crop moisture.

BASIC TITLES FOR MOROCCO

Title	ISBN
Morocco A "Spy" Guide - Strategic Information and Developments	1433034530
Morocco A Spy" Guide"	1438733909
Morocco Air Force Handbook	1433034549
Morocco Air Force Handbook	1438733917
Morocco Banking & Financial Market Handbook	1433034557
Morocco Banking & Financial Market Handbook	1438733925
Morocco Business and Investment Opportunities Yearbook	1433034565
Morocco Business and Investment Opportunities Yearbook	1438733933
Morocco Business and Investment Opportunities Yearbook Volume 1 Strategic Information and Opportunities	1438777426
Morocco Business and Investment Opportunities Yearbook Volume 2 Leading Export-Import, Business, Investment Opportunities and Projects	1577519949
Morocco Business Intelligence Report - Practical Information, Opportunities, Contacts	1433034573
Morocco Business Intelligence Report - Practical Information, Opportunities, Contacts	1438733941
Morocco Business Law Handbook - Strategic Information and Basic Laws	1438770553
Morocco Business Law Handbook - Strategic Information and Basic Laws	1433034581
Morocco Business Law Handbook - Strategic Information and Basic Laws	1438770553
Morocco Business Law Handbook - Strategic Information and Basic Laws	143873395X
Morocco Company Laws and Regulations Handbook	1433070359
Morocco Constitution and Citizenship Laws Handbook - Strategic Information and Basic Laws	1438779437
Morocco Country Study Guide - Strategic Information and Developments	143303459X
Morocco Country Study Guide - Strategic Information and Developments	1438733968
Morocco Country Study Guide - Strategic Information and Developments Volume 1 Strategic Information and Developments	1438775091
Morocco Customs, Trade Regulations and Procedures Handbook	1433034603
Morocco Customs, Trade Regulations and Procedures Handbook	1438733976
Morocco Diplomatic Handbook - Strategic Information and Developments	1433034611
Morocco Diplomatic Handbook - Strategic Information and Developments	1438733984
Morocco Ecology & Nature Protection Handbook	143303462X
Morocco Ecology & Nature Protection Handbook	1438733992
Morocco Ecology & Nature Protection Laws and Regulation Handbook	1433074451
Morocco Economic & Development Strategy Handbook	1433034638
Morocco Economic & Development Strategy Handbook	143873400X
Morocco Energy Policy, Laws and Regulation Handbook	1433072211
Morocco Energy Policy, Laws and Regulations Handbook	1433034646
Morocco Energy Policy, Laws and Regulations Handbook	1438734018
Morocco Export-Import Trade and Business Directory	1433034654
Morocco Export-Import Trade and Business Directory	1438734026
Morocco Foreign Policy and Government Guide	1433034662

Title	ISBN
Morocco Foreign Policy and Government Guide	1438734034
Morocco Healthcare Sector Organization, Management and Payment Systems Handbook - Strategic Information, Programs and Regulations	9781433085925
Morocco Immigration Laws and Regulations Handbook - Strategic Information and Basic Laws	1438783043
Morocco Industrial and Business Directory	1433034670
Morocco Industrial and Business Directory	1438734042
Morocco Internet and E-Commerce Investment and Business Guide - Strategic and Practical Information: Regulations and Opportunities	1433034689
Morocco Internet and E-Commerce Investment and Business Guide - Strategic and Practical Information: Regulations and Opportunities	1438734050
Morocco Investment & Business Guide	1433034697
Morocco Investment & Business Guide Volume 1	1438734069
Morocco Investment and Business Guide - Strategic and Practical Information	1438768273
Morocco Investment and Business Guide - Strategic and Practical Information	1438768273
Morocco Investment and Business Guide - Strategic and Practical Information	1433034700
Morocco Investment and Business Guide - Strategic and Practical Information Volume 2	1438734077
Morocco Investment and Business Guide Volume 2 Business, Investment Opportunities and Incentives	1577519167
Morocco Investment and Trade Laws and Regulations Handbook	1433076365
Morocco Labor Laws and Regulations Handbook - Strategic Information and Basic Laws	1438781245
Morocco Land Ownership and Agriculture Laws Handbook	1438759606
Morocco Mineral & Mining Sector Investment and Business Guide - Strategic and Practical Information	1433034719
Morocco Mineral & Mining Sector Investment and Business Guide - Strategic and Practical Information	1438734085
Morocco Mining Laws and Regulations Handbook	1433077906
Morocco Oil & Gas Industry Business Intelligence Report - Practical Information, Opportunities, Contacts	1433034727
Morocco Oil & Gas Industry Business Intelligence Report - Practical Information, Opportunities, Contacts	1438734093
Morocco Oil & Gas Sector Business & Investment Opportunities Yearbook	1433034735
Morocco Oil & Gas Sector Business & Investment Opportunities Yearbook	1438734107
Morocco Oil and Gas Exploration Laws and Regulation Handbook	1433078813
Morocco Privatization Programs and Regulations Handbook	1433034743
Morocco Privatization Programs and Regulations Handbook	1438734115
Morocco Recent Economic and Political Developments Yearbook	1433064146
Morocco Recent Economic and Political Developments Yearbook	1433064146
Morocco Recent Economic and Political Developments Yearbook	1433064146
Morocco Starting Business (Incorporating) in....Guide	1433067269
Morocco Taxation Laws and Regulations Handbook	1433080508

Title	ISBN
Morocco Telecom Laws and Regulations Handbook	1433082233
Morocco Telecom Sector Investment and Business Opportunities Handbook	1433034751
Morocco Telecom Sector Investment and Business Opportunities Handbook	1438734123
Morocco Telecommunication Industry Business Opportunities Handbook	143303476X
Morocco Telecommunication Industry Business Opportunities Handbook	1438734131
Morocco Transportation Policy and Regulations Handbook	1433067277
Morocco: How to Invest, Start and Run Profitable Business in Morocco Guide - Practical Information, Opportunities, Contacts	9781433084072

33.	Equatorial Guinea Business and Investment Opportunities Yearbook
34.	Eritrea Business and Investment Opportunities Yearbook
35.	Estonia Business and Investment Opportunities Yearbook
36.	Estonia Business and Investment Opportunities Yearbook
37.	Ethiopia Business and Investment Opportunities Yearbook
38.	Falkland Islands Business and Investment Opportunities Yearbook
39.	Faroes Business and Investment Opportunities Yearbook
40.	Fiji Business and Investment Opportunities Yearbook
41.	Finland Business and Investment Opportunities Yearbook
42.	Finland Business and Investment Opportunities Yearbook
43.	France Business and Investment Opportunities Yearbook
44.	France Business and Investment Opportunities Yearbook
45.	Gabon Business and Investment Opportunities Yearbook
46.	Gambia Business and Investment Opportunities Yearbook
47.	Georgia Business and Investment Opportunities Yearbook
48.	Germany Business and Investment Opportunities Yearbook
49.	Germany Business and Investment Opportunities Yearbook
50.	Ghana Business and Investment Opportunities Yearbook
51.	Gibraltar Business and Investment Opportunities Yearbook
52.	Greece Business and Investment Opportunities Yearbook
53.	Greenland Business and Investment Opportunities Yearbook
54.	Grenada Business and Investment Opportunities Yearbook
55.	Guam Business and Investment Opportunities Yearbook
56.	Guatemala Business and Investment Opportunities Yearbook
57.	Guernsey Business and Investment Opportunities Yearbook
58.	Guinea Business and Investment Opportunities Yearbook
59.	Guinea-Bissau Business and Investment Opportunities Yearbook
60.	Guyana Business and Investment Opportunities Yearbook
61.	Haiti Business and Investment Opportunities Yearbook
62.	Honduras Business and Investment Opportunities Yearbook
63.	Hungary Business and Investment Opportunities Yearbook
64.	Hungary Business and Investment Opportunities Yearbook
65.	Iceland Business and Investment Opportunities Yearbook
66.	India Business and Investment Opportunities Yearbook
67.	India Business and Investment Opportunities Yearbook
68.	Indonesia Business and Investment Opportunities Yearbook
69.	Indonesia Business and Investment Opportunities Yearbook
70.	Iran Business and Investment Opportunities Yearbook
71.	Iraq Business and Investment Opportunities Yearbook
72.	Ireland Business and Investment Opportunities Yearbook
73.	Israel Business and Investment Opportunities Yearbook

74. Italy Business and Investment Opportunities Yearbook
75. Jamaica Business and Investment Opportunities Yearbook
76. Japan Business and Investment Opportunities Yearbook
77. Jersey Business and Investment Opportunities Yearbook
78. Jordan Business and Investment Opportunities Yearbook
79. Kazakhstan Business and Investment Opportunities Yearbook
80. Kenya Business and Investment Opportunities Yearbook
81. Kiribati Business and Investment Opportunities Yearbook
82. Korea, North Business and Investment Opportunities Yearbook
83. Korea, South Business and Investment Opportunities Yearbook
84. Kuwait Business and Investment Opportunities Yearbook
85. Kyrgyzstan Business and Investment Opportunities Yearbook
86. Laos Business and Investment Opportunities Yearbook
87. Latvia Business and Investment Opportunities Yearbook
88. Lebanon Business and Investment Opportunities Yearbook
89. Lesotho Business and Investment Opportunities Yearbook
90. Liberia Business and Investment Opportunities Yearbook
91. Libya Business and Investment Opportunities Yearbook
92. Liechtenstein Business and Investment Opportunities Yearbook
93. Lithuania Business and Investment Opportunities Yearbook
94. Luxembourg Business and Investment Opportunities Yearbook
95. Macau Business and Investment Opportunities Yearbook
96. Macedonia Republic Business and Investment Opportunities Yearbook
97. Madagascar Business and Investment Opportunities Yearbook
98. Malawi Business and Investment Opportunities Yearbook
99. Malaysia Business and Investment Opportunities Yearbook
100. Maldives Business and Investment Opportunities Yearbook
101. Mali Business and Investment Opportunities Yearbook
102. Malta Business and Investment Opportunities Yearbook
103. Man Business and Investment Opportunities Yearbook
104. Marshall Islands Business and Investment Opportunities Yearbook
105. Mauritania Business and Investment Opportunities Yearbook
106. Mauritius Business and Investment Opportunities Yearbook
107. Mayotte Business and Investment Opportunities Yearbook
108. Mexico Business and Investment Opportunities Yearbook
109. Micronesia Business and Investment Opportunities Yearbook
110. Moldova Business and Investment Opportunities Yearbook
111. Monaco Business and Investment Opportunities Yearbook
112. Mongolia Business and Investment Opportunities Yearbook
113. Monserrat Business and Investment Opportunities Yearbook

114. Morocco Business and Investment Opportunities Yearbook
115. Mozambique Business and Investment Opportunities Yearbook
116. Myanmar Business and Investment Opportunities Yearbook
117. Namibia Business and Investment Opportunities Yearbook
118. Nauru Business and Investment Opportunities Yearbook
119. Nepal Business and Investment Opportunities Yearbook
120. Netherlands Business and Investment Opportunities Yearbook
121. New Caledonia Business and Investment Opportunities Yearbook
122. New Zealand Business and Investment Opportunities Yearbook
123. Nicaragua Business and Investment Opportunities Yearbook
124. Niger Business and Investment Opportunities Yearbook
125. Nigeria Business and Investment Opportunities Yearbook
126. Niue Business and Investment Opportunities Yearbook
127. Northern Mariana Islands Business and Investment Opportunities Yearbook
128. Norway Business and Investment Opportunities Yearbook
129. Oman Business and Investment Opportunities Yearbook
130. Pakistan Business and Investment Opportunities Yearbook
131. Palau Business and Investment Opportunities Yearbook
132. Palestine Business and Investment Opportunities Yearbook
133. Panama Business and Investment Opportunities Yearbook
134. Papua New Guinea Business and Investment Opportunities Yearbook
135. Paraguay Business and Investment Opportunities Yearbook
136. Peru Business and Investment Opportunities Yearbook
137. Philippines Business and Investment Opportunities Yearbook
138. Pitcairn Islands Business and Investment Opportunities Yearbook
139. Poland Business and Investment Opportunities Yearbook
140. Polynesia French Business and Investment Opportunities Yearbook
141. Portugal Business and Investment Opportunities Yearbook
142. Romania Business and Investment Opportunities Yearbook
143. Russia Business and Investment Opportunities Yearbook
144. Rwanda Business and Investment Opportunities Yearbook
145. Saint Kitts and Nevis Business and Investment Opportunities Yearbook
146. Saint Lucia Business and Investment Opportunities Yearbook
147. Saint Vincent and The Grenadines Business and Investment Opportunities Yearbook
148. Samoa (American) A Business and Investment Opportunities Yearbook
149. Samoa (Western) Business and Investment Opportunities Yearbook
150. San Marino Business and Investment Opportunities Yearbook
151. Sao Tome and Principe Business and Investment Opportunities Yearbook
152. Saudi Arabia Business and Investment Opportunities Yearbook
153. Senegal Business and Investment Opportunities Yearbook
154. Serbia Business and Investment Opportunities Yearbook
155. Seychelles Business and Investment Opportunities Yearbook
156. Sierra Leone Business and Investment Opportunities Yearbook
157. Singapore Business and Investment Opportunities Yearbook
158. Slovakia Business and Investment Opportunities Yearbook
159. Slovenia Business and Investment Opportunities Yearbook
160. Solomon Islands Business and Investment Opportunities Yearbook
161. Somalia Business and Investment Opportunities Yearbook

162. South Africa Business and Investment Opportunities Yearbook
163. South Sudan Business and Investment Opportunities Yearbook
164. Spain Business and Investment Opportunities Yearbook
165. Sri Lanka Business and Investment Opportunities Yearbook
166. St. Helena Business and Investment Opportunities Yearbook
167. St. Pierre & Miquelon Business and Investment Opportunities Yearbook
168. Sudan Business and Investment Opportunities Yearbook
169. Suriname Business and Investment Opportunities Yearbook
170. Swaziland Business and Investment Opportunities Yearbook
171. Sweden Business and Investment Opportunities Yearbook
172. Switzerland Business and Investment Opportunities Yearbook
173. Syria Business and Investment Opportunities Yearbook
174. Taiwan Business and Investment Opportunities Yearbook
175. Tajikistan Business and Investment Opportunities Yearbook
176. Tanzania Business and Investment Opportunities Yearbook
177. Thailand Business and Investment Opportunities Yearbook
178. Timor Leste Ecological and Nature Protection Guide
179. Togo Business and Investment Opportunities Yearbook
180. Tonga Business and Investment Opportunities Yearbook
181. Trinidad and Tobago Business and Investment Opportunities Yearbook
182. Tunisia Business and Investment Opportunities Yearbook
183. Turkey Business and Investment Opportunities Yearbook
184. Turkmenistan Business and Investment Opportunities Yearbook
185. Tuvalu Business and Investment Opportunities Yearbook
186. Uganda Business and Investment Opportunities Yearbook
187. Ukraine Business and Investment Opportunities Yearbook
188. United Arab Emirates Business and Investment Opportunities Yearbook
189. United Kingdom Business and Investment Opportunities Yearbook
190. Uruguay Business and Investment Opportunities Yearbook
191. Uzbekistan Business and Investment Opportunities Yearbook
192. Vanuatu Business and Investment Opportunities Yearbook
193. Venezuela Business and Investment Opportunities Yearbook
194. Vietnam Business and Investment Opportunities Yearbook
195. Virgin Islands, British Business and Investment Opportunities Yearbook
196. Yemen Business and Investment Opportunities Yearbook
197. Zambia Business and Investment Opportunities Yearbook

38.	Cayman Islands Investment and Business Guide
39.	Central African Republic Investment and Business Guide
40.	Chad Investment and Business Guide
41.	Chile Investment and Business Guide
42.	China Investment and Business Guide
43.	Colombia Investment and Business Guide
44.	Comoros Investment and Business Guide
45.	Congo Investment and Business Guide
46.	Congo, Democratic Republic Investment and Business Guide
47.	Cook Islands Investment and Business Guide
48.	Costa Rica Investment and Business Guide
49.	Cote d'Ivoire Investment and Business Guide
50.	Croatia Investment and Business Guide
51.	Cuba Investment and Business Guide
52.	Cyprus Investment and Business Guide
53.	Czech Republic Investment and Business Guide
54.	Denmark Investment and Business Guide
55.	Djibouti Investment and Business Guide
56.	Dominica Investment and Business Guide
57.	Dominican Republic Investment and Business Guide
58.	Ecuador Investment and Business Guide
59.	Egypt Investment and Business Guide
60.	El Salvador Investment and Business Guide
61.	Equatorial Guinea Investment and Business Guide
62.	Eritrea Investment and Business Guide
63.	Estonia Investment and Business Guide
64.	Ethiopia Investment and Business Guide
65.	Falkland Islands Investment and Business Guide
66.	Faroes Islands Investment and Business Guide
67.	Fiji Investment and Business Guide
68.	Finland Investment and Business Guide
69.	France Investment and Business Guide
70.	Gabon Investment and Business Guide
71.	Gambia Investment and Business Guide
72.	Georgia Investment and Business Guide
73.	Germany Investment and Business Guide
74.	Ghana Investment and Business Guide
75.	Gibraltar Investment and Business Guide
76.	Greece Investment and Business Guide
77.	Greenland Investment and Business Guide
78.	Grenada Investment and Business Guide
79.	Guam Investment and Business Guide
80.	Guatemala Investment and Business Guide
81.	Guernsey Investment and Business Guide
82.	Guinea Investment and Business Guide
83.	Guinea-Bissau Investment and Business Guide
84.	Guyana Investment and Business Guide
85.	Haiti Investment and Business Guide
86.	Honduras Investment and Business Guide
87.	Hungary Investment and Business Guide
88.	Iceland Investment and Business Guide

89. India Investment and Business Guide
90. Indonesia Investment and Business Guide
91. Iran Investment and Business Guide
92. Iraq Investment and Business Guide
93. Ireland Investment and Business Guide
94. Israel Investment and Business Guide
95. Italy Investment and Business Guide
96. Jamaica Investment and Business Guide
97. Japan Investment and Business Guide
98. Jersey Investment and Business Guide
99. Jordan Investment and Business Guide
100. Kazakhstan Investment and Business Guide
101. Kenya Investment and Business Guide
102. Kiribati Investment and Business Guide
103. Korea, North Investment and Business Guide
104. Korea, South Investment and Business Guide
105. Kosovo Investment and Business Guide
106. Kurdistan Investment and Business Guide
107. Kuwait Investment and Business Guide
108. Kyrgyzstan Investment and Business Guide
109. Laos Investment and Business Guide
110. Latvia Investment and Business Guide
111. Lebanon Investment and Business Guide
112. Lesotho Investment and Business Guide
113. Liberia Investment and Business Guide
114. Libya Investment and Business Guide
115. Liechtenstein Investment and Business Guide
116. Lithuania Investment and Business Guide
117. Luxembourg Investment and Business Guide
118. Macao Investment and Business Guide
119. Macedonia Investment and Business Guide
120. Madagascar Investment and Business Guide
121. Madeira Investment and Business Guide
122. Malawi Investment and Business Guide
123. Malaysia Investment and Business Guide
124. Maldives Investment and Business Guide
125. Mali Investment and Business Guide
126. Malta Investment and Business Guide
127. Man Investment and Business Guide
128. Marshall Islands Investment and Business Guide
129. Mauritania Investment and Business Guide
130. Mauritius Investment and Business Guide
131. Mayotte Investment and Business Guide
132. Mexico Investment and Business Guide
133. Micronesia Investment and Business Guide
134. Moldova Investment and Business Guide
135. Monaco Investment and Business Guide
136. Mongolia Investment and Business Guide
137. Monserrat Investment and Business Guide
138. Morocco Investment and Business Guide
139. Mozambique Investment and Business Guide

140. Myanmar Investment and Business Guide
141. Namibia Investment and Business Guide
142. Nauru Investment and Business Guide
143. Nepal Investment and Business Guide
144. Netherlands Investment and Business Guide
145. New Caledonia Investment and Business Guide
146. New Zealand Investment and Business Guide
147. Nicaragua Investment and Business Guide
148. Niger Investment and Business Guide
149. Nigeria Investment and Business Guide
150. Niue Investment and Business Guide
151. Northern Mariana Islands Investment and Business Guide
152. Norway Investment and Business Guide
153. Oman Investment and Business Guide
154. Pakistan Investment and Business Guide
155. Palau Investment and Business Guide
156. Palestine (West Bank & Gaza) Investment and Business Guide
157. Panama Investment and Business Guide
158. Papua New Guinea Investment and Business Guide
159. Paraguay Investment and Business Guide
160. Peru Investment and Business Guide
161. Philippines Investment and Business Guide
162. Pitcairn Islands Investment and Business Guide
163. Poland Investment and Business Guide
164. Polynesia French Investment and Business Guide
165. Portugal Investment and Business Guide
166. Qatar Investment and Business Guide
167. Romania Investment and Business Guide
168. Russia Investment and Business Guide
169. Rwanda Investment and Business Guide
170. Saint Kitts and Nevis Investment and Business Guide
171. Saint Lucia Investment and Business Guide
172. Saint Vincent and The Grenadines Investment and Business Guide
173. Samoa (American) A Investment and Business Guide
174. Samoa (Western) Investment and Business Guide
175. San Marino Investment and Business Guide
176. Sao Tome and Principe Investment and Business Guide
177. Saudi Arabia Investment and Business Guide
178. Scotland Investment and Business Guide
179. Senegal Investment and Business Guide
180. Serbia Investment and Business Guide
181. Seychelles Investment and Business Guide
182. Sierra Leone Investment and Business Guide
183. Singapore Investment and Business Guide
184. Slovakia Investment and Business Guide
185. Slovenia Investment and Business Guide
186. Solomon Islands Investment and Business Guide
187. Somalia Investment and Business Guide
188. South Africa Investment and Business Guide
189. Spain Investment and Business Guide
190. Sri Lanka Investment and Business Guide

191. St. Helena Investment and Business Guide
192. St. Pierre & Miquelon Investment and Business Guide
193. Sudan Investment and Business Guide
194. Sudan South Investment and Business Guide
195. Suriname Investment and Business Guide
196. Swaziland Investment and Business Guide
197. Sweden Investment and Business Guide
198. Switzerland Investment and Business Guide
199. Syria Investment and Business Guide
200. Taiwan Investment and Business Guide
201. Tajikistan Investment and Business Guide
202. Tanzania Investment and Business Guide
203. Thailand Investment and Business Guide
204. Togo Investment and Business Guide
205. Tonga Investment and Business Guide
206. Trinidad and Tobago Investment and Business Guide
207. Tunisia Investment and Business Guide
208. Turkey Investment and Business Guide
209. Turkmenistan Investment and Business Guide
210. Turks & Caicos Investment and Business Guide
211. Tuvalu Investment and Business Guide
212. Uganda Investment and Business Guide
213. Ukraine Investment and Business Guide
214. United Arab Emirates Investment and Business Guide
215. United Kingdom Investment and Business Guide
216. United States Investment and Business Guide
217. Uruguay Investment and Business Guide
218. Uzbekistan Investment and Business Guide
219. Vanuatu Investment and Business Guide
220. Vatican City Investment and Business Guide
221. Venezuela Investment and Business Guide
222. Vietnam Investment and Business Guide
223. Virgin Islands, British Investment and Business Guide
224. Wake Atoll Investment and Business Guide
225. Wallis & Futuna Investment and Business Guide
226. Western Sahara Investment and Business Guide
227. Yemen Investment and Business Guide
228. Zambia Investment and Business Guide
229. Zimbabwe Investment and Business Guide

www.ingramcontent.com/pod-product-compliance
Ingram Content Group UK Ltd.
Pitfield, Milton Keynes, MK11 3LW, UK
UKHW051509290926
15471UKWH00008B/1527

9 780739 708859